Futuring Our Past

Studies in Latino/a Catholicism

A series sponsored by the Center for the Study of Latino/a Catholicism
University of San Diego

Previously published

Orlando O. Espín and Miguel H. Díaz, editors, *From the Heart of Our People: Latino/a Explorations in Catholic Systematic Theology*

STUDIES IN LATINO/A CATHOLICISM

Futuring Our Past

Explorations in the Theology of Tradition

Edited by
Orlando O. Espín
and Gary Macy

ORBIS BOOKS

Maryknoll, New York 10545

Library of Congress Cataloging-in-Publication Data

Futuring our past : explorations in the theology of tradition / edited by Orlando O. Espín and Gary Macy.
    p. cm. — (Studies in Latino/a Catholicism)
  ISBN-13: 978–1–57075–647–4 (pbk.)
  1. Hispanic Americans—Religion—Congresses. 2. Tradition (Theology)—Congresses. I. Espín, Orlando. II. Macy, Gary. III. Series.
  BR563.H57F88 2006
  230.089'68073—dc22

                                    2006008458

Para Ricardo, compañero y amigo.
Y para Nery, Carlos, Vivianna, Mario y Dee.
O.O.E.

For Saralynn, who keeps me honest.
G.M.

Contents

Introduction   ix

Contributors   xi

1   **Traditioning**
Culture, Daily Life and Popular Religion,
and Their Impact on Christian Tradition   1
Orlando O. Espín

2   **Authority and/or Tradition**   23
Bernard Cooke

3   **The Iberian Heritage of US Latino/a Theology**   43
Gary Macy

4   **Reading between the Lines**
Toward a Latino/a (Re)configuration of Scripture
and Tradition   83
Jean-Pierre Ruiz

5   **Reinventing the Biblical Tradition**
An Exploration of Social Location Hermeneutics   113
Francisco Lozada, Jr.

6   **Tradition as Conversation**   141
Gary Riebe-Estrella

7   **A Trinitarian Approach to the Community-Building Process
of Tradition**
Oneness as Diversity in Christian Traditioning   157
Miguel H. Díaz

8 What about *Mulatez?*
   An Afro-Cuban Contribution   180
   Michelle A. González

9 Traditioning
   The Formation of Community, the Transmission of Faith   204
   Nancy Pineda-Madrid

10 The Politics of Tradition in the Protestant Educational
    Endeavor for Colonial Puerto Rico   227
    José R. Irizarry

11 *El gran avivamiento del '33*
    The Protestant Missionary Enterprise, Revival, Identity,
    and Tradition   249
    Daisy L. Machado

12 *La Quinceañera*
    Traditioning and the Social Construction
    of the Mexican American Female   277
    Theresa L. Torres, OSB

Index   299

Introduction

In January 2003, and again in January 2004, twelve scholars met at the invitation of the Center for the Study of Latino/a Catholicism at the University of San Diego.[1] The present volume is the result of those two week-long meetings and of many months spent in conversation, research, and writing.

In keeping with the Center's mission to reflect theologically on Latino/a Catholicism from interdisciplinary perspectives, the gathered researchers included historians, educators, biblical scholars, and theologians in various disciplinary fields: women and men, Latinos/as and others, young and not so young, Roman Catholics and Protestants. The diversity of perspectives, contexts, and backgrounds was intentional. This too was in keeping with the Center's mission and with its commitment to Latino/a theology's methodological *teología de conjunto*.

Before gathering for the 2003 meeting in San Diego, all scholars were asked to reflect on a series of issues revolving around two central questions: How is the Christian tradition "traditioned" among Latinos/as? and What impact (if any) does this "traditioning" have on the tradition?

During the 2003 gathering the two central questions, and many issues revolving around them, were discussed. Inevitably, new ideas, new perspectives, and new questions arose as the result of the lively conversation. Not all was agreement, but a consensus did arise indicating that the "how" Latinos/as transmit the Christian tradition (and how it was transmitted to them) has a significant impact on what Latinos/as (Roman Catholic and Protestant) have come to understand as Christianity.

The second meeting in San Diego, in 2004, brought the participants together again, after nearly a year of more informal conversations, individual research, and writing, to review and critique papers presented by the participating scholars. Important suggestions were made, further questions were raised, and new ideas and questions arose. Reluctantly, common sense dictated that eventually we had to draw discussion to a close and commit the participants to the publication of a manuscript that reflected not only the individual authors' scholarship but also the dynamics of the group's many conversations.

The papers included herein were not written mainly *for* Latinos/as, although we hope they too will benefit from the insights and research reflected here. The chapters in the present volume were written for the entire theological academy, which in its diversity is as ethnic and contextual as Latino/a theologies, since *all* theologies and *all* theologians everywhere are ethnically and contextually bound. The included texts, however, do reflect a particular set of contextualities that are reflective of the demographic half of the US Catholic church that, in turn, constitutes the largest minority in the country. This is *American* theology, perhaps more so today than others under the same label.

No attempt was made by the authors or the editors to force agreement among these papers. The texts reflect the individual author's ideas and perspectives as shaped by eighteen months of lively conversations.

We thank the participants for their hard scholarly work, for their research and writing, their often brilliant ideas, and the many months they spent on this project. We thank them too for their collaboration with the Center's mission.

Robert Ellsberg and the staff of Orbis Books also deserve our thanks for supporting this new volume. It is the second in a series published by Orbis in conjunction with the Center, reflecting some of the research sponsored and conducted by the Center for the Study of Latino/a Catholicism.

We hope these texts will contribute significantly to the growing theological study of tradition and traditioning.

Note

[1] For information on the Center's projects, mission, rationale, research interests, and assumptions, as well as for very complete Internet and other resources for research on US Latino/a and Latin American Catholicism, see http://www.sandiego.edu/theo/Latino-Cath/index.php.

Contributors

Bernard Cooke
Loyola Professor of Theology Emeritus
College of the Holy Cross

Miguel H. Díaz
Associate Professor of Systematic Theology
St. John's University, Collegeville

Orlando O. Espín
Professor of Systematic Theology
Director, Center for the Study of Latino/a Catholicism
University of San Diego

Michelle A. González
Independent Theologian
(formerly at Loyola Marymount University)
San Lucas Tolimán, Guatemala

José R. Irizarry
Dean of Doctoral Programs
Associate Professor of Religion and Culture
McCormick Theological Seminary

Francisco Lozada, Jr.
Professor of Biblical Studies
French Chair in Religion
University of the Incarnate Word

Daisy L. Machado
Vice President for Academic Affairs and Dean
Lexington Theological Seminary

Gary Macy
Professor of Church History
Associate Director, Center for the Study of Latino/a Catholicism
University of San Diego

Nancy Pineda-Madrid
Assistant Professor of Theology
Boston College

Gary Riebe-Estrella
Academic Vice-President and Dean
Professor of Practical Theology
Catholic Theological Union

Jean-Pierre Ruiz
Professor of Biblical Studies
St. John's University, New York

Theresa L. Torres, OSB
Assistant Professor of Religious Studies
Benedictine College

1

Traditioning

Culture, Daily Life and Popular Religion, and Their Impact on Christian Tradition

Orlando O. Espín

"TRADITION" AND "TRADITIONING"

Christianity has transmitted itself across generations and beyond cultural boundaries; otherwise it could not have survived in history or expanded beyond its Palestinian origins. This is historically self-evident. The Christianity we know today is not identical or coextensive with first-century Palestinian Christianity, and yet the claim has always been made that the Christian religion has remained identifiably the same. In other words, Christianity claims that throughout twenty-one centuries it has been able to change, grow, adapt, and modify itself while somehow managing to hold loyally to its core message and necessary memories.

Evidently, the various denominational branches of Christianity understand that core message and those necessary memories differently (or at least somewhat differently), but all Christian churches—regardless of their understanding of the core message and the necessary memories— have depended on means of transmission in order to survive and further expand. Some Christian denominations might comfortably refer to and acknowledge their particular means of transmission, while others might appear or actually are uncomfortable with any reference to tradition. The degree of denominational comfort with some types of tradition terminology, however, does not cancel the reality: Christianity in all of its branches has had to transmit itself throughout the generations and across cultural boundaries, or Christianity would have ceased to exist as a living religion.

One significant difficulty with tradition terminology among Christians is that the term *tradition* is often misunderstood as referring almost exclusively to ecclesial customs. First, in this chapter I do not understand *tradition* to include ecclesial customs—although a reasonable and important argument can be made to the effect that all contents of tradition must somehow be expressed and transmitted through cultural means that might be or become "customary." Second, the claimed contents of tradition are themselves difficult to ascertain or assume throughout the centuries—some (for example, the belief that the Bible is the inspired word of God) have been unquestionably and constantly held and received as one of the contents of Christian tradition, but some other doctrines and ethical expectations cannot claim such unquestioned, constant reception throughout Christian history (for example, papal infallibility or the moral acceptability of slavery). That some Christian churches have in time come to define this or that doctrine or ethical expectation as part of their understanding of the core message of Christianity or of its necessary memories, or as authentic and required development thereof, does not in any way cancel the difficulty of ascertaining or assuming the contents of a universal Christian tradition throughout history.[1]

But regardless of what Christian denominations might debate among themselves in reference to the claimed contents of tradition, they cannot disagree with the fact that there has been and continues to be "traditioning." Without "traditioning"—the transmission of Christianity across generations and across cultural boundaries—there would not be a Christian religion in the twenty-first century.

In this chapter I focus on traditioning of and within Catholic and non-Catholic Christianity—on traditioning as transmission of the religion in history and across cultures—and not on tradition as contents (except as it is evidently necessary to recognize that all traditioning implies and requires that *something* be "traditioned"). The intent is explicitly ecumenical, and I hope the methodological approach is too. And more to the point, I explicitly suggest that when we consider tradition from the perspective of traditioning, all sorts of unexpected and perhaps dangerous considerations arise in the study of Christian tradition. Traditioning does something significant to tradition—historically and theologically.

I have further chosen, in this article, to examine traditioning benefiting from theological reflections within my own church (Roman Catholic), not only because of professional familiarity with these studies but because the Roman Catholic communion is the largest Christian body on earth, sharing much (on traditioning) with the two other large Christian communions, the Anglican and the Orthodox. However, I make no claim of presenting here the official theological views of my own church or of others. It seems to me that much of what is said herein is applicable to the churches of the Roman Catholic, Anglican, Orthodox, and Old Catholic communions, as well as to a number of other historical Christian churches—and, if an ecumenical spirit were to guide all, I would venture to say that evangelical and Pentecostal denominations might also see themselves engaged by the argument, *mutatis mutandi*, were they to acknowledge their own evident (if denominationally distinct or differently labeled) processes of traditioning.

One more clarification. The reader should realize that this chapter is by no means a full-length study of traditioning and/or of the theological issues and consequences involved therein; rather, it is a *limited experimental suggestion* on a possible methodological approach to tradition by way of traditioning, beyond the usual denominational "battle lines" drawn at the very mention of either term.[2] Consequently, much that needs to be examined in an ecumenical theology of "traditioning" cannot and will not be dealt with here.

One distinction, however, needs repeating. The reader should recall that in this chapter I am using the term *tradition* to mean *contents* of Christianity (for example, core message and necessary memories, and authentic developments thereof) and the term *traditioning* (and the verb *to tradition* and the noun *traditioners*) to mean or to refer to the *processes* whereby Christianity transmits itself across generations and across cultural boundaries. And, as I just indicated above, it doesn't seem possible to speak of traditioning without somehow implying tradition, but I believe it is very important to distinguish the two.

TRADITIONING: THE PROCESSES OF TRANSMISSION

How has Christianity transmitted itself across generations and across cultures? The extraordinarily complex answer to this question would require a detailed and complete history of the Christian church—because that is what the study of church history is ultimately about. It is evident that this brief essay cannot engage in that kind of historical reconstruction. So, dramatically short of a complete history of Christianity, what can we distill here from that history that might suggest, reasonably, what have been some of the key traditioning processes displayed by Christians throughout their history? More concretely, we must search for the traditioning processes that appear to have been most *ordinary*, most *common*, among Christians.

Consider Culture

When considering the ordinary transmission of Christianity, we have to reflect on the importance of culture.[3] In my understanding, culture is primarily the historically and ecologically possible means and ways through which peoples construct and unveil themselves (to themselves, and secondarily to others) as meaningfully human.[4] And, as I have argued elsewhere,[5] nothing human is *a*cultural—hence, the transmission of Christianity, its doctrines and polities, and their development, are all cultural products too.

Traditioning is cultural because it is human activity. It implicates a crucial human(izing) activity: the construction, discovery, clarification, and affirmation of life's meaning and for Christians, consequently, the meaning of revelation. In theological terms the source of revelation (God) is not necessarily bound by culture, but given that revelation exists only there where/when it is received as word of God, then, in the revelatory divine-human dialogue, culture plays an extraordinarily important role because the human partner is intrinsically shaped and bound by culture. When revelation is received and understood as word of God, when it is reflected upon, and when Christianity results from that reception and reflection, culture acts as a necessary medium. Indeed, anytime that Christianity is transmitted (expressed, taught, preached, ecclesially organized, and so on), and anytime that Christianity is lived by human communities, culture acts as the unavoidable means and prism.[6]

If culture is primarily the historically and ecologically possible means and ways through which a people unveil themselves (to themselves) as meaningfully human, and if revelation unveils for Christians the most foundational grounding of their humanness, then it is also legitimate to ask if culture is a *necessary condition* for revelation. In other words, it might be reasonably argued, Christian revelation *requires* culture as much as it requires the divine initiative. It could be further argued that culture is not only the necessary means, condition, and possibility of revelation; the revelatory event *itself* is intrinsically and necessarily cultural.

On the other hand, theological reflection has shown the impact of sin on culture and on the unveiling of the meaningfully human (which depends on culture). What consequences for traditioning are implicated by the impact of sin on culture, if the latter is understood as necessary for revelation, and indeed if the revelatory event is itself cultural?

It would be totally unacceptable to think that because of sin's evident and profound mark on all things human, and hence on culture, that the latter's importance or necessity for revelation and Christian traditioning is diminished, or that it can be theologically ignored. Revelation does not depend on or require sinless humanity or a sinless church, but it does require human cultures.[7]

Consider *lo cotidiano*

The expression *lo cotidiano*, in Spanish, refers to that which occurs and recurs daily.[8] It is everyday reality—with its routines and its surprises, its mysterious depths and its pedestrian quality. *Lo cotidiano* is another way of saying daily life as it actually exists and as it is lived. Thus, it is a constitutive dimension and element of the ordinary transmission of Christianity *because* Christian revelation and preaching, and the beliefs and practices which evolve from it, can only be engaged by humans in real, daily life. Indeed, revelation could *only* happen (as revelation) in *lo cotidiano*.

Traditioning does not occur, and it has never occurred, in some extraterrestrial space, apart from daily human life. On the contrary, the transmission of Christianity across generations and across cultural boundaries has happened more often than not as a direct consequence of questions, circumstances, crises, stresses, tendencies and antagonisms common in real, daily human life. *Lo cotidiano* is context and "shaper" of ordinary traditioning because it *is* daily life as daily life is lived by Christians. We will be able to argue that popular Christianity is also context and shaper of this ordinary traditioning precisely because popular Christianity is found in and is itself a constitutive part of *lo cotidiano*.[9]

It must be emphasized (at the risk of redundancy) that real life only exists in lived and living everyday reality, and not in our reflections (regardless of degree of sophistication or lack thereof) about real life. Furthermore, *lo cotidiano* is not reducible to the "domestic," the "private," or the "individual." What is experienced and lived within *lo cotidiano* is not just domestic or private—if by these is meant a sphere somehow secondary to the most significant events and trends within a supposedly more important national or international "public" sphere. Employment and unemployment, violence and war, educational systems, famine or plenty, mass media, global economics, information systems, international and national political decisions, and so on, and so forth, all have a very direct impact on the *daily* realities of individuals, families, and communities and do in fact all occur within daily life and as part of it. Indeed, it might be argued that the so-called public sphere only has any *real* effect on people's lives if, when, and to the degree that it existentially affects them in their daily life.

If "daily relationships constitute the foundation and image for the totality of social relationships,"[10] then it is from within daily relationships, as imaged in them, that human beings engage in the process of transmitting their religious faith. But, as I explained earlier, traditioning is not a sinless process, because sin affects daily relationships and daily reality *(lo cotidiano)* as much as it influences culture. And, as I argued earlier, the requirement of sinlessness as ground for legitimacy is also unacceptable here because *lo cotidiano* is human reality and nothing human is sinless. Hence, the legitimacy of the ordinary traditioning of Christianity cannot depend on the sinlessness of human daily life.

Consider Popular Christianity

As we have seen, familial, neighborhood and community relational networks are the foundation of *lo cotidiano*, its popular religious mediations, and its epistemology. But the dynamics of conflict, which so deeply wound and shape our society, also affect these relationships. Indeed, familial, neighborhood, and social relationships are the "social sacrament" of society's conflicts.

Popular Christian religion (and perhaps more specifically, popular Catholicism) embodies and epistemologically organizes these daily relationships and symbolically expresses their connections to/with the broader social networks—including the "sacred" networks—through the rites, beliefs, objects, and experiences of the people's religion.[11]

That there is popular Catholicism is today an unquestioned fact. Much has been written on popular Catholicism, and much in it has been analyzed from the perspectives of theology, history, and the social sciences. But is there such a religious universe as popular Protestantism? I believe there is, and we will see it as long as we are willing to apply to denominational variations within Protestantism the same criteria scholars typically apply to the popular variations within Catholicism. If we did, we would discover devotional and ritual practices (for example, *coritos*, some "revivalist" customs and expectations, many congregational ways of "doing things here," everyday home devotions and personal practices of church members, numerous local devotional customs and rules, religious items such as paintings, and more) fitting the criteria of popular religion. I realize that many within Protestant congregations feel uncomfortable with the label popular religion when it is applied to what they simply consider an authentic analysis or interpretation of the Christian message and/or of specific biblical texts, but if we are to be consistent and ecumenical, we must admit that the "official" denominational versions of Protestant Christianity are neither the only versions nor, I might add, the ones that ordinarily nourish the hearts and faith of many Protestant Christians. Their popular devotions are.[12]

Christians are convinced, mostly because of experiences mediated by their popular religion, that God is on their side, fighting with them their battles, suffering with them their pains and humiliations, in solidarity with them in their struggles for dignity and justice, and empowering them to overcome the sin that seeks to overwhelm them in society and family.

But, on the other hand, the *same* popular religious mediations seem to derail the people's solidarity with each other, often blind them to compassion and social responsibilities, condone domestic violence and the perpetuation of dehumanizing gender and family roles, and at times to reinforce their self-image as victims. Popular Christianity suffers from, and does not seem to undo, many of the consequences of patriarchal society mostly because its main leaders and interpreters (who very frequently are mature women) are themselves victims of that society.[13] This (in my mind) also explains why in some instances (in many instances?) popular Christian religion can display many of the sins and wounds of culture and of daily relationships, promoting or justifying behaviors or attitudes that might be judged unacceptable. It would be a grave analytical error to assume that because popular Christianity is *popular*[14] that, ipso facto, it must be wholly defended, wholly supported, or wholly romanticized.

Popular Christianity exists within the context of *lo cotidiano*. Its various elements intertwine with and are shaped by the public and private spheres, which in turn exist (equally intertwined) in *lo cotidiano*—in daily life. Popular Christianity is not a parenthesis to real life or a side show to so-called mainstream Christianity. It is part, mirror, and hermeneut of daily life and of Christianity. Indeed, it has been shown that popular religion has been and is one of the key bearers (if not *the* key bearer) of cultural identity. Within this religious universe life (all of life) is interpreted and symbolized as nowhere else in a cultural milieu.[15]

Popular Christianity does not refer solely to those relationships or contents that might be typically labeled religious in contemporary European-American culture; it refers to *all* human relationships (including, of course, the "religious" ones). Popular Christianity is like an epistemological womb within and through which all of daily reality is produced and reproduced. Furthermore, the culture, social place, and gender of individuals and/or groups will profoundly shape and mark their particular style of and participation in popular Christianity. Groups and individuals will utilize the hermeneutic tools made available to them by their standing in society, thereby making their interpretation and understanding of Christianity "acceptable" and "respectable" in society to the same manner and degree given to the culture, gender, and social place of that individual or group.[16] Consequently, any attempt at retrieving and/or authentically constructing a theology of traditioning *must* not only go to and through popular religion, but must *also* realize that not all versions of popular Christianity will necessarily lead to the same processes of traditioning. This is certainly one very important reason why popular Christianity, as bearer of the *sensus fidelium* in the ordinary transmission of Christianity, needs to be discerned. Traditioning *by itself* is not exclusive of doctrinal error.

Christians interpret and attempt to remember, symbolize, and live by that which they experienced in and interpret to be a (coherent) part of the Christian religion. In theological terms there is Christianity only where the experience of God (as proclaimed and made possible by the gospel) has become truly incarnate in the culture, history, and life of the believing people. Among other consequences this implies, for example, that the Christianity of the hegemonic groups and their allies in a society will express itself through the symbols, the images, and the lifestyles of hegemony, which are not those of the socially marginalized Christian groups in that same society.[17] But to the degree that shared religious symbols, teachings, and lifestyles are "received" by both the marginalized and the hegemonic, and to the degree that the memory of Christianity's origins is acknowledged as the source of religious identity among both groups, to those degrees people on all sides of society's divide(s) can claim to participate in the same Christian religion.[18]

If it is true that Christianity, of its very nature, must incarnate in and symbolize the social and historical realities of its believers, then *there cannot be one single way of being Christian or of experiencing and interpreting the Christian religion*. The different ways will reflect the conflicts, the social places, the classes, the cultures, the genders, and everything else that is common part and parcel of human societies.[19]

Popular Christianity has great importance in the daily lives of ordinary Christians. This religious universe, as it has been shown, is *not* mainly or more significantly the sum of devotions, rituals, beliefs and doctrines that may be retrieved from the people's religion. Popular Catholicism is, arguably, and above all else, an epistemology—a way of knowing and constructing the "real."[20] Indeed, it has been shown that popular Christianity is one of the most foundational bearers of social and cultural identity among the majority of Christians. And, among

Latinos/as, it is the meaningful home of our collective, daily being. The people's religion may be compared, no more and no less, to any human family where humanization *and* dehumanization mix in *lo cotidiano*, and where neither dimension alone defines or exhausts it.

Scholars are sometimes inclined to seek long lists of odd rituals or of theologically exotic beliefs when searching for popular Christianity's religious and/or theological core. This approach assumes and perpetuates the marginalization of ordinary people's real-life faith, casting it into a secondary, "folk," "curious," or "popularized" mold vis-à-vis an otherwise (assumed to be) "real and official" Christianity. The same may be said in reference to other forms of popular Christianity. Thus, the ecclesiastical institution is held up by many scholars as the witness to "true" mainstream Christianity, while the real-life, daily-life religion of most Christians is regarded as an adulterated or simplistic (or simplified) version of the official norm.

I have serious philosophical and theological difficulties with a scholarly method such as the one just described—because it studies the outward, sociological, cultural, and even doctrinal forms (necessary as these might be) without a *methodologically* significant regard for the religious *experiences* that ultimately legitimize, ground, and sustain the forms. That sort of approach to popular Christianity misses the main reason for this religion's extraordinary staying power and resilience, covers up popular Christianity's more significant threats to dominant culture and religious doctrinal/institutional forms and transmission processes, and it implies or assumes as self-evident an ecclesiology that is woefully inadequate.[21] As I said before, popular Christianity is, arguably, and above all else, *an epistemology: a way of constructing and interpreting the "real" by means that are culturally-specific,* grounded in equally culturally specific experiences of God and of the Christian message.

To speak of the role(s) of popular Christianity in traditioning is to speak of the ordinary means through which Christianity transmits itself across generations and across cultural boundaries. And because these means are affected by sin (as are all things human), then the role(s) of popular Christianity in traditioning must also be regarded as limited, wounded by sin, and in need of discernment.

Popular Christianity can be theologically understood as a legitimate bearer of the *sensus fidelium*—indeed, its most common bearer. Furthermore, as a way of constructing and interpreting the real (hence, as epistemology), popular Christianity acts as an indispensable lens through which revelation, as received and elaborated by the *sensus fidelium* within Christianity, evolves and adapts itself to ordinary Christians' ever-changing sociocultural and historical circumstances. Popular

Christianity, consequently, acts as inculturation and transculturation of revelation, making it possible for the latter to become understandable and received by the people (thus empowering ongoing evangelization and conversion). But, as I keep repeating, this positive and important evaluation of popular Christianity, in order to be theologically useful and adequate, must be accompanied by a parallel critical evaluation that takes into account popular Christianity's cultural woundedness and sinfulness.

Ordinarily, in the Christian universe it is in the context of *lo cotidiano* and, therefore, in the context of popular Christianity that the religion transmits itself. It is the familial, communal, daily life that traditions what one generation (or one cultural group) considers to be Christianity to another generation (or to another cultural group). Although preaching and more formal religious education can and almost certainly are involved in the traditioning process, it is clear that styles of living and witnessing, family practices and assumptions, ethical expectations and counseling, wisdom phrases, rites and symbols, and many other elements combine to express what is understood (and wants to be transmitted) as the core Christian message and the necessary Christian memories (and what are regarded as authentic developments thereof). Most Christians received Christianity through a diverse set of processes, acting together. Most Christians can truthfully be said to have "caught" Christianity more successfully through the ordinary and often unawares processes of traditioning than by their having been formally "taught" it. And although the diverse set of processes of traditioning probably included more formal and intentional ecclesial means too, the familial and communal means were by far more successful and widespread. This is especially important, theologically, when we recall that Christianity is a lifestyle before it is a body of doctrines.[22]

The power of devotions, of prayer life, and so on, it seems, far outweighs the power of creedal formulations and doctrinal explanations in the faith life of everyday Christians. The direct experience of God is immensely more important than the knowledge of being doctrinally orthodox. The strength of the witness of compassion unquestionably surpasses whatever importance might be given to ecclesial polities. This is not to say that ordinary Christians give no importance to creeds, doctrines, or polity; it is, however, a reminder of where the crucial weight is placed in ordinary people's understanding of what is most necessary in Christianity. And thus, if Christianity is transmitted ordinarily by ordinary Christians through the ordinary means available to them in *lo cotidiano*, then *that which* is transmitted (the contents) will consequently express the ordinary appreciation and understanding of the core message of Christianity and its necessary memories (and whatever is understood as authentic developments thereof) as held by ordinary Christians. Hence the important role of popular Christianity, and the crucial role of culture and *lo cotidiano* for and in Christian traditioning—because even the contents of traditioning (that which is transmitted—the tradition) are recalled, shaped, and conveyed by the common and ordinary processes usually associated with popular Christianity.

Said differently, and perhaps more theologically, the main and ordinary subjects (traditioners) of Christian tradition are the ordinary Christians in and through their ordinary (popular) Christianity within the cultural context of *lo cotidiano*. All other subjects (traditioners) of Christianity are, at most, ancillary and extraordinary, even if in Christian history they have at times proven to be of immense importance.

Consider the Extraordinary Traditioners

Christianity is first a faith commitment and lifestyle, and then secondarily a body of doctrines. It can be easily argued, however, that the faith commitment and lifestyle cannot be understood or even assumed without some development and acceptance of doctrine. Therefore, even the ordinary means of traditioning must acknowledge that it is traditioning *something*—the core message of Christianity, its required memories, and the developments thereof that are held to be authentic and at times also required. There is no traditioning, then, without tradition.

The problems arise (and certainly have frequently arisen in Christian history) when divergent perspectives appear regarding the contents of the core message, the selection and nature and implications of the required memories, or the criteria for developments and for determining the authenticity of these developments. Sometimes ordinary Christians and their popular Christianity have not had the means or the ability to settle differences of perspectives, or perhaps have themselves widened the differences. What then?

The history of Christianity, across generations and across cultures, shows that denominational separations and varieties have often resulted from the situation described above. I do not think I exaggerate if I say that neither Luther, nor Calvin, nor Zwingli, nor any of the other reformers in church history, including Roman Catholic and Anglican reformers, could have proven successful simply or mainly by elaborating coherent theologies or reform plans. The same could be said of others responsible for newer (post-sixteenth century) denominational forms and reforms of Christianity across the world.

Ordinary people had to listen, had to understand sufficiently, had to be convinced, in order for *any* reformer and *any* reformation movement to be successful. Ordinary people listened, understood, and were convinced, and committed to any of the several reform movements, within and from within *their* ordinary ways of understanding, of listening, and so on. Said in other words, neither Luther, nor Calvin, nor Trent, for example, could have succeeded had they not been able to connect, at the cultural levels and contexts of *lo cotidiano*, with ordinary Christians' faith and experience.[23] Which then allows me to say that what actually became the reform movements of the sixteenth century (as well as other reform movements of later centuries) were shaped and transmitted, in ways that were clearly not extrinsic or tangential or merely contextual to the reform movements, by ordinary Christians in and through their ordinary ways of traditioning, thereby "producing" denominational strands of Christianity that today should not understand themselves mainly or exclusively through academic theological analyses of doctrines (if they pretend really to understand themselves) but which must engage in a thorough study of the *ordinary* means and assumptions through which the reformers' doctrines and programs were accepted, reshaped, and implemented in Christian history by ordinary Christians in and through their cultures. Furthermore, it must be recalled as hermeneutically very relevant for that theological study (and not merely as the horrid or embarrassing context—historical, doctrinal, and ethical—that needed reforming) that the *common* and *ordinary* perspective from which *all* Western Christians at the time of the reformations listened to, understood, and committed to one or another reform movement was the perspective of popular Catholicism (and in this perspective I am explicitly including all those Christians who eventually broke with Rome as well as those who remained in the Roman communion).

The dissolution of Christian unity has often resulted, historically, when divergent perspectives have appeared regarding the contents of the core message of Christianity, or the selection and nature and implications of Christian required memories, or the criteria for doctrinal or polity developments and for determining the authenticity or not of these developments. It does not seem an exaggeration to say, therefore, that the role of the extraordinary transmitters of Christianity (the extraordinary traditioners) have, at best, been partially successful and mostly ancillary to ordinary Christian traditioning.

But what was just stated cannot be taken to assume that the extraordinary traditioners can be dismissed as irrelevant or unnecessary. Indeed, most Christian churches will explicitly admit the necessary role of bishops and/or other ministers (or synods, general conventions or councils) in affirming and guiding even ordinary Christian traditioning. What arguably cannot be claimed and is not claimed by any Christian church is that its bishops and/or other ministers (or synods, general conventions or councils), *without the rest of the Christian community*, are the exclusive and *only* transmitters of Christianity, because theologically this simply cannot be said without explicitly denying what is ordinarily understood as the baptismal responsibility of all Christians and the overall mission of the whole church.

What, then, is the role of bishops and/or other ministers (or of synods, general conventions, and councils) in Christian traditioning? I think this is a question that must not be answered merely or mainly from canonical perspectives—in other words, from legal and/or institutionally customary role descriptions—because the intent and content of the question is not directed at what *customarily* is done or has been done, but at what *theologically* has been done and should be done.

What is the role of bishops and/or other ministers (and of synods, general conventions, and councils) in traditioning? Extraordinary in crises (in the sense of, literally, being "extra" or "outside" of the ordinary) but ordinarily ancillary. And this without disregarding or undervaluing their recognized and important ministry.

It might be denominationally customary, and perhaps even canonically required, that bishops and/or other ministers coordinate the ecclesial processes involved in overall traditioning. It is often the case that bishops and/or other ministers (and synods, general conventions, and councils) provide denominational spaces and means for learning and reflection for and with other members of their Christian communities, as well as develop guidelines and styles of traditioning deemed to be consistent with their communities' understanding of the core Christian message, its required memories, and its authentic developments. Bishops and/or other ministers (and synods, general conventions, and councils) are frequently responsible, or perhaps exclusively responsible in some Christian churches, for the creation and adaptation of official liturgical forms and styles, of some devotional practices, and of art, literature, and symbols that contribute to overall traditioning. But few if any of these contributions, important as they might be in the churches' life, are as crucial as the bishops' and/or other ministers' (or synods', or general conventions', or councils') role vis-à-vis what is perceived as (factually or potentially) heretical or heterodox.

When Christianity faces a doctrinal or moral crisis, or when what is deemed necessary is judged to be compromised by processes of ordinary

traditioning, bishops and/or other ministers (and synods, general conventions, and councils) play or can play a crucial role that serves as
resolution to the crisis. In this case their role might imply adopting and
adapting elements or perspectives, often borrowed from non-Christian
contexts, which are judged to serve as tools for clarification of what is
contested or doubted, or borrowed from other Christian communities
with the same justification, or simply fashioned afresh to resolve the
doctrinal crisis. In all cases the judgment is made, by the bishops and/or
the other ministers (in synod, in general convention, or in council), that
their proposed resolution is indeed consistent with and required by the
core Christian message, its necessary memories, and/or its authentic developments. But the resolution proposed is a proposal, presented with as
much weight as the bishops' and/or other ministers' role (in synod, in
general convention, or in council) might be endowed in their respective
churches, but in every case requiring the consent (or reception)[24] on the
part of ordinary Christians, however this consent (or reception) is expressed or understood customarily or doctrinally in each church. Once
consent (or reception) occurs, the role of bishops and/or other ministers
(and of synods, general conventions, and councils) is legitimized in its
function as bulwark against heresy or heterodoxy, as guiding and affirming the Christian community in its understanding of the core Christian message, its necessary memories and authentic developments.

But *ordinarily,* Christian doctrinal or moral development and
traditioning unfolds peacefully and slowly, and it is only recognized
post factum.[25] It occurs ordinarily through popular Catholicism or other
forms of popular Christianity, their symbols and practices, and within
the contexts of daily life; Christian traditioning as well as doctrinal and
moral developments occur, therefore, very typically through witnessing,
informal conversation, ritual, symbol and aphorism, acquiring any technical, theological expression later on, *after* the church's *sensus fidelium*
has *already* believed, acknowledged, and accepted the doctrine or the
moral option.[26] Only rarely, and usually in the midst of crises, do the
bishops and/or other ministers involved in the process exercise a role
distinguishable from that of ordinary Christians—a role welcomed or
expected by most Christian communities, whose outcome commonly
requires the consent (or reception) of the people.

In their daily lives Christians experience God, believe and practice
their faith, and (probably unawares) attempt to adapt and explain better
(to themselves and to others) what they experience, believe, and practice. These adaptations and explanations are themselves grounded on
earlier ordinary doctrinal and ethical developments and consequently
(and necessarily) will lead to further doctrinal and ethical developments.

TRADITIONING'S IMPACT ON TRADITION

If the ordinary traditioners of Christianity are ordinary Christians, *and* if the ordinary means of traditioning are those typical of ordinary Christians, *and* if this is and has been so across generations and across cultural and denominational boundaries throughout twenty-one centuries of Christian history, *and* if, further, the role of bishops and/or other ministers (and of synods and councils) has been especially important in moments of doctrinal or moral crises, being otherwise ancillary and commonly participatory in the ordinary processes of traditioning, *and* if all traditioning (ordinary and extraordinary) is necessarily cultural and inescapably located within *lo cotidiano, and*, lastly, if all traditioning assumes that something is traditioned, *then* it seems reasonable to suggest that *whatever is traditioned (the tradition or contents of Christianity) is shaped, selected, presented, and received according to the social position, gender, culture, and so forth,[27] of those who ordinarily transmit Christianity as well as of those who ordinarily listen to the gospel and accept it across generations and across cultural boundaries.*

The social locations, classes, cultures, genders, and so forth of the Christians who transmit their religion across generations and across cultural boundaries will affect and shape the contents of that religion and its various presentations to new listeners, as well as affect and shape the new listeners' understanding of the religion and their decision to accept, reject, or further modify it.

We can, consequently, wonder about the ecumenical possibilities that might open if Christians of different denominations were to (admittedly with some degree of artificiality) put temporarily "on the back burner" their doctrinal differences and focus their attention on the social locations, classes, cultures, genders, and so forth, of themselves and others (regardless of denomination) who also claim to be Christian. My suspicion is that the denominational lines, so far established in history by doctrinal differences, would yield in true radical importance to other differences (class, gender, race, culture, and so forth) perhaps more profound and perhaps more diabolical because they have been hidden from most ordinary Christians by the hegemonic groups in societies and churches. And thus, consequently, if among those of the same class, gender, race, ethnic background, and so forth, there were to perdure denominational differences grounded in doctrinal questions, then these questions must first submit themselves to deep and systematic analyses—to make sure, indeed, that the differences are doctrinal and not the introjection of the ideological arguments put forth by those whose hegemony depends on the supposed evidence of the arguments.

It thus seems to me that, after careful historical, social, and cultural studies, theologians of different denominations might find their ecumenical enterprise confounded by the hidden realities of ideological hegemony's arguments, by the contextualizing circumstances of all Christians and of all denominations, and by the less-than-convincing doctrinal argumentation the hegemonic often put forward as part of the construction of their hegemonic status (which, of course, necessitates their introjection as "evident" by those who do not share in hegemonic status).[28]

I am not making light of doctrinal differences. I am simply saying that I strongly suspect there have been three enormous impacts on Christian tradition (contents, doctrines) by the traditioning of the religion throughout the centuries and the cultures:

1. Doctrinal differences that have emerged (although, granted, not always) among Christians have very often more to do with hegemonic arguments than with real necessities of doctrinal development and/or clarification.

2. At the level of ordinary traditioning and traditioners of Christianity there has been much introjection of the doctrinal arguments of the hegemonic in society and church.

3. These introjected hegemonic arguments are much more divisive in their theory than in their daily reality, role, and ordinary impact on ordinary Christians' lives, unless, of course, the ideological powers of hegemony successfully convince them otherwise, for the benefit of the hegemonic (although hegemonic interests are often subsumed into an apparent—but sometimes not transparent—concern for truth and orthodoxy).

A CONCLUDING CHALLENGE

After the (admittedly partial) reflections on traditioning offered in the preceding pages, I conclude simply by wondering whether Christian theologians of the various denominations would be willing to take up the risks implied in studying tradition from the perspective of traditioning; and furthermore, if they are willing to expose their denominations' doctrinal claims (that is, the supposed grounds for denominational distinctiveness) to the rigorous analysis of hegemonic, contextualizing relationships and circumstances. It might be wise for the future of Christianity and of the ecumenical movement to pick up the methodological challenge, but will we be willing to assume the risks?

Notes

[1] See José Irizarry's chapter in the present volume, as well as the chapter by Gary Riebe-Estrella.

[2] There is a long list of theologies of tradition, from many denominational perspectives—some supportive of (e.g., Congar, Geiselmann, Tilley) and some opposed to (e.g., Cullmann, Ebeling) the normative necessity of tradition in Christianity. To a large degree these options are expected, given that five hundred years of animosity among Christians have had much to do with their options on tradition's role and understanding in their various denominations. However, this article is on traditioning, and on this latter topic there has been (understandably) much less animosity among Christians. For two remarkable works, both by non-Catholic authors, see Dale T. Irvin, *Christian Histories, Christian Traditioning: Rendering Accounts* (Maryknoll, NY: Orbis Books, 1998); and David Brown, *Tradition and Imagination: Revelation and Change* (Oxford: Oxford Univ. Press, 1999). I am currently working on a book-length ecumenical and intercultural proposal on tradition and traditioning (which I think is directly pertinent to what is discussed in the present article): *Power and Memory: Toward an Ecumenical and Intercultural Theology of Tradition* (Maryknoll, NY: Orbis Books, forthcoming).

[3] On culture, besides and beyond the classical and/or expected texts, see, for example Marcello Santos, *Técnica, espaço, tempo* (São Paulo: Editora HUCITEC, 1997); Jere P. Surber, *Culture and Critique: An Introduction to the Critical Discourses of Cultural Studies* (Boulder, CO: Westview Press, 1998); Mary McCanney Gergen, ed., *Feminist Thought and the Structure of Knowledge* (New York: New York Univ. Press, 1988); Homi K. Bhabha, *The Location of Culture* (London: Routledge, 1994); Samuel Fleischacker, *The Ethics of Culture* (Ithaca, NY: Cornell Univ. Press, 1994); Robert Wuthnow et al., *Cultural Analysis: The Work of Peter L. Berger, Mary Douglas, Michel Foucault, and Jürgen Habermas* (London: Routledge, 1984); Renato Rosaldo, *Culture and Truth: The Remaking of Social Analysis* (Boston: Beacon Press, 1993); Uma Narayan, *Dislocating Cultures: Identities, Traditions, and Third World Feminism* (New York: Routledge, 1997). And certainly see Peter L. Berger and Thomas Luckmann, *The Social Construction of Reality* (New York: Doubleday, 1966); Hugues Portelli, *Gramsci y la cuestión religiosa* (Barcelona: Editorial Laia, 1977); Pierre Bourdieu, *A economia das trocas simbólicas* (São Paulo: Edições Perspectiva, 1974); idem, *The Logic of Practice* (Stanford, CA: Stanford Univ. Press, 1990); David Swartz, *Culture and Power: The Sociology of Pierre Bourdieu* (Chicago: Univ. of Chicago Press, 1997); and Renato Ortiz, *A consciência fragmentada: Ensaios de cultura popular e religião* (Rio de Janeiro: Editorial Paz e Terra, 1980).

[4] It seems to me that the "unveiling" role of culture is a "constructing" role too, so that, in the process of unveiling us to ourselves (and to others) as meaningfully human, culture *constructs* us as meaningfully human. I am, therefore, not affirming or assuming that there is some sort of communal "self" underlying us that is *then* unveiled to us by culture. Rather, unveiling implies and is itself the construction of ourselves as meaningful humans. We must also remember that cultural processes are historical.

[5] See, for example, Orlando O. Espín, *The Faith of the People* (Maryknoll, NY: Orbis Books, 1997), chaps. 1 and 6; idem, "Grace and Humanness," in *We Are a People! Initiatives in Hispanic American Theology,* ed. Roberto S. Goizueta, 133–64 (Minneapolis: Fortress Press, 1992); idem, "A Multicultural Church? Theological Reflections from Below," in *The Multicultural Church: A New Landscape in U.S. Theologies,* ed. William Cenkner, 54–71 (New York: Paulist Press, 1995); and idem, "An Exploration into the Theology of Grace and Sin," *From the Heart of Our People,* ed. Orlando Espín and Miguel Díaz (Maryknoll, NY: Orbis Books, 1999).

[6] I am increasingly uncomfortable with the tendency to romanticize Latino/a cultures (acknowledging that I too have done this in the past). Our cultures are not, and have never been, "innocent." I am clearly in agreement with Professor Justo González's evaluation, as presented several years ago in *Mañana: Christian Theology from the Hispanic Perspective* (Nashville, TN: Abingdon, 1990), 31–42. I think most Latino/a theologians are on target in their attempt to theologically describe and analyze the "both/and" existence of Latinos/as as source and locus of theology, and especially agree with their growing *critical* analysis and appropriation of the categories of *mestizaje* and *mulataje*. Michelle González's chapter in the present volume contributes to a much needed corrective dialogue on Latino/a identity building, and so does Miguel Díaz's chapter. At the fifty-ninth convention of the Catholic Theological Society of America (2004) I presented a paper on the possible contours of a Latino/a theology of religions that, in dialogue with the Afro-Cuban Lukumí religion, also significantly challenged the "canonical" version of Latino/a history and identity (for a synthesis of the paper, see the *Proceedings of the Catholic Theological Society of America,* 2004).

[7] Cf. Mário de França Miranda, *Libertados para a práxis da justiça: A teologia da graça no atual contexto latino-americano* (São Paulo: Edições Loyola, 1980).

[8] It is evident that *lo cotidiano* is not and cannot be referred solely or mainly to domesticity or to "women's spheres." It is also clear that feminist theorists and historians have been at the forefront of critical studies on and retrieval of *lo cotidiano* as reality and category of analysis. On *lo cotidiano*, see, for example, Orlando O. Espín, "Exploration in the Theology of Grace and Sin," in Espín and Díaz, *From the Heart of Our People,* which offers a more complete bibliography than the one offered here, especially in reference to Latinos/as. For a thorough discussion and bibliographical references in the Latin American context, see María Pilar Aquino, *Our Cry for Life* (Maryknoll, NY: Orbis Books, 1993); originally published as *Nuesto clamor por la vida* (San José, Costa Rica:

DEI, 1992). Among the pioneering authors on the critical study of daily life, are Agnes Heller, *Historia y vida cotidiana* (Mexico City: Editorial Grijalbo, 1972); idem, *Sociología de la vida cotidiana* (Barcelona: Editorial Península, 1977); idem, *La revolución de la vida cotidiana* (Barcelona: Editorial Península, 1982); Teresa de Barbieri, *Mujeres y vida cotidiana* (Mexico City: Fondo de Cultura Económica, 1984); Ana Sojo, *Mujer y política. Ensayo sobre feminismo y sujeto popular* (San José, Costa Rica: DEI, 1985); B. Welter, "The Cult of True Womanhood: 1820–1860," *American Quarterly* 18 (1966): 151–74; and Michel de Certeau, *The Practice of Everyday Life* (Berkeley: Univ. of California Press, 1984). See also, L. K. Kerber, "Separate Spheres, Female Worlds, Woman's Place: The Rhetoric of Women's History," *Journal of American History* 75 (1988): 9–39; Nancy F. Cott, *The Bonds of Womanhood: "Woman's Sphere" in New England, 1780–1835* (New Haven, CT: Yale Univ. Press, 1977), esp. 63–100 and 197–206. See also, Ada María Isasi-Díaz, *En la lucha/In the Struggle: A Hispanic Women's Liberation Theology* (Minneapolis: Fortress Press, 1993); and idem, *Mujerista Theology* (Maryknoll, NY: Orbis Books, 1996), 66–73.

[9] Very pertinent to this discussion, and to any reflection on *lo cotidiano*, is the third chapter, "*Nosotros*: Community as the Birthplace of the Self," in Roberto S. Goizueta, *Caminemos con Jesús: Toward a Hispanic/Latino Theology of Accompaniment* (Maryknoll, NY: Orbis Books, 1995), 47–76.

[10] Aquino, *Nuestro clamor por la vida*, 75 (my translation).

[11] For a more thorough discussion of Latino/a popular Catholicism, and abundant bibliographical references to its study, see Espín, *The Faith of the People*; idem, "Religiosidad popular: Un aporte para su definición y hermenéutica," *Estudios Sociales* 58 (1984): 41–57; and Espín, "An Exploration into the Theology of Grace and Sin." The reader must have noticed that, in the text, I say that popular Christianity embodies, epistemologically organizes, and symbolically expresses daily relationships and their broader networks and connections. From this it must *not* be deduced that popular Christianity is the *only* Latino/a cultural creation that embodies, organizes, and expresses daily relationships and their networks within and for the Latino/a milieux. What should be understood is that popular Christianity is an extraordinarily important, culturally authentic manner for accomplishing those tasks.

[12] Another consideration to keep in mind is that within evangelical and/or Pentecostal Christianity separate denominations (including those that understand themselves as nondenominational) can come into being with some ecclesiological ease and legitimacy if severe circumstances appear to lead to irreconcilable variations within the denomination of origin, whereas within the historic Protestant churches there would be greater inclination to accommodate severe intra-denominational variations without formal separation. Occasionally, therefore, we may find an entire denomination, usually of evangelical and/or Pentecostal origins, fitting the criteria of popular religion, although in their self-appreciation the members would judge themselves to be a legitimate (perhaps *the* legitimate or even mainstream) denominational interpretation of the core Christian message, of its required memories, and of its authentic developments.

Within the historic Protestant churches the application of the criteria of popular religion would uncover, as it does in Roman Catholicism and in Anglicanism, widely and popularly held beliefs and practices, as well as much that is religiously cultural.

[13] There is no need to romanticize the role of mature women in Latino/a culture and religion, or to freeze or stereotype it in time. There is no guarantee that future generations of Latinas will preserve or continue the role that mature Latinas have had and currently still have among us. Reason and history clearly suggest that there will be significant changes. The impact of the dominant culture, certainly, will be felt on the cultural role of mature Latinas. But whatever the changes, it is very important to remember that these will happen *from* the current situation, as this situation was itself molded from past circumstances. To understand the present cultural status of mature, older Latinas is an essential step in preparing for and understanding their future. For discussions and bibliographies on issues relating to women within popular Catholicism, and especially on how the social victimization of women affects popular Catholicism, see Espín, *The Faith of the People*, esp. chaps. 3, 4, and 6; and Espín, "An Exploration into the Theology of Grace and Sin."

[14] *Popular* meaning "of and by the common people." *Popular* does not mean widespread here, although popular religion evidently is.

[15] Espín, *The Faith of the People*, 63–103.

[16] On this, see Espín, "A Multicultural Church?" See also Linda Alcoff and Elizabeth Potter, eds., *Feminist Epistemologies* (New York: Routledge, 1993); and Kathleen Lennon and Margaret Whitford, eds., *Knowing the Difference: Feminist Perspectives in Epistemology* (New York: Routledge, 1994). I found invaluable, for understanding *lo cotidiano* as well as for the overall discussion of epistemology, Alessandra Tanesini, *An Introduction to Feminist Epistemologies* (Oxford: Blackwell, 1999), as well as Sojo, *Mujer y política*.

[17] See Portelli, *Gramsci y la cuestión religiosa*, 141–62.

[18] Ibid., 43–94.

[19] See François Houtart, "Religion et champ politique: cadre théorique pour l'étude des sociétés capitalistes périphériques," *Social Compass* 24, no. 2–3 (1977), 265–72; and, idem, "Weberian Theory and the Ideological Function of Religion," *Social Compass* 23, no. 4 (1976), 345–54.

[20] See Orlando O. Espín, "Popular Catholicism as an Epistemology (of Suffering)," *Journal of Hispanic/Latino Theology* 2, no. 2 (1994): 55–78.

[21] In addition, it assumes a definition of *religion* that is far from acceptable or evident. On this, see Orlando O. Espín, "Popular Catholicism: Alienation or Hope?" in *Hispanic/Latino Theology: Challenge and Promise*, ed. Ada M. Isasi-Díaz and Fernando F. Segovia (Minneapolis: Fortress Press, 1996), 307–24.

[22] Very important, in this regard, is Terrence Tilley, *Inventing Catholic Tradition* (Maryknoll, NY: Orbis Books, 2000). Tilley's "practical" theology of tradition and traditioning is pertinent to our entire discussion, specifically the third and fourth chapters in his book. Tilley's book is one of the best recent theologies of tradition. For a study of continuity in (Catholic) tradition's development, see

John E. Thiel, *Senses of Tradition: Continuity and Development in Catholic Faith* (New York: Oxford Univ. Press, 2000).

[23] But, we must admit, the acceptance by the people of the different reformations (Catholic, Anglican, or Protestant [Lutheran, Calvinist, and so on]) has been historically accompanied and assisted, all too frequently, by nonreligious pressures. Kings and princes and other leaders often involved themselves (and perhaps still involve themselves) in the promotion of this or that religious perspective or polity. And in the sixteenth and seventeenth centuries (and later too) the people's compliance with the leaders' religious choices were not simply left to the people's freedom. But regardless of the pressures on the people, ordinary Christians had (indispensably) to "receive" the reformations for these to have survived in history. In this regard we can fruitfully read José Irizarry's article in the present volume.

[24] Reception of a doctrine does not create the doctrine but merely affirms that it is in fundamental accord with scripture and tradition or already present there. More important, reception of doctrine points to a constitutive dimension of Christianity, since Christianity exists because the apostolic preaching was and is accepted (that is, *received*, assented to) by all who become members of the church. Theologically speaking, the reception of a doctrine or teaching occurs as a consequence of the guiding action of the Holy Spirit, who preserves the entire church from error. Today, some theologians use the expression "reception of doctrine" also to refer to the acceptance of a doctrine that originated in one Christian church (or denomination) by another Christian church (or denomination). The reception of a conciliar or papal doctrine is not historically guaranteed. There have been cases of doctrines officially proposed by a council (e.g., the conciliarist teaching of the council of Constance) or by a pope (e.g., Boniface VIII's teaching that salvation requires submission to papal authority) that were not received by the members of the church. The specific manner or procedure through which a doctrine is received in and by the church has never been established because it has greatly varied throughout history. Any contemporary attempt at describing the process of reception will also have to contend with the very serious questions raised by inculturation. The idea that doctrine has to be received by the members of the church emerged during the first centuries of Christianity, when the prevalent ecclesiological model understood the universal church to be a community of communities. After the Council of Trent (1546–63), and especially after the First Vatican Council (1869–70), the idea of reception of doctrine began to be slowly transformed in Western Roman Catholicism to mean obligatory assent to the doctrinal decisions of the magisterium. However, after the Second Vatican Council (1962–65) Catholic theology started reflecting again on the nature, importance, and need of reception of doctrines, on the role the *sensus fidelium* plays in that reception, and on how reception occurs in contemporary Roman Catholicism's ecclesiological model. This newer and yet very traditional reflection is important because the reception of doctrine is a process that involves the entire church, and it cannot be reduced to assent to a juridical or magisterial determination. Furthermore, reception of

doctrine must not be confused with modern democratic processes because what is sought by reception is not doctrinal agreement among the members of the church but *agreement with and assent to apostolic preaching and tradition*, as this preaching and this tradition must be received and understood by every generation.

[25] Although this *post factum* recognition might not always be peaceful, as evidenced by history.

[26] For an explanation of *sensus fidelium*, see the pertinent section in Espín, *The Faith of the People*, chap. 3; and Daniel J. Finucane, *Sensus Fidelium: The Use of a Concept in the Post–Vatican II Era* (San Francisco: International Scholars Publications, 1996).

[27] This "and so forth" includes a longer list of other contextualizing circumstances, whether individual Christians or specific denominations want to admit it or not. Among the evident and non-dismissable factors included in this "and so forth" are race, ethnic origin, immigration status, sexual orientation, and access to health, education, and other services. The list could be longer. There is, of course, a direct connection between social position, gender, and culture and these other contextualizing circumstances. And all must be analyzed for the power relations implicit in their social existence and roles.

[28] I remind the reader that feminist and Latin American liberation theologians have been making similar suggestions for at least the past four decades.

2

Authority and/or Tradition

Bernard Cooke

Implicit in all the discussion of tradition in this volume's essays is the issue of *normativity*: in what way(s) do the various agents and forms of tradition provide a guideline or a law for individual and community behavior? To express it differently, what *authority* attaches to a specific element of tradition, to a specific bearer of a tradition, or to the process of traditioning as a whole?[1] Any response to these questions demands a clarification of the kinds of authority that function in the process of traditioning and of the manner in which they apply to the bearers of tradition. Such clarification is the intent of this essay which, fortunately, can draw from a considerable body of reflection about authority during recent decades.[2]

Authority is a multi-form kind of power that functions both to govern relationships in the public sphere and to affect the motivation of individuals. One could also describe authority as the operative influence of a person, text, event, custom, or institution upon the thinking and action of a community or an individual. Much recent explanation of authority has insisted that in practice it is a modality of the complex relationships of influence among people, and there is disagreement whether authority can be viewed as a "quality" residing in one or other agent.[3] In an important and provocative essay Orlando Espín has elaborated the way in which the phenomenon of globalization is fundamentally affecting the way in which traditioning occurs and the resultant perspective that must guide research into tradition. While the essay does not explicitly deal with the element of authority in traditioning, the entire essay can be read as an analysis of the way in which globalization has changed the reality and the theoretical consideration of authority.[4]

Though in some cases authority is made effective by enforcement of one sort or another, authority as such operates by persuasion directed to people's free choices. Dependent upon the function of authority in a particular instance, it is specified by and grounded in a distinctive base; for example, authority in the case of teaching can flow from the knowledge of the teacher, in the political sphere from the office of the office-holder, in the case of a charismatic prophet from divine inspiration and commission. From among the many forms of authority that exist, this essay will deal only with those that impinge or depend upon tradition.

Actually, the relation of authority and tradition is very close, almost one of inseparability; traditioning always involves an aspect of authority, and most instances of authority are grounded in and draw from traditioning for their legitimation and their implementation.[5] Tradition is a primary source of authority in thinking and acting; conversely, elements of a people's tradition are embodied in those persons, texts, rituals, and offices that are viewed as bearing authority. Tilley, in his recent study of tradition, criticizes much of the discussion of tradition because "the practices of institutional authority are absent. . . . An understanding of the authority of office is so absent that such theories [of tradition] are simply not adequate to account for the multifaceted reality that is an enduring faith tradition."[6]

The intimate link between authority and tradition is immediately apparent if one examines the broad experiential context of a culture and the role within it of a people's "religious" faith. David Stagaman (following Gadamer) has in his monograph on authority in the church drawn attention to what he calls the authoritative, that is, the implicit, taken-for-granted evaluation of events, persons, and institutions that implicitly passes judgment as good or evil, appropriate or inappropriate. The normativity of a culture's "hermeneutic of experience" is a fluid, constantly shifting influence on people's outlook and choices—pervasive and for the most part unrecognized.[7] Such an over-arching, authoritative influence has in any particular case emerged from the previous experiences and wisdom evaluations of that people, especially from those evaluations that because "religious" are considered in some form to have come from God. This constitutes a broad, lived tradition that guides the activity and ethical judgments of a group, even when scarcely recognized, much less enunciated. It is often seen as simply natural, what has always been done, and therefore acceptable.

It is not a long leap to associate this value-bearing general cultural judgment with the faith notion of *sensus fidelium*.[8] In a culture such as the Latino/a, in which a presence of the divine is part of the "atmosphere" of experience, a faith perspective is intrinsic to people's awareness of themselves and their world regardless of whether they are "religious" or not. Because life is experienced and carried on *latinamente*, there is a shared assumption of what is appropriate and "true," not only as humans but also as Christians. To some extent, cultural memory extends beyond the influence of faith, but it is impossible to establish any bounds of demarcation. The ongoing process of traditioning provides a fundamental hermeneutic by which the occurrences of daily life are interpreted in the light of faith, and faith is interpreted in the light of *lo cotidiano*.[9]

AUTHORITY OF TRADITION-BEARING TEXTS

Beyond this amorphous, over-arching "authoritative" that accompanies traditioning as it unfolds,[10] there is a number of identifiable agencies that combine to shape and legitimate Tradition. When one thinks of the agents that have carried traditioning, one of the first that comes to mind is the canon of texts, religious or secular, that is recognized as bearing explicitly the ideas, values, hopes, world view, and identity of a group. For Latino/a cultures the place of privilege among such texts has been the sacred scriptures of Israel and Christianity, texts that carry unparalleled authority across a range of differing faith communities because they are regarded as the inspired word of God.[11]

That is not to say that scripture is authoritative in the same way for all its readers/hearers; instead, it speaks to individuals and communities in distinctive ways dependent upon their social location and especially the nature and extent of their educational background.[12] For many fundamentalists, the Bible acts as an icon in which they believe they encounter a present revelation of the will of God. For those in a context of scripture being proclaimed in worship, the word can be heard, dependent upon the expertise of the homilist explaining the text, with more critical understanding. For a trained scripture scholar, the text can constitute a means of uncovering the revelation communicated to people at the origin of the text, revelation communicated through this text during centuries of interpretation by faith communities, revelation that is accepted as faith guidance. In short, a person regards the authority of scripture according to the tradition(s) of interpretation that he or she has inherited and accepted.[13]

Justo González, reflecting on his own evolving experience of reading the Bible, points out the way in which the precise authority of scripture depends upon the life context of a person and at any given moment of that experience can be multiple.[14] Childhood and adolescent confidence in the vision of the biblical word of God can for some individuals fade in adulthood as the Bible no longer seems to speak to life's happenings. Technical study of scripture can provide the tools for evaluating the text as historical evidence or as source of theological reflection, with a result quite different from the religious authority the text has for the ordinary believer. While the latter person can share the centuries-old traditions of a faith community, the exegete draws as well from the scholarly evaluation of methodology and insights handed down in the academy.

Within academic worlds, for example, biblical scholarship in nineteenth-century German universities, there develop schools of exegesis, each with its traditional interpretation of many texts. The fact that they are handed down relatively unchanged from one generation to another gives these interpretations an authority that can endure unchallenged for decades.[15] The German scripture scholar Luise Schottroff has drawn attention to the extent to which biblical interpretation had been dominated and truncated because all the interpreters of the Bible until very recently have been men who assumed the validity of an androcentric perspective.[16]

It is not only professional biblical scholars, however, who accept certain meanings of biblical texts as authoritative because those meanings have always been assumed as the true sense of the text. Among the ordinary faithful many texts are understood the way they are because that has been the meaning passed down from one generation to the next. In evaluating the way in which scripture operates authoritatively for the bulk of Latino/a Christians, it is good to keep in mind the remark of Jean-Pierre Ruiz in the theological discussion that produced *From the Heart of Our People*:

> A *teologia de conjunto* that seriously engages in critical dialogue with the ancient voices that emerge from the biblical texts, voices that testify to a self-disclosing God, must attend respectfully to voices outside of the academy, to those who bring their own language and their own experience to their dialogue with the biblical text.[17]

AUTHORITY OF NON-BIBLICAL "OFFICIAL" RELIGIOUS TEXTS

The variation in authority that religious texts bear is even more pronounced when one looks at the actual impact of key historical statements that are considered officially normative, such as the creed of the Council of Chalcedon. Indirectly, through the recognition it receives as dogma, and therefore through preaching and catechisms and guiding the transmission of faith understandings to those not theologically sophisticated, such a text does help shape Tradition, but on the level of immediately influencing people's faith the text is unknown and irrelevant. Such texts function only within professional circles as normative guides in the community's official transmission of traditional beliefs.

One can attribute to other historical statements of belief, especially the explanations of Christian faith provided by the great figures of the Patristic period, like Augustine or Ambrose, an authority because of the intrinsic genius of their insights and their influential role in shaping Christian thought. Such authority has also been attributed over the centuries to prominent theologians like Aquinas or Alexander of Hales. During the past two centuries papal statements have increasingly acquired, whether justifiably or not, this kind of authority, to some extent supplanting the influence of earlier ecclesiastical statements.[18]

CANONICAL "SECULAR" TEXTS

Biblical or ecclesiastical texts can claim no monopoly in the transmission of Tradition. Along with canonical religious scriptures, other literary classics play a canonical or semi-canonical role in a culture's traditions—and in some instances function cross-culturally. One need only reflect on the communication of human insights and values through Shakespeare's *King Lear* or Sophocles' *Antigone* or Cervantes' *Don Quixote*. Nor need such sharing in a people's traditions be limited to "great" pieces of literature; popular songs and nursery rhymes that pass on interpretations of human experience very likely have a broader effect on popular understanding of what it means to be human.[19] One can point, for instance, to the immense influence on religious understandings and attitudes of the hymns of the Wesley brothers in the Methodist movement. Moreover, in many cases it is not easy, sometimes impossible, to say when texts carry religious or secular meaning [20]

Linked with the cultural authority of literary classics is the subtle but widespread impact of the arts. Elusive though it is to define or identify in a given culture, *style* exerts a broad and profound effect on people's decisions and lifestyle. Closely connected though it is with custom and memory, style is a very fluid force in people's perception of the good life and with their judgment of acceptable social behavior. The aesthetic appreciation belonging to those who are genuinely "stylish" is, however, not a natural endowment but a sensibility that must be acquired by education, essentially by exposure to the beautiful. It is in this realm that the arts make an indispensable contribution to a people's culture and in which objects of true quality possess an authority as guides in forming aesthetic judgments.[21]

Schools of artistic production with their distinctive traditions come and go, but they unquestionably shape people's perception of the beautiful in some enduring fashion. Museum exhibits witness the extent to which artists and their work constitute an important influence in a people's traditioning. Despite the overall fickleness of style, truly beautiful artistic creations—whether paintings or symphonies or poems or buildings—transcend time's changes and provide a heritage that is not limited by ethnic or temporal boundaries.

"Texts" can and do acquire an authority of their own, but that authority is generally rooted in the authority (real or presumed[22]) of their authorship. Biblical texts possess unique authority for believers because of their "divine" origin, though (as we saw earlier) this is conditioned by the manner and extent of their reception. Key dogmatic creeds derive authority because they come from the "infallible" voice of church councils. Great literary classics reflect the genius of their creators. Subsequently, the attribution of authority to these texts and the authority of any particular exegesis comes because of the personal authority of "teachers." Under this general rubric of *teacher* there is a wide range—parents and other family members, credentialed teachers in schools, experts through research, religious pastors and church authorities, charismatic prophets, saintly models of faith and behavior, well-informed friends.

Most basic, of course, in any person's beginning to share in his or her cultural heritage or religious traditions are the members of the individual's immediate family. Orlando Espín has repeatedly pointed to older women, especially the grandmother, the *abuela*, as key authority figures in the transmission of Latino/a tradition.[23] Teaching authority within the family is, however, a shifting influence and one that is challenged by other social forces such as peer pressures on adolescents. For children in their early years, the authority of parents is unquestioned, but with the onset of adolescence, this authority is often diminished by discovery that the older generation is not infallible, not "in synch" with the surrounding dominant culture, not always honest. Eventually, as persons grow into maturity, their measured "conformity" to tradition grows out of their own understandings and experienced choices. They have been taught by life itself, but shared memories and continued interchange still wield a powerful influence in closely knit families.

Other teachers enter the picture as children go to school. These figures are assumed to "know their stuff" and possess the authority that implies. But their authority is often enhanced by other factors: many of us can remember the religious women who presided over the classroom, women whose authority (symbolized by their garb) came at least as much from their ecclesial and professional role as from their knowledge. In some cases there is the influence of a charismatic teacher, one who with a unique kind of authority represents what it means to be human as well as learned, one who epitomizes what is best in a cultural tradition.

Along with academic teachers there are parish pastors. Within the broader influence of a parish community that embodies people's outlook on life, often as an island in the midst of an alien culture, the symbolic role of the ordained pastor is unique.[24] His (or, in some cases, hers) is a voice of established religious authority. He is the one representing God as well as the official church, designated by ordination to guide the faith and, in somewhat prophetic fashion, through sermons and teaching, to explain ethical precepts as the will of God. In the realm of "the sacred" his words bear an authority beyond teaching, for they confect the great mystery of eucharistic transformation; his words of confessional absolution are believed to have power over sin. This is true even when the priest is not personally an exemplar of his role.

However, in the concrete context of Christians' lives, the authority of a pastor is conditioned by such factors as his knowledge, his skill in communicating, the authenticity of his faith, and even his personality traits. It is not uncommon for the exhortation given during Sunday worship to be neutralized for children by a parent's criticism of the sermon. Simply put, in addition to the authority that comes with special relation to "the sacred," a pastor must gain human authority by what he himself is and does. Moreover, today, when greater opportunities exist for people to develop an accurate and adult conscience, the authority of a person's own conscience at times conflicts with and overrules the authority of religious leaders.

AUTHORITY OF SCHOLARLY HISTORICAL RESEARCH

In the past few centuries, associated with the overall respect for science, critical historical research has exerted increasing authority as a guide to people's memory of their antecedents. The supposed objectivity of this scholarly effort had inescapably been affected by the differing social locations of the researchers, but this influence was not always recognized nor admitted by those historians who have claimed to be and have often been considered to be "mainstream history." Confronting this hegemonic claim, Gary Macy has rejected the view that Latino/a historical scholarship is marginal to such a mainstream; instead, he details a centuries-long recording of remembered events that provides a rich heritage and resource for Latino/a traditioning.[25]

AUTHORITY OF RITUAL

In families, parishes, schools, and neighborhoods a key agency in traditioning is ritual. Among Latinos/as this is accentuated because of the cultural prominence of fiestas. In his essay in *From the Heart of Our People*, Roberto Goizueta has provided a penetrating analysis of the central and complex role played by fiestas of various kinds in the life of Hispanic peoples.[26] He has pointed out how fiesta celebration involves much more than the element of play, because the basic forces of ritual present in fiestas work to shape a culture and the individuals within it.

Rituals make clear, as perhaps no other exercise of traditioning, the interplay of authority and power. In the realms of teaching and social administration authority is at times claimed when it is not truly possessed, and in its place dominating power is employed. This is accentuated in religious rituals, in which an official leader can claim to be a necessary and irreplaceable mediator between the divine and humans. This implies that the very possibility of human salvation, of humans attaining their destiny, lies in the hands of these designated religious officials. Such a view is, of course, a misconception of the manner in which ritual is meant to function.[27]

Ritual has its own distinctive dynamic, which comes into play in proportion to the authenticity of the ritualizing activity. Recent studies of ritual[28] have highlighted four effects of genuine ritual celebration: (1) it expresses and creates the group's self-identification; (2) it shapes the character of the group; (3) it alerts the group to its purpose for existing and demands a commitment to that goal; and (4) it reflects and confirms or challenges the structure of power within the group. Properly conducted ritual achieves these goals, not by dominating control of the participants but by appeal to their free decisions and the communal conversion of their understandings, attitudes, and behavior.

The authority of ritual lies, then, not in a personal prerogative of the presiding leader but in the shared actions and relationships of the persons engaged in the ritual. It is precisely because of this engagement of persons in confronting together the meaning of their lives and the decisions that are needed to shape a shared future that ritual has an inescapable ethical dimension, a distinctive authority in directing people's moral behavior. And it is for this reason that rituals, unofficial as well as official, play a key role in the process of traditioning.

Specific elements of ritual celebration have their own role in passing on understandings and attitudes. There has been a good deal of attention given recently to the cultural impact of the "bloody" crucifixes that are common in Latinos/as' homes and churches,[29] crucifixes where in symbol the religious memory of the suffering of Jesus intertwines with the popular memory of conquest and painful domination. In similar fashion popular religious music carries from one generation to the next the world view and outlook, the emotional response to life, that is central to the diachronic process of tradition.[30]

I saw the authoritative teaching influence of these popular rituals illustrated in dramatic fashion in the Good Friday "passion play" in San Antonio. During the years I lived in that city I had the opportunity not only of observing but also of sharing in that ritual. It began in the Mercado, where, on a raised stage, the condemnation of Jesus by Pilate was reenacted. Because a good-sized crowd had gathered, the actual drama itself was preceded by a long line of greetings delivered by local Mexican American politicians; the present-day relevance of Latino religious roots was quite evident. The judgment scene was not simply observed by the crowd; they entered into it, the shared communal memory of Jesus' passion was obviously being reinforced. As I looked around the crowd, I was struck by something that made clear how traditioning was occurring: much of the crowd was made up of children with their grandmothers, these *abuelas* quite obviously using the occasion to catechize. The memory of those passion plays, with the interpretation given them by their grandmothers, will remain for those children in the imagination's storehouse of "exegesis" along with the overtone of reality that will give authority to Christian religious beliefs in later years.

From the Mercado we processed for several blocks on a Way of the Cross, along a city street that bears the name Dolorosa, to the cathedral. There, in front of the church, three crosses were raised bearing the "stand-ins" for Jesus and the thieves. Illustrating again the mixture of past and present, a long pole with a microphone was raised to "Jesus," so that the crowd in the cathedral plaza could hear the seven last words. Though that song was not used, experiencing this Good Friday liturgy could not but bring to mind the words of the old Negro spiritual, "Were You There When They Crucified My Lord?"

This folk liturgy exemplified quite clearly the authoritative power of ritual in Tradition as a process of people's culture and faith. It was not accidental to the drama that it began and ended in the two locations in San Antonio, the Mercado and San Fernando Cathedral, that continue to play important roles for the Mexican American populace in celebrating and reinforcing their folk memories in fiesta.

In her essay in this volume (Chapter 9) Nancy Pineda-Madrid details the character and impact of what may be the most important of Latino/a folk rituals, those associated with Our Lady of Guadalupe. She highlights the power of these traditional rituals to provide for the participants both individual and group identity, enabling them to draw from familiar rituals to name themselves and their life experience. Moreover, these rituals have, as she points out, the power to build and shape faith communities, communities of memory and hope.[31]

In principle, celebration of Eucharist should be for Roman Catholics (and similarly for other "catholic" communities like the Anglican and Lutheran) the most important ritual to bear the process of traditioning. As the ultimate instance of *anamnesis* it carries through history for communities of Christian faith not just the memory and proclamation of Jesus' Passover but the very presence of the risen Christ. Eucharist is, of its essence, however, a *ritual,* and its effective authority as normative of faith is conditioned by the extent to which it is actually enacted as ritual. For centuries, however, the experience of Christians at Eucharist has not been that of sharing actively in a ritual; instead, it has been basically that of attendance at a sacred spectacle. It is only with Vatican Council II's *Constitution on the Sacred Liturgy (Sacrosanctum concilium)* that official teaching of the Catholic church has directed eucharistic celebration back to ritual. Given its traditional understanding and exercise of fiesta, and its frequent linking of fiestas with celebration of the Eucharist, the Latino/a community can be a valuable resource in the US Catholic church's reassessment and "reconstruction" of its eucharistic activity.

In Protestant denominations that do not have as explicitly eucharistic forms of worship, the basic principles of ritual traditioning still apply.[32] In proportion as those in attendance are actively engaged, individually and communally, in response to the proclaimed word of God, the ceremony creates a lively faith in the saving presence of God and is thereby transformative. This supposes that such gathering for worship relates to and gives a deepened Christian meaning to people's present faith experience at the same time that it draws upon the shared religious memory of the past.

Before leaving this topic of the authoritative function of ritual, we need to stress again the centrality of festive activity within family circles. It is the experience of such folk festivity that will develop the mentality that must flow into larger community liturgies. Authentic liturgy cannot be taught in classrooms; it must be learned by doing.

AUTHORITY OF CHURCH STRUCTURES

Usually when people refer to the exercise of authority within the church, they are thinking of official structures and those who function in that arena. Even though we are today questioning the monopolistic exercise of authority by ecclesiastical officialdom and becoming more aware of a multitude of other authoritative influences—the discussion shared in *teologia de conjunto* is a leading example of this—there is no question of the abiding importance of official authority and the influence it has had and still has on the process of Tradition. It was only in the mid-twentieth century, with the research of Geiselmann and Jungmann in Germany and the *nouvelle theologie* in France, that the static view of Tradition that had prevailed for decades was finally challenged. Many of us who studied theology in the pre–Vatican II years can remember how we resonated with the movement to think about Tradition as more than official ecclesiastical statements, to view it as a process that involved the entire Christian people. This important change was furthered by Vatican II, but continuing monopolistic use of the term *magisterium* to refer to the Vatican (and by extension to the bishops) indicates that the struggle is far from over.

Genuine advance in our understanding of official exercise of authority in the church and its role in the process of Tradition will not be aided, however, by simply rejecting the authority of officeholders. Rather, it must come by assessing not only the distribution of religious authority in Christianity but also the very nature of the authority that is appropriate to the life and mission of the church. The standard historical narrative, especially as it developed in academic circles and then trickled down into the post-Reformation polemic theology taught in seminaries, pointed to three basic exercises of authority by church officials: (1) normative explanation of doctrine, especially through regional or church-wide gatherings of bishops (in recent centuries this activity has focused increasingly on the authority of papal teaching as the indispensable channel of Tradition); (2) modeling and then gradually controlling the structure of sacramental rituals (while liturgical similarity had gradually been established over the centuries, it was in reaction to the Protestant Reformers that the rubrical approach to ritual unity became absolute); and (3) with increasing monopoly of ministry by the ordained, participation in the active ministry of the church depended upon permission or mandate of church officials. Vatican II, of course, helped break this pattern by its recognition of the responsibility and right of ministry for all the baptized, but its theory still needs to be implemented thoroughly.

In all three of these ways, ecclesiastical structures and personnel ruled the public aspects of Tradition, with a clear stress on orthodoxy. The voice and activity of church officials was for all practical purposes identified in academic ecclesiology with the process of Tradition. While all this was happening, however, there was always an unofficial development that somewhat independently and in supposedly non-authoritative ways carried on faith and wisdom through channels such as family life and informed conversation of devoted Christians. In evaluating the actual authority of these parallel, sometimes complementary, sometimes conflicting, paths of traditioning, research is needed into the range of authority that extends beyond officialdom. This research is being importantly assisted by recent study of popular Christianity. It is to be hoped that this will not result in opposing authentic official guidance but rather in recognizing and fostering a healthy though tensive relationship between the institutional and prophetic aspects of the Christian community.

AUTHORITY OF SOCIAL LOCATION

Current discussion of authority relationships within society has drawn attention to the influence of an individual's or a group's "social location." Feminist scholars in particular have pointed out the subtle or not so subtle discriminations that occur in power relationships because of gender differences. Significantly, as leading feminist reflection deepened, women realized that within their own ranks there was such discrimination—study of sexist imbalance had been unconsciously focused on Euro-American women to the neglect of Hispanic and African American women. This awareness led, in turn, to greater appreciation of the extent to which wealth, education, ethnic identity, class, and sexual orientation give hidden but important weight to people's speech and actions. Those who are on the receiving end of such discrimination are naturally more aware of it than are those who profit from it. So, it is not surprising that much of the important research on the impact of social location is currently being done by Latina scholars.[33]

Though one ordinarily thinks of social location as a force within secular society, it functions also within religious circles. It is difficult to find any situation in which there are advantages of social location more traditional and more firmly entrenched than that of clergy in the Catholic church. While the ordained are generally considered to be set apart as a sacramental reality, *clergy* itself is not a sacramental designation but rather refers to a set-apart group whose privileges go back at least as far as Constantine. To an extent, even some who are clearly not ordained, such as vowed women religious, tend to possess some of the "superiority" attached to the clergy. On a less structured level, wealthier members of parishes and dioceses generally have closer links and more influence with church officials, and therefore a stronger voice in decision-making.

Over the centuries the social location of the wealthy has meant that those with financial ability to provide for publication of their ideas have disproportionately influenced the narrative of history and therefore people's traditions. It has been remarked, somewhat cynically but truly, that history is the story of those who have won. Yet the apparent monopoly of elites in fashioning Tradition has been matched to some extent by the folk-level memories and customs of the poor and powerless.

One aspect of social location providing authority that is distinctive to modern times is the prestige and respect given professionals. We have become accustomed to the importance attached to physicians, lawyers, and clergy, especially in smaller towns—in some countries teachers can be added to this list. Whenever there are public gatherings of one sort or another it is common practice to invite some of these professional people in order to give prestige to the gathering. Even when an individual who is, let us say, a physician, steps outside his or her particular domain to become active as a political figure, some of the authority of the profession still clings to the person. It is assumed that one trained as a lawyer is more responsible in the public realm—an assumption not always justified. In many instances the views of professionals are sought in matters outside their field. A reflection of this esteem for professionals is the desire on the part of many new immigrants to have their children attain the prestige of being a doctor or lawyer.

It is clear that, rightly or wrongly, traditional views within a given culture underpin the authority with which certain individuals or institution are endowed. Medical practice was for many centuries an activity reserved for men.[34] Then, during the early medieval period in the West, it was increasingly associated with the healing practices of women. With the approach of modern times it again reverted to men, with the accompanying "memory" of women's healing being superstitious and untrustworthy and medical practice by men now considered "scientific."

There is an interesting (and for some people troubling) shift at present in the public identification of imitable professionals. Instead of those presumably dedicated to public service, the models of admiration and imitation are professionals in sports and entertainment. Particularly among young people, it is athletes or movie stars or rock musicians who enjoy a prominent authority as "important" humans, and the level of their monetary income reflects a broader societal evaluation of their role in society. Given this phenomenon, it is interesting to speculate about the basis for the "charismatic" authority they enjoy, whether they do embody the values of the culture and symbolize "success," or whether the attention they receive comes from people's regard for unusual physical or artistic endowments. More traditionally, among Christians there is still a widespread devotion to those models of faith and virtue referred to as saints, whether formally canonized or not. An interesting instance of this that is prominent in Latin American cultures is the respect, even veneration, paid to some *curanderos/as*.

AUTHORITY OF ESTABLISHED STRUCTURES

It is not only individuals to whom authority is attributed. Institutional structures and processes, both civil and ecclesiastical, can acquire and exercise authority. The US Constitution, for example, grants the Supreme Court the authoritative power to influence decisions made by lower courts and in cases of legal dispute to be the final authoritative voice. True, individuals—in this case Supreme Court justices—exercise this authority, but it is precisely the authority attached to their office.

Authoritative structures can be directly and explicitly established, as was the case when the government of the United States was brought into being by a representative group selected by the people from whom the authority was ultimately drawn. In other cases a structure can be set up by an authority-bearing individual who delegates designated authority to it; an example would be an official commission appointed by the president. In the religious sphere a structure such as the Law of Israel can be seen to have its authority because of direct divine establishment.

In other instances a structure can gradually acquire authority through authoritative actions to which people have acquiesced. This seems to have been the case with the papacy, which in the course of history came to be viewed in the West as an arbiter in cases of dispute among "lower-level" authorities.[35] In some such cases the authority being claimed and exercised is justified by a process of legitimation, a process that attempts to ground authority in historical tradition. Such claims to tradition are not always validated by solid historical evidence. Basing papal primacy as ruling authority on the grant of authority to Peter by Jesus was unquestioned for centuries; today such an exegesis of Matthew 16:14 is regarded as uncertain at best. Some of the most solidly established patterns of institutional authority are today being challenged, historical research indicating that their claimed authority derived from a less than justified grab of power. Perhaps the most drastic such reassessment has to do in many cultures with the long presumed headship of the family by a male patriarch.[36]

Christianity has not escaped this challenge. To an extent considered alarming in many quarters, the traditional authority of Christian churches is being questioned because of the rapidly changing social situations in many "traditional" Catholic or Protestant regions. The structured experience that created the seemingly unchanging outlook of so many, an outlook reflected in religious beliefs and practices, has been fragmented by wars and migration and economic globalization. Life is no longer what it seemed to be, and the explanations of life previously given have lost their authority as interpretations of reality. Not only has the longstanding Catholic religious hegemony in Latin America been confronted with a new prominence of Protestantism, but mainline churches, Protestant and Catholic, have been "threatened" by the explosion of Pentecostal groups. For millions of people the social situations that fostered the old allegiances no longer exist, and in their new "neighborhoods" they are often drawn to what seems to be more relevant acknowledgment of the divine. The question is unavoidable: Has "the traditional" lost its authority?[37]

Gradual acquisition of an institution's authority can occur in several ways.[38] Long use of certain practices can give the impression of their intrinsic validity; custom can even be elevated to law on the basis of being what has always been done. Women in the Catholic church are familiar with this argument because of the appeal in the papal prohibition of women's ordination to the "fact" that women have never been ordained.[39] In other cases certain structures and processes come to be considered authoritative because in practice they have proved to be successful. Their authority is challenged, of course, when social conditions shift and these formerly profitable ways of doing things are no longer advantageous.

ABUSE OF AUTHORITY

The theory is quite clear regarding legitimate appeal to authority, especially when it is based on religious traditions. Religious authority should be claimed and exercised, not for obtaining or retaining power, but as a means of furthering the reign of God by nurturing the faith of individuals and communities. Still, human nature being what it is, there have been and still are instances of abuse when authority is claimed without foundation or when those in authoritative positions attempt to legitimate unjust activity by appealing to their authority.

To pass fair judgment on any specific instance of abuse would require knowledge and appraisal of many influences bearing on the case, something that the space limitations of this essay do not allow. Suffice it to mention a few of the more common infractions. Those in position of official power can control the information that people need in order to make informed judgments. Again, those occupying positions of official authority can misrepresent the reality of historical happenings so that the distorted account can appear to be a tradition that legitimates their claims to power. Again, those in official positions can claim to speak for God and demand of their "subjects" submission rather than justified obedience, using the threat of divine punishment or socioreligious ostracism to underpin their rule. Finally, there can be the attempt to suppress legitimate dissent from official decrees by characterizing it as disloyal, heterodox, or irrelevant. The basic corrective to such injustices is the careful research that determines what has been the genuine Tradition of the living church.

SUMMARY

A final word about the relation between Tradition and authority. It is intrinsic to Tradition as the distilled wisdom of a people that it be an authoritative guide to thinking and acting. Conversely, acceptance of Tradition as authentic and normative depends on the authority of the agencies that in the course of traditioning create and transmit it.

Notes

[1] Drawing from the group's recognition of the need to nuance use of the term *tradition,* this essay will employ the following usage: (1) When the term *Tradition* is capitalized, it refers to the official use of the term, which for most of the past has pointed to the content of faith formulations. (2) There are any number of traditions (celebrations, texts, practices, etc.) that are handed down in family or ethnic or religious or territorial groups; and such traditions always involve some understandings that can be referred to as content. The tendency is to consider content as objective and unchanging, but in actuality it is diversified and conditioned by changing circumstances. (3) There is growing recognition that in using the term *tradition,* whether capitalized or not, one is dealing with a process of handing on an entire way of life and belief; groups *traditionalize.* When the focus is on this process, this essay will use the term *traditioning,* but when *tradition* is used, the assumption is that one is dealing with a process of traditioning that involves one or another developing content.

[2] For a more extensive discussion of authority, see Bernard Cooke, *Power and the Spirit of God: Toward an Experience-based Pneumatology* (New York: Oxford Univ. Press, 2003), chap. 3.

[3] See T. Tilley, *Inventing Catholic Tradition* (Maryknoll, NY: Orbis Books, 2000), 66–87. In similar fashion David J. Stagaman writes: "Authority, then, is an attribute of human interaction among human agents and the objects that surround them" (*Authority in the Church* [Collegeville, MN: Liturgical Press, 1999], 39).

[4] Orlando O. Espín, "Towards the Construction of an Intercultural Theology of Tradition," *Journal of Hispanic/Latino Theology* 9 (2002): 22–59. Espín's essay provides a complement to what Stagaman describes as the diachronic approach to understanding authority (*Authority in the Church*, 51–55).

[5] Stagaman goes so far as to identify authority and tradition: "Authority considered in the light of the temporal before and after is called *tradition*" (*Authority in the Church*, 51).

[6] Tilley, *Inventing Catholic Tradition*, 154.

[7] On the need to include a diachronic consideration in any definition of authority, see Stagaman, *Authority in the Church*, 51–55. This indicates the need to apply such an approach to a study of Tradition.

[8] See Orlando O. Espín, *The Faith of the People* (Maryknoll, NY: Orbis Books, 1997), 63–90.

[9] See Chapter 1 in this volume, in which Orlando Espín points out that popular Christianity involves the entire life experience of a people, including the overtly religious elements.

[10] Though Stagaman and others are correct in stressing the importance of studying the development of Tradition, a caution must be kept in mind. It is typical of the modern mentality to consider the historical sequence as a gradual, cumulative gain of insights and wisdom. However, until modern times, it was assumed that the normative *auctores* were figures of the past and that the wisdom of the ancient sages was sometimes dimmed or distorted with the passage of time. It is interesting to compare this older view with recent focus on *ressourcement*. On the attitude of medieval theologians, like Thomas Aquinas, to the creative use and rethinking of ancient wisdom, see M.-D. Chenu, *Towards Understanding Saint Thomas* (Chicago: Univ. of Chicago Press, 1964), 20–38.

[11] In Catholic reflection on the "inspiration" of the Bible there was an important advance in official teaching at the Second Vatican Council; its document *Dei Verbum* opened up the notion of revelation as an ongoing process in the life of the church, instead of the previously prevalent understanding that revelation ended with the death of the last of the apostles. This "new" view was linked with mid-twentieth-century advances in understanding the nature of Jesus' resurrection and the continuing presence of God to history in the gift of the Spirit.

[12] Jean-Pierre Ruiz's essay in this volume (Chapter 4) and the ensuing discussion emphasized the manner in which the invention of printing and the increase of literacy affected both the transmission and the interpretation of the biblical text.

[13] On the influence of an "audience" on the identity and interpretation of a test, see Jorge Gracia, *Texts: Ontological Status, Identity, Author, Audience* (Albany: State Univ. of New York Press, 1996), 141–69.

[14] Justo González, *Santa Biblia: The Bible through Hispanic Eyes* (Nashville, TN: Abingdon Press, 1996). González describes the ways in which popular Latino interpretation of the Bible is influenced by marginalization, poverty, *mestizaje,* and cultural solidarity. While the Bible provides out of the traditions of the people an authoritative interpretation of their life, their experience furnishes the hermeneutic that governs the religious understanding of the sacred text. In a nonconformist essay in this volume (Chapter 5), Francisco Lozada, Jr., goes further: he questions the assumed ultimacy of the biblical traditions themselves and points to the creative insights that come with reading biblical texts along with parallel texts drawn from other religious and literary traditions.

[15] On the need to reassess the authoritative (traditional) interpretation of scripture, see F. Segovia, *Decolonizing Biblical Studies* (Maryknoll, NY: Orbis Books, 2000), reviewed in *Journal of Hispanic/Latino Theology* 9 (2001): 60.

[16] Luise Schottroff, *Lydia's Impatient Sisters* (Louisville, KY: Westminster Knox, 1995). Her critique runs throughout the book as she proposes, in contrast to the exclusively androcentric view that has predominated, the feminist perspective on various texts that has been developed by current biblical scholarship by women.

[17] Jean-Pierre Ruiz, "The Bible and U.S. Hispanic American Theological Discourse," in *From the Heart of Our People: Latino/a Explorations in Catholic Systematic Theology*, ed. Orlando O. Espín and Miguel H. Díaz, 100–120 (Maryknoll, NY: Orbis Books, 1999), 112.

[18] On the authority of official statements, especially the teaching of the papacy in recent times, see F. Sullivan, *Magisterium: Teaching Authority in the Catholic Church* (New York: Paulist Press, 1983). For a discussion of papal teaching's relation to the broader "ordinary magisterium," see R. Gaillaretz, *Witness to the Faith* (New York: Paulist Press, 1992).

[19] Poetry is a specially powerful instrument for shaping people's religious understandings. See H. Pena, "The Thousand Faces of God in Central American Poetry," *Journal of Hispanic/Latino Theology* 6 (1999): 35–77.

[20] One of the more intriguing instances of such double meaning is the way in which apparently completely secular texts such as some Shakespearean plays carried encoded elements of the Hermetic religious tradition. See the writings of Frances Yates, especially *Giordano Bruno and the Hermetic Tradition* (Chicago: Univ. of Chicago Press, 1964) and *The Occult Philosophy in the Elizabethan Age* (London: Routledge, 1979).

[21] On the resources of cultural traditions in development of a Latino theology of art, see A. García-Rivera, "A Wounded Innocence," *Journal of Hispanic/ Latino Theology* 8 (2002): 5–20. Also, R. Goizueta's study of the influence of José Vasconcelos draws attention to the aesthetic aspect of the over-arching "authoritative" dimension of a people's culture ("La Raza Cosmica? The Cosmic

Vision of José Vasconcelos," *Journal of Hispanic/Latino Theology* 2 [1994]: 5–27).

[22] The classic case of such presumption is that of Pseudo-Dionysius, whose alleged connection with Saint Paul gave widespread and lasting authority to his writings.

[23] See, for instance, his discussion of the role of older women in Espín, *The Faith of the People*, 4–5.

[24] On the role of the parish and its pastor in the transmission of tradition, see W. Taylor, *Magistrates of the Sacred* (Stanford, CA: Stanford Univ. Press, 1996), reviewed in *Journal of Hispanic/Latino Theology* 7 (1999): 72. It is obvious, then, how desirable it is to have as pastors indigenous priests who share the culture of the people.

[25] See Gary Macy's essay (Chapter 3) in this volume.

[26] Roberto Goizueta, "Fiesta: Life in the Subjunctive," in Espín and Díaz, *From the Heart of Our People*, 84–99.

[27] For Roman Catholics, the first major document of Vatican Council II, *Sacrosanctum concilium (Constitution on the Sacred Liturgy)*, constituted a revolution in this regard. By characterizing the Eucharist as a ritual rather than a spectacle, the decree began to reverse centuries of passive congregational attendance by insisting on ritual involvement.

[28] See, for example, R. Firth, *Symbols, Public and Private* (Ithaca, NY: Cornell Univ. Press, 1978); and V. Turner, *Dramas, Fields, and Metaphors* (Ithaca, NY: Cornell Univ. Press, 1974). I have found Catherine Bell, *Ritual Theory, Ritual Practice* (New York: Oxford Univ. Press, 1992) particularly helpful, especially the chapter on ritual and power, 171–223.

[29] On the symbolic power of the crucifix in Hispanic devotion and catechesis, see Espín, *The Faith of the People*, 46–48.

[30] On the role in transmitting belief that can be played by familiar songs, see E. Aponte, "*Coritas* as Active Symbol in Latino Protestant Popular Religion," *Journal of Hispanic/Latino Theology* 2 (1995): 57–66.

[31] It is interesting that Elizabeth Johnson, in her pioneering book on Christian belief in the communion of saints, *Friends of God and Prophets* (New York: Continuum, 1998), also focuses on communities of memory and communities of hope.

[32] There is among Catholics a prevalent view that Protestants, especially in the Reformed and Pentecostal traditions, lack a ritual approach to worship. Actually, there has been for some decades an increase of Protestants' interest in their own liturgical history and present practice. A striking example of Protestant scholarly study of ritual is the research and reflection of James White, for twenty-two years professor of liturgy at Perkins School of Theology and more recently at the University of Notre Dame. See particularly his *Sacraments as God's Self Giving* (Nashville, TN: Abingdon Press, 1983).

[33] For summary descriptions of theology from the social location of African American and Hispanic women, see Ada María Isasi-Díaz, *Mujerista Theology*

(Maryknoll, NY: Orbis Books, 1997); and S. Mitchem, *Introducing Womanist Theology* (Maryknoll, NY: Orbis Books, 2002).

[34] On the rise and then decline of women's role in the healing arts, see R. Bridenthal, S. Stuart, and M. Wiesner, *Becoming Visible: Women in European History* (Boston: Allyn Bacon, 1998), 222–24.

[35] See R. Southern, *Western Society and the Church in the Middle Ages* (Baltimore: Penguin Books, 1970), 91–169.

[36] See G. Lerner, *The Creation of Patriarchy* (New York: Oxford Univ. Press, 1986).

[37] For an interesting study of the dynamics of such "conversion"—in this case the religious interaction of a received tradition (Lutheranism) with a changing social context and experience in El Salvador—see Mary Solberg, "Working on the Church: A Contribution to Lutheran Ecclesiology," *Journal of Hispanic/ Latino Theology* 2 (1994): 60–77.

[38] On the process by which church structures have come to be considered authoritative, see M. Ejido, "Theoretical Prolegomenon to a Sociology of Hispanic Popular Religion," *Journal of Hispanic/Latino Theology* 7 (1999): 27–55.

[39] For evidence of women's "ordination" to various offices in the course of church history and of the arguments against this practice, see the essays of Gary Macy and Hilary Martin in *A History of Women's Ordination*, vol. 1, ed. Bernard Cooke and Gary Macy (Lanham, MD: Scarecrow Press, 2003).

3

The Iberian Heritage
of US Latino/a Theology

Gary Macy

PART 1: METHODOLOGY

Why This Topic?

The purpose of this paper is to provide a skeletal outline of the Iberian background to the *theological tradition* of Latino/a theology in the United States in the opening decade of the twenty-first century.[1]

Classifying Theologies

The impetus for this project is very simple, even perhaps simplistic. In meetings of professional theological associations, there are separate sessions on Latino/a theology. Books are written and classified specifically as Latino/a theology and scholars are identified as such by their colleagues and by themselves. The question that sparked this study asks, Why have a separate category, Latino/a theology, which is not somehow just plain theology?

The classification does have some distinct advantages. Such a designation highlights the particular strengths of the approach taken to different theological topics by Latino/a theologians. These theologians have insights based on their experience and the experience of Latinos/as in the United States that other groups do not have. Thus, to refer to Latino/a theology can indicate the particular contributions that this group of theologians can make to the larger theological enterprise that cannot be made by any other group. The very purpose of this volume is an indication of the value of such an approach.

But this answer, while certainly true and important to pursue, does not sufficiently answer the question. If it were simply a matter of identifying theologians by their traditions in order to highlight the strengths and weaknesses of those traditions, there should also be sessions at professional theological meetings on Celtic theology, Franco theology, Teutonic theology, Anglo theology, and so on. There are no such sessions. Rather, there are sessions on Latino/a theology and just theology. The clear implication is that there is traditional theology and Latino/a theology. The same could be said of feminist and African American theologies. Somehow these *other* theologies stand outside the mainstream discourse of theology; they are different, odd, new, and definitely marginal to *real* theology.

Purposes of the Present Study

One purpose of this essay is to demonstrate that whatever can be said of Latino/a theology, it cannot be said that it is out of the mainstream of Western European theological tradition. On the contrary, it is the heir of an ancient tradition that was greatly responsible not only for the preservation of the Western European traditions and learning, but also was one of the most influential creators of that tradition and of that learning. From this historical vantage point, then, Latino/a theology is as much, or even more so, a part of mainstream theology than any other theological grouping.

A second purpose of the essay is to challenge the usefulness of the expression *mainstream theology,* or of the more common undifferentiated term *theology,* to indicate the dominant theological discourse of the academy. Rather, it will be suggested that there is no theology that is not intrinsically "ethnic" in the sense that it is based in a particular historical tradition. More accurately, use of the terms *mainstream theology* or just *theology* indicates which ethnic theologies presently dominate and hence marginalize other ethnic theologies.

Traditions and *the* Tradition

Underlying this approach are certain methodological assumptions based on the recent work on tradition by several scholars. Rather than present a complete recapitulation of this scholarship, I rely here on the work of three of the more influential scholars in this area, Dale Irvin, Terrence Tilley, and Orlando Espín.[2]

History and Tradition: Never Innocent

According to these authors, history is never just "telling it like it is." Rather, it is a political, social, and economic activity that influences the present by highlighting a particular set of historical events and personages in order to justify or explain a present social, cultural, or economic reality. History always exists in the present and for the present. We write history for a reason. We are interested in something *now* that can be explained by looking at certain events and persons *then*.

No event, no document, no history that we have exists in the past—otherwise we wouldn't have it. Some mention of even lost artifacts must exist in the present or we wouldn't even know such artifacts ever existed. There is no history in the past. This may seem so obvious as to be not worth mentioning, but the idea of an objective history that simply relates indisputable facts in a disinterested fashion still dominates much scholarly work.[3]

History, then, is always in the present and about the present. The same is true for historians. Historians first of all study what interests them. Why waste hours and hours on something about which one cares nothing? Historians pick issues they think are important. Further, the issues that concern historians arise from their own particular economic, social, cultural, and political setting.[4] Historians sense that some aspect of the story told about the past is misrepresenting the present. According to their political, social, economic, and cultural point of view, a misunderstanding or even a lie has crept into the story of present society, and the historians wish to correct that for some purpose in the present. One often hears the phrase, "History will show . . . ." Nothing could be further from the truth. There is no "history." There are only historians who demonstrate the importance of some person or event for their own culture or society or economic grouping. History is what historians decide it is, and those decisions inevitably take place within particular economic, social, and political settings.[5]

For a study to become part of "history," however, it is not enough for a particular historian to be passionate, thorough and convincing. The historian's work also has to be accepted by a larger audience of scholars. To be published in a journal that will receive serious attention, for instance, the study will need to be reviewed by other scholars. These scholars are far more likely to view as acceptable those publications that already share certain assumptions of the larger academic community. For a study to be published as a book, the hurdles are higher still. Not only does the study need to pass muster with other scholars who will review the study for publication, but the publisher must be convinced that enough people will be interested in buying the book that the publisher will make money in producing that particular volume.

Historians whose work cannot meet these requirements can, of course, put up their own website or pay for their work to be published. It is unlikely, however, that this work will reach a large enough audience to change the dominant understanding of the past.[6]

This means that writing history is also inevitably a process of choosing. First, there are the choices made *by* the historian. One could hardly relate all the events that happened at any particular moment (even if one had the data to do so). The relating would take longer than the happening itself. So historians must pick and choose which events best explain how the society they are studying became the way it is. These events themselves are often related in documents that were not neutral when they were produced and were preserved by those who had a vested interest in their preservation. Sources are never free of political, social, and economic baggage. Sources exist because someone cared about creating them and then preserving them. Second, there are the choices made *for* historians. Other scholars, quite possibly with other presuppositions and agendas, will decide whether or not a particular historian's work is worth dissemination. If these scholars do so decide, economic and political considerations will determine how wide will be the distribution of that work. Before the printing press, this meant how many manuscript copies of a work would be produced in a process that was available almost exclusively to the wealthy. Since the invention of the printing press, this has meant how many copies of a book a publisher decides must sell in order to make a profit on the printing of it. It is these products (manuscripts and books) that in time become sources for further studies—these now subject to the same exigencies. In short, the sources of history are already the result of economic and social forces before a scholar even begins the process of selecting sources, and whether a scholar's work itself becomes a source will be determined by economic and social choices outside of the scholar's control.[7]

Implications from Lack of Innocence

Two important implications follow from these assumptions. First, different histories emerge from different perspectives. History depends on who is writing the history and for whom the history is being written, and also on who allows the history to be disseminated. Second, history is itself a political act because it helps create the present insofar as telling us who we are and who we can become. "We are always reinventing our traditions in order to make them relevant, for the changes that occur through the passage of time refuse us the opportunity to lay claim to the timeless relevance of an unchanging memory. We are always excluding some aspects of our collective memories, recalling others, and reinventing tradition as we contend with new questions that emerge to confront us in faith."[8]

First Implication

The first of these implications suggests that to understand tradition as a multiplicity of histories and traditions in dialogue is more faithful to the actual global situation of Christianity than any search for a universal history of Christianity.[9] The assumption that there is *one* identifiable history or tradition of Christianity is actually an attempt to silence all other interpretations. More precisely, such an endeavor was, and remains, an attempt to universalize one particular Western European view of its history to all peoples in all places at all times. In Irvin's words, "What is essentially a tribal theological tradition (variously described as 'the West,' 'Western Christianity,' or 'Christendom') has been universalized and thus has become an idol."[10] The same point can be made about theology as described above. The assumption that there is a theology different from or opposed to Latino/a theology or black theology or feminist theology is an attempt to universalize another particular theological tradition. It is also, consequently, an attempt to deny legitimacy to any tradition apart from a rather narrowly defined (tribal) theology arising from one part of Western Europe.

It should be noted that the creation of a universal and monolithic history of Christianity involved not only the choices made by a myriad of historians, as Irvin would seem to suggest, but also a scholarly community that marginalized all other versions of history. When such versions are not simply silenced, they are relegated to a separate scholarly enterprise and to their own specialized journals. The creation of a dominant theological tradition involves not only scholars, but journal editors, publishers, and organizers of conferences. In short, the term *mainstream theology* is shorthand for hegemonic theology.

Second Implication

This brings us to the second important implication. Writing history and allowing that history to be disseminated are political, social, economic, and ultimately moral acts. If the purpose of writing history is to help define who we are and can be, then it is essential that we not lie about who we were (and are), and yet recall that we have been in other ways (and therefore can be different, and hopefully better) than we presently are. Education is freedom from the tyranny of the present.

We can rewrite the past to re-create the present. Irvin quotes Jacques LeGoff on the obligation that historians have to create a history that liberates and not enslaves: "'We can, indeed we must, beginning with each and every historian, work and struggle so that history, in both senses of the word, may become different.' This critical imperative impinges on various forms of social and collective memory as well, calling us in LeGoff's words again 'to act in such a way that collective memory may serve the liberation and not the enslavement of human beings.'"[11]

One important role that history can play in liberating our collective memories is to insist upon and to allow a multiplicity of histories and traditions which demand mutual respect. To quote Espín: "There are no multiple particularities and one evident human universality; rather there are multiple historical, cultural, human universalities which can encounter one another, which can challenge one another, and which through intercultural dialogue might engage in the process of unveiling universally relevant truth."[12]

In this particular case, then, it is a moral and liberating act to argue that all theologies are culturally, socially, and economically determined and all theologies are equally engaged in a process of dialogue that will, it is to be hoped, enrich all of humankind. It is to expose one form of hegemony that is marginalizing, silencing and minimizing all voices but its own. "No culture, and no cultural situation, may be considered as the definitive locus of truth."[13]

Why This Tradition?

All traditions are the traditions, then, of someone by someone who has been allowed by someone else to be heard. They are the creation of a multiplicity of social, economic, and political forces that directly affect how one thinks about oneself and about the possibilities for one's future. These traditions tell one who one is and, ultimately, who one might become.

To ask, then, why one wants to "create" or "remember" this particular tradition is really quite simple. One undertakes such an exploration to determine who Latino/a theologians in the United States are and, ultimately, who they are becoming. To "remember" such a long and distinguished history is, first of all, to reject the notion that US Latino/a theology deserves less respect than other theologies because of its novelty or specificity. Rather, today's Latino/a theology is, as it has always been in the history of Christianity, a deeply engaged and creative theology—one part of a dialogue of many different theologies, no doubt, but not somehow separate, or subordinate, or marginal.

The first step in this process of remembering is to point out that there has been, and continues to be, an unbroken succession of distinguished and influential Christian theologians in this theological tradition, stretching from the fourth to the twenty-first centuries. This long line of theologians were creatively engaged with the important issues of their day and offered new and creative answers to those issues. US Latino/a theology today is the heir to such brilliant thinkers as Gregory of Elvira, Isidore of Seville, Ramón Lull, Teresa of Avila, and Juan de la Cruz. Sometimes these theologians challenged the dominant theological paradigm, and sometimes they reinforced that paradigm, but they were never considered somehow a different enterprise, a separate undertaking, from theology in general, that is, a "Hispanic" theology apart from "real" theology.

To trace the lineage of US Latino/a theology, then, is a first step in moving this theology from the margins of theology. This is not for a moment to say that the approach US Latinos/as take to theology will not seriously challenge other theologies that may politically claim a form of cultural hegemony. There certainly are distinctive characteristics to US Latino/a theology, but so are there distinctive features to US Irish theology, and US German theology, and US Anglo theology.

First and foremost, then, to trace the lineage of Latino/a theology reminds present-day US Latino/a theologians that they are part of an ancient theological tradition and certainly not a novelty in Christian theological history. If they do not recognize this, they cannot expect others to do so.[14] Second, it insists that all theologians recognize the theologies they do as equally ethnic theologies, equally based on the historical experience of particular groups of people, and equally influenced by a particular tradition of academic theology.

Of course, this is only a first step. The delineation of such a tradition would also have to receive acceptance by both Latino/a scholars and by non-Latino/a scholars. This acceptance will need to be sufficient for a significant distribution of a series of studies in order to influence how both Latinos/as and non-Latinos/as think of themselves and their history. Only then can a constructive dialogue between equals commence.

Continuities and Discontinuities

To argue that the tradition of Iberian theology mentioned above somehow constitutes an identifiable unity is not without problems.

Discontinuities and Questions to This Project

Questions of Cultural and National Identity

Surely Hosius of Córdoba or Prudentius would have understood themselves as Roman, not as Hispanic in any modern sense of the word. The
same would probably be true of Isidore of Seville and his brother Leander.
In later centuries the theologians included in the list that follows would
much more likely identify themselves as Castilian, Aragonese, or
Catalonian than Iberian. Muslim theologians might have felt more culturally at one with Cairo or Baghdad.

During the modern period the relationship between Spain and its
former colonies of Mexico, Cuba, and Puerto Rico are also problematic.
Not all citizens of those countries would wish to associate themselves so
closely and clearly with an Iberian heritage because, as pointed out below, their own traditions include far more than just the contributions of
Spain. Finally, the histories of Mexico, Cuba, and Puerto Rico are hardly
a unity. These three rich cultures are quite distinctive and deserve to be
treated as such.[15]

Questions of Denominational Identity and Applicability

The objection could also be raised that while the tracing of such a
tradition might be meaningful to those Christians of the larger catholic
community, particularly Roman Catholics, Orthodox, and Anglicans,[16]
it may not speak to Latino/a Christians who belong to churches in the
Reformed tradition.[17] The Reformed tradition is by self-definition a pro-
test against precisely the theologians included in the broad catholic tradition. Why or even how could the Reformed churches understand themselves to be formed by a catholic tradition?

In the end, perhaps, the connection cannot and should not be made.
This decision will be made, if made at all, by members of the Reformed
churches themselves. Two suggestions will be offered, nevertheless, as to
why the memory of the catholic theological tradition may be of value for
those in the Reformed churches.

First, the history of the Christian West is as much part of the Reformation as it is part of Roman Catholicism and Anglicanism. The preach-
ers of reform include Priscillian, Julian of Toledo, Arnald of Vilanova,
Juan Luis Vives, and Michael Servetus, as well as Valdez of Lyon, Jan
Hus, John Wyclif, and finally, Luther and Calvin. The church before the
sixteenth century was as much the background to the Reformation as it
was to Trent or to the Thirty-Nine Articles.[18]

Second, the way in which Latinos/as in the Reformed churches live
out this faith cannot help but be informed by their own centuries-old

traditions. For example, Latino/a Presbyterians, it can be argued, have a specific way of being Presbyterian that distinguishes them from their Anglo counterparts. This is not to suggest that Latino/a Presbyterians are somehow less Presbyterian than others. To suggest that would be to imply that there is a Presbyterian mainstream tradition into which Latino/a Presbyterians have to fit. But that would be simply to reinforce the hegemonic theological tradition already rejected by Presbyterianism. The suggestion here is rather that Latino/a members of the Presbyterian churches are as much a part of that tradition as Anglo members. Latinos/as do not "give up" their Latino/a traditions to become part of the Reformed churches. Their own long tradition contains elements of reform that helped form the shared Latino/a tradition and continue to do so. Even if one argues that Latinos/as only joined the Reformed churches in significant numbers in the last two centuries, one can also argue that they did so because they found something in the Reformed churches that was compatible with their own Latino/a traditions.[19] This chapter hopes to offer one source for uncovering what that compatibility might be.

Continuities and Choices in This Project

With all these disjunctures, why even suggest a unified tradition for Latino/a theology? Doesn't the artificial unity suggested by such a project disintegrate as soon as one looks more closely at the individual historical periods and cultures summarily lumped together? No doubt this is true, but it is true of all traditions. Traditions are inventions, as indeed are histories. The unity of such projects is imposed, and to some degree it is always artificial. The real question, then, is what justifies this particular artificiality.

Mexico, Cuba, and Puerto Rico

Today's US Latino/a theologies do look to Latin American countries and cultures not only for roots of identity but also as a source of theology. The vast majority of US Latino/a theologians have ties, more or less personal, either to Mexico, to Cuba, or to Puerto Rico—simply because these three groups make up the majority of Hispanics in the United States. Of course, there are important and growing exceptions to this, and the names of theologians of Central and South American heritage should begin to be added to the following list.

All of the three aforementioned cultures, to a larger or lesser extent, share a similar background in colonial history. They were colonies of Spain. Further, that colonial background was shaped by sixteenth-century Iberian theology, which in turn was influenced by the *Convivencia* that continued into that century of encounter and mutual discovery. Despite all the very real disjunctures mentioned above, there are identifiable influences, heritages, and traditions at work in Latino/a theology.

Centrality to Theology

To trace this heritage challenges the assumption that there is a so-called mainstream theology that does not itself also have identifiable influences, heritages, and traditions. Latino/a theology is as central to Western European theological thought as are any of the other theologies that today claim a form of hegemony over the Western Christian tradition. Even the most cursory examination of the list of Iberian theologians given below corroborates the centrality of Latino/a theology's theological lineage. It would be hard to imagine a history of Western European theology without Hosius of Córdoba, Isidore of Seville, Moses Maimonides, Averroes, Raymond of Peñafort, Ignatius Loyola, or Teresa of Avila. These are some of the greatest shapers of the Western theological tradition, and many others could be mentioned. Latino/a theological tradition may be only one legitimate tradition among many others but, as such, it must be granted the same legitimacy as any other.

A Model of Theological Dialogue and Equality?

A larger hope of this project is that it might nudge theological discourse closer to a model of dialogue between different equally valid theologies rather than prejudice some particular theologies over others. The move toward this form of dialogue involves many difficulties. First and most obviously, scholars would need to see that such a model is desirable. Those who judge themselves to be part of the mainstream tradition may strongly object to the suggestion that even to claim such a mainstream may be morally unacceptable. On the other hand, those marginalized by the mainstream may not want to give up the "advantages" of victimization and marginalization. If different theological traditions actually ever dialogue as equals, no one group can claim any special status, even that of victim. Of course, this does imply real equality that may well be more of a heuristic category than an attainable historical state.[20]

PART 2: OUTLINES OF A TRADITION

This project aims at providing the barest outline of this extensive tradition. It is a start, a suggestion for a much larger study. As such, it admittedly does not even touch on some essential elements in that tradition.

The aim of this project is to demonstrate that there has been a continuous tradition of serious theological discourse by Iberian and Latin American theologians for seventeen hundred years and that this tradition directly feeds present-day Latino/a theologies. That is a very long time, but even here there are serious gaps.

One Heritage Stream among Several

The following list is hardly exhaustive or authoritative, even within its self-circumscribed limits. There are certainly authors that should have been included and were not. There are authors that were also excluded because of lack of space. Hopefully, both these lacunae can be filled in future studies, and the author gladly welcomes suggestions from scholars more knowledgeable than himself.

This list presents *only one stream* of tradition that feeds Latino/a theology as it presently exists in the United States. The tradition represented here is Iberian and Latin American. The following genealogy lists theologians who were active in the Iberian peninsula from the fourth through the sixteenth centuries, and then those theologians active particularly in the Mexican, Cuban, and Puerto Rican areas of the Spanish colonial empire, and finally those theologians active in Mexico, Cuba, and Puerto Rico after independence up to approximately the 1960s. The rationale for this limited choice is admittedly artificial.

This approach was taken because the author's expertise is in European history, and so this is one area of the tradition to which the author could make a contribution. Also, this was an area that had not been explored by earlier scholars. The *terminus ad quem* of the study, again admittedly arbitrary, was chosen to coincide with the emergence of the identification of Latino/a theology.[21]

Other Heritage Streams to Be Researched

There are clearly other important areas to be mapped out. A full presentation of the influence of Visigothic tribal tradition should be explored, as well as that of Muslim and Jewish theologians—an area merely hinted at in this chapter. Extremely important and not at all present here is the influence of the religions of the indigenous peoples on Latino/a theology in the United States. Particularly in the case of the Antilles, there is also the very strong influence of the West African peoples who were brought into that region as slaves. In fact, no presentation of the roots and heritages of US Latino/a theological tradition could be considered complete without an exploration of all these influences.[22]

Further, the admittedly limited tradition laid out here did not occur in a vacuum. Fourth-century theologians were in constant dialogue with other theologians of the Roman Empire. The medieval theologians were part of a much larger body of discourse throughout Europe. The theologians of the colonial period often moved back and forth across the Atlantic and retained close ties with European thought. More recent Latino/a theology has influenced and been influenced by not only European thought, but also Asian and African theology. No theology occurs in a vacuum, and theology that for centuries has been in dialogue with other cultures and religions cannot be understood as if it were an isolated and monolithic entity.

Influence of Dominant Theological Paradigms

More challengingly, part of the heritage of Latino/a theology is intimately bound to the dominant theological paradigm that has in turn marginalized it. As was pointed out above, several of the theologians included in this list could and would be identified as instrumental in forming dominant theological paradigms. This has several serious implications both for US Latino/a theologians and for theologians of other theological traditions who see themselves as working within the dominant paradigm. For Latino/a theologians this means that they are the heirs of an ancient tradition—in fact, one of the most ancient. But this carries all of the challenges and dangers of any ancient tradition.[23]

Patriarchal and Clerical

The list given here has been shaped by a particular understanding of the history of theology that is patently patriarchal and clerical. This is clear from the fact that the overwhelming majority of those listed are males and clerics. There is a good reason for this. These are the authors whose works have been preserved, valued, and studied by succeeding generations of scholars, who were for the most part males and clerics, with a vested interest in preserving a patriarchal and clerical dominance. Not surprisingly, then, some of the influential theologians on this list not only accepted the essentially patriarchal, clerical, and imperialist norms of their own times but actively defended those norms. This, in turn, helped embed them even more deeply into the Western European theological tradition. In short, the theologians on this list shaped theological tradition for both good and ill. In turn, the understanding of *who* constitutes the tradition has been influenced by the dominant theological premises, good and ill, of that tradition. If Latino/a theologians acknowledge their roots in this ancient Iberian theological tradition, they will necessarily also need to address the shadow side of the tradition that has formed them.[24]

But Who Is a Theologian?

The list below contains almost exclusively professional theologians. But in any tradition, and most importantly in the US Latino/a tradition, the influence of informal, popular sources of theology is essential.[25] This has been amply demonstrated and developed by Latino/a theologians.

Characteristics of This Stream
Feeding Latino/a Theological Tradition

The following is nothing more than a skeletal outline of *one* of the traditions that nourish Latino/a theology. Such a list needs the further elaboration, analysis, and evaluation that this study does not supply. The list is no more, but not less, than an invitation to other scholars to put flesh on the skeleton, to bring to life a tradition whose bare bones are laid out below. It is my hope that this slightest of hints of what the tradition might hold will entice other scholars to bring a great feast to this graveyard of the living in a wonderful rich celebration of a theological Day of the Dead. With ancestors such as these, it should be great fun.

To start the party, a few brief comments might be in order. Even a cursory overview of the tradition must recognize some obvious and distinctive characteristics.

An Intercultural Theology

First and most clearly, this is an inherently intercultural theology. Iberian Christian theology emerged from a continuous dialogue with other peoples and faiths. In the sixth century that dialogue was with the Visigothic Arians. In the great period (eight centuries) of the *Convivencia*, that dialogue was with the greatest minds of Islam and Judaism as well as with the recovered classics of ancient Greece and Rome. In the sixteenth century Hispanic theology not only embraced the Enlightenment and met the challenge of the Reformation, but also faced the greater problems raised by the entirely different world of the Americas. Hispanic theology, and hence US Latino/a theology, is intercultural by heritage, history, and almost by instinct.

In the Americas, as in the *Convivencia*, theologians themselves became personally the focus of interculturality. Abner of Burgos, the Jewish scholar, was *also* Alfonso of Valladolid, the Christian theologian. Solomon Ha-Levi the Jew was *also* Pablo de Santa María, the Christian, and Joshua Lorki converted to become Gerónimo de Santa Fe. Not all Jewish conversions were by free will, unforced by social circumstance or physical force. But then, intercultural encounters are not usually simple, peaceful encounters.

Intercultural theology is a theology fully and personally aware of dominance, fear, violence, and confusion as well as toleration and mutual respect. Both are present in the *Convivencia,* and both are present in the encounter with the indigenous peoples of the New World. Just as scholars personally embodied the clash of cultures of the *Convivencia,* so did, for instance, Francisco de Florencia, Juan de Zumárraga, and particularly, Diego Valadés embody the clash of cultures caused by the conquest of the Americas. The experience of living in and being torn by two cultures is not new to such a tradition.

Concern for Social Justice

A second prominent feature of this tradition is a concern for social justice. Otto Maduro has already traced this concern in the theology of the Americas.[26] But this concern within the tradition, I suggest, predates the arrival of Europeans in the New World. One aspect of this concern is the readiness, for good or ill, to work with secular governments to address the perceived ills of the day. For example, Hosius of Córdoba advised Constantine for years, immersing himself in the complexities of the Arian controversy and calling the bishops together in the name of the emperor at Nicea. Braulio, Bishop of Zaragoza, helped compile the Visigothic code to standardize law in Visigothic territory. Isidore and Leander of Seville, and later Julian, Bishop of Toledo, convoked the famous Councils of Toledo to deal with abuses and regulate ecclesial life. Medieval Spain saw a plethora of famous lawyers: the two Peters of Spain, Raymond of Peñafort, Pedro de Luna, and even Nicolás Eimeric. Francisco de Vitoria, the political theorist of the sixteenth century, is still studied today.

It is no wonder, then, that there were a series of strident voices in the defense of the indigenous peoples in the colonial period—Antonio de Montesinos, Bartolomé de Las Casas, Bernardino de Sahagún, Juan de Zumárraga, and Vasco de Quiroga, to name but a few. Today's Latino/a theologians inherit, then, a legacy of political and social involvement.

Incarnational Theology

For good or ill, this is a truly incarnational theology, accepting that human institutions are capable of providing great good and that using human institutions can be part of God's will. But the tradition also accepts that this power can be abused, and abused even more readily if political domination is seen as God's will. In such a theology, sin is very real and a constant, just as it is unavoidable temptation for those who wish to solve political, social, and economic problems in the real world.

These are just three possible themes for exploration in the evaluation of the heritage outlined below. Surely others will point out other distinctive features, just as other distinctive features will accompany explorations of the indigenous and African heritage of Latino/a theologians. There is much work to be done. Let the following suggestions begin the exploration.

PART 3: A SELECT ANNOTATED LIST OF HISPANIC THEOLOGIANS

The bibliographical references given here are to recent dictionary and encyclopedia articles on Hispanic theologians. These articles, in turn, provide a fuller list of studies. The purpose of the bibliographical references, then, is to provide the reader with *a guide to further literature* rather than a complete bibliographical list of entries for each theologian, historical period, or country mentioned below. When possible, two references are provided for each author.

The reader should keep in mind, when using the list below, the reflections, assumptions, limitations, and caveats expressed in the preceding two parts of this essay, including the time-frame and geographic limits I have imposed on the following list. The list includes names from the fourth century to the first half of the twentieth century.

Today's political/national divisions in the Iberian peninsula and in Latin America cannot be projected back to the medieval or colonial past. Consequently, authors born in one area of the peninsula or the continent could have worked and lived in another while remaining within the territories of the same sovereign. Furthermore, "immigration" to one or another kingdom or viceroyalty was common during the medieval and colonial periods.

As stated and explained in the preceding two parts, no attempt has been made to be complete and exhaustive in the list of names and works, which is only indicative and suggestive.

Abbreviations

Borges	*Historia de la Iglesia en Hispanomérica y Filipinas.* Edited by Pedro Borges. 2 vols. Madrid: Biblioteca de Autores Cristianos, 1992.
DMA	*Dictionary of the Middle Ages.* Edited by Joseph R. Strayer. New York: Charles Scribner's, 1982–89.
EEC	*Encyclopedia of the Early Christian Church.* Edited by Angelo Di Berardino. Translated by Adrian Walford. 2 vols. New York: Oxford Univ. Press, 1992.
EJ	*Encyclopedia Judaica.* 16 vols. Jerusalem: Keter Publishing House, 1971.
Fronteras	*Fronteras: A History of the Latin American Church in the USA since 1513.* Edited by Moisés Sandoval. San Antonio: Mexican American Cultural Center, 1983.
Materiales	*Materiales para una historia de la teología en América Latina.* Edited by Pablo Richard. San José, Costa Rica: Comisión de Estudios de Historia de la Iglesia en Latinoamericana (CEHILA), 1980.
Maza Miquel	*Esclavos, patriotas y poetas a la sombra de la Cruz: Cinco ensayos sobre catolicismo e historia cubana.* Edited by Manuel P. Maza Miquel. Santo Domingo, Dominican Republic: Centro de Estudios Sociales Padre Juan Montalvo, 1999.
Murray	Paul V. Murray, *The Catholic Church in Mexico, vol. 1 (1519–1910).* Mexico City: Ediciones de Libros con Fines Culturales, 1965.
NCE2	*New Catholic Encyclopedia,* 2nd edition. 15 vols. Washington, DC: Thomas-Gale, 2003.
ODCC	*Oxford Dictionary of the Christian Church.* Edited by F. L. Cross and E. A. Livingston. 3rd edition. Oxford: Oxford Univ. Press, 1997.

Polcari Ramón Suárez Polcari, *Historia de la Iglesia Católica en Cuba.* 2 vols. Miami: Ediciones Universal, 2003.

Raíces *Raíces de la teología latinoamericana.* 2nd ed. Edited by Pablo Richard. San José, Costa Rica: Comisión de Estudios de Historia de la Iglesia en Latinoamericana (CEHILA), 1987.

Saranyana *Teología en América Latina: Desde los Orígenes a la Guerra de Sucesión (1493–1715)*, vol. 1. Edited by Josep Ignasi Saranyana, et al. Madrid: Interamericana; Frankfurt: Vervuert, 1999.

Valverde y Telles Emeterio Valverde y Telles, *Bio-bibliografía eclesiástica del Estado de México.* Estado de México: Biblioteca Enciclopédica del Estado de México, 1976.

Vilanova Evangelista Vilanova. *Historia de la teología cristiana.* 3 vols. Barcelona: Herder, 1987–92.

Additional Bibliographical Sources

Andrés, Melquíades, ed. *Historia de la teología española.* 2 vols. Madrid: Fundación Universitaria Española, 1983–87.
Blancarte, Roberto. *Historia de la Iglesia Católica en México.* Mexico City: Fondo de Cultura Económica, 1992.
Campo Lacasa, Cristina. *Historia de la Iglesia en Puerto Rico (1511–1802).* San Juan: Instituto de Cultura Puertorriqueña, 1977.

The Select Annotated List

Fourth Century
Juvencus (early fourth century): Wrote a poetic *Life of Christ* based on Virgil. EEC, 1:466; ODCC, 916–17.
Hosius (or Osius) of Córdoba (c. 256–357/8): Ecclesiastical adviser to Emperor Constantine. Investigated the Arian controversy in Alexandria and organized the Councils of Antioch and Nicea in 325 to deal with Arianism. EEC, 1:626; ODCC, 792–93.
Gregory, Bishop of Elvira (c. 359): A prolific theologian who joined Hosius in defense of orthodoxy against the Arians. EEC, 1:363; ODCC, 711. Saint of the church.

Potamius of Lisbon (d. after 359): A Catholic bishop who turned Arian and wrote on the Trinity. EEC, 2:706; ODCC, 1313.

Priscillian, Bishop of Avila, (active c. 370–86): A controversial theologian who advocated a rigorous, ascetic life. He was condemned and executed by the government in Trier, in 386. EEC, 2:711–12; ODCC, 1:329–30.

Prudentius (348–c. 410): Called the prince of Christian poets, Prudentius was also an influential theologian (whose theology was set to poetry). EEC, 2:721–22; ODCC, 1341–42.

Eutropius the Presbyter (probably Iberian; late fourth–early fifth century): Wrote works about sin and perfection. EEC, 1:304.

Pacianus, Bishop of Barcelona (fourth century): Wrote on penance. Jerome dedicated his *De viris illustribus* to Pacianus' son. ODCC, 1207; EEC, 2:628b. Saint of the church.

Fifth and Sixth Centuries

Paul Orosius (early fifth century): An Iberian presbyter who befriended Augustine and was involved in the Pelagian controversy. He wrote what is considered the earliest universal Christian history, the *Historiarum adversus paganos*. EEC, 1:624–25; ODCC, 1197.

Severus, Bishop of Minorca (early fifth century): The disputed author of an encyclical letter describing, among other things, Minorca's liturgy. EEC, 1:774.

Idatius (or Hydatius), Bishop of Chaves (mid fifth century): A church historian for the period 379 to 468. EEC, 1:404.

Martin, Bishop of Braga (c. 520–579) and Abbot of Dumium: Originally from Hungary, Martin is considered the apostle to the Suevi. EEC, 1:530–31; ODCC, 1044. Saint of the church.

Apringius of Beja (mid sixth century): Wrote a commentary on the Apocalypse. EEC, 1:64.

Justinian, Bishop of Valencia (from 527 to 547): Wrote on Christology and baptism. He was the brother of Justus of Urgel. EEC, 1:465.

Justus of Urgel (mid sixth century): Composed a commentary on the Song of Songs and was the brother of Justinian of Valencia. EEC, 1:466.

Severus, Bishop of Málaga (late sixth century): Wrote on the Arian controversy and on virginity. EEC, 1:774.

Eutropius, Bishop of Valencia (late sixth century): Wrote on sin and on monastic discipline. EEC, 1:304.

Licinianus of Cartagena (late sixth century): A friend of Severus of Málaga, of Eutropius of Valencia, and of Leander of Seville, and a correspondent of Gregory the Great. He was interested in and wrote about theological questions arising from the Arian controversy. EEC, 1:489.

The Visigothic Period

Leander, Bishop of Seville (c. 545–c. 600): Isidore's elder brother and teacher. While in exile in Constantinople, Leander met Gregory the Great, who dedicated the *Moralia in Job* to him. Only two of Leander's works survive: his closing address to the Third Council of Toledo and a rule for holy women. EEC, 1:478; ODCC, 961. Saint of the church.

Isidore, Bishop of Seville (c. 560–636): One of the most influential and prolific of Christian theologians. His twenty-volume *Etymologiae* was one of the most copied and theologically influential books in medieval Western Europe. EEC, 1:418–19; ODCC, 851–52. Saint of the church.

Braulio, Bishop of Zaragoza (bishop c. 631–651): One of the most renowned literati of the Visigothic renaissance. He wrote many letters and hagiographies, and he helped compile the Visigothic legal code. EEC, 1:127. Saint of the church.

Taio, Bishop of Zaragoza (651–683): A great lover of the writers of the early church, wrote a five-volume *Sententiae*. EEC, 2:812.

Masona, Bishop of Mérida (from after 573 until c. 605): Left no writings but was deeply involved in disputes with the Arians. EEC, 1:542.

Eugenius, Bishop of Toledo (from 646 to 657): Renowned as a poet and presided over the Eighth, Ninth, and Tenth Councils of Toledo. EEC, 1:296.

Idefonsus, Bishop of Toledo (from 657 to 667): Wrote on the virginity of Mary, on baptism, on spiritual progress and continued the *De viris illustribus* of Jerome, Gennadius, and Isidore. EEC, 1:405; ODCC, 819. Saint of the church.

Julian, Bishop of Toledo (642–690): Presided over the Twelfth through Fifteenth Councils of Toledo. He was famous for learning and for his defense of the Iberian church against Rome. He wrote numerous works in scripture, history, and polemical theology. EEC, 1:458–59; ODCC, 909–10.

John, Abbot of Biclaro and Bishop of Gerona (sixth century): Wrote a history of events from 567 to 590. EEC, 1:444.

Fructuosus, elected Bishop of Braga (in 656): Founded several monasteries and wrote a Rule for one of his foundations. EEC, 1:330–31. Saint of the church.

Valerius of Bierzo (c. 630–695): An ascetic who produced extensive hagiographical and spiritual writings, as well as an autobiography. EEC, 2:860.

The Iberian *Convivencia*

Muslim Scholar

Abul Wabid Mohammed ibn Ahmad ben Mohammed Hafid ibn Roshd (Latin name: Averroes; 1126 to 1198): The famous Muslim scholar from Córdoba. Although learned in several areas, he is most famous for his influential commentaries on Aristotle. Was read widely throughout Western Europe, becoming very influential among Christian theologians and philosophers of his time. ODCC, 137–38; Vilanova, 1:621–26.

Jewish Scholars

Solomen Ibn Gabirol (Latin name: Avicebron or Avicebrol; 1026–1050): Born in Málaga. A Jewish philosopher in the Muslim courts of the Iberian peninsula, he wrote *The Source of Life*, the Latin translation of which became very popular during the Western Middle Ages. ODCC, 138; Vilanova, 1:633–34.

Bahya ben Joseph Ibn Paquda (second half of the eleventh century): Probably from Zaragoza, he was a moral philosopher, who wrote *Duties of the Heart*. EJ, 4:105–8.

The Kabbalist School of Gerona (twelfth to fourteenth centuries) includes the following (EJ, 3:1012–14):

Isaac ben Judah

Jacob ben Sheshet

Moses ben Solomon d'Escola

Samuel ben Meshullam

Solomon ben Isaac

Zerahiah ben Isaac Ha-Levi. Vilanova, 1:1648–49; EJ, 7:505–10.

Azriel of Gerona (early thirteenth century): Perhaps the most famous.

Abraham bar Hyya of Barcelona (d. c. 1136): Jewish philosopher, mathematician, astronomer, and translator who wrote on the soul, penance, and messianism. Vilanova, 1:635; EJ, 2:130–33.

Judah ben Barzilai of Barcelona (twelfth century): Wrote, among other works, a commentary on *The Book of Creation*. Vilanova, 1:636; EJ, 10:341–42.

Abraham Ibn Daud of Toledo (d. c. 1180): Historian, philosopher, physician, and astronomer. He was the first Jewish philosopher of Aristotle. His principal work is *The Exalted Faith*. He collaborated with Domingo Gundisalvo in translations. Also known as John of Spain (see below). Vilanova, 1:636; EJ, 8:1159–63.

Moses Maimonides (1135–1204): Born in Córdoba, he spent significant parts of his life in Cairo, where he did much of his work. A great

Talmudic scholar, his most widely known work is the *Guide for the Perplexed*. ODCC, 1021; Vilanova, 1:637–40; EJ 11:754–81.

Judah Ha-Levi of Toledo (1080–1141): A famous and influential poet and philosopher. Vilanova, 1:644–46; EJ, 10:355–66.

Abraham ben Samuel Abulafia (1240–after 1291): Mystical writer and Kabbalist. Was born in Zaragoza but traveled much, including time in Barcelona. EJ, 2:185–86.

Moses ben Sem Tov of León (1250–1305): A Kabbalist and author of the bulk of the *Zohar*. Vilanova, 1:649–50; EJ 12:425–27.

Abner of Burgos (Alfonso of Valladolid) (c. 1270–1340): A Jewish convert to Christianity who wrote *Teacher of Righteousness*, a defense of Christianity, in Hebrew. This work was answered by the *Touchstone* of Shem Tov ben Issac Shaput. DMA, 10:5.

Solomon Ha-Levi (also known as Pablo de Santa María; late fourteenth century): Jewish convert who was moved to conversion by Vincent Ferrer (see below). Ha-Levi received his doctorate from the Sorbonne and later became Bishop of Burgos. He wrote the *Scrutiny of the Scriptures*. DMA, 10:6.

Joshua Lorki (Gerónimo de Santa Fe): Jewish scholar who rebuked Solomon Ha-Levi (see above) for his conversion but later became a convert himself and was the leading Christian contender at the debate between Christians and Jews at Tortosa in 1413–14. DMA, 10:6.

Hasdai Crescas of Barcelona (d. 1412): Poet, philosopher and official with the court of Aragón. H wrote a refutation of Christianity in 1387–88. EJ, 5:1079–85.

Joseph ben Arbraham Hayyun (d. 1497): The last rabbi of the Jewish community in Lisbon before the expulsion. He wrote theology and scriptural commentary. EJ, 7:1514.

Joseph Albo (fifteenth century): Wrote on Jewish articles of faith and took part in several theological disputations with Christians. EJ, 2:535–37.

Christian Scholars

Prudentius of Galindo (d. 861): Chaplain at the court of Louis the Pious and Bishop of Troyes. He wrote on predestination. ODCC, 1342.

Raymond, Archbishop of Toledo (bishop 1124–52): Started the century-long translation program based in Toledo (and consequently, what came to be known as the very influential Toledo School of Translators). Villanova, 1:650–53 (for an excellent summary of the scholars who worked for Raymond of Toledo and for Alfonso X, see http://faculty.washington.edu/petersen/alfonso/esctra12.htm).

The following scholars of the Toledo School of Translators should be noted:

John of Spain (also known as Abraham Ibn Daud—see above): A Jewish scholar who collaborated closely with Domingo Gundisalvo from 1130 to 1150. He continued to translate up until his death in 1180. One of the most important translators, his fields included astrology, philosophy, mathematics, and medicine. In philosophy he translated Ibn Sina (Avicena), Qusta ben Luqa, and Avicebron, among others.

Domingo Gundisalvo, Archdeacon of Cuéllar: Worked with John of Spain as one of the founding scholars of the Toledo School of Translators. His activity extends from 1130 to 1180. Vilanova, 1:651–53; DMA, 12:135–36.

Gerald of Cremona: Gerald came to Toledo in 1167 and was a prolific translator of seventy-one works.

Plato of Tivoli: An Italian mathematician, astronomer, and astrologer who resided in Barcelona and then in Toledo, where he translated from Arabic and Hebrew into Latin either from 1116 to 1138 or from 1134 to 1145. He was assisted by Abraham bar Hyya (see above).

Alfred of Sareshel: An English translator and philosopher who resided in the north of Spain toward the end of the mid twelfth century.

Rudolf of Bruges (second quarter of the 13th century): A Flemish astronomer and translator residing in Toledo.

Robert of Chester, Archdeacon of Pamplona (mid twelfth century): Translated the Qur'an, among other works. He resided in Toledo from around 1140 to 1147.

Alfonso X, King of Castile and Léon (from 1252 to 1284): Employed fifteen different translators to turn the works of Aristotle from Arabic into Castilian, continuing the work started by Archbishop Raymond in the Toledo School of Translators. Alfonso himself was a very influential scholar. Perhaps his most famous work is the *Cantigas de Santa María*, a classic of Iberian literature written in early Castilian. DMA, 12:137.

The following scholars should be noted among Alfonso's collaborators and translators:

Michael the Scot (mid thirteenth century): Translated several of Aristotle's works while in Toledo. Some of his translations were still being used in the sixteenth century.

Marcos of Toledo (c. 1191–1234): Castilian physician and canon of the cathedral of Toledo, who translated the Qur'an, scientific works, and a series of Muslim religious treatises.

Herman the German: Worked in Toledo between 1240 and 1256. He later became a citizen of the kingdom of Castile and Bishop of

Astorga (from 1266 to 1272). He produced a Castilian translation of the Hebrew Psalter text as well as translations of philosophical works.

Theologians of the High Middle Ages

Peter of Spain, the Elder: A canon lawyer who wrote both a commentary on the *Decretum* (1170s) and on the *Decretals*. DMA, 9:519–20.

Raymond of Peñafort (c. 1180–1275): Studied and taught philosophy in Barcelona and later studied and taught canon law in Bologna. In 1222 he entered the Dominican convent of Barcelona. Peñafort became master general of the Dominicans in 1238. He dedicated his later life to the conversion of Jews and Muslims, establishing schools of Hebrew and Arabic. He is best known for his collection of the *Decretals* and his arrangement of the Dominican constitutions. He seems to have had considerable personal influence on Thomas Aquinas. Vilanova, 1:867–72; ODCC, 1369; DMA, 10:266; NCE2, 11:936–37. Saint of the church.

John XXI (1276–1277, baptized Pedro Juliano Rebolo and also known as Peter of Spain; b.c. 1205): Born in Lisbon, he studied arts and theology at Paris and taught medicine at Siena. He became court physician to Pope Gregory X in 1272, cardinal in 1273, and was elected pope in 1276. He wrote influential works in philosophy, theology, and medicine. ODCC, 884–85; DMA, 9:519–20; NCE2, 7:929–31.

Ramón Martí, also known as Raymond Martini (b. c. 1220–d. 1285): Born in Subriat, Catalonia. Taught in the School of Hebrew Studies in Barcelona. Among his numerous works is *The Dagger of the Faith*, a refutation of Judaism in Latin, Hebrew, and Aramaic. Vilanova, 1:889–95; DMA, 7:77 and 10:5; NCE2, 11:934–35.

Ferrar of Catalonia (late thirteenth century: Dominican master who succeeded Thomas Aquinas (after 1272) in the Dominican chair of theology at the University of Paris. Vilanova, 1:887–88.

Ramón Lull (c. 1233–1316): Lay missionary, philosopher, and mystical writer. Born in Majorca, he became seneschal to the son of the king of Aragón. At the age of thirty he dedicated himself to the conversion of the Muslims. To this end he convinced the king to establish a school for Oriental languages in Majorca; this foundation led to the Council of Vienne establishing such schools at five universities. He taught at Paris, Montpellier, and Naples; produced a large number of theological works; and went on three missionary trips to North Africa. One of the first to write what later came to be known as a Christian theology of religions. Vilanova, 1:872–87; DMA, 7:685–87. Beatification approved by the church.

Peter of Spain, the Younger (thirteenth century): A native of Lisbon and canon lawyer who became an important professor of canon law in Bologna. DMA, 9:519–20.

Arnald of Vilanova (c. 1240–1311): Catalonian physician, religious reformer, and author of spiritual works who became physician to Pedro III, king of Aragón. Arnald studied Hebrew and scripture in Barcelona, and preached the coming of the Anti-Christ. His teachings were condemned in Paris in 1299, but Arnald was absolved when he submitted to Boniface VIII. Besides spiritual works, Arnald translated Avicenna (see above) from Arabic and was one of the earliest writers in Catalan. Vilanova, 1:896–902; DMA, 1:537–38.

Paul the Christian (mid thirteenth century): Dominican master and convert from Judaism. Paul disputed with Rabbi Moses ben Nahman in Barcelona in 1263. Vilanova, 1:888.

Antoni Andreu, called Doctor Dulcifluus and Doctor Fundantissimus; b. c. 1280–d. 1333): A Franciscan born near Zaragoza, he was an influential commentator on Aristotle. Vilanova, 1:910.

Bernard Oliver (b. end of the thirteenth century-d. 1348): Augustinian friar. He studied at Paris, taught in Valencia, and became successively Bishop of Huesca (1336–45), of Barcelona (1345–46), and of Tortosa (1346–48). He wrote *Against the Jewish Blindness.* Vilanova, 1:907–8.

William Rubio (fourteenth century): A master of theology in Paris in 1334 who became the Dominican provincial of the province of Aragón. Vilanova, 1:911.

Francesc Eiximenis (c. 1327–1409): Franciscan theologian, born in Gerona, who lived in Barcelona. He was the confidant of the royal family of Aragón. In 1408 he was named Patriarch of Jerusalem by Benedict XIII, and later Bishop of Elna. He is the author of several works in Latin and Catalan. Vilanova, 1:911–18; DMA, 4:146–47.

Nicolás Eimeric (1320–1399): Dominican friar born in Gerona. Had two separate appointments as Inquisitor in Valencia but spent much of his time in Avignon. He wrote the influential *Directorium inquisitorum* in 1376. Vilanova, 1:921–24.

Vincent Ferrer (1350–1413): Entered the Dominican order in his native Valencia in 1367. He lectured on philosophy at Lérida and on theology at Valencia. He was confessor to the queen of Aragón (1379–83) and to the anti-pope Benedict XIII (1391) (see below). In 1395 he became preacher general of his order, and from 1339 toured Europe preaching with great success. Vilanova, 1:925–31; ODCC, 1699; DMA, 12:452–53. Saint of the church.

Benedict XIII (1394–1417); baptized Pedro de Luna (d. 1423): Born in Illueca, Aragón, he served in the court of the king of Castile and studied medicine at Montpellier, where he also taught. In 1375 Pope Gregory XI made him a cardinal, and in time he became an important member of the Curia of Clement VII in Avignon, after the papal schism. Elected pope while still a deacon, he immediately was ordained a priest and bishop, becoming the anti-pope Benedict XIII. He was deposed by the Council of Constance but refused to step down. He wrote in both canon law and theology. NCE2, 2:245–47.

Felip de Mallá (d. 1431): Dominican preacher and spiritual writer who, while a canon of the cathedral at Barcelona, was ambassador to the courts of Castile and England; he attended the Council of Constance. Vilanova, 1:936–39; DMA, 3:168.

Ramón de Sibiuda (c. 1436): Dominican master of arts, medicine, theology, and canon law. He wrote a massive *Theologia naturalis*. Vilanova, 1:939–43.

Martín of Córdoba (d. 1476): Augustinian scholar who wrote commentaries on the Bible and the *Art of Preaching*. DMA, 11:422.

The Sixteenth Century in Spain

Francisco Jiménez de Cisneros (1436–1517): Born in Torrelaguna in Castile. After studies in Alcalá de Henares, Salamanca, and a brief stay in Rome, he became vicar general for Spain's Cardinal Mendoza. He left this position to become an Observantine friar in Toledo. In 1492 he reluctantly accepted the position of confessor to Queen Isabel and, on the death of Cardinal Mendoza, the Archbishopric of Toledo (thereby becoming Primate of Spain). He became an influential member of the court, and in 1499 became both a cardinal and Inquisitor General. In 1516, he became regent of Castile during the minority of Charles V. An outstanding patron of learning, he founded the University of Alcalá de Henares in 1500, revived the Mozarabic rite and sponsored the famous Complutensian Polyglot Bible. He was widely known as a spiritual writer (for example, his *Ejercitaciones*) and a Castilian church reformer. Vilanova, 2:645ff.; ODCC, 1771.

Elio Antonio de Nebrija (1442–1522): Studied theology in Bologna but dedicated himself to the study of scripture in 1495. He became the first apostolic vicar to the West Indies in 1493 and accompanied Columbus on his second voyage. He worked on the Conplutensian Polyglot Bible in Alcalá de Henares. Vilanova, 2:129–30; NCE2, 1:2366 and 12:188–89.

Ignatius Loyola (1491–1556): Born of a noble family, he spent his youth in the household of the royal treasurer of Castile but eventually followed a military career. Wounded in the battle of Pamplona in 1521, he experienced a conversion and dedicated his life to God. The time he spent in Manresa became pivotal in his life. After a trip to Jerusalem he spent eleven years studying in Barcelona, Alcalá de Henares, Salamanca, and Paris. In 1540 the group organized by him was recognized by the pope as the Society of Jesus. Loyola is known for founding the Jesuits and for reviving religious fervor in Europe. He is also known for his classic and influential *Spiritual Exercises*. Vilanova, 2:178; ODCC, 818–19. Saint of the church.

Juan Luis Vives (1492–1540): One of the greatest sixteenth-century humanists. Born to converted Jews in Valencia, he studied in Valencia and Paris and taught at Louvain, where he befriended Erasmus. He also taught at Alcalá de Henares and at Oxford, where he befriended Thomas More. In 1524 he settled in Bruges, Belgium, where he lived most of his life as an independent scholar, despite being designated a cardinal and becoming Archbishop of Toledo. He wrote extensively in several areas, but his most influential theological work is the five-volume *De veritate fidei christianae*. Vilanova, 2:118–27; NCE2, 12:119, 124.

Juan de Valdés (c. 1490–1541): Born in Cuenca in Castile, he studied at Alcalá de Henares. Under accusation from the Inquisition, he fled to Italy in 1531, there becoming *camerario* to Pope Clement VII in 1533. Living in Naples, he was the focal point for reformers. He translated the Hebrew Psalter into Castilian and wrote several spiritual works. ODCC, 1674–75; NCE2, 14:368–69.

Francisco de Vitoria (1483–1546): Entered the Dominicans in 1505 and studied in Burgos and Paris, where he taught from 1513 to 1522. From 1522 until 1526 he taught theology at Valladolid, and from 1526 at Salamanca. He began the practice of replacing the *Sentences* of Peter Lombard with the *Summa theologiae* of Thomas Aquinas as the standard theological textbook. He was also a philosopher of law. His writings on the rights of Amerindians were extremely influential and are still studied as foundational to modern international law. One of the famed sixteenth-century Salamanca theologians. Vilanova, 2:606–9; ODCC, 1705–6; NCE2, 14:570–72.

Domingo de Soto (1494–1560): Entered the Dominicans in Burgos in 1524 after studying in Alcalá de Henares and Paris. He taught in Burgos until 1532, when he took a chair in theology in Salamanca. In 1545 he was chosen imperial theologian to the Council of Trent. In 1550 he returned to Salamanca, where he taught until his death. Very influential, and one of the famed sixteenth-century Salamanca theologians. Vilanova, 2:609–11; ODCC, 1520.

Peter of Alcántara (1499–1562): Born at Alcántara and studied at Salamanca from 1511 to 1515. He joined the Franciscans soon after and was ordained in 1524. He served as provincial from 1538 to 1541, and in 1557 he became commissary general of the reformed Conventuals. He is best known for his guidance of Teresa of Avila (see below) and his *Tratado de la oración y meditación*. ODCC, 1263; NCE2, 11:195. Saint of the church.

John of Avila (1499 or 1500–1569): Known as the Apostle of Andalusía, John studied law at Salamanca, and arts and theology at Alcalá de Henares. Ordained in 1526 he undertook a preaching campaign in Andalusía until ill health forced him to stop in 1554. He encouraged church reform and established at least fifteen colleges for the laity and two for the clergy. He had great influence through his spiritual guidance, both in person and through correspondence. Vilanova, 2:649–52; ODCC, 887–88. Saint of the church.

Melchor Cano (1509–1560): Entered the Dominicans in Salamanca in 1523 under Francisco de Vitoria (see above). He taught at Valladolid and Alcalá de Henares before succeeding Vitoria as professor of theology in Salamanca. He was actively involved at the Council of Trent, and in 1557 was elected provincial of the Dominicans in Castile (although papal confirmation of this appointment was at first withheld). His most famous work is the *De locis theologicis*. Influential as a theologian and as royal adviser in Castile. One of the famed sixteenth-century Salamanca theologians. Vilanova, 2:611–14; ODCC, 276.

Miguel Servetus (c. 1509–1553): Born in Navarre, he studied law in Toulouse. He traveled to Basle and Strasbourg, where he met the Reformation leaders Oecolampadius and Bucer. In 1531 he published a treatise attacking the doctrine of the Trinity. He subsequently studied medicine at Paris and Montpellier and was appointed physician to the Archbishop of Vienne. In 1546, in correspondence with Calvin, he again attacked the doctrine of the Trinity and also questioned the traditional view of the Incarnation. Under Calvin's orders he was arrested by the Inquisition. He was condemned as a heretic and burned at the stake in Geneva in 1553. He is also remembered for first discovering the circulation of the blood in the human body. Vilanova, 2:508–12; ODCC, 1487.

Diego Laínez (1512–1565): The son of Jewish converts, Laínez studied at Alcalá and Paris, where he joined Ignatius Loyola (see above) as one of his earliest companions. He taught at the Sapienza in Rome and was very active at the Council of Trent. He succeeded Loyola as the second general of the Jesuits in 1558. ODCC, 943–44; NCE2, 8:287–88. Cause of beatification has been introduced.

Teresa of Avila (1515–1582): Entered the Carmelite convent in Avila in 1535, converting to a life of asceticism and mystical experiences in

1555. In 1560 she received guidance from Peter of Alcántara (see above), moving to the newly founded Convent of Saint Joseph in Avila. There she wrote *The Way of Perfection; The Interior Castle*, her spiritual autobiography; and other works. Teresa worked to establish convents of the primitive Carmelite observance for both nuns and friars. Declared a doctor of the church in 1970, Teresa is one of the greatest mystical writers. Vilanova, 2:65970; ODCC, 1598–99. Saint of the church.

Bartolomé de Medina (1527–1580): Dominican friar who taught at Alcalá de Henares and, from 1576 on, at Salamanca. He is best known for his commentary on Aquinas and is sometimes credited with authoring the doctrine of probabilism in moral theology. One of the famed sixteenth-century Salamanca theologians. Vilanova, 2:615–16; ODCC, 1065; NCE2, 9:464–65.

Luis de León (1527–1591): Became an Augustinian hermit at Salamanca in 1544, becoming a professor there in 1561. Both John of the Cross (see below) and Francisco Suárez (see below) were his students. He edited the works of Teresa of Avila (see above). He clashed with the Inquisition in 1572 because of his preference for the Hebrew Old Testament but was cleared of all charges. He is famous as a poet, a spiritual writer, and a biblical scholar. ODCC, 970; Vilanova, 2:627–28.

Domingo Báñez (1528–1604): Studied philosophy at Salamanca, joining the Dominicans in 1547. He taught at Avila and Valladolid, returning to Salamanca in 1577. An advocate of Aquinas in his theology, he was also the confessor of Teresa of Avila. One of the famed sixteenth-century Salamanca theologians. Vilanova, 2:616–17; ODCC, 149.

Juan Maldonaldo (1533–1583): Studied at Alcalá, joining the Jesuits in 1546. He taught at the Jesuit college in Paris from 1564 until 1576, when he was cleared of charges of heresy by the Bishop of Paris. He is most famous for his commentary on the Gospels. Vilanova, 2:619; ODCC, 1024.

Luis de Molina (1536–1600): Entered the Jesuits in 1553 and taught in Coimbra and Evora. He is best known for his theology of grace. Vilanova, 2:624–5; ODCC, 1100.

John of the Cross (1542–1591): Entered the Carmelite monastery of Medina del Campo in 1563, studied theology at Salamanca, and was ordained in 1567. Following the advice of Teresa of Avila (see above), John helped found the reformed Discalced Carmelites. He was confessor of the Convent of the Incarnation in Avila from 1572 to 1577, at the time when Teresa was prioress. From 1579 to 1582 he was rector of the college he had founded at Baeza, and from there he was appointed prior of Granada and then of Segovia. In 1591 he was banished to Andalusía, where he died. One of the great mystical writers in the Christian tradition, he was declared a doctor of the church in 1926. Vilanova, 2:670–82; ODCC, 889–90. Saint of the church.

Francisco Suárez (1548–1617): Known as Doctor Eximius et Pius, Suárez, a Jesuit, studied philosophy and theology at Salamanca. He taught there from 1564 to 1570. He also taught in Rome from 1580 to 1585, in Alcalá de Henares from 1585 to 1593, and in Coimbra from 1597 to 1616. Often considered the greatest of the Jesuit theologians of his day, Suárez was an original thinker who contributed not only to theology but to law. He was also influential in his day and after through his commentaries on Thomas Aquinas. Vilanova 2:621–23; ODCC 1550–51.

Tomás Sánchez (1550–1610): Entered the Jesuits in 1567 and taught moral theology at Granada. He is most famous for an extensive study of marriage. Vilanova, 2:621; ODCC, 1451.

Gabriel Vázquez (1549–1604): Became a Jesuit in 1569 and taught moral theology at Madrid, Ocaña, Alcalá de Henares, and Rome. He is best known for his extensive commentary on the *Summa theologiae* of Thomas Aquinas, in which he disagrees with Francisco Suárez (see above). ODCC, 1684.

The Colonial Period

Emphasis on Mexico, Cuba, and Puerto Rico from the Sixteenth to Eighteenth Centuries[27]

Ramón Pané: Joined Columbus on his second voyage; studied the religion, customs, and oral traditions of the indigenous Taíno people of the Caribbean. He completed his work sometime around 1498. The original of his *Relación acerca de las antigüedades de los indios* has been lost, but it was used by Bartolomé de Las Casas (see below), and some notes survive. A modern reconstruction of his original text has been published. Borges, 1:615–16; Saranyana, 35–37.

Antonio de Montesinos (c. 1486–c. 1530): Originally at the Dominican convent in Salamanca, he traveled to Santo Domingo in 1510. He immediately worked to free the natives from slavery, preaching there his famous Advent sermons. Montesinos returned to Spain several times to defend his position. When his mission failed, he returned to Puerto Rico, from where he joined the expedition to Virginia in 1526. His work for the indigenous people was taken up by Bartolomé de Las Casas (see below). NCE2, 9:835; Saranyana, 37–38.

Bartolomé de Las Casas (1474–1566): Known as the Apostle of the Indies and Defender of the Indians. Las Casas, a lawyer, accompanied the

Spanish governor to Hispaniola in 1502. Ordained in 1507, he celebrated his first Mass in Hispaniola in 1510. Beginning in 1514 he
dedicated himself to protecting the indigenous peoples from the Spanish
settlers. In 1515 he successfully presented his cause to the court of
Spain. He joined the Dominicans in 1522 and became Bishop of
Chiapas in 1543. He returned to Spain, where he continued his efforts until his death. Vilanova, 2:715; ODCC, 952; Jean-Pierre Ruiz,
"Cardinal Francisco Ximénez de Cisneros and Bartolomé de las Casas,
the 'Procurator and Universal Protector of All Indians in the Indies,'"
Journal of Hispanic/Latino Theology 9, no. 9 (2002): 60–77. Cause
of beatification has been introduced.

Bernardino de Sahagún (1499–1590): Studied in Salamanca, where he
became a Franciscan. In 1529 he was sent to Mexico, where he taught
at the college of Santa Cruz in Tlaltelolco, near Mexico City. He is
most noted for his exhaustive study of the Aztec religion, culture, and
language. He also wrote shorter theological works, some in the native
language. Vilanova, 2:720; NCE2, 12:528–29.

Juan de Zumárraga (1468–1548): Born in the Basque country, Zumárraga
entered the Franciscans and in time became custodian of the convent
at Abrojo. In 1527 he was chosen first Bishop of Mexico. He arrived
in 1528 in Mexico City before being ordained bishop. He immediately objected to the mistreatment of the indigenous people and was
opposed by the Spanish authorities in Mexico. He placed the city under interdict in 1530. In that same year a new administration arrived
from Spain including the lawyer Vasco de Quiroga (see below). In
1532 Zumárraga returned to Rome, successfully defending his administration. He was finally ordained bishop in 1533. He returned to
Mexico City in 1534 and continued, despite great difficulties, to deal
justly with the native population. He is responsible for establishing
new institutions and introducing several innovations including a school
for Indian girls, the famous Colegio de Tlaltelolco; the first printing
press of the New World; and the foundation of various hospitals,
especially those of Mexico City and Veracruz. Borges, 1:618–19;
Saranyana, 49–55.

Vasco de Quiroga (c. 1470–1565): Trained in law rather than theology,
and as a lawyer traveled to Mexico in 1530. Upon his arrival he began advocating for the just treatment of the indigenous peoples. Having been chosen Bishop of Michoacán, he was immediately ordained
priest and bishop. As bishop he continued his advocacy for the natives and founded the Colegio de San Nicolás for the training of native clergy. *Raíces*, 37–48; NCE2, 11:870–71; Bernardino Verástique,
Michoacán and Eden: Vasco de Quiroga and the Evangelization of

Western Mexico (Austin: Univ. of Texas Press, 2000). Cause of beatification has been introduced.

Alonso de la Vera Cruz, baptized Alonso Gutiérrez y Gutiérrez (1507–1584): Born in Caspueñas (Spain) and studied in Alcalá and Salamanca. He was ordained in 1535 and arrived in Veracruz in 1536, where he became an Augustinian friar (thereby changing his name). He soon moved to Mexico City where from 1553 he was the first professor of scripture at the newly founded University of Mexico. He authored the first philosophical treatise written and printed in Mexico and is considered the father of Mexican philosophy. Borges, 1:409–10; Saranyana, 290–98.

Diego Valadés (1533–c. 1583): Born in Extremadura (Spain) of a *conquistador* father and a Tlaxacaltec mother. He went to the New World as a child in 1541–42 and entered the Franciscans sometime between 1548 and 1550. Diego published the first book to appear in Europe by a Mexican, the *Rhetorica catholicum* (one of the first books on indigenous Mexican culture). NCE2, 14:367–68; Saranyana, 231–36.

José de Acosta (1540–1600): Born at Medina del Campo, Acosta joined the Jesuits at age thirteen. After lecturing in theology at Ocaña, he was sent in 1569 to Lima, where he occupied the chair of theology. He also taught in Cuzco and founded colleges in Arequipa, Potosí, Chuquisaca, and Panamá. Returning to Europe, he taught in Rome and was rector of the University of Salamanca. He is most famous for his descriptions of nature and society in the New World. He also wrote on the evangelization of the indigenous populations. Vilanova 2:723; *Raíces*, 5, 9–10.

Gerónimo Mendieta (1525–1604): Born in Vitoria (Spain). He became a Franciscan in Bilbao and arrived in Mexico in 1554. Soon thereafter he became an expert in native languages. Mendieta returned to Europe to take part in the Franciscan general chapter of 1569. While in Spain, he argued against the harsh treatment of the indigenous population and suggested that the native population be completely separated from the Spanish with its own towns, courts, and even bishops. He returned to Mexico in 1571 and held several posts there. His most famous work is the *Historia Eclesiástica Indiana,* completed in 1596. NCE2, 9:492; Saranyana, 535–39, 630–34.

Alonso de la Mota y Escobar (1556–1625): Born and educated in Mexico City, he was sent to Spain where became tutor to the future king. He earned his degree in canon law in Salamanca, returned to Mexico, and was consecrated Bishop of Guadalajara in 1597. In 1608 he was transferred to the see of Puebla de Los Angeles. Throughout his career he worked for better treatment of the indigenous people and wrote (between 1602 and 1605) a description of missionary activities in northern Mexico and the (now) US Southwest entitled *Descripción geográfica de las Reynos de Nueva Galicia, Nueva Vizcaya y Nuevo León. Fronteras,* 17, 27–28; NCE2, 10:11.

Francisco Pareja (d. 1628): Born probably near Toledo, he became a Franciscan and was sent to Florida in 1593 or early in 1594. There he became guardian of the convent of the Immaculate Conception in St. Augustine. He is noted for having published the first books in the language of an Indian tribe within the United States, the Timuquanan. In 1616 he was elected provincial of the Franciscans' Province of Santa Elena, including what is now Cuba, Florida and Georgia. NCE2, 10:882; Saranyana, 228–30. (For another Francisco Pareja, see below.)

Martín Vázquez de Arce (1599–1609): The first *criollo* Bishop of New Spain. He was born in Lima and appointed Bishop of Puerto Rico before moving to Mexico. A Dominican, he served as rector and professor at Santo Tomás in Seville and published a *Catecismo* and *Constituciones.* He is remembered for his concern for the indigenous peoples and the sick. Borges, 2:11.

Bernardo de Balbuena (1568–1627): Born in Val de Peñas (Spain), he moved to Mexico at an early age and was educated there. He became Bishop of Jamaica in 1610 and of Puerto Rico in 1620. He is best known for his learned poetry. Borges, 2:12; NCE2, 3:110.

Damián López de Haro: Bishop of Puerto Rico from 1642 to 1648. During that time he held the important synod of 1645 and published the *Constituciones sinodales*—guides to diocesan governance that were reprinted (and some still used) until 1989. Borges, 2:12–13.

Alonzo Benavides: Born on the island of San Miguel in the Azores. He became a Franciscan in Mexico in 1603. After being master of novices at the convent of Puebla, he was put in charge of the missions of New Mexico. He returned to Europe in 1630, where he was made Archbishop of Goa in 1636. He died on his return to the Americas. He worked hard for the betterment of the missions of New Mexico, for which purpose he wrote and published two books important for the ethnography and ethnology of New Mexico. NCE2, 2:235.

Francisco Pareja (d. 1688): Probably studied at the Mercedarian convent in Mexico City. He was sent to Spain in 1652. In 1654 he became the first rector of the San Ramón Nonato College in Mexico City, where he became professor of theology in 1656. He was twice elected provincial of the Mercedarians. He is most known for his extensive history of the Mercedarians in Mexico. NCE2, 10:881–82. (For another Francisco Pareja, see above.)

Antonio Vieira (1608–1697): Born in Lisbon, he moved to Bahia (Brazil) when he was six. He entered the Jesuits in Brazil in 1623 and returned in 1641 to Lisbon, where he gained considerable influence in the court of King John IV. Returning in 1652 to the Jesuit missions of Brazil, he worked relentlessly to uphold the freedom of the indigenous peoples. In 1661 he was forced to return to Portugal, where he was condemned by the Inquisition and spent two years in jail. In 1669 he went to Rome to plead his own case and that of converted Jews. His preaching won a hearing, and Rome exempted him from jurisdiction of the Inquisition and imposed a seven-year ban on Inquisitional trials. In 1681 he returned to Brazil, where he later became visitor general of the missions, a position he used to continue his defense of the indigenous people. His writings in defense of Indians and Jews were influential in Spain's colonies, but his exaggerated views of the world mission of the Portuguese monarchy were seen as dangerous by Spain. ODCC, 1695; NCE2, 3:4127, 7:785.

Francisco de Florencia (1619–1695): The first Latino/a theologian of the New World. He was born in Florida and studied at the College of San Ildefonso in Mexico City. He entered the Jesuits in 1641, moving first to Rome and then to Seville as *procurador* for the New World. He wrote both history and theology. *Fronteras*, 45; Saranyana, 550–52.

Juana Inés de la Cruz, baptized Juana de Asbaje y Ramona (1651–1695): Born in San Miguel Nepantla, México, in 1669 she entered the convent of the Order of Saint Jerome in Mexico City in 1669, where she lived the rest of her life. Juana Inés was the first woman theologian in the New World. She also wrote plays, poems, and songs (many with theological themes) that are now considered classics of the Spanish language. She received an encyclopedic education and was influential in the Mexican learned society of her day. *Raíces*, 49–52; Borges, 1:758–60; Michelle A. González, *Sor Juana: Beauty and Justice in the Americas* (Maryknoll, NY: Orbis Books, 2003).

Isidro Félix de Espinoza, (1679–1755): Born in Querétaro, Mexico, and educated at the Franciscan College there. He was ordained in 1703, and in 1714 was elected superior of the Franciscan missions in Texas. In 1731 he founded the *Hospicio de San Fernando*, which soon became a college of which he became the first president. Among several other works he wrote the *Crónica Apostólica y Seráphica de todos los Colegios de Propaganda Fide*, published in Mexico City in 1746. *Fronteras*, 47; NCE2, 5:539.

Francisco Antonio de Lorenzana (1722–1804): Born in León (Spain), he studied at the Jesuit college in that city. In 1765 he was ordained

Bishop of Plasencia, and the next year he was elected Archbishop of Mexico City. He published the Acts of the first three provincial councils of Mexico, as well as an extensive *Historia de Nueva España* in 1770. In 1772 he became Archbishop of Toledo and Primate of Spain. In Toledo he built a remarkable library and published a collection of church writers from that city; he also published an edition of the Mozarabic missal. To all these works he attached learned introductions. He became a cardinal in 1789 and, while in Rome, founded the Catholic Academy. He left his entire inheritance to the poor. NCE2, 8:786.

Francisco Javier Alegre (1729–1788): Born in Veracruz, he entered the Jesuits in 1747. He taught at the Jesuit colleges in Havana and in Mérida. In 1767 (because of the expulsion of the Jesuits from all Spanish territories) he moved to Bologna, where he died. He wrote a number of books, but is most widely known for his multi-volume *History of the Society of Jesus in New Spain*—a veritable mine of information, references, and analyses on Mexico's colonial history. NCE2, 1:249.

Francisco Palau (1732–1790): Born in Majorca, he became a Franciscan and traveled to New Spain in 1749. He worked with Junípero Serra in the establishment of the missions of Alta California. He was elected superior of the College of San Fernando in Mexico City in 1784, and he published his history of the California missions in 1787. *Fronteras*, 49; Borges, 1:628–29. Cause of beatification has been introduced.

Bartolomé García (mid eighteenth century): Published the *Manual para la administración de los Santos Sacramentos* in Mexico City in 1760. This work contains a wealth of information on the customs and cultures of the indigenous peoples of Texas. *Fronteras*, 47.

Mexico, Cuba, and Puerto Rico, Nineteenth and Early Twentieth Centuries[28]

Miguel Hidalgo y Costilla (1753–1811): Born in Guanajuato, he studied in Morelia (at the time called Valladolid). He was ordained in 1778. Hidalgo became professor of theology and later rector of the College of San Nicholas. While a parish priest he translated the works of Molière and Racine. Hidalgo worked first secretly and then openly for Mexican independence from Spain. On September 16, 1810, Hidalgo led the first public cry for freedom; Mexico has celebrated this day up to the present as the anniversary of its Declaration of Independence. Selecting the banner of the Virgin of Guadalupe for his standard, he raised an army and took the important city of Guanajuato. After the victory of Las Cruces outside Mexico City he lost battles at

Aculco and Puente Grande, where he was forced to surrender his army. He was executed in Chihuahua. Given his very important role in Mexican history, most forget that he was first a professor of theology and often explained his pro-independence stance in theological terms. Murray, 86–89; NCE2, 6:820–21.

Juan José Díaz de Espada y Landa (1756–1832): Born at Arroyave (Spain), Espada studied at Salamanca, where he earned a doctorate in canon law. He was ordained in 1782 and for eleven years did pastoral work in Spain. In 1792 he became professor of philosophy and canon law. He was named Bishop of Havana in 1800 and arrived in Cuba in 1802. He worked tirelessly for the benefit of education, the arts and public health. Espada was a very important modernizing force in Cuba. He established several schools and published a pastoral letter in favor of vaccination, then still in its experimental stages. He inspired and supported the work of Félix Varela (see below) and other notables of the Cuban church. Polcari, 291–339; NCE2, 5:357.

Manuel Hechavarría y Peñalver (1774–1845): Born in Havana, he began his studies in the diocesan seminary there but obtained his doctorate in canon law in Bologna in 1797. He was ordained in the same year and returned to Cuba in 1803. In 1838 he became vice-rector of the Pontifical University in Havana, as well as theologian for the diocese. In addition to teaching theology, he also published a book on medicine. He is particularly noted for his work in moral theology. Polcari, 347–48.

Félix Varela (1788–1853): Born in Havana, as a child he moved with his family to St. Augustine, Florida, where his grandfather was military governor. Varela entered the Havana diocesan seminary, where he obtained degrees in humanities and in theology. He was ordained a priest in 1811. Varela held the chairs of Latin, rhetoric, philosophy, physics, and chemistry at the Havana seminary, which by then had become Cuba's paramount academic institution, far surpassing the universities. In 1822–23 he represented Havana in Spain's parliament. Condemned to death for his opposition to the Spanish monarchy and his support for the abolition of slavery, he escaped to the United States. After some time in Philadelphia, he moved to New York. There he became a parish priest and later vicar general of that diocese, dedicating his life to the pastoral care of the thousands of poor Catholic immigrants. Varela received a doctorate in theology from St. Mary's in Baltimore. He also wrote several important books in philosophy including *Institutiones Philosophiae Eclecticae ad usum studiosae juventutis* and *Miscelánea, Etica y Elencos anuales*. In New York he founded and edited several English-language periodicals (mostly to explain and defend Catholicism from Protestant attacks in New York), and a Spanish-language defense of Catholicism *(Letters to Elpidio)*; he is credited with having founded the US Catholic press. He also founded and edited (and wrote much for) a Spanish-language periodical in the United States *(El Habanero)*. He established free schools and found work for the poor. He is one of the most important and revered names in Cuban history and was the first Latino to receive a doctorate in theology from a US institution. Needing to recuperate from tuberculosis, he moved to St. Augustine (Florida) again, where he died in 1853 and was buried. After Cuba's independence from Spain, his body was transferred to the island, where it was reburied with honors in the *aula magna* at the University of Havana. Polcari, 351–53. Cause of beatification has been introduced.

Francisco García-Diego y Moreno (1785–1846): Born in San Juan de los Lagos, Jalisco, he completed his studies at the seminary in Guadalajara. He entered the Franciscans in 1802 and was ordained in 1808, becoming prefect and then vicar of the Franciscan college in Guadalajara. In 1833 he was sent by the government of Mexico to take over the California missions whose secularization he later opposed. When California (Alta and Baja) was separated from the diocese of Sonora in 1840, he became the first Bishop of California, with his see in San Diego. The see was later moved to Santa Barbara and Monterey. He founded a seminary at Santa Ines, (Alta) California, in 1844. NCE2, 6:93.

Remigio Cernadas (1779–1859): Entered the Dominican priory in Havana in 1779. He earned the doctorate in philosophy and theology at the University of Havana in 1817. Cernadas served as chancellor of the Real y Pontificia Universidad de San Jerónimo de La Habana on several occasions. In 1836 he became secretary to the bishop of Havana. He is known for his skills as an orator and preacher. He worked closely with Félix Varela (see above) and with Bishop Espada (see above). Polcari, 351–53.

Basilio Arrillaga (1792–1867): Born in Mexico City, he became a Jesuit in 1816. In a series of learned books and pamphlets Arrillaga defended the Mexican church against liberal Catholicism and the antireligious actions of successive Mexican governments. He was dean of the Jesuit college in Puebla and then in Mexico City. He was one of the founders of the Academia Nacional de la Historia. From 1844 to 1849 he was rector of the University of Mexico. Murray, 230–33; NCE2, 1:724.

José María de Yermo y Parrés (1851–1904): The founder of the Christian Mercy Program and of the Congregation of the Servants of the Sacred Heart of Jesus and the Poor. He was educated by tutors and then by the Vincentians, whom he joined in 1867. He was sent to Paris for theological studies in 1873, but when he returned to Mexico he left the Vincentians and was ordained as a diocesan priest. He founded numerous schools, hospitals, and homes for the needy. He wrote many works, not all published, on social work, education, and spirituality. Valverde y Telles, 135–40; NCE2, 14:888. Saint of the church (canonized in 2000).

Desiderio Mesnier (1852–1913): Born in Santiago del Prado del Cobre, in eastern Cuba, he studied at the seminary in Santiago de Cuba, where he received his bachelor's degree in 1869. He was then expelled from the seminary for his sympathies with Cuban independence. He joined the insurgent army as a medic. He was later received back into the seminary and was ordained in 1880. He received his doctorate in education from the University of Havana in 1909. During and after the independence war years of 1895–98 he worked to support the struggle while still defending a church whose hierarchy was openly pro-Spanish. He wrote during this time, as he put it, to explain that the war for independence was not "a war against God or his ministers, but against the Spanish government." Maza Miquel, 237–54.

Leopoldo Ruíz y Flores (1865–1941): Born in Amealco, Querétaro, he studied at the clerical college in Tacuba and in Rome at the Gregorian University, where he earned doctorates in philosophy, theology, and canon law. He taught philosophy at the archdiocesan seminary of Mexico City until he became Bishop of León in 1900. He was progressively Bishop of León (1900–1907); Archbishop of Lenares-Monterrey (1907–11), and Archbishop of Morelia (1912–41). He served as apostolic delegate from 1929 to 1937. Twice he fled to the United States because of the relationship between the Vatican and the Mexican government, a relationship he worked to ameliorate. He strove to improve education, founding several schools. He stressed the social apostolate among workers. Valverde y Telles, 97–119; NCE2, 12:408–9.

Emeterio Valverde y Telles (1864–1948): Born in Villa del Carbón, he entered the seminary in Mexico City in 1876. He was professor at the seminary from 1882 to 1890. He became vicar general of the archdiocese of Mexico City in 1903, and Bishop of León, Guanajuato, in 1909, where he remained until his death. He promoted Catholic education, wrote extensively in philosophy and mystical theology, and composed extensive bibliographies. Valverde y Telles, 141–77; NCE2, 380–81.

Angel María Garibay Kintana (or Quintana) (1892–1967): Born in Toluca, he entered the archdiocesan seminary in Mexico City. He was appointed librarian there, and then began his studies in Hebrew, Greek, Náhuatl, and Otomí. He was ordained a priest in 1917. In 1924 he became professor of humanities and rhetoric at the seminary. In 1952 he was named extraordinary professor of the faculty of philosophy and letters at the National Autonomous University of Mexico, and in 1956 he became director of the prestigious national Seminar on Nahuatl Culture. Garibay was responsible for printing many of the early accounts of the native cultures of Mexico and for the preservation of their histories and texts. Valverde y Telles, 208–12.

Pedro Velásquez Hernández (1913–1968): Born in Valle de Bravo, near Mexico City, he entered the archdiocesan seminary in Mexico City. He also studied in Rome at the Gregorian University, where he earned a doctorate in theology. He became director of the Secretariado Social Mexicano, where he worked to demonstrate the relevance of Catholic social teaching to the social problems of the day. He toured South America, the United States, Canada, and Europe espousing his cause. He also published widely in the area of Catholic social teaching. Valverde y Telles, 230–36.

Notes

[1] As described in more detail below, this chapter deals with the Iberian and particularly Spanish background as opposed to either Native American or African, or the wider European background to Latino/a theology. It also deals with the theological as opposed to the popular tradition that informs that theology. In this regard the essay is only one small part of a much larger project.

[2] Dale Irvin, *Christian Histories, Christian Traditioning: Rendering Accounts* (Maryknoll, NY: Orbis Books, 1998); Terrence Tilley, *Inventing Catholic Tradition* (Maryknoll, NY: Orbis Books, 2000); and Orlando O. Espín, "Toward the Construction of an Intercultural Theology of Tradition," in *Journal of Hispanic/Latino Theology* 9 (2002): 22–59. I have also discussed these issues in the introduction to *Treasures from the Storehouse: Essays on the Medieval Eucharist* (Collegeville, MN: Liturgical Press, 1999), xi–xx; and more recently in "The Future of the Past: What Can History Say about Symbol and Ritual," in *Practicing Catholic: Ritual, Body, and Contestation in Catholic Faith*, ed. Bruce Morrill, Susan Rodgers, and Joanna E. Ziegler (New York: Palgrave-Macmillan, forthcoming).

[3] On the historical background to this approach, see Irvin, *Christian Histories, Christian Traditioning*, 21–27 and Tilley, *Inventing Catholic Tradition*, 45–65.

[4] Tilley describes well how scholars are themselves situated within an Enlightenment tradition that itself has its own cultural, economic, and political problems: "The tradition of critical inquiry assumes that this search is not only

good for the scholars but also (at least potentially) liberating for all. Critical scholarship is to be done because because it benefits the common good. Why should we accept the claim that participating in the Enlightenment tradition of critical scholarship is a good and truly liberating experience? Why should we assume that criticism of a tradition is a force to free human minds?" (Tilley, *Inventing Catholic Tradition*, 18–19).

⁵ "Tradition is not merely or mainly the recall of the past or a reference to it. Rather, it is a present interpretation of the past in reference to the future. And, in doing this, the present 'creates' a past which is then declared to be stable, self-evident, 'objectively there,' and ready to be mined for justifications to the present's legitimation needs" (Espín, "Toward the Construction of an Intercultural Theology of Tradition," 52). "Redefining and reworking the heritage of the past actually creates the past, creates a new past, by creating the present which is to become the past that future generations will take over or reject on their own, and as their own" (Irvin, *Christian Histories, Christian Traditioning*, 14).

⁶ "An individual cannot reform a tradition any more than an individual can change other social patterns like racism or sexism (which themselves can be understood as traditions). Any proposal for reformation must be accepted by the practioners who put it into practice. If the participants in the tradition, through whatever mechanism from horrible coercion to completely free choice, put into practice the proposal for reform, then and only then, is a tradition reformed" (Tilley, *Inventing Catholic Tradition,* 80). This principle is important not only for the future of Latino/a theology, but for this very essay and the changes it proposes.

⁷ Tilley, relying on the work of Yves Congar, emphasizes that traditions can only survive by communication: "But essential to tradition, as Congar's definition highlights, is the fact that it is a process of the communication of tradition, what Congar calls transmission" (Tilley, *Inventing Catholic Tradition,* 50–51). If there is no transmission, there can be no tradition, and transmission is itself a act bound by the economic, social, political and cultural constraints.

⁸ Irvin, *Christian Histories, Christian Traditioning*, 41; see also Tilley, *Inventing Catholic Tradition*, 66–86.

⁹ Espín, "Toward the Construction of an Intercultural Theology of Tradition," 38–51.

¹⁰ Irvin, *Christian Histories, Christian Traditioning,* 4, see also 72; and Espín, "Toward the Construction of an Intercultural Theology of Tradition," 28–30.

¹¹ Irvin, *Christian Histories, Christian Traditioning,* 21. For a similar sentiment in the writing of Otto Maduro, see note 14 below.

¹² Espín, "Toward the Construction of an Intercultural Theology of Tradition," 46–47.

¹³ Ibid., 41.

¹⁴ In the words of Otto Maduro, "Dicho de otro modo, hacer historia escrita es hacer historia real, es una de las maneras de influir en la historia de un pueblo y de participar en la construcción de sus alternativeas, de su devenir y de

su destino histórico. Insisto: que lo deseemos o no, que nos demos cuenta or no, así es" (Maduro, "Apuntes epistemolólogico-políticos para una historia de la teología en América Latina," in *Materiales para una historia de la teología en América Latina*, ed. Pablo Richard [San José, Costa Rica: CEHILA, 1980], 19).

[15] See, for example, the distinctive theologies discussed in the popular devotions and movements in the Puerto Rican, Cuban, and Mexican cultures, in Chapters 4, 7, 9, 10, and 11 in this volume.

[16] I want to thank Carla Roland for suggesting this consideration. In this essay *Anglican* refers to all the churches that belong to the Anglican communion.

[17] In this essay *Reformed tradition* or *Reformed churches* refers to all those churches that belong to the tradition influenced by the reforms instituted by John Calvin, including churches in the broad evangelical and Pentecostal traditions.

[18] For a more extensive discussion of this issue and the political ramifications of it for Latinos/as in the United States, see Gary Macy, "Demythologizing 'the Church' in the Middle Ages," *Journal of Hispanic/Latino Theology* 3 (1995), 23–41; and idem, "Was There a 'the Church' in the Middle Ages?" in *Unity and Diversity in the Church*, ed. Robert Swanson, Studies in Church History 52 (Blackwell: Oxford, 1996), 107–16.

[19] On the political nature of the creation of tradition in the Latino/a Protestant tradition, see Chapter 10 in this volume.

[20] For a discussion of the complexities of the political nature of tradition, see Chapter 5 in this volume.

[21] "Identification" here means both self-identification and identification by other theologians. On the history of this identification, see, for example, Orlando Espín, "The State of U.S. Latino/a Theology: An Understanding," *Perspectivas* (Fall 2000): 19–55, esp. 19–34.

[22] See Chapter 8 in this volume.

[23] On the influence of church authority in forming tradition, see Chapter 2 in this volume.

[24] For attempts to address the issue of patriarchy and *machismo* in the Latino/a theological tradition, see Elsa Tamez, ed., *Against Machismo* (Oak Park, IL: Meyer-Stone, 1987); María Pilar Aquino, *Our Cry for Life: Feminist Theology from Latin America* (Maryknoll, NY: Orbis Books, 1994); Miguel A. de la Torre, "Beyond Machismo: A Cuban Case Study," *Annual of the Society of Christian Ethics* 19 (1999): 213–33; David Tombs, "Honor, Shame and Conquest: Male Identity, Sexual Violence, and the Body Politic," *Journal of Hispanic/Latino Theology* 9 (2002): 21–40; and Eduardo Mendieta, "Making *Hombres*: *Feo, Fuerte, Formal*: On Latino Masculinities," *Journal of Hispanic/Latino Theology* 9 (2002): 41–51.

[25] On the central role of popular religion in forming tradition, see Chapter 1 in this volume.

[26] Maduro, "Apuntes epistemolólogico-políticos para una historia de la teología en América Latina," 19–38.

[27] A more complete list of theologians can be found in Saranyana.

[28] For a more complete list of theologians in Mexico, see Valverde y Telles.

4

Reading between the Lines

Toward a Latino/a (Re)configuration of Scripture and Tradition

Jean-Pierre Ruiz

MARELA: He doesn't like lectors.

OFELIA: He doesn't understand the purpose of having someone like you read stories to the workers.

JUAN JULIAN: But that has always been the tradition.

CONCHITA: He's from another culture.

MARELA: He thinks that lectors are the ones who cause trouble.

JUAN JULIAN: Why? Because we read novels to the workers, because we educate them and inform them?

MARELA: No. It's more complicated than that. His wife ran away from home with a lector.

—NILO CRUZ, ANNA IN THE TROPICS

INTRODUCTION

Anna in the Tropics, the play by Nilo Cruz that won him the 2003 Pulitzer Prize for drama, is set in a Cuban American cigar factory in Ybor City, Florida, in 1929.[1] In this factory cigars are still hand rolled in the traditional way, and a lector is employed to entertain and educate the workers as they engage in their repetitive routine day after day. When Juan Julian Ríos, "the best lector west of Havana," arrives to take up his post, he gets the cold shoulder from Cheché—Chester—the factory owner's half-Cuban half-brother. Ofelia Alcazar, the owner's wife, has paid for the lector's trip from Cuba, and in this scene she and her daughters Marela and Conchita do their best to make excuses for Cheché. As Juan Julian reads aloud to the workers from Leo Tolstoy's *Anna Karenina* (the Anna of the title of the play), the novel's tragic tale of love and adultery unfolds in the plot of the play, in the lives of the characters who are Juan Julian's attentive *oidores*. Borne across time and space and language from Tolstoy's St. Petersburg to the Ybor City *tabaquería*, the novel's illicit romance between Anna and Vronsky is replicated in Juan Julian's affair with the cigar factory owner's younger daughter, Conchita, whose husband, Palomo, assumes the role of Anna Karenina's wronged husband Alexei Karenin. In the end, Cheché shoots Juan Julian to death, taking vengeance against one lector for the offense of another.

After its October 12, 2002, premier at New Theatre in Coral Gables, Florida, and a production that opened at the Roger S. Berlind Theatre of the McCarter Theater Center in Princeton, New Jersey, on September 18, 2003, *Anna in the Tropics* opened at the Royale Theater on Broadway on November 15, 2003, with Jimmy Smits cast in the role of Juan Julian Ríos and Daphne Rubin-Vega as Conchita. The Broadway production closed on February 22, 2004, after 15 previews and only 113 performances. In an interview with *Theatermania*, Cuban American playwright Nilo Cruz explains his decision to spotlight what interviewer Dan Bacalzo called "a piece of America's past that most people probably don't know about." The first Latino playwright to win a Pulitzer Prize, Cruz told Bacalzo: "I felt it was important to write about this group of people that came here in the late 1800s and built a city. Tampa really flourished with the tobacco industry. And we [Latinos] didn't just make the economy boom in Tampa; we were also bringing traditions and culture to that society."[2] While reviews of the Broadway production of *Anna in the Tropics* were mixed, it received favorable nods from Latinos/as and others who applauded the play's Pulitzer and its high profile (albeit short-lived) Broadway production as examples of the increased visibility of Latinos/as in mainstream venues.[3] At the same time, it could be said that *Anna in the Tropics* catered to the appetite of the theater-going public for stereotypical steamy, spicy Caribbean flavors, while perpetuating caricatured *machista* constructions of gender, as well as dancing altogether too lightly around the historical context in which the play is set.[4] In this regard it is sadly ironic that a Latino playwright may well have contributed—albeit inadvertently—to the continued marginalization of Latinas and Latinos in the United States.

While this cannot be denied, *Anna in the Tropics* effectively opens the door for this Latino postcolonial (re)configuration of scripture and tradition in several ways. First, the play's setting in the Cuban American community in South Florida foregrounds the already complicated dynamics of the neocolonial relationship between Cuba and the United States, a relationship that continues to increase in complexity in the twenty-first century.[5] For the purposes of this essay, the play's setting early in the twentieth century is an occasion for the exercise of a hermeneutics of retrieval with respect to more remote elements of the Spanish colonial legacy, for tracing colonial trajectories about language and text and tradition from the past into the present. Second, the play's focus on the role of the lector in the *tabaquería* offers an effective entrée into consideration of the permeable border between textuality and orality, and between medium and message, and also into reflection on the transmission *(traditio et redditio)* of significant information and on the technologies of transmission (acting, reading, writing, speaking, printing). Negotiating these intersections (in the peculiar embrace of postmodernity's emphasis on life on the hyphen) makes it possible to imagine a reconfiguration of scripture and tradition that is this essay's specific contribution to this project's effort to understand tradition *latinamente* as product and as process.[6] Third, as an artifact of popular culture *Anna in the Tropics* mediates important questions of language, culture, and canon that have direct bearing on the construction of an adequate theology of tradition. While, curiously, *Anna in the Tropics* makes no reference to the rich and complex religious experience of the Cuban diasporic community in Florida, the twofold emphasis of US Latino/a theologies on daily lived experience *(lo cotidiano)* and on popular culture as sources and stimuli for theological reflection calls attention to religious dimensions implicit even in discourses where these are not immediately apparent.[7] Before proceeding further, I should also be clear about my aims: this essay is not intended to be a study *of* the play. Rather, I hope to make use of *Anna in the Tropics* to make a move toward a rethinking of the complex relationship between scripture and tradition, in what the title of this essay suggests will be a Latino reading between the lines, even a reading "on the hyphen" between scripture and tradition.[8]

(POST)COLONIAL READING:
"THAT HAS ALWAYS BEEN THE TRADITION"

In scene one of act two, Cheché and Palomo offer two very different takes on the meaning and value of tradition. Cheché is eager to mechanize the time and labor-intensive process of producing cigars, yet not without giving thought to the fact that the noise of the machines will drown out the voice of the lectors, rendering them superfluous. He offers a strange ode to industrial modernity:

> We are stuck because we are not part of the new century. Because we are still rolling cigars the same way that Indians rolled them hundreds of years ago. I mean, we might as well wear feathers and walk half naked with bones in our noses. There are machines that do tobacco stuffing at the speed of light: bunching machines, stripping machines.[9]

Palomo raises an objection, reverently citing the views of Leonardo, the lector at the Aurora factory:

> He doesn't talk about machines like you do. But I can tell you what he says. He's always talking about maintaining our ways. Our methods. The old process we use. What we brought with us from the island. *(Raises his hands.)* We brought these to roll our cigars, so we don't need an apparatus or whatever you want to call it.[10]

Cheché dismisses Palomo's objection out of hand: "I'm not interested in giving any more money from my pocket, from my wages to listen to a lector read me romantic novels."[11] In turn, the lector Juan Julian responds by linking the present to the past in what amounts to a myth of origins:

> Señor Chester, allow me to say something. My father used to say that the tradition of having readers in the factories goes back to the Taino Indians. He used to say that tobacco leaves whisper the language of the sky. And that's because through the language of cigar smoke the Indians used to communicate to the gods. Obviously I'm not an Indian, but as a lector I am a distant relative of the Cacique, the Chief Indian, who used to translate the sacred words of the deities. The workers are the *oidores*. The ones who listen quietly, the same way Taino Indians used to listen. And this is the tradition you're trying to destroy with your machine.[12]

More than just an effort to rehabilitate the image of the Tainos that is tarnished by Cheché's tirade, Juan Julian's intervention challenges Cheché's view that the vocation of the lector is peripheral, even superfluous. This myth of origins argues that reading matters more than manufacturing, that telling is more valuable than making.[13] Juan Julian invokes precolonial indigenous religious practices, binding the "tradition of having readers in the factories" to the ritual use of tobacco among the

Tainos. As a lector, he claims kinship with "the Cacique, the Chief Indian, who used to translate the sacred words of the deities," an anti-
modern appeal to a remote but authoritative past. By invoking this myth
of origins, the lector sacralizes his vocation and claims a hierarchical
authority over his audience: "The workers are the *oidores*. The ones
who listen quietly, the same way Taino Indians used to listen." According to Juan Julian, the lector is the latter-day mediator of meaning on
behalf of his *oidores*, heir to Taino tradition as he has constructed it.

Juan Julian's appeal to this myth of origins notwithstanding, Darien
Cavanaugh explains that, in fact,

> the story of the lectors began in Cuban jails in the early nineteenth
> century, where they read to inmates. By the mid nineteenth century,
> Cuban cigar factories began adopting the practice. Workers, who
> democratically selected readings, further adapted the role of the
> lector, including materials from the proletariat press and fiction
> with social themes. From Cuba, the lectors spread through cigar
> cities in America, bringing their tradition of political intellectual-
> ism and proletariat propaganda dissipation with them.[14]

Here the truth fascinates more than fiction, for what began among
deliberately marginalized Cubans—the incarcerated—became a practice
that sparked labor activism and political organizing among Florida cigar-factory workers. As Cavanaugh notes, "As a result of the lectors'
readings, a predominantly illiterate workforce became familiar with the
writings of the great novelists and theorists of the time, as well as working conditions in other parts of the world. . . . This informal working-
class education and the lectors' direct involvement with labor activity
cut to the heart of the factory owners' distaste for the readers."[15] In the
end, technology won the day and the lectors disappeared. In a playwright's
note that accompanies his spare stage directions, Nilo Cruz explains:
"After 1931, the lectors were removed from the factories, and what remained of the cigar rollers consisted of low-paid American workers who
operated machines. The end of a tradition."[16]

The relationship between lectors and *oidores* was by no means the
sort of straightforward asymmetrical hierarchy suggested in Juan Julian's
myth of origins. Nancy A. Hewitt paints a much different picture:

> Since most immigrant workers in the United States left school at an
> early age to earn a wage, the reader offered tobacco workers some-
> thing quite rare in American industry, a cosmopolitan education
> on the factory floor. Workers, in turn, provided the reader with

something equally rare—the freedom to present radical ideas to a captive but willing audience—for *el lector* was beholden not to the employer but to the employees. Cigar workers donated a specified amount each week to sustain the position and selected, by a majority vote, the individual to fill it. As a result, cigar workers in South Florida heard the latest news on labor strife and anticolonial rebellion around the world, and listened to literary classics, such as *Les Miserables*, or utopian fantasies, such as *Don Quixote*, that nurtured class consciousness.[17]

The readers were, in fact, employees of the cigar-factory workers, a curious partial inversion of the way in which modernity attributes higher status to those who work with ideas and lesser status to those who work with their hands. If knowledge is power, then the *oidores* did not listen only for respite from the repetitive tedium of the *tabaquerías* through escape into the imaginary realm of fiction. By hiring the lectors with a share of their own wages, the cigar-factory workers distanced themselves from the mere materiality of their work: they used the earnings from their making to invest in knowing. As they listened to the lectors, they were empowered by what they learned, emboldened to become participants and not mere spectators.

That the truth can be more fascinating than fiction is likewise confirmed in the story of Luisa Capetillo (1879–1922), a Puerto Rican who was among the few women chosen as a cigar-factory reader. Capetillo worked as a lector in Puerto Rico, in New York, and in Florida. In her case, "the reader would have been dressed in the standard fashion— white shirt, tie, dark pants, and, so early in the day, the jacket still on and a panama hat tossed to the side. Only when Capetillo began to read would the listener realize, with a start, that *el lector* was *la lectora*, a woman in men's clothing chosen by a mixed-sex work force to fill a traditionally masculine role."[18] This cross-dressing Puerto Rican lector was, in Hewitt's words, "in the vanguard of labor organizing, anticolonial agitation, and the crusade for sexual emancipation. She was an anarcho-syndicalist and working-class agitator, a suffragist and a 'New Woman.' She chose, moreover, to wear men's clothes, not only on the reader's platform but in her everyday life as well. She did so not to emulate men's power but to declare her independence as a woman."[19]

The cigar-factory readers straddled the border between textuality and orality, between reading and writing. For many readers, including Luisa Capetillo, their role as performers of texts written by others prompted them to produce texts of their own. For example, Victoriano Manteiga, who arrived in Tampa from Cuba in 1913 and who worked as a lector in

West Tampa's Morgan Cigar Factory, co-founded *La Gaceta* (with Dr. José Avellanal) in 1922. Still published more than eighty years later, *La Gaceta* boasts that it is "the nation's only trilingual newspaper," its founders producing a newspaper in English, Spanish, and Italian to serve the ethnically diverse immigrant community in and around Tampa.[20]

Luisa Capetillo herself published in a variety of genres, including essays and short plays. As a reader and as an author, she insisted, "La instrucción es la base de la felicidad de los pueblos" [education is the foundation of the happiness of the peoples].[21] In 1910 she also became editor of the magazine *La Mujer*, funded from the royalties of her own books, among them *Ensayos libertarios* (1907) and *La humanidad en el futuro* (1910).[22] Lara A. Walker suggests that Capetillo's short plays are of particular interest, writing that they "were performed to inspire audiences already politicized in union ideology and social oppression."[23] As Norma Valle observes, "no podemos dudar que [estas obras] probablemente fueron presentadas durante veladas dramáticas, auspiciadas por la Federación Libre de los Trabajadores o por la Federación de Torcedores de Tabaco, durante huelgas o actividades de sindicato" [We can't doubt that these works were probably presented during evenings devoted to dramatic theater, sponsored by the Free Federation of Workers or by the Federation of Cigar Rollers, during strikes or union activities].[24] Faithful to the conventions of the stage, Capetillo's short dramas employs them with a twist, in order to communicate a message that advances her intersecting egalitarian, feminist, anarchist, and trade-unionist agendas.[25] For example, Lisa Sánchez González points out: "Unlike the hapless Anna Karenina in Tolstoy, as well as many other adulterous tragic heroines in 19th and 20th century literature, Capetillo's adulteresses live happily ever after."[26] If indeed truth can be more fascinating than fiction, how much more compelling might Nilo Cruz's play have been if its protagonist had been the real but unconventional Luisa Capetillo rather than the fictitious but altogether conventional Juan Julian Ríos? Would such a play have won a Pulitzer Prize? Would such a play have made it to Broadway, and, if so, might it have enjoyed a longer run than *Anna in the Tropics* did? One can only speculate.

This brief consideration of the role of lectors in the cigar factories poses a significant challenge to the commonplace assumptions that tradition is always and necessarily conservative, that "traditional" institutions and practices always and necessarily function to maintain the status quo, and that tradition is the enforcer of fixed hegemonic hierarchies of race, class, and gender. Far from endorsing business as usual, the *lectores* (and *lectoras*) often were progressive activists who sowed the seeds of restlessness among the cigar-factory workers. While the production methods in these factories may have been traditional in the conventional sense, and while those methods traveled to Florida from Cuba and Puerto Rico along with the tradition of the readers, the practices of the readers themselves were anything but conventional, as was the democratic process by which they were selected and retained by the factory workers. This shows that tradition—as process, as project, and as product—can function as a dynamic vehicle of social change.[27] Even so, when we consider the ways in which the lectors negotiated the border between textuality and orality, we hear echoes of ancient traditions, and it is to these echoes that I now direct our attention.

(CON)TEXT AND TRADITION:
"HE'S FROM ANOTHER CULTURE"

Despite the anticlericalism of a number of the Cuban immigrants to South Florida (a sentiment that was certainly nourished by the socialist texts that the cigar-factory workers heard from the readers), when one studies photographs of Ybor City *tabaquerías* taken in the early decades of the twentieth century, with rows of workers at their benches and the well-dressed reader perched on a raised *tribuna* or platform in the middle of the room, one cannot help but notice that the factory scene bears more than a passing resemblance to a church and that the reader's formal attire amounts to ritual vesture that sets the lector apart from the factory workers.[28] There the *oidores* sit, listening more or less attentively to an activist "gospel" proclaimed from a secular pulpit, a scene that transposes the ancient Christian liturgical practice of the oral proclamation of scripture, and the monastic practice of reading during meals into a distinctly modern key.[29]

This transposition clears the way for us to attend to the relationship between (biblical) text and tradition in specifically Christian and explicitly theological terms. For this essay, to do so *latinamente* calls for attention to Iberian Christianity and its encounter with the aboriginal populations of the lands Spain colonized in the Western hemisphere as an encounter among different literacies. To do so from the standpoint of postcolonial criticism makes it necessary for us to recognize that these literacies were different *and unequal*, with the literacy of the colonized disparaged by their Christian colonizers.[30] While the Tainos with whom Nilo Cruz's lector Juan Julian Ríos claims kinship have left us no texts, several of the aboriginal peoples encountered by the *conquistadores* and the missionaries who accompanied them *did* transmit and record knowledge in ways that the recently arrived colonizers could not help but recognize as texts.[31]

Sixteenth-century European Christians—Iberian ones among them—had recently begun to reflect on the transmission and preservation of *revealed* knowledge as they wrestled with the thorny question of relationship between text and tradition that the Reformation principle *sola scriptura* had precipitated. As John Thiel explains:

The status of "tradition" as a dimension of divine revelation identifiable in its own right and distinguishable from "scripture" is a more recent development in Catholic belief, dating from the later Middle Ages. Its arrival occurred at the contentious threshold of Reformation polemics, where its affirmation or denial was taken to be the mark of true or false faith. Since the sixteenth century—when the Council of Trent's 1546 *Decretum de libris sacris et de traditionibus recipiendis* raised a distinguishable "tradition" to the authority of a conciliar teaching—theologians (and to a certain extent the magisterium too) have struggled with the problem of defining tradition's relationship to scripture and thus the authority scripture and tradition hold as media of God's inspired Word.[32]

Martin Luther's assertion of the principle of *sola scriptura* did not imply an a priori rejection of tradition per se.[33] As a principle of reform, it specifically targeted what Luther regarded as the problem of authority. According to Maurice Bévenot:

The application of the Word of God to the life of the Church had been in the hands of the officials of the Church: henceforth all office in the Church must be judged by the Word of God. This was a . . . dogmatic reason for the rejection of Tradition; for once all authoritative interpretation of the Word of God was denied to the Church's official ministers, the 'Word' was reduced to a self-explanatory Scripture which could not tolerate alongside itself any such independent factor as "Tradition." It meant the canonization of "sola Scriptura."[34]

In this respect the nagging concern that presented itself before the participants at the Council of Trent was the question of how to configure the relationship of tradition to scripture. If tradition could not be considered independent of the Bible, then how might their relationship be understood, and how might both be recognized as valid and normative media for the transmission of divine revelation? The March 22, 1546, draft of the *Decree on the Acceptance of the Holy Scriptures and the Apostolic Traditions* suggested that revelation is contained partly in the Sacred Scriptures, and partly in the unwritten traditions which the apostles received from Christ's own lips or which, under the inspiration of the Holy Spirit, were by them, as it were, passed down to us from hand to hand. Following the example of the Fathers, the Council receives with utmost reverence as holy and authentic all the books of the Old and New Testaments, since the one God is the author of both, as well as the traditions which proceeded either from Christ's own mouth or from the Holy Spirit and have been preserved in the Catholic Church by an unbroken succession of the ministry, and to which is due the same loving adhesion.[35]

During the debate of this draft, Agostino Bonuccio, the superior general of the Servites, voiced serious objections, arguing that "the stream of New Testament revelation does not divide into Scripture and Tradition. . . . Scripture is complete as to its content and contains all truths necessary for salvation. . . . 'Tradition' is essentially an authoritative interpretation of Holy Writ, not its complement."[36] Jedin notes that Bonuccio's argument did not win the day. Despite some uneasiness about the draft's formulation that revelation was contained *partly* in scripture and *partly* in tradition, there was agreement "that dogmatic tradition was a channel of revelation which supplemented the Scriptures."[37] Yet the debate continued over whether scripture and tradition ought to receive "the same loving adhesion." The Dominican Giacomo Nacchianti, Bishop of Chianti, exclaimed: "To put Scripture and Tradition on the same level . . . is ungodly," to which the Bishop of Badajoz, Francisco de Navarra, objected, regarding Nacchianti's remark as an insult to the majority of the council, "Are we ungodly people?" Yet Nacchianti did not back off, instead pursuing his point still more aggressively, "Yes, I repeat it! How can I accept the practice of praying eastward with the same reverence as St. John's gospel?"[38]

As promulgated on April 8, 1546, the Council's *Decree concerning the Canonical Scriptures* concluded that revelation is contained "in the written books and in the unwritten traditions," a shift from the earlier draft's formulation that revelation was contained *partly* in scripture and *partly* in tradition. While the decree went on to enumerate the books of the biblical canon, it did *not* elaborate an analogous canon of the specific contents of authoritative tradition, leaving that question open in what amounted to a somewhat uneven response to *sola scriptura*.[39] The Second Vatican Council's *Dogmatic Constitution on Divine Revelation (Dei Verbum)* actually maintains a similar reticence about the scope and content of tradition even as it underscores the unity of scripture and tradition more clearly than the Tridentine "two source" formulation:

> There exists a close connection and communication between sacred tradition and Sacred Scripture. For both of them, flowing from the same divine wellspring, in a certain way merge into a unity and tend toward the same end. For Sacred Scripture is the word of God inasmuch as it is consigned to writing under the inspiration of the divine Spirit, while sacred tradition takes the word of God entrusted by Christ the Lord and the Holy Spirit to the Apostles, and hands it on to their successors in its full purity, so that led by the light of the Spirit of truth, they may in proclaiming it preserve this word of God faithfully, explain it, and make it more widely known. Consequently it is not from Sacred Scripture alone that the Church draws her certainty about everything which has been revealed. Therefore both sacred tradition and Sacred Scripture are to be accepted and venerated with the same sense of loyalty and reverence. Sacred tradition and Sacred Scripture form one sacred deposit of the word of God, committed to the Church. (*DV*, nos. 9–10).[40]

For our purposes, it is important to note that the Tridentine debate over scripture and tradition and the Reformation principle *sola scriptura* that precipitated that debate were consequences of the prominent place that printed books—the Bible among them—had acquired in the decades since Gutenberg's mechanization of printing in 1453 (just less than a century earlier than the Council of Trent). The diffusion of printed books had already begun to dramatically alter the flow of information and the dynamics of knowledge creation and knowledge diffusion.[41] The ever-increasing availability of books led Luther and Trent to very different positions on the question of authority over access to religious information and over its transmission. In 1534, Luther himself produced a translation of the Bible into German—a project that was as momentous for the development of the German language as the publication of the so-called King James Version was for the development of the English language.[42] He did so in order to put the text in the hands of ordinary literate German laypeople, to provide them with access to the word of God—the normative foundational Christian deposit of faith—in German words.

At the Council of Trent there were significant disagreements over the propriety and the liceity of translating the Bible into vernacular languages. One Spaniard at the council, the Franciscan Alfonso de Castro, theologian to Cardinal Pedro Pacheco, the Bishop of Jaén, had written a book in which he warned that the vernacular Bible is "the mother and origin of heresies."[43] When Piero Bertano, the Bishop of Fano, argued that translations of the Bible ought to be tolerated—including those produced by the Protestant Reformers—he met with the strenuous objections of Pacheco and de Castro. To these he replied, "If we forbid such translation . . . do we not act like the pharisees who hold the key to sacred knowledge, but will not allow anyone else to enter? Can we snatch the word of God from the hands of the people who read it? Neither youth nor age, man or woman, noble or lowly, may be precluded from reading the Bible."[44] For Pacheco and de Castro, the advancing technologies of book production posed a threat to the hierarchy's interest in suppressing heresy, and that compelling interest called for strict control over the diffusion of the biblical text. Pacheco went so far as to insist that "all translations other than the Vulgate, even the Septuagint, must be forbidden."[45] For Bertano, on the other hand, the benefits of the broad diffusion of the Bible through the publication of vernacular translations far outweighed any possible risks. In the end the Council of Trent made no pronouncement either explicitly encouraging or expressly prohibiting the translation of the Bible from the original languages into vernacular languages. Sidestepping this issue, the council chose instead to endorse the Vulgate in its *Decree concerning the Edition and Use of the Sacred Books*:

> The same holy council considering that not a little advantage will accrue to the Church of God if it be made known which of all the Latin editions of the sacred books now in circulation is to be regarded as authentic, ordains and declares that the old Latin Vulgate Edition, which, in use for so many hundred years, has been approved by the Church, be in public lectures, disputations, sermons and expositions held as authentic, and that no one dare or presume under any pretext whatsoever to reject it.

Three factors—the Tridentine reluctance to describe the specific contents of tradition, the opposition by some to vernacular translations of the Bible, and the endorsement of the Vulgate (in an era when Latin was no longer commonly used outside ecclesiastical and academic circles)— converged to suggest that tradition-as-content ultimately mattered less at Trent than the question of control over who could be considered authorized tradents. The Reformation's invocation of *sola scriptura* and the increasing availability of books (especially of vernacular translations of the Bible) were seen as significant threats to ecclesiastical control over the diffusion of information. While struggling to articulate the parity of tradition alongside scripture as a medium of revelation, Trent indirectly endorsed the biblical text-as-technological-product (especially the Vulgate) as a vehicle of tradition and underscored the function of translation in the transmission of tradition-as-content *(tradita)*.[46]

There is a curious irony in the fact that during the Tridentine debate the most vocal opposition to the translation of the Bible into the vernacular came from a Spanish prelate and his Franciscan theologian. Was not Spain the birthplace of the *Biblia de Alba* (1430)? This manuscript was a glossed translation of the Old Testament into Castilian, commissioned by Luis de Guzmán, grand master of the Order of Calatrava, and produced by Rabbi Mose Arragel.[47] More proximately, was not Spain the birthplace of the Complutensian Polyglot Bible (1522)? That massive work of philological erudition was sponsored by the Archbishop of Toledo, Cardinal Francisco Ximénez de Cisneros, who was also responsible for appointing Bartolomé de las Casas "Procurator and Universal Protector of All Indians in the Indies."[48] Deeply committed to furthering a humanist agenda, the Franciscan Cisneros very deliberately designed the six-volume Complutensian Polyglot as an instrument of church reform, explaining to Pope Leo X in the dedicatory prologue that his intention was "that the hitherto dormant study of Holy Scripture may now at last begin to revive."[49] While the Complutensian Polyglot did not include a translation into Castilian, it presented the text of the Bible in its original languages, based on the best manuscripts then available.[50] The first complete translation of the Bible into Spanish did not actually appear until 1569, when Casiodoro de Reina published the so-called Biblia del Oso in Geneva, the city in which he took refuge. Described by Pym as "certainly a man of protestant ideas influenced by Erasmus and the Complutense project," Reina's escape from Seville did not keep the Inquisition from burning him in effigy! While the translator never returned to his homeland, his work did; once Reina's version of the Bible was printed, twenty-six hundred copies were sent to Flanders, to be shipped to Spain from there.[51]

There is still further irony in the Spanish opposition to vernacular translations of the Bible in the debates of the Council of Trent, inasmuch as this was the era in which Spanish was being imposed as the language of empire in Spain's American colonies, just as it had been used as the instrument through which the *Reconquista* was solidified in the Iberian peninsula. To justify his *Gramática castellana*—the first complete Spanish grammar—Antonio de Nebrija explained to Queen Isabella that language has always accompanied empire ("siempre la lengua fue compañero del imperio").[52] He went on in greater detail about the function of language as a medium of colonial control:

When Your Highness has subdued many barbarous peoples and nations that have strange tongues, and when those peoples need to receive not only the laws that the victor applies to the vanquished but also, with those laws, our language, then they may use this my art to gain knowledge of the language, just as we now must learn the art of Latin grammar in order to learn Latin.[53]

As Anthony Pym comments, we have here "a reasoned language policy for European colonialism, although Nebrija was more probably thinking of nothing beyond the conquest of Granada and a few military adventures in northern Africa."[54] The language of the conquerors colonized the ears and the tongues, the pens, and the books of the conquered. As for the role of Cardinal Ximénez de Cisneros in all this, Pym tells us that he

instructed Hieronymites in the Caribbean to teach Castilian to the sons of Amerindian leaders, helping to instigate the policy that could have produced an intercultural control caste. The polyglot project at home might thus have corresponded in part to the polyglot preaching in the Americas, in both cases setting up intercultural groups in such a way that reigning discourses could ideally stand unchallenged. In both cases risks would be run, although the Vulgate would remain the authoritative bible and Castilian would persist as the language of empire.[55]

In the territory of the Iberian peninsula as in the nascent overseas possessions of the *reyes Católicos*, the medium (the Castilian language) was the message, and that message was the grammar of empire that displaced competing languages and competing traditions. As a grammar of exclusion, the imposition of the crown's language as an integral part of the overall strategy of the *Reconquista*, paralleled the Catholic monarchs' displacement of Jews with their own language(s), traditions, and sacred texts, and of the Muslims, with their own language, traditions, and sacred text. In the preface to his 1492 *Gramática de la lengua castellana*, Nebrija wrote:

Now that the Church has been purified, and we are thus reconciled to God, now that the enemies of the Faith have been subdued by our arms, now that just laws are being enforced, enabling us all to live as equals, what else remains but the flowering of the peaceful arts. And among the arts, foremost are those of language, which is the unique distinction of man, the means for the kind of understanding which can be surpassed only by contemplation.[56]

What else remained? Spain's westward colonial expansion led to un-expected and transformative encounters with other traditions and different literacies. Anthony Grafton emphasizes the enormity of the challenges these encounters posed:

> After the Portuguese began to explore Africa, Western explorers and writers had to deal with lands and societies, customs and religions, men and women whose very existence they had not expected. After 1492 the problems became critical. The encounter between Europe and the Americas juxtaposed a vast number of inconvenient facts with the elegant theories embodied in previously authoritative books. The discoveries gradually stripped the books of their aura of completeness as repositories of information and their appearance of utility as tools for interpretation.[57]

For the missionaries who traveled westward, the New World posed new and vexing challenges to the transmission of the substance of Christianity, and they struggled mightily to incorporate their new experiences into a religious world view that had been shaped principally by the Bible.[58]

LANGUAGES, TEXTS, AND THE COLONIZATION OF TRADITION

Orlando Espín has argued convincingly that, in large measure, the Christianity that arrived in the Americas aboard the Spaniards' ships was still substantially medieval in character:

> The Spaniards of the late fifteenth and early sixteenth centuries were still medieval in their approach to religion. Theirs was a Christianity that communicated the gospel by means of graphic symbols (verbal or otherwise). . . . The united Spain of the sixteenth century, though continuing the tradition of high scholarship did not go beyond the best medieval models of education. The Christian catechesis available to the rural majority tended to emphasize religious storytelling (often Bible stories or the lives of the saints) and religious dramas *(autos da fe)*. . . . The Catholicism that came to the Americas was one used to catechizing through symbols, stories and dramas.[59]

The point is well taken, for it is clear that the catechetical tools and methods that the earliest generations of missionaries employed in communicating the Christian faith in the Americas were the time-tested techniques used to catechize the illiterate majority of the European Christian population.[60] The Franciscan Pedro de Gante, who was actually Flemish, the first missionary to reach Mexico after the capture of Tenochtitlán, wrote to Philip II that Mexicans were "people without writing, without letters, without written characters, and without any kind of enlightenment."[61] Arriving without any knowledge of Nahuatl and without any interpreters, the Franciscans began their work by communicating the gospel in sign language, in the words of Gerónimo de Mendieta, "por señas, como mudos" (with signs, like mutes).[62] They quickly set about the work not only of learning the indigenous languages themselves, but also of compiling grammars of these languages so that other Europeans could learn them and to prepare the way for the production of Nahuatl and bilingual catechisms and other materials for religious instruction.[63] The struggles and difficulties of some of the missionaries with learning the indigenous languages were such that in 1607, for example, the Dominican Friar Gregorio García suggested in his book *Orígen de los indios del Nuevo Mundo* "that the devil had incited the original inhabitants of the New World to invent their diabolically difficult languages as a way to hide and distort the true word of God."[64]

In that respect, to borrow a phrase from Mignolo, the missionary grammarians brought Nebrija to the New World, for they used Nebrija's Latin grammar as the template for their grammars of Amerindian languages. The composition of the grammars dealt with difference by recontextualizing it, by organizing it according to European patterns. In that respect the Franciscan contribution to the colonial enterprise represented a step beyond the medieval intellectual practices, in what amounted to at least a limited embrace of the currents of humanism that were making significant headway throughout Europe, even in Counter-reformation Spain.[65] Indeed, as Walden Browne has suggested, the Franciscan encounter with the indigenous populations of the new Spanish colonies precipitated the demise of the medieval conceptualization of knowledge.[66]

In the Spanish encounter with the different literacy and the different textuality of the peoples they encountered, we note an acute concern for the permanence and continuity that texts bring to the transmission of tradition. As Elizabeth Hill Boone explains: "The Aztecs and Mixtecs never doubted that their books contained writing. Manuscript painting was simply their way of writing in books and on paper. . . . It was the activity that fulfilled the written needs of the ancient Mexicans. It recorded the past, it preserved the prognosticatory guides that suggested the future, and it documented the many features of the present."[67] Yet, because these documents used pictographical rather than alphabetical conventions, Europeans regarded them with a measure of puzzlement. Motolinía, says Boone, "recognized that the Aztecs had books, but he could not quite accord them writing because to him, as to most of his contemporaries, writing was alphabetic script that recorded speech."[68] Linking alphabetical script to accuracy in the transmission of information across time, the Jesuit José de Acosta (1540–1600) wondered, "since the Indians did not have writing, how could they preserve such a quantity and variety of matters for so long a time?"[69] Yet Acosta *did* eventually come to admit that

> among the nations of New Spain there is great knowledge and memory of their ancient customs. And when I desired to learn how the Indians could preserve their histories in so much detail I realized that, although they did not possess the care and refinement of the Chinese and Japanese, still they did not lack some kind of letters and books, in which they preserved after their fashion the deeds of their ancestors.[70]

The intercultural encounter between the missionaries and the different literacy they encountered led the Spaniards to "set about transcribing Aztec oral and pictorial traditions into a written, alphabetic form," and so "as the friars transcribed the Indians' reconstructed and selective memories" these were transformed such that "knowledge that had once been oral, pictorial and memory based became immutably fixed and literal."[71] Living tradition, so to speak, became fixed scripture. Nebrija's axiom, "to write as we pronounce and to pronounce as we write," was the key to understanding a European model of literacy that was based on alphabetic scripts.[72] On the other hand, for readers of pictographic scripts, interaction with a text was not a matter of the mechanical recitation of alphabetically encoded sounds. "The members of a culture without letters tell or narrate what they see written on a solid surface, although they do not necessarily read in the sense we attribute to this word today."[73] Motolinía complained: "The memory of man being weak and feeble, the elders in the land disagreed in expounding the antiquities and the noteworthy things of this land, although some things pertaining to ancient times and the fixing of the succession of the lords who took possession of and ruled over this great land have been gathered and explained by their figures."[74] For Motolinía, variations among the performances by tradents who used pictographic documents "that evoke memorized recitations presented interpretational difficulties that could be attributed to fading and failing memory."[75] Motolinía's European attitude toward texts and toward the practices of reading as a matter of accurate reproduction in speech of alphabetically encoded words ("we pronounce as we write") kept him from recognizing a different relationship between indigenous Mexican texts and their performers. Curiously enough, this reveals something of a bias toward texts *(scriptura)* as a fixed and authoritative medium for the accurate transmission *(traditio* as process) of information. This bias prevented him from recognizing that indigenous practices of encoding information in texts supported performative practices that were dynamic and fresh.

The historic dialogue in 1524 between the first twelve Franciscan missionaries in Mexico and the Mexican nobles and sages, documented by Bernardino de Sahagún in the diglot (Nahuatl and Spanish) *Coloquios y doctrina cristiana,* sheds light on the religious dimension of the encounter between European and Mexican literacies.[76] Mignolo calls attention to the point in the dialogues at which "the question of reading, writing, books, and knowledge come to the foreground."[77] The Franciscans explain their evangelizing mission:

> He, the holy father on the earth,
> The great speaker of divine things,
> Who sent us hither
> (us twelve side by side)
> who commanded us *by the divine word*
> to make known to you
> this One, the Only One God, the Very True God
> Speaker, He by Whom All Live,
> Possessor of the Near, Possessor of the Surrounding,
> Possessor of Heaven, Possessor of Earth,
> He Who created them, He Who made them,
> the heaven, the earth,
> and the region of the dead.[78]

The Franciscans clearly frame their mission in terms of language. They are charged by the pope to employ the divine word to bring their audiences to knowledge of the Christian God. Their mission is about words—God's word—and they go on to assure their listeners that the message they bring is to be found in the divine book, the Bible: "Todo lo que habéis escuchado está pintado en el libro divino"[79] ("everything you have heard is painted in the divine book").[80] The Franciscans' Mexican interlocutors reply in their turn, attending in their own way to the place of texts and of reading in the transmission of religious information:

And these, oh our lords,
indeed they are there, they still guide us,
these who carry us, these who govern us,
in relation to these being served,
indeed, these who are our gods, these who have their
    merit,
that of the tail, that of the wing,
the ones who offer things, the ones who offer incense,
and those named the feathered serpents.
These are the knowers of the word,
and their charge with which they trouble themselves,
by night, by day,
is the act of burning *copal,*
the act of offering incense,
thorns, *acxoyatl*
the act of bloodletting.
These see, these trouble themselves,
with the journey, the orderly course of the heavens,
according to how the night is divided.
And these continually look at it,
these continually relate it,
these continually cause the book to cackle.
The black, the color
is in the paintings they continually carry.
Indeed, they are the ones who continually carry us,
they guide us, they cause the path to speak to us.
They are the ones who put it in order,
such as how a year falls,
such as how the count of the destinies-feasts follows its
    path,
and each one of the complete counts.
They trouble themselves with it,
they have their charge, their commission,
their duty which *is the divine word.*[81]

Mignolo asks, "What does it mean to be 'in charge' of the paintings, to read the red and black ink? Does it mean that they are in charge of interpreting them or writing them?" He concludes: "Those who have the wisdom of the word are those who can 'look' at the sky or at the painted books and interpret them to tell stories based on their discerning of the signs. The oral narrative of the wise men seems to have a social function as well as a rank superior to the *tlacuilo,*" that is, the scribes.[82]

For the Franciscans, what mattered most was the faithful reproduction and transmission of the word of God available in the Bible, whereas for their Mexican interlocutors the oral transmission of information had a higher priority and texts were employed to provide mnemonic cues for oral performance. Reformation and Counter-reformation debates over scripture and tradition notwithstanding, the missionaries brought European Christian notions of text and tradition with them, notions that would be challenged and transformed by encounters like these with indigenous traditions and texts, notions that would shape the ways in which Christianity took shape in the Americas.

CONCLUSION:
"LECTORS ARE THE ONES WHO CAUSE TROUBLE"

In her exceptionally lucid introduction to postcolonial theory, Leela Gandhi notes: "Despite its interdisciplinary concerns, the field of postcolonial studies is marked by a preponderant focus upon 'postcolonial literature.'"[83] She goes on to explain:

> Following the impact in the mid-1980s of "cultural materialism" upon literary theory, critical practice has been urged to concede the material underpinnings of all culture. Texts, as is now commonly agreed, are implicated in their economic and political contexts. Few critics would dispute the understanding that all literature is symptomatic of and responsive to, historical conditions of repression and recuperation. While postcolonial literary theory invokes these cultural materialist assumptions in its account of textual production under colonial and postcolonial conditions, it goes a step further in its claim that textuality is endemic to the colonial encounter. Texts, more than any other social and political product, it is argued, are the most significant instigators and purveyors of colonial power and its double, postcolonial resistance.[84]

By placing texts at the center of attention, postcolonial literary criticism at least implicitly privileges "the role and function of the postcolonial literary critic—whose academic expertise suddenly provides the key to all oppositional and anti-colonial meanings."[85] Gandhi sounds a salutary note of caution by calling into question the presuppositions of a narrowly cultural materialist approach to texts and by exposing the self-interest latent in the affirmations of postcolonial theorists and literary critics about the priority of texts. Framing the critical agenda more modestly, R. S. Sugirtharajah turns to Gloria Anzaldúa to clarify the particular role of postcolonial analysis and to identify the questions it raises: "Who has the voice? Who says these are rules? Who makes the law? And if you're not part of making the rules and the laws and the theories, what part do you play?"[86] Focusing more specifically on postcolonial *biblical* criticism, Sugirtharajah identifies the following as key questions: "Who has the power to interpret or tell stories? To whom do the stories/texts belong? Who controls their meaning? Who decides what texts we choose? Against whom are these stories or interpretations aimed? What is their ethical effect? Who has power to access data?"[87]

These are among the key questions that have animated this essay and its take on the relationship between texts and tradition as process and as product. Our consideration of readers in early twentieth-century cigar factories, of the controversy over vernacular translations at the Council of Trent, and of the consternation of the missionaries over the different literacy of the indigenous peoples of the American colonies established by the nascent Spanish empire leads us to recognize the importance of the questions that Sugirtharajah identifies as the agenda of postcolonial inquiry. However peripheral the lectors may have been in the production process, cigar-factory owners knew that the lectors were "the ones who cause trouble" by offering workers alternate texts that threatened the very *oikonomia* of production. For their part, the fathers of the Council of Trent recognized full well the importance of control over access to and interpretation of authoritative texts, and this concern is clearly evident in their ambivalence vis-à-vis the specific contents of tradition and in their opposition to the widespread diffusion of the text of the Bible in vernacular languages. Who has voice? The *Coloquios y doctrina cristiana* documents the challenges faced by the first Franciscan missionaries as they came to terms with the different voices, the different texts, and the different traditions of the indigenous "keepers of the word."

Poised on the permeable boundary between medium and message, reading can be risky business because it does not merely transmit received *tradita* intact, bringing the contents of the past unchanged into the present. As performance—whether public or private—reading actively participates in the process of shaping tradition, re-presenting it in the vernacular of the here and now of reader and audience (even if the reader is his or her own audience). This is no less true when the texts that are being read are invested with special and normative authority as scripture, for, as Wilfred Cantwell Smith has aptly observed: "People— a given community—make a text into scripture, or keep it scripture by treating it in a certain way. . . . Scripture is a human activity. . . . The quality of being scripture is not an attribute of texts. It is a characteristic of the attitude of persons—or groups of persons—to what outsiders perceive as texts. It denotes a relationship between a people and a text."[88]

Reading between the lines and across the centuries we have seen that, as often as not, texts have functioned as catalysts of social change and not only as repositories for the reliable storage and convenient dissemination of information. That this is the case for religious texts is plainly evident from the Tridentine response to the protestant principle *sola scriptura*, that is, the council's invocation of tradition as a source of revelation that could be controlled by ecclesiastical authorities *precisely because* the council did not (or could not?) detail its contents. In the reconfiguration of scripture and tradition that I have begun to sketch in these pages, I have sought to call attention to the tension between the dynamic and the conservative qualities and effects of each, qualities and effects that are best understood when scripture and tradition are appropriately situated in their sociopolitical contexts. At the same time I have underscored the tradition-bearing quality of texts, recognizing that the border between scripture and tradition is permeable in both directions: the encoding of tradition in texts (as *tradita*), and the performance and reformulation of tradition in the reading and translation of texts (as *traditio et redditio*).

Here the unsettling questions posed by postcolonial criticism are an abiding call of conscience to those who would formulate an adequate theology of tradition: Who decides what traditions we choose? Against whom are these stories or interpretations aimed? What is their ethical effect? Who has power to access data? Likewise, who decides what traditions we ignore or suppress, what we inscribe and what we delete? What are the ethical effects of such exclusion? Who are the authorized tradents and what tradents and alternative traditions are effectively disempowered?

Nilo Cruz's Cheché had it right: "Lectors are the ones who cause trouble." For people like Cardinal Pacheco at the Council of Trent, allowing just anyone to read the Bible was regarded as risky business. For the first missionaries in Spain's new colonies, the tradition-bearing texts of the peoples they encountered proved troublesome inasmuch as they prompted the Franciscans to rethink what reading and writing might mean for the non-Europeans to whom they sought to bring the word of the Christians' God. For the indigenous peoples of the Americas, the arrival of the Europeans and their texts spelled trouble for them and even for their books, so many of which were seized and burned in the effort to obliterate the different traditions that these texts mediated. In the fiction of *Anna in the Tropics*, reading proved to be the undoing of Juan Julian Ríos, the lector who brought Anna Karenina to Santiago's Ybor City *tabaquería*, his oral performance translating Tolstoy's novel so effectively that its fiction became fact in that factory. That reading was, in fact, risky business was recognized by the cigar factory owners whose workers were educated and empowered by the words of readers like Luisa Capetillo, readers-become-writers who tapped into the transformative power of drama to organize emancipatory action. Such reading, as *traditio* and *redditio*, as the retrieval of unsettling histories to which we are heirs and as the articulation of meanings we author, is well worth the risk.

Notes

[1] Nilo Cruz, *Anna in the Tropics* (New York: Theater Communications Group, 2003), 53.

[2] Dan Bacalzo, "Tropical Cruz," *Theatermania*, October 10, 2003 (available online). See also Robert P. Ingalls and Louis A. Pérez, Jr., *Tampa Cigar Workers: A Pictorial History* (Gainesville, FL: Univ. Press of Florida, 2003).

[3] Among the lukewarm reviews of *Anna in the Tropics*, see Michael Feingold, "Southern Discomforts," *The Village Voice*, November 19–25, 2003 (available online). Among the favorable reviews, see Robert Brustein, "Shotover's Apocalypse," *The New Republic* (November 17, 2003), 28–30. On the Broadway production as an example of the heightened visibility of Latinos/as in mainstream entertainment venues, see Mireya Navarro, "Actors in All-Latino Cast Savor a 'Historic Moment,'" *New York Times*, December 2, 2003. On Nilo Cruz's Pulitzer Prize, see Amy Lennard Goehner and Richard Zoglin, "Break Out the Cigars," *Time* 162, no. 14 (November 3, 2003), 73 (available online); Gigi Anders, "Work and All Play," *Hispanic* (June 2003), 34–35.

[4] In his *Village Voice* review Michael Feingold complains: "The realities of factory life are scanted—Emily Mann's production doesn't suggest what the place must look like until the epilogue—and there are even fewer hints of the anomalous position Cubans, with their own complex racial mix, must have occupied in segregated Florida. Nor is there any mention of the world beyond Florida, except for a passing reference to Valentino movies. Russia is alluded to, of course, as the setting for Anna's doomed affair, but you'd never know that there had recently been a revolution there, or that Tolstoy was important to workers not only as a literary genius, but as a quasi-religious socialist and pacifist. Lectors, in fact, were often an irritant to factory management because their reading matter gave the workers political and economic, as well as cultural, inspiration: Samuel Gompers, founder of the American Federation of Labor, began his career as a lector in a New York cigar factory. But labor-management problems have no more to do with this factory play than the realities of cigar making, about which you learn next to nothing" (Feingold, "Southern Discomforts").

[5] From the standpoint of postcolonial criticism, I recognize—following Walter D. Mignolo—that the history of the colonial and postcolonial periods in Latin America offers Latin American (and Latin American diaspora) postcolonial critics

a different orientation than that of postcolonial critics, whose points of reference are in former British colonial possessions. See Walter D. Mignolo, *Local Histories/Global Designs: Coloniality, Subaltern Knowledges, and Border Thinking,* Princeton Studies in Culture/Power/History (Princeton, NJ: Princeton Univ. Press, 2000). Also see Walter D. Mignolo, "Human Understanding and (Latin) American Interests: The Politics and Sensibilities of Geohistorical Locations," in *A Companion to Postcolonial Studies,* ed. Henry Schwarz and Sangeeta Ray (Malden, MA: Blackwell, 2000), 180–202; and J. Jorge Klor de Alva, "The Postcolonization of the (Latin) American Experience: A Reconsideration of 'Colonialism,' 'Postcolonialism,' and 'Mestizaje,'" in *After Colonialism: Imperial Histories and Postcolonial Displacements,* ed. Gyan Prakash (Princeton, NJ: Princeton Univ. Press, 1995), 241–75.

[6] I borrow the expression "life on the hyphen" from Gustavo Pérez Firmat, *Life on the Hyphen: The Cuban-American Way* (Austin: Univ. of Texas Press, 1994).

[7] Recent Latino/a theologies have begun to take a fresh look at hitherto unexplored dimensions of popular culture. This essay takes up the challenge articulated by Carmen M. Nanko: "We need as theologians to more actively engage popular culture and to be far more intentionally interdisciplinary in our conversations" ("A Marginalized Majority? Hispanic Theologians and the Latino/a Presence in the U.S. Catholic Church," paper presented at the Fifty-Eighth Annual Convention of the Catholic Theological Society of America, Cincinnati, Ohio, June 7, 2003). See also Carmen M. Nanko, "Elbows on the Table: Ethics of Doing Theology/A U.S. Hispanic Perspective," *Journal of Hispanic/Latino Theology* 10, no. 3 (February 2003): 52–77. As a biblical scholar's contribution to this project's study of tradition *latinamente* conceived, this essay pursues the agenda of critical interdisciplinary engagement I set out in my paper, "Good Fences and Good Neighbors? Biblical Scholars and Theologians," constructed in conversation with Carmen M. Nanko and presented at the 2003 Annual Convention of the Catholic Theological Society of America (see Gary Riebe-Estrella, "Hispanic/Latino/a Theology," *CTSA Proceedings* 58 [2003], 147–48).

[8] In his stimulating contribution to this volume, Francisco Lozada, Jr., problematizes the attribution of authority to the biblical tradition.

[9] Cruz, *Anna in the Tropics,* 51.

[10] Ibid., 51–52.

[11] Ibid., 52.

[12] Ibid., 52–53.

[13] Roberto Goizueta's distinction between poiesis and praxis is helpful here. See Roberto Goizueta, *Caminemos con Jesús: Toward a Hispanic/Latino Theology of Accompaniment* (Maryknoll, NY: Orbis Books, 1995), esp. 111–19.

[14] Darien Cavanaugh, "Huelga! Labor Activism and Unrest in Ybor City: 1886 to 1950," guide to the exhibit at the Ybor City Museum State Park, August 2 to October 20, 2003 (available online). On cigar-factory readers, see María Elena Rodríguez Castro, "Oír leer: Tabaco y cultura en Cuba y Puerto Rico," *Caribbean Studies* 24, no. 3–4 (1991): 221–39; Louis A. Pérez, Jr., "Reminiscences of

a Lector: Cuban Cigar Workers in Tampa," *Florida Historical Quarterly* 53 (April 1975): 443–49.

[15] Cavanaugh, "Huelga!" 7. During the 1890s South Florida cigar workers were deeply involved in the movement for Cuban independence. Cavanaugh notes that "a cigar made at the O'Halloran Cigar Factory in West Tampa carried the note directing Cuban separatists to start the rebellion" ("Huelga!" 3).

[16] Cruz, *Anna in the Tropics*, 6. According to Nancy A. Hewitt, "Workers were forced to give up the tradition of readers, who were replaced with radios offering music and baseball in place of labor news, political tracts, and literary classics" (*Southern Discomfort: Women's Activism in Tampa, Florida, 1880s-1920s* [Urbana: Univ. of Illinois Press, 2001], 273).

[17] Hewitt, *Southern Discomfort*, 3.

[18] Ibid.

[19] Ibid., 3–4. See also Norma Valle Ferrer, *Luisa Capetillo: Historia de una mujer proscrita* (Río Piedras: Editorial Cultural, 1990); Lara A. Walker, "Luisa Capetillo: Beyond Border Feminism and Class Struggle," *Selected Proceedings of the Annual Symposium on Hispanic and Luso-Brazilian Literature, Language and Culture*, Univ. of Arizona, Tucson (available online). According to Walker, "one of her most infamous moments was her arrest for wearing men's trousers in public" ("Luisa Capetillo," 95).

[20] *La Gaceta* is available online. See also Gary R. Mormino and George E. Pozzetta, *The Immigrant World of Ybor City: Italians and Their Latin Neighbors in Tampa, 1885–1985* (Gainesville: Univ. Press of Florida, 1988); Susan D. Greenbaum, *More than Black: Afro-Cubans in Tampa* (Gainesville: Univ. Press of Florida, 2002).

[21] Luisa Capetillo, "Situación del trabajador puertorriqueño," in *Amor y anarquía: los escritos de Luisa Capetillo*, ed. Julio Ramos (Río Piedras: Ediciones Huracán, 1992), 89.

[22] Luisa Capetillo, *Ensayos libertarios* (Arecibo, Puerto Rico: Imprenta Unión Obrera, 1907); idem, *La humanidad en el futuro* (San Juan: Tipografía Real Hermanos, 1910). See Evelina López Antonetty, *Luisa Capetillo (1879–1922): Bibliografías puertorriqueñas* (New York: City Univ. of New York Hunter College Center for Puerto Rican Studies, 1986). See the selection of Luisa Capetillo's writings in Ramos, *Amor y anarquía*. Lara A. Walker explains: "Her hybrid style of writing and production includes essays, short propaganda plays, fiction, and experimental prose. In each case Capetillo denounces Catholic dogma, elite class corruption and gender/class oppression" ("Luisa Capetillo," 95).

[23] "Walker, "Luisa Capetillo," 96.

[24] Norma Valle, "El Teatro de Luia Capetillo," *Ateneo Puertorriqueño. XVII Festival de Teatro* (1985), 38, cited in Walker, "Luisa Capetillo," 96.

[25] Walker offers Capetillo's play "Matrimonio sin amor, consecuencia, adulterio" as an example: "Upon hearing (or reading) the title the traditional semantic interpretation would be: an unhappy marriage can lead one to look outside those legal bonds in infidelity and commit the sin and crime of adultery. Yet, by the end of the play the meaning will have changed. . . . Capetillo allows

her female protagonist (as she does with all of them) to be a thinking, intelligent agent of power and change. . . . Capetillo ruptures the tradition to highlight her didactic message and now at the end of the play the semantics of the title have changed: a marriage without pure (free) love is adultery, even though it be legal and lawful" (Walker, "Luisa Capetillo," 96–97).

[26] Lisa Sánchez González, "Luisa Capetillo: An Anarcho-Feminist Pionera in the Mainland Puerto Rican Narrative/Political Tradition," in *Recovering the U.S. Hispanic Literary Heritage*, ed. Erlinda González-Berry and Chuck Tatum (Houston: Arte Público Press, 1996), 2:162, cited in Walker, "Luisa Capetillo," 97.

[27] See the treatment of tradition, traditioning and the agents of tradition by Orlando O. Espín in Chapter 1 in this volume. Also see Orlando O. Espín, "Toward the Construction of an Intercultural Theology of Tradition," *Journal of Hispanic/Latino Theology* 9, no. 3 (February 2002): 22–59.

[28] On immigrant anticlericalism in South Florida, see Hewitt, *Southern Discomfort*, 316 n. 36.

[29] See the *Rule of St. Benedict*, chap. 38, "The Reader for the Week": "Reading will always accompany the meals of the brothers. The reader should not be the one who just happens to pick up the book, but someone who will read for a whole week, beginning on Sunday. After Mass and Communion, let the incoming reader ask all to pray for him so that God may shield him from the spirit of vanity. Let him begin this verse in the oratory: Lord, open my lips, and my mouth shall proclaim your praise (Ps. 50[51]:17), and let all say it three times. When he has received a blessing, he will begin his week of reading. Let there be complete silence. No whispering, no speaking—only the reader's voice should be heard there. The brothers should by turn serve one another's needs as they eat and drink, so that no one need ask for anything. If, however, anything is required, it should be requested by an audible signal of some kind rather than by speech. No one should presume to ask a question about the reading or about anything else, lest occasion be given [to the devil] (Eph 4:27; 1 Tim 5:14). The superior, however, may wish to say a few words of instruction. Because of holy Communion and because the fast may be too hard for him to bear, the reader for the week is to receive some diluted wine before he begins to read. Afterward he will take his meal with the weekly kitchen servers and the attendants. Brothers will read and sing, not according to rank, but according to their ability to benefit their hearers" (Timothy Fry, et al., eds., *The Rule of St. Benedict in Latin and English with Notes* [Collegeville, MN: Liturgical Press, 1981], 237, 239).

[30] See Fernando F. Segovia, *Decolonizing Biblical Studies: A View from the Margins* (Maryknoll, NY: Orbis Books, 2000), 119–32.

[31] On the Tainos, see Irving Rouse, *The Tainos: Rise and Decline of the People Who Greeted Columbus* (New Haven, CT: Yale Univ. Press, 1992); Samuel M. Wilson, ed., *The Indigenous People of the Caribbean*, The Ripley P. Bullen Series (Gainesville, FL: Univ. Press of Florida, 1997); and Sebastián Robiou Lamarche, *Taínos y Caribes: Las culturas aborígenes antillanas* (San Juan: Editorial Punto y

Coma, 2003). On the texts of the aboriginal peoples of Mesoamerica and the Andes, see Elizabeth Hill Boone and Walter D. Mignolo, *Writing without Words: Alternative Literacies in Mesoamerica and the Andes* (Durham, NC: Duke Univ. Press, 1994); Elizabeth Hill Boone, *Stories in Red and Black: Pictorial Histories of the Aztecs and Mixtecs* (Austin: Univ. of Texas Press, 2000).

[32] John E. Thiel, *Senses of Tradition: Continuity and Development in Catholic Faith* (New York: Oxford Univ. Press, 2000).

[33] As Hubert Jedin writes, "There is no denying that Luther accepted the creeds of the ancient Church as being in accordance with the Scriptures and to that extent set himself within the continuing dogmatic tradition of the Church—but with the reservation: 'in so far as it conforms with the Scriptures.' . . . The fight against 'tradition' as 'human statutes' occupied a large place in his polemics" (*A History of the Council of Trent*, vol. 2, *The First Sessions at Trent 1545–47*, trans. Ernest Graf (St. Louis: B. Herder, 1957), 58. Also see Gerhard Ebeling, *Wort Gottes und Tradition: Studien zu einer Hermeneutik der Konfessionen*, 2nd ed., Veröffentlichungen des Konfessionskundlichen Instituts des Evangelischen Bundes 7 (Göttingen: Vandenhoeck and Ruprecht, 1966), 91–143.

[34] Maurice Bévenot, "Scripture and Tradition in Catholic Theology," in *Holy Book and Holy Tradition*, ed. F. F. Bruce and E. G. Rupp (Grand Rapids, MI: Eerdmans, 1968), 174.

[35] Jedin, *A History of the Council of Trent*, 74.

[36] Agostino Bonuccio, quoted in ibid., 75.

[37] Jedin, *A History of the Council of Trent*, 75.

[38] Giacomo Nacchianti and Francisco de Navarra, quoted in ibid., 86–87.

[39] Does this reticence even indirectly imply that the canon of authoritative tradition is *not* definitively closed, unlike the biblical canon?

[40] See the succinct and nuanced treatment of tradition, with attention to Trent and Vatican II, by Hermann Pottmeyer, "Tradition," in *Dictionary of Fundamental Theology*, ed. René Latourelle and Rino Fisichella (New York: Crossroad, 1995), 1119–26.

[41] On the relationship between oral tradition and written texts in early Christianity, and on the relationship between the technologies of knowledge production and knowledge diffusion, see Harry Y. Gamble, *Books and Readers in the Early Church: A History of Early Christian Texts* (New Haven, CT: Yale Univ. Press, 1995). Also see David Diringer's wide-ranging work, *The Book before Printing: Ancient, Medieval, and Oriental* (New York: Dover, 1982; originally published as *The Hand-Produced Book*, 1953). On the place of texts in the European imagination at the beginning of the colonization of the Americas, see Anthony Grafton, April Shelford, and Nancy Siraisi, *New Worlds, Ancient Texts: The Power of Tradition and the Shock of Discovery* (Cambridge, MA: Belknap Press of Harvard Univ. Press, 1992).

[42] See, for example, Benson Bobrick, *Wide as the Waters: The English Bible and the Revolution It Inspired* (New York: Penguin, 2002; original edition New York: Simon and Schuster, 2001).

[43] Alfonso de Castro, quoted in Jedin, *A History of the Council of Trent*, 71. Also see Jesús Enciso, "Prohibiciones españolas de las versiones bíblicas en romance antes del Tridentino," *Estudios bíblicos* 3 (1944), 523–60; and Anthony Pym, *Negotiating the Frontier: Translators and Intercultures in Hispanic History* (Manchester: St. Jerome Publishing, 2000), 175–78.

[44] Piero Bertano, quoted in Jedin, *A History of the Council of Trent*, 71.

[45] Pedro Pacheco, quoted in Jedin, *A History of the Council of Trent*, 83–84.

[46] On the issue of translation, see Pym, *Negotiating the Frontier*, 108–31.

[47] See Moshe Lazar, "Moses Arragel as Translator and Commentator," in *Companion Volume to la Biblia de Alba: An Illustrated Manuscript Bible in Castilian*, ed. Jeremy Schonfeld (Madrid: Fundación Amigos de Sefarad; London: Facsimile Editions, 1992), 157–200; A. A. Sicroff, "The Arragel Bible: A Fifteenth Century Rabbi Translates and Glosses the Bible for His Christian Master," in *Américo Castro: Essays to Mark the Centenary of His Birth*, ed. Jaime Ferrán, Ronald E. Kurtz, and Daniel P. Testa, 173–82 (Madison, WI: Hispanic Seminary of Medieval Studies, 1988).

[48] See Jean-Pierre Ruiz, "Cardinal Francisco Ximénez de Cisneros and Bartolomé de las Casas, the 'Procurator and Universal Protector of All Indians in the Indies,'" *Journal of Hispanic/Latino Theology* 9, no. 9 (February 2002): 60–77.

[49] Francisco Ximénez de Cisneros, quoted in John C. Olin, *Catholic Reform from Cardinal Ximenes to the Council of Trent 1495–1563* (New York: Fordham Univ. Press, 1990), 64.

[50] See Pym, *Negotiating the Frontier*, 164–73. Also see Marcel Bataillon, *Erasmo y España*, trans. Antonio Alatorre (Mexico: Fondo de Cultura Económica, 1966).

[51] Pym, *Negotiating the Frontier*, 171.

[52] Could the Tridentine insistence on the priority of the Vulgate be understood after the analogy of Nebrija's argument for the strategic deployment of his Castilian grammar as an instrument of centralization, an exercise of language as power?

[53] Antonio de Nebrija, *Gramática castellana*, ed. Miguel Ángel Esparza and Ramón Sarmiento (Madrid: Fundación Antonio de Nebrija, 1992) 107–9, as translated in Pym, *Negotiating the Frontier*, 137.

[54] Pym, *Negotiating the Frontier*, 137. Also see Walter D. Mignolo, *The Darker Side of the Renaissance* (Ann Arbor: Univ. of Michigan, 1995), 29–67.

[55] Pym, *Negotiating the Frontier*, 167.

[56] Translation from Mignolo, *The Darker Side of the Renaissance*, 39.

[57] Grafton, Shelford, and Siraisi, *New Worlds, Ancient Texts*, 5.

[58] As Grafton tells us: "Benito Arias Montano, an influential Spanish theologian who worked on the great multivolume Polyglot Bible published at Antwerp in 1572, insisted that one could easily find New Spain in his old text. The origins of New World settlement he tied to Joctan, son of Eber, of the family of Shem. He had given his name, after all, to that 'very old city Ivktan' which lay in the midst of the Andean mountains" (*New Worlds, Ancient Texts*, 149).

[59] Orlando O. Espín, "Tradition and Popular Religion: An Understanding of the *Sensus Fidelium*," in *Frontiers of Hispanic Theology in the United States*, ed. Allan Figueroa Deck, SJ (Maryknoll, NY: Orbis Books, 1992), 68.

[60] For one fascinating example of the transmission and transformation of popular drama from Spain to Mexico, see Max Harris, *Aztecs, Moors, and Christians: Festivals of Reconquest in Mexico and Spain* (Austin: Univ. of Texas Press).

[61] Pedro de Gante, translation in Mignolo, *The Darker Side of the Renaissance*, 45.

[62] Pym, *Negotiating the Frontier*, 145.

[63] See, for example, Arthur J. O. Anderson, *Bernardino de Sahagún's Psalmodia Christiana (Christian Psalmody)* (Salt Lake City: Univ. of Utah Press, 1993).

[64] Gregorio García, cited in Walden Browne, *Sahagún and the Transition to Modernity* (Norman: Univ. of Oklahoma Press, 2000), 190.

[65] See Mignolo, *The Darker Side of the Renaissance*, 29–67. On the humanism of the sixteenth-century Franciscan missionaries in Mexico, see Ellen T. Baird, *The Drawings of Sahagún's Primeros Memoriales: Structure and Style* (Norman: Univ. of Oklahoma Press, 1993), 6–10.

[66] Browne, *Sahagún and the Transition to Modernity*, esp. 185–213. Browne argues that "throughout the Middle Ages, social institutions in general (including knowledge) were perceived as fundamentally unchanging" (201) and "curiosity was perceived as nothing more than a distraction from true knowledge—a knowledge that can only be revealed by God and safeguarded with the memory provided by the written word" (209).

[67] Boone, *Stories in Red and Black*, 28. Also see Boone and Mignolo, *Writing without Words*.

[68] Boone, *Stories in Red and Black*, 28.

[69] Ibid., 29.

[70] José de Acosta, *Natural and Moral History of the Indies*, ed. Jane E. Mangan, trans. Brances López Morillas (Durham, NC: Duke Univ. Press, 2002), 339 (bk. 6, chap. 7).

[71] Baird, *The Drawings of Sahagún's Primeros Memoriales*, 10. On orality and literacy, see Walter J. Ong, *Orality and Literacy* (London: Methuen, 1982); Jack Goody, *The Interface between the Written and the Oral* (Studies in Literacy, Family, Culture, and the State (Cambridge: Cambridge Univ. Press, 1987); idem, *The Power of the Written Tradition* (Washington, DC: Smithsonian Institution Press, 2000).

[72] Mignolo, *The Darker Side of the Renaissance*, 41.

[73] Ibid., 344 n. 39.

[74] Toribio de Benavente (Motolinía), *Motolinía's History of the Indians of New Spain*, trans. Frances Borgia Steck (Washington, DC: Academy of American Franciscan History, 1951), 74, cited in Baird, *The Drawings of Sahagún's Primeros Memoriales*, 9.

[75] Baird, *The Drawings of Sahagún's Primeros Memoriales*, 9. See Goody, *The Interface between the Written and the Oral*, 174–82.

[76] Bernardino de Sahagún, *Los diálogos de 1524 según el texto de Fray Bernardino de Sahagún y sus colaboradores indígenas,* ed. and trans. Miguel León-Portilla (Mexico City: Universidad Nacional Autónoma de México, 1986).

[77] Mignolo, *The Darker Side of the Renaissance*, 97.

78 Translation from J. Jorge Klor de Alva, "The Aztec-Spanish Dialogues of 1524," *Alcheringa: Ethnopoetics* 4, no. 2 (1980): 79–80. Emphasis added.

79 Sahagún, *Los diálogos de 1524*, lines 575–76.

80 Translation from Klor de Alva, "The Aztec-Spanish Dialogues of 1524," 94.

81 Translation from Klor de Alva, "The Aztec-Spanish Dialogues of 1524," 108–10.

82 Mignolo, *The Darker Side of the Renaissance*, 104.

83 Leela Gandhi, *Postcolonial Theory: A Critical Introduction* (New York: Columbia Univ. Press, 1998), 141.

84 Ibid., 141–42.

85 Ibid., 142.

86 R. S. Sugirtharajah, *The Bible and the Third World: Precolonial, Colonial, and Postcolonial Encounters* (Cambridge: Cambridge Univ. Press, 2001), 258, citing Andrea A. Luncford, "Toward a Mestiza Rhetoric: Gloria Anzaldúa on Composition and Postcoloniality," in *Race, Rhetoric, and the Postcolonial*, ed. Gary A. Olson and Lynn Worsham (Albany: State Univ. of New York Press, 1999), 62.

87 Sugirtharajah, *The Bible and the Third World*, 259.

88 Wilfred Cantwell Smith, *What Is Scripture? A Comparative Approach* (Minneapolis: Fortress Press, 1993), 18. Also see Jean-Pierre Ruiz, "Reading across Canons: U.S. Hispanic Reflections on Globalization and the Senses of Scripture," *Journal of Hispanic/Latino Theology* 10, no. 4 (May 2003): 22–44. On the ways in which texts are invested with authority, see Chapter 2 in the present volume.

5

Reinventing the Biblical Tradition

An Exploration of Social Location Hermeneutics

Francisco Lozada, Jr.

INTRODUCTION

It is not uncommon today to find many rereadings of the biblical tradition using one's social location, such as ethnic/racial, gender, geographical, or sexual orientation, as a point of departure in rereading the biblical tradition, namely, the Christian scriptures. This way of rereading scriptures, which I call social location hermeneutics, among biblical scholars has in many ways become—and is very much still in the process of becoming—a new constructed and creative "tradition" on *how* to reread the biblical tradition within the field of contemporary biblical hermeneutics. In this chapter, *biblical tradition* refers not only to content (the texts of scripture) but also to the history of biblical hermeneutics that involves all global readers and reading strategies that continuously remake and broaden the content.[1]

Social location hermeneutics is informed by a wide range along the theoretical continuum of ideological criticism and by the theological positions of liberation. It is a reading strategy that aims to reread the biblical tradition with the aim of acknowledging the identity(ies) of the interpreter (intratextual) and/or the identity of the group (extratextual) for whom the interpreter is writing, and for seeking to uncover the ideological world views of both the interpreter and the text in the quest to sift out a liberating interpretation.[2] In other words, social location hermeneutics aims to contextualize fully the reading process in order to construct a rereading of the biblical tradition with the objective of liberation and empowerment in mind.

113

Social location hermeneutics has been quite valuable and essential to the field of contemporary biblical hermeneutics over the last fifteen years or so.[3] In addition to overturning the notion that the rereading process is an objective, universalistic, and positivistic enterprise, it has raised the consciousness of the interpreter's identity as well as that of many "minority" groups who struggle to change current negative viewpoints or representations of their group.[4] Most important, it has breathed life back into the biblical tradition, thus making the biblical tradition much more meaningful to the people (church) than ever before. As such, social location hermeneutics deserves commendation and respect for its contribution to expanding the traditional modus operandi for rereading the biblical tradition, namely, the historical critical approach in its many forms. However, I am at a point in my own hermeneutical journey—as one who locates himself deeply within the tradition of social location hermeneutics—where this new modus operandi for rereading the tradition (that is, social location hermeneutics) needs a brief exploration or examination. This, it seems to me, is necessary in order to prevent this approach from becoming stagnant or fixed—a tendency I do not want to see happen to social location hermeneutics as it has happened with other approaches.

One of my concerns with the social location approaches to rereading the biblical tradition is that the reading strategy has yet to challenge the authority of the biblical tradition. As indicated above, the social location approach has made the biblical tradition much more relevant for many minority groups as a way to recognize their identities within a guild that marginalizes these groups as well as their approach to rereading the tradition. However, it is pertinent that minority groups reflect upon the ramifications and consequences of their reading strategy vis-à-vis their own representation as Other. In other words, in the attempt to use the biblical tradition to legitimate their participation within the Christian tradition, it is the biblical tradition itself that confirms their "otherness."[5] Rather than challenging the authority of the biblical tradition, minority readers use the biblical tradition to harmonize their otherness with the otherness represented within the biblical tradition.[6] For instance, it is not uncommon to find US Latino/a readers harmonizing their otherness with the marginalized Galilean experience in the Gospels, or Latin American readers correlating their experience of poverty with poverty in the biblical tradition, or feminist readers paralleling their legitimacy as leaders within today's *ekklesia* with the women who held leadership roles within the biblical tradition.[7]

Much of this way of rereading the biblical tradition is very important and has done much to raise consciousness of "otherness." It has also sensitized many readers to the present situation of marginalization that these minority readers are experiencing and hopefully will overcome. However, these minority readers are legitimating their otherness using an authoritative biblical tradition. In other words, the biblical tradition is maintaining their otherness every time the tradition is used to challenge—in the name of liberation—an existing, troubling representation. From my point of view, I wonder if this is the most effective strategy to change the perception of otherness, not so much vis-à-vis the mainstream individuals of their respective societies, but within their own respective minority communities.

In this essay I intend to examine three particular readings that legitimate otherness using the authorized biblical tradition. I am not arguing that they are wrong in their chosen reading strategies, but rather I focus on how their readings support otherness in the process of trying to bring about liberation. I argue that less attention should be given to the biblical tradition as authoritative.

When we encounter tradition today, a question that I believe is lacking is whether that tradition has authority or not, as well as the value of the tradition for continuing on into the globalized future. In this period of globalization, when many religious traditions are retreating to their sacred scriptures as a way to identify themselves against the homogenization by the world, these traditions are at the same time reinforcing their authority.[8] Christianity is no exception, given the rise of fundamentalism throughout the West with regard to the biblical tradition and also its teachings and practices.

I think minority groups, in an unconscious way, are reacting in a similar fashion when they provide social location readings. It is a way to resist the assimilation of their varied cultures. However, these social location readings, I believe, are also contributing to a perspective among minority groups that confirms that they are indeed outside the mainstream. At the same time, they buttress the biblical tradition and fortify its authority. I believe that to reinforce the power of the biblical tradition could be dangerous for minority groups in the future. Such authorization, I believe, is potentially dangerous because identity is constructed using the Bible as source rather than using the experiences of the groups.

I am not arguing to dispense with the biblical tradition, but rather that the notion of authority associated with biblical tradition needs revamping or eradication. It is this notion of authority that contributes strongly to the continual marginalization of many within the present-day *ekklesia* and society.

In order to examine further how "minority' readers contribute to the "othering" of themselves and their communities through the use of the authority of the biblical tradition, I examine critically three recent studies that I believe demonstrate this process of marginalization, namely, C. Gilbert Romero, "Biblical Anti-Monarchic Tradition and a U.S. Latino Theology"; J. Severino Croatto, "Recovering the Goddess: Reflections on God-Talk"; and Elsa Tamez, "1 Timothy: What a Problem!"[9] Since my social location and my hermeneutics are strongly informed by my US Latino/a and Latin American identities, it is apropos that I begin with studies from this particularity.[10]

The secondary goal of this essay is to begin thinking of alternative ways to engage a nonauthoritative biblical tradition. I believe each one of these readings provides glimpses of different ways or stances toward the biblical tradition that minimize the authority of the biblical tradition. The conclusion briefly explores these alternative stances vis-à-vis the authorized biblical tradition.

SOCIAL LOCATION READINGS
WITHIN THE BIBLICAL TRADITION

C. Gilbert Romero,
"Biblical Anti-Monarchic Tradition
and a U.S. Latino Theology"

C. Gilbert Romero's reading of the biblical anti-monarchic tradition and US Latino/a theology asks three main questions. First, how can scripture contribute to alleviating the palliative responses, such as *Es la voluntad de Dios* (It is God's will) or *Que Dios haga su santa voluntad* (May God do his holy will) that are so common among many US Latinos/as as practitioners of *religiosidad popular* or devotional piety (popular Catholicism)? Second, how does 1 Samuel 8—15 and its anti-monarchic tradition contribute to alleviating the aforementioned palliative responses? Third, what is the relationship between the anti-monarchic tradition and *religiosidad popular*? As such, these questions are fully entrenched in the question of tradition.

Informed by historical criticism, Romero examines the monarchic tradition within 1 Samuel 8—15. At the same time, his reading of 1 Samuel 8—15 is informed by ideological criticism, since he aims to examine how the monarchic tradition, and particularly the *anti*-monarchic tradition, assists in encouraging Latinos/as to challenge the above palliative responses. All in all, using a combination of historical and ideological criticisms, Romero argues that the anti-monarchic tradition that exists in 1 Samuel 8—15 is an excellent biblical tradition for Latinos/as to

embrace. It is one that can help them understand and contest such palliative responses so they can struggle against civil and ecclesiastical injustices. In other words, Romero, with the best of intentions, sets out to
reread 1 Samuel 8—15 in a liberative fashion to help Latinos/as challenge their oppression. However, at the end Romero simply confirms
Latinos/as' otherness by using the very biblical tradition he is examining
to solidify their otherness.

Romero's applied reading of 1 Samuel 8—15 occurs in four stages:
(1) "Introduction," (2) "The Anti-Monarchic Tradition in Its Biblical
Context," (3) "Kingship and the Two Covenant Traditions," and (4)
"The Anti-Monarchic Tradition and *Religiosidad Popular*." I will sum-
marize this reading along these sections.

Introduction

Romero begins his article with the argument that one of the most
important sources for Latinos/as in doing US Latino theology is
religiosidad popular or devotional piety, which is confirmed in the tradition history of the Bible (biblical analogues).[11] He has argued this point
before.[12] However, in this particular article, he aims to develop this argument further with a reading of the anti-monarchic tradition found in
1 Samuel 8—15. This reading begins with particularity, namely, the oppression experienced by U.S. Latinos in and through civil and ecclesiastical institutions. One way that Latinos[13] have dealt with such suffering,
according to Romero, has been through *religiosidad popular*, either as a
palliative or as a valiant response. Palliative responses, reflective of the
way Latinos think, influence them to behave in a subdued and passive
fashion. These expressions lead Romero to search for a way to help
Latinos not only recognize the oppressive nature of these expressions,
but also construct new ones that will liberate them from the negative
ramifications of these ideas. This search, for Romero, begins with the
font of divine revelation and the locus of the divine will, namely, the
scriptures.[14] It is Romero's theological belief, therefore, that the anti-
monarchic tradition (that he will explore in 1 Samuel 8—15) is consonant with the divine will of God and, therefore, useful as a tool for
Latinos to overturn any sort of oppression that they experience in society.

His argument is thus: 1 Samuel 8—15 is based on two covenant traditions, a Sinaitic and a Davidic. The anti-monarchic tradition is founded
on the Sinaitic covenant. The monarchic tradition, which Romero calls
the *pro*-monarchic tradition and which exists side by side with the
anti-monarchic tradition in 1 Samuel 8—15 is based on the Davidic

covenant tradition. In 1 Samuel 8—15, a tension exists between these two traditions. The anti-monarchic tradition is contending with the pro-monarchic tradition's exclusivist theological position that the only way to relate to God is through the Davidic dynasty. The anti-monarchic tradition reflects the world view of those Israelites who disagree with this position. For Romero, as indicated above, this anti-monarchic tradition is a way to challenge oppression. For Romero, tradition (part of the living word of God) not only serves to unite Latinos, but also functions as a tool to fight against oppression.[15]

The Anti-Monarchic Tradition in Its Biblical Context

Romero begins the delineation of his argument with a brief discussion of the sociopolitical context of Israel (ca. eleventh century BCE). Prior to the period of the monarchy in Israel (when Saul, David, and Solomon were kings), the people were organized as a tribal federation. In other words, the tribes of Israel who functioned autonomously came together, under the direction of a judge or military leader, as a nation whenever an outside group threatened the tribes. This model of governance was based on the Sinai model of covenant. The Sinaitic covenant was a bilateral agreement between God and the Israelites, which happened to be a conditional one as well. That is, God would support the Israelites in their time of need on the condition that the Israelites would repent those sins that led them to call upon God's help. This form of governance, the bilateral agreement, changed after the settlement in Canaan, giving way to a unilateral type of governance called monarchy. The anti-monarchic tradition is opposed to this new form of governance, whereas the pro-monarchic tradition is supportive of monarchal rule. Thus, both the politics of the day and different theological positions (*sitz im leben*) gave rise to both of these biblical traditions in 1 Samuel 8—15.

Romero then proceeds to a rereading of 1 Samuel 8—15. This reading, based on the results of redaction criticism, aims to show the tension between the anti-monarchic and the pro-monarchic traditions. The first major point that Romero makes is that the reason behind the unhappiness of Samuel, the last judge prior to the monarchic rule, is due to the tribes' choice for a change of governance styles. For Romero, this unhappiness is really a "reading back" by the anti-monarchic tradition (1 Samuel 8). A second major point is that Saul, the first king selected to lead the nation, is being set up for failure by the pro-monarchic tradition in order to pave a way for David, the king of their choice. For Romero, this pro-monarchic tradition is somehow divinely sanctioned because this tradition also legitimates Jesus' descent from the family of David—a must for salvation purposes (1 Samuel 9—10).[16] Third, the anti-monarchic tradition shifts its focus a bit and begins to challenge not the ideal of kingship per se, but the style of kingship that accompanies this office. What matters is how the king (Saul) behaves, justly or unjustly, as discussed in the text (1 Samuel 11—12). Fourth, the pro-monarchic tradition appears again and begins to prepare for David's kingship by portraying Saul in a negative light. Saul's actions, wrongly assuming Samuel's authority in offering sacrifice, are not in line with tradition (1 Samuel 13—14). Therefore, finally, as Saul's power continues to decline, with the help of the pro-monarchic tradition, David's power is gradually ascending politically and theologically (1 Samuel 15).

Kingship and the Two Covenant Traditions

Romero's reading of 1 Samuel 8—15 demonstrates that there did exist two dominant traditions or sources, an anti-monarchic tradition and a pro-monarchic tradition, which were eventually redacted together in 1 Samuel 8—15. Both are divinely inspired, but it is the anti-monarchic tradition that he will encourage Latinos to embrace in their context of oppression.

As mentioned above, both of these traditions are influenced by two covenant traditions. The anti-monarchic tradition is based on the Sinai covenant and the pro-monarchic one on the Davidic covenant tradition. This is a very important point in Romero's essay, because both covenant traditions carry certain characteristics.

For instance, the Sinai covenant tradition is characterized as bilateral and conditional. Yahweh makes a covenant with the Israelites on the condition that they keep the Law. For Romero, the Sinai covenant aims to democratize the relationship with Yahweh.[17] This Sinai covenant also tends to emphasize the community in that God is relating to a people rather than to an individual. The conditional Sinai covenant provides the people the choice of either accepting the covenant or rejecting it. Romero's point here is that if one understands the underlying influences of the anti-monarchic tradition (the Sinai covenant tradition), one begins to understand why the anti-monarchic tradition was against the pro-monarchic style of kingship. This latter emphasized the characteristics of the Davidic covenant tradition which were not bilateral (God and the Israelites) but unilateral (God and the Davidic dynasty) and unconditional (God asks nothing in return; no accountability).

In other words, the Davidic covenant tradition influenced the pro-monarchic tradition in 1 Samuel 8—15. The anti-monarchic tradition existed to serve to challenge the pro-monarchic tradition as well as the abuses incurred by it later. Romero's point here is that this ant-imonarchic tradition found in 1 Samuel 8—15, colored by the Sinaitic covenant's characteristics of bilateralism and conditionality (accountability), could be used as a model for those experiencing oppression. Latinos or practitioners of *religiosidad popular* could use this tradition to critique civil and ecclesiastical abuses of leadership in the world—as the anti-monarchic supporters did against the pro-monarchic supporters. It is interesting to note that, in my opinion, Romero is subtly using tradition (scripture) to challenge his own tradition (ecclesiastical structures).

The Anti-Monarchic Tradition and *Religiosidad Popular*

For Romero, *religiosidad popular* can be of divine revelation. However, Romero is cautious: "This revelatory dimension is supplementary to and does not supersede the foundational revelation as found in our Catholic creedal formulae."[18] Yet, Romero still holds that *religiosidad popular* is a means of communication with God without mediators. As such, *religiosidad popular* can be used to challenge the dominant religious beliefs if these are oppressive—in the same way the anti-monarchic tradition in 1 Samuel 8—10 challenged the dominant beliefs of the pro-monarchic tradition.

To justify this reading of both the anti-monarchic tradition and *religiosidad popular*, Romero digresses a bit to discuss the history of Catholic biblical interpretation. I now address briefly several of Romero's points. First, as *Dei Verbum (The Dogmatic Constitution on Divine Revelation)* suggests, according to Romero, foundational revelation is dependent upon cultural expressions for tradition to make progress in the Roman Catholic Church. *Religiosidad popular* is such an expression.

Second, in order to understand the *developing* tradition within cultures that employ scriptures, it is necessary to use a methodology or reading strategy that allows for cultural expressions like *religiosidad popular* to participate in the ongoing life of tradition as guided by the Holy Spirit. The methodology or reading strategy that Romero is proposing is reader-response criticism, which he argues is the best critical method, along with historical criticism, to use to challenge oppression. He can make this argument because he believes *Dei Verbum* is calling upon the reader/hearer to participate in the living development of tradition. Reader-response is not meant to replace the historical-critical methodology, which is predominant among Catholic biblical scholars, but to work with it.[19]

Third, the value of adopting the reader-response approach is that it is compatible with the world of traditions and symbols that characterize Latino culture. What is more, reader-response criticism is a development closely related to narrative criticism, and since the biblical narrative deals with feelings and human attitudes, Latinos—who also understand and function in this way, according to Romero—would be best served by reader-response criticism.

Finally, reader-response criticism involves both the reader and the text (bipolar entity) as well as active imagination. Such a method allows Latinos, in dialectical relationship with the text, to bring their *religiosidad popular* into dialogue with tradition. In short, Romero's short history of the history of Catholic biblical interpretation and his argument for the use of reader-response criticism alongside historical criticism suggest that his reading of the anti-monarchic tradition in 1 Samuel 8—15 and *religiosidad popular* is an embodiment of Vatican II's guidelines for addressing scriptures. Romero believes he is in keeping with his tradition.

Romero begins his conclusion by arguing that *religiosidad popular*, through its many devotions, best represents the bilateral and conditional characteristics of the Sinai covenant tradition and thus of the anti-monarchic tradition. It best represents the anti-monarchic tradition of leadership because there is no mediator to communicate with God, and there is conditionality—both features of *religiosidad popular*. In other words, practitioners are both obligated to carry out their devotion and to be responsible for their choices. Also, *religiosidad popular* best reflects the anti-monarchic tradition because both have tendencies toward democracy and toward liberation. What is more, *religiosidad popular* and the anti-monarchic tradition both invoke a sense of community. God made a covenant not with a dynasty but with a people. *Religiosidad popular*, therefore, can be used to challenge any abuses, whether in civil or ecclesiastical structures. *Religiosidad popular,* like the anti-monarchic tradition, is theologically and biblically affirmed.

In conclusion, Romero calls on all leaders who facilitate Latino (Roman Catholic) Bible study groups to be aware of how to use historical and reader-response criticism. He believes that to do so would be in line with the tradition of the church, for practitioners "would be tending toward a 'growth in insight' of the Bible so desired by Vatican II."[20] He concludes with a call to biblical scholars, theologians, and pastoral agents to continue to search for the characteristics of the anti-monarchic tradition in *religiosidad popular*.

Summary: This reading of 1 Samuel 8—15 in relationship to US Latino/a theology by Romero is simply a rereading of authorized biblical tradition that maintains Latinos/as as "other." I do not find the reading all that liberative. In other words, in his attempt to provide a liberative reading of a particular biblical tradition for Latinos/as who practice *religiosidad popular*, Romero reaches back to tradition (biblical and ecclesiastical) to authorize a construction that supports an essentialist identity of Latinos/as—an identity that is homogenous, patriarchal, and marginalized. He legitimates with tradition the notions that all Latinos/as are Catholic and practitioners of *religiosidad popular*. He uses a tradition (biblical and ecclesiastical) that is steeped in patriarchy without any consideration to the fact that the tradition itself regards women as second-class citizens. Furthermore, he plays right into the hands of the mainstream ecclesiastical tradition by portraying *religiosidad popular* as marginal, by trying to legitimate it within his church's traditional teachings. At the end, Romero prefers a reading consonant with his church's tradition. However, such a reading does not go far enough to change the perception of Latinos/as as "other."

J. Severino Croatto,
"Recovering the Goddess: Reflections on God-Talk"

Croatto, like Romero, employs primarily ideological criticism. He aims to deconstruct and then reconstruct the tradition concerning the sexuality of God as masculine. What Croatto aims to do is to unsettle this tradition (God as masculine) to make space for another (Goddess as feminine).

He is fully aware that the tradition of God as masculine is steeped in the rhetoric and discourses of the biblical tradition as well as in the Christian teachings, but he believes that to bring equality and justice to women a divine model of the Goddess is necessary. To do this, he makes several methodological moves in his essay. First, he argues that it is not possible to speak of God in a meta-sexual way. The divine is indeed gendered. Second, he argues for a recovering of the Goddess who is gendered just as God is gendered. Third, Croatto contends that one of the reasons for the disappearance of the Goddess is due to the monotheization of religion in ancient Israel. Fourth, he argues for new ways to recover the Goddess in the divine person. And fifth, Croatto makes a case for theologians to invoke the Goddess-Mother language. All in all, Croatto's thesis is that women have no divine models of God that they can reflect upon for self-understanding. This is the reason why the recovery of the Goddess is so pertinent.

As such, Croatto, unlike Romero, critically engages the biblical tradition. Croatto, like most social location readers, is after legitimating the identity not of himself but of women within the biblical tradition. He does so by recovering a divine model of the Goddess for them. However, like Romero, he does so by using the biblical tradition. Croatto argues that the femininity of the Divine was eliminated due to the patriarchal world view of the biblical tradition; at the same time that he is dismantling the authority of this biblical tradition, however, he is giving it more potency with a case for the Goddess as the divine being using the biblical tradition. Unfortunately, Croatto conforms to the status of the Goddess (and of women, for that matter) as "other." I will critically review his essay along five stages of development.

Meta-sexual God

Croatto begins his essay by challenging the position of some feminists that God can be spoken about in a meta-sexual way. But, he says, to speak of God in a meta-sexual way is to imply that God is not gendered. There is no question for Croatto that the biblical tradition portrays God as masculine, patriarchal, and kyriarchal—and thus God is masculine. However, such characterization leaves no room for the feminine, which for Croatto disallows an egalitarian image.

The way feminists have dealt with this characterization is to go beyond the sexuality of God (meta-sexual) in order to avoid attaching a gender to God, an approach that Croatto finds insufficient. God is indeed gendered. Croatto is not interested in denying God as masculine, but rather in denying that God is *only* masculine. For Croatto, the name of the Divine is both God and Goddess. It is not a question of either/or but rather both/and in naming the Divine. What is more, according to Croatto, God/Goddess is a person. One cannot speak about a gendered God/Goddess without speaking of the Divine as male and female. Even trying to transcend the gender of the divine person, and resorting to the neuter case in order to speak about the Divine, is unsatisfactory for Croatto. A person is not a neuter—one cannot speak of/to the Divine as if the Divine were neuter.

Croatto contends that in feminist theology there is an emphasis on placing a gender upon God, even if that gender is feminine, such as in emphasizing God as *hokmâ* (wisdom) and *rûah* (spirit). Yet, when this is done, he argues, the masculine identity of God remains. That is, the feminine identity is infused within God—who remains masculine. For Croatto, *hokmâ* (wisdom), *rûah* (spirit), and even Sophia should be the equivalent of the Goddess. However, to speak of God with feminine personifications does not make God feminine, according to Croatto.

Therefore, the recovery of the Goddess remains most pertinent for Croatto.

Recovery of the Goddess

Croatto begins the process of recovering the Goddess by contending that one way to establish the Goddess is to multiply "the feminine functions, representations, and names" attributed to her, such as Sophia/Wisdom.[21] This keeps the Goddess as an alternative to God.

Second, another path of exploration for rediscovering the Goddess is to emphasize the Divine as heterosexually integrated (Goddess beside God). What this means for Croatto is that divinities throughout history have typically been represented as having a consort, either a male complement or a female complement. Yahweh had a female consort by the name of Asherah, until the feminine counterpart was removed to conform to the patriarchal context of ancient Israel, thereby getting rid of the feminine counterpart. Croatto is not entirely happy with this second path, for it still tilts the balance of representation toward the masculine side of things. In fact, he argues that this is exactly what happened in the case of Yahweh and Asherah. Yahweh reflected the patriarchal context of ancient Israel and therefore remained as the representation of the Divine, while the Goddess vanished.

Monotheization

Croatto believes that the disappearance of the Goddess is due to the monotheization of religion in ancient Israel. This process took place along a sixfold path. First, the disappearance of the Goddess is due to the increasing attention given to the figure of Yahweh in ancient Israel. Yahweh alone is in control of the destiny of the people. Second, on Yahweh is bestowed the role of the one God above all other gods (for example, Dt 32). Third, even though Yahweh was identified with or linked to the Goddess Asherah, she was eradicated to emphasize Yahweh's singularity. Croatto supports this point with a reference to Josiah's reform and his rage against this Goddess (2 Kgs 23:6). There is evidence from Ugaritic texts to the effect that Yahweh-Asherah were replaced with El-Asherah (an older couple) when Yahweh was confirmed as the only God; there is also evidence from inscriptions found in southern Israel that mention several times "Yahweh and his Asherah."[22] Asherah, who is represented as a person, will eventually be removed in ancient Israel, if not in words surely in thought.

Fourth, during Josiah's reform (seventh century BCE), a suppression of other gods and goddesses took place as a way to purify the cult of Yahweh. Fifth, by the time of the final redaction of the biblical texts, God was monotheized, masculinized, and functioned in a patriarchal and kyriarchal fashion. Even grammatically the name of God, Elohim, which is plural, became singular and masculine as well. Finally, in the history of ancient Israel, there existed a process of masculinization of the divinity that aimed to erase any trace of a feminine divine being. As such, the suppression of the Goddess is based on conformity to patriarchy's emphasis of having one God who is masculine.

The Divine as Goddess

Croatto is fully aware that recovery of the Goddess is a difficult process and that it is very easy to fall back on attributing feminine words to God to affirm the femininity of God, or to resort to Deuteronomy 4:15–20 and the Decalogue (Ex 20:4 and Dt 5:8), where an absolute monotheism is mistakenly promoted as fixed.

But Croatto points to other ways to recover the Goddess.[23] One possible way, according to him, is to shift attention away from God's phallus. In other words, to focus on God as primarily the creative force, which is the common way of looking at God, takes away from talking about other gendered representations of God as man. For Croatto, the phallus is not the essence of a man. Second, this centering of attention on the phallus of God erases God's "feminine counterpart in our conception of the divinity."[24] As such, another way to rediscover the Goddess is to conceptualize the Goddess as taking part in the creative act. The problem here, for Croatto, is not that God is masculine, but rather that the Goddess is invisible in our way of thinking about the Divine. Croatto believes that favoring the masculinity over the femininity of the Divine leads to entrenching patriarchy and kyriarchy in Christian discourse. Finally, another possible way to rediscover the Goddess is to provide rereadings of the Bible with greater attention from the perspective of gender. This will lead both women and men to produce readings that promote an egalitarianism that will eventually contribute to approaching the Divine as Goddess.

Feminine Divine Model

Croatto hopes that these discernible ways of rediscovering the Goddess, using the biblical tradition, will lead to a feminine divine model—

so that women will have a referent to communicate with the Divine. Some have tried to use Mary as a model, but Croatto finds this attempt lacking. Mary of Nazareth cannot function as a divine model because she is not a goddess; neither can "Mary serve as a foundational figure," for example, in confirming a healing practice.[25] Croatto suggests four actions to try to create a feminine divine model.

All four actions argue for the bisexuality of the Divine. First, Croatto argues that the practice of attributing feminine traits to a masculine God only supports "the 'masculine unicity' of God."[26] This practice promotes the idea that God is ultimately father but not mother. To establish a feminine divine model, the Divine must appear as the one divine being that is both God (father) and Goddess (mother). Second, Croatto argues that, rather than using the "God-mother" language to name the divinity as Goddess, the "Goddess-mother" language allows naming and representing the divinity as God as well as Goddess—instead of collapsing the feminine within the masculine as in the "God-mother" language. Croatto, in other words, is arguing for the bisexuality of God-Goddess. That is, God and Goddess are not separate beings; they are "complementary . . . and are hypostatized in the man and the woman, who complement each other at that very moment when they become 'one flesh' through love."[27] Third, to establish a feminine divine model, Croatto argues that the unification of the masculine and the feminine of God must not be based on an essentialized identity of the Divine as masculine. Such practices will lead to negative effects, such as constructing an unreal image of God; creating a divine model for men only; reaffirming the divine's masculine character in function, representation, and name; excluding women both symbolically and in fact from the bosom of the divinity; and possibly falling back on a notion of eternity as the masculine in history and in "our 'monotheistic religions.'"[28] Finally and fourth, Croatto finds Elisabeth Schüssler Fiorenza's ideogram $G*d$ a bit troublesome, for it does not allow one who wishes to pray to speak to the Divine. Croatto does, however, see some merit with this ideogram if it allows the reader to speak of the Divine as God and Goddess. This latter line of thinking would allow the Goddess to exist.

In conclusion, Croatto leaves the readers with three suggestions with regard to the "ideal in our speaking about God and to God."[29] First, a feminine divine model would be ideal in order to allow women to have a divine archetype in order to do thealogy. Monotheism should be thought of as bisexual rather than unisexual. Second, the recovery of the Goddess in tradition would be ideal as well. The Goddess that corresponds to a divine model would allow patriarchy and kyriarchy and their practices to be unsettled so that they do no reify symbols and practices based on a masculine God. Third, another ideal in speaking about the Divine is to think in terms of a utopia. In other words, Croatto calls upon his readers to imagine a utopia of egalitarianism in order to encourage them to change "stagnant traditions."[30]

Summary: Croatto provides a very strong argument for understanding the Divine as God and Goddess. Unlike Romero, Croatto challenges the biblical tradition as patriarchal and kyriarchal. He understands this patriarchal tradition as intentionally setting out to eliminate the feminine divine being. Attempts in the past by feminists to rediscover the feminine either by way of a meta-sexual argument or by searching for feminine personifications of the Divine does not construct God as feminine; they only highlight the masculinity of God. Therefore, only a model of the divine being as Goddess *and* God is able to break through the patriarchal world view within the biblical tradition, as well as within the Christian tradition, to provide women a means to relate to the divine being.

It is quite courageous for Croatto to take up this very complex and divisive issue, namely, that the divine is Goddess *and* God. His identity hermeneutics is creative and challenging—the way I argue that hermeneutics needs to continue moving forward in these globalized and postcolonial contexts.

However, Croatto chooses not to engage the basic assumption of the biblical tradition, which he uses to construct his argument for a feminine divine model. He has merit in arguing that women have no divine model of the feminine in the biblical tradition, but why argue for a divine feminine model using the very biblical tradition that eliminated this model, especially when this biblical tradition is still viewed by Croatto as authoritative? Such a hermeneutical move conforms the status of women as authoritatively marginal.

To convince women universally that Christianity is respectful to both women and men, I believe, some of the basic assumptions about the biblical tradition need to be engaged. Again, I am not contending to eradicate the biblical tradition but to challenge the assumption of the authoritativeness of that tradition. If continually overlooked, I am afraid that with the increasing turn toward the biblical tradition to legitimate and authenticate one's identity (by fundamentalists or by readers espousing social location hermeneutics) more potency will be given to the biblical tradition and thus used once again, if not already, in dogmatist and colonialist ways. I do not believe minority groups will benefit from such a turn.

Elsa Tamez,
"1 Timothy: What a Problem!"

Tamez provides an ideological reading of 1 Timothy. However, unlike Romero and Croatto, she is a bit more conscious of the hermeneutical moves to "dress up" the biblical tradition in order to identify and to authenticate the "other"—moves more similar to Romero's than to Croatto's.

Tamez, similar to Croatto, chooses a reading strategy that sensitizes the reader to the "other," but a strategy that does not aim to unsettle or to de-emphasize the biblical tradition. This hermeneutics will turn to other authoritative texts as well as to the Jesus movement to argue for the importance of an egalitarian *ekklesia*.

In her essay Tamez provides a rereading of 1 Timothy from the perspective of Latin America, and more particularly, from the social location of the excluded: the poor and women. 1 Timothy is well known in the biblical tradition for its harsh discourse against women participating in the household of God in the late first century of early Christianity. However, in this particular essay Tamez is not interested in, as she says, "dressing up" 1 Timothy for liberating purposes.[31] Rather, she is interested in engaging critically the text of 1 Timothy and its subjugating discourse toward women and the oppressed, as well as the "attitude of ecclesiastical and verticalist authoritarianism" found throughout the text.[32] In this way Tamez's hermeneutics is quite different from Romero's and closer to Croatto's. Fully aware that it is very easy to discard as not normative 1 Timothy and its imposition of a patriarchal household on the household of God, Tamez strongly believes that it is important to take on 1 Timothy, especially since it is considered inspired. Texts like 1 Timothy are used by hierarchical and patriarchal churches in a normative fashion to exclude women and the oppressed. If Latin American women wish to use these sacred texts to challenge injustices in their societies, it is important that they also challenge patriarchal discourses. Tamez will take on this challenge.

Tamez achieves two objectives in this essay. First, she delineates the four major concerns preoccupying 1 Timothy, and then she shows how the letter's author responds to these concerns. Tamez's overall argument is that the author of 1 Timothy consistently begins to provide a response in line with the tradition of the Jesus movement but falls short by espousing a discourse of patriarchy upon the household of God. This thesis is founded on Tamez's vocational and theological commitment to the marginalized in Latin America, particularly Central American communities of poor women.[33] All popular readings of the Bible, for Tamez, must connect to a concrete history in the present.

Similarly, Tamez has four historical and fundamental concerns in 1 Timothy that she aims to explore further. The first involves a conflict between different theological interests in 1 Timothy. The second engages the wealthy in the *ekklesia*. The third involves women in the *ekklesia*, and the fourth addresses the public opinion of outsiders. In fact, all of the concerns deal one way or another with controlling the behavior of the members of the *ekklesia*.

After a brief justification for each fundamental concern, Tamez proceeds to the first historical tension in 1 Timothy, namely, the divergent or alien ideas/theologies entering the community of 1 Timothy. However, Tamez is not interested in trying to classify these alien ideas, especially since they are very difficult to classify; she is instead interested in how the author of 1 Timothy responds to these alien ideas.

As expected, the author of 1 Timothy responds quite negatively to new, alien ideas. The author is concerned that these new ideas that have seeped into the Christian community are too abstract and do not pertain to any concrete history or good works.[34] Thus, the author is troubled that the community of believers is being led astray from its inherited tradition (Jesus movement). In other words, the author of 1 Timothy responds by arguing that abstract or a-historical theology is meaningless without good stewardship (1:4). What the community of believers needs to concern itself with is good works *(erga agatha)*.[35] For instance, the wealthy women should not be concerned with decorating themselves with fine accessories but with dressing themselves up with good works. Poor widows should not be worried about adorning themselves with the financial support given to them by the *ekklesia* but with "caring for their children, giving hospitality, washing the feet of the saints, and helping the oppressed (5:10)."[36] The repeated emphasis on good works, according to Tamez, is to remind the community of believers of the redemptive work of Christ; God is revealed through the works of real flesh (3:16a) rather than any abstract ideas that remove the importance of the real.

Tamez actually agrees with the author of 1 Timothy in that she also has an aversion to a theology that does not take reality seriously. However, drawing upon her emphasis on praxis, Tamez is troubled that the author of 1 Timothy did not ask *why* the women of the community were attracted to these new alien ideas. More specifically, Tamez strongly objects to the author's correspondence of women's good works with keeping the household. In other words, "for the author, therefore, good works include not only hospitality and help for the oppressed but also

the proper training of children and obedience in the patriarchal household."[37] Tamez is quite troubled with the patriarchal correlation between
good works and the behavior of women in the assembly. She is challenging the author's patriarchal vision of *ekklesia*, which is founded on a
community of hierarchy in which "women do not teach and remain silent; slaves obey; good men manage their houses well and do not raise
rebellious children."[38] What Tamez would like to have seen instead of
this hierarchical community is a community where everyone is equal, a
community that is consonant with the gospel of Jesus rather than with
patriarchy. Tamez, very early in her essay, is making an argument for
another tradition more powerful than 1 Timothy. This other tradition is
the gospel.

The second concern within the community of 1 Timothy that Tamez
engages is the wealthy in the *ekklesia*. According to Tamez, there existed
a strong presence of rich members in the *ekklesia* and other members
who would have liked to become rich, possibly to buy influence or obtain positions of leadership in the *ekklesia*. This strong desire to become
rich was a great concern for the author of 1 Timothy. These members
(men only according to Tamez) were placing their trust in wealth rather
than following the gospel. According to Tamez, the rhetoric directed
toward the established wealthy is not as harsh as the rhetoric toward
those who are seeking to be wealthy. Nonetheless, the author attacks
those seeking to be wealthy for seeking the new teachings that outsiders
are bringing into the *ekklesia*. What we have here, according to Tamez,
is 1 Timothy's author trying to control the behavior of the wealthy and
of those seeking wealth within the *ekklesia*. The author's response, similar to his response to those members attracted to the new abstract theology mentioned above, is one of hierarchical authoritarianism.

Tamez, and many other Latin American theologians, are very familiar
with this oppressive economic form of control in Latin America. Such a
desire for wealth leads to unjust economic structures throughout the
Latin American continent. Tamez challenges the response of the author
of 1 Timothy in light of this economic experience. How so? The author's
response aims to control the behavior of the wealthy, which includes
both women and men. This desire to control behavior is the very same
tool of oppression that the wealthy tried to use upon the *ekklesia*. This
regulating of behavior is "the same as that of the *paterfamilias* of a rich
family," in which the father controls the behavior of the women, children, and slaves through the ideology of patriarchy.[39] Rather than responding to the wealthy with an option for the excluded (for example,
poor widows), the author of 1 Timothy aims to control their behavior
with exclusion from the community. A patriarchal household of God is

preferred over an egalitarian household of God, in which, for example, women's ministerial gifts could be utilized to benefit the community rather than remaining in the private sphere of the home.

The third fundamental historical concern is the participation of women in the *ekklesia*. Tamez works with the assumption that women did indeed play an active role in the administration and ministry of early Christianity, and this is why there are very strong prescriptions against women teaching, baptizing, and preaching in the *ekklesia* throughout the Pastoral Letters. What is more, debates among the opponents of the Gnostics and the Montanists, as well as the debates in apocryphal books such as *The Acts of Paul and Thecla*, also affirm women's involvement in the public sphere in the first century.

It is the wealthy women, although not exclusively those women, that the author is addressing in terms of submitting to patriarchy in the assembly (2:11–12). Tamez notes that the author attacks young widows (5:13) as well as slaves indirectly (6:2) for not abiding by the rules of the patriarchal household. Tamez believes that the author of 1 Timothy, who himself is not wealthy, is opposed to the wealthy women who have influence and power in the *ekklesia*. The author aims to control their behavior by ordering them to be silent (2:11–12), as well as by commanding the men to rule over the women (2:12). These oppressive commands are based on a patriarchal understanding of the household, informed by a misogynistic attitude. Women are to remove themselves from positions of leadership and adapt themselves to the patriarchal system. The author of 1 Timothy continues to support this unjust perspective by making an analogy between the women (in 1 Timothy's community) and Eve—both are responsible for the first transgression against God and, as a result, must bear children for the sake of their salvation. Tamez believes that this response by the author is another example of the author's using the weapon of the oppressor against wealthy women. In fact, this tool of oppression (i.e., controlling behavior) affects poor women much more. The preferential option for the excluded, particularly the poor, is overlooked by the author of 1 Timothy as a viable response to the wealthy women. Tamez strongly believes in the correlation between patriarchal theology and patriarchal practices. For Tamez, this must be challenged by the marginalized in order to bring forth a community consonant with the egalitarian Jesus movement.

The final concern that Tamez discusses within the community of 1 Timothy is the opinion of "those outside" the community (for example, 2:2; 3:7; 4:10) "with regard to the testimony of leaders and slaves."[40] As a way to respond to the Greco-Roman antagonism of the day, 1 Timothy represents a discourse, characterized by some as "love patriarchialism," that is quite sympathetic to the opinion of those outside the community in order to establish good relations with those unbelieving leaders or rulers in the greater society. This strategy might also possibly serve to evangelize or convert unbelievers to Christianity. In other words, the author of 1 Timothy's response to the public opinion of "those outside" the community is to avoid conflict with them and hopefully to also save them. In other words, "the author asks all members, men and women, to pray for all human beings as well as kings *(basileon)* and rulers *(hyperoche)* (2:2)."[41] For Tamez, this response by the author of 1 Timothy allows the public opinion of "those outside" to influence the Christian community, in order to adopt a stance of non-resistance to the greater society's pressure to conform to the values and beliefs of the pagan world. The voice of the (Christian) minority is subsumed under the voice of the majority Greco-Roman world.

This tendency to submit the community to the public opinion of "those outside" is also witnessed among many churches in Latin America, according to Tamez. For instance, when many governments try to promote unjust political and economic policies with the help of minority evangelical churches, and these policies are opposed by the majority Catholic church in Latin America, evangelical churches too easily sell out the gospel of Jesus in order to feel important and significant by siding with the government against the Catholic church. For Tamez, "fidelity to the gospel of justice and social equality comes first," even in the face of possible oppression by the majority public.[42] As such, Tamez does not find 1 Timothy to be a good example of resistance for Latin Americans. She concludes that better examples for the *ekklesia* can be found in Mark and John, where a community of equals is promoted rather than the community of unequals of 1 Timothy.

Summary: Tamez is arguing that 1 Timothy does not possess the best strategy to challenge oppression, particularly patriarchal and economic, within the biblical tradition. Texts such as 1 Timothy, which aim to control the behavior of the members with patriarchal discourse, are very dangerous and must be contested within the tradition. She takes on 1 Timothy not because it is a liberating archetype to follow, but rather because too many Latin American women are reading texts like 1 Timothy and thinking that this is the way Christian women ought to behave, namely, in a submissive fashion. For Tamez, the issue is not what alien ideas and public opinion were entering the community—or the wealthy members of the community. Rather, the issue is how 1 Timothy responded to difference. And it consistently reflected a patriarchal, controlling discourse that was consistently directed primarily to women, the poor, and the slaves.

Tamez's reading of the biblical tradition, I believe, is the one that challenges the authority of the biblical tradition the most. She does not conform to the status of women as "other." She has unsettled and made 1 Timothy less important. She, like me, is not arguing to do away with 1 Timothy; rather, texts like 1 Timothy must find their authority anew, perhaps reading them along other texts such as Mark and John, which she turns to in order to challenge patriarchal texts elsewhere within the biblical tradition. She even turns to *The Acts of Paul and Thecla* to "de-authorize" 1 Timothy. Living in such a globalized world, I believe more of this type of reading is necessary, that is, reading the biblical tradition alongside other religious texts (howsoever defined) throughout the globe. Again, I argue this point not to discard the sacred texts of the Christian religion but rather to lessen their importance and dilute the potency of the biblical tradition to control our behavior, as has been done traditionally by dogmatist and colonial interests.

CONCLUDING COMMENTS

What I am proposing in this essay is a reading strategy that does not keep minority communities marginalized after a "liberative" reading of a biblical tradition, a reading strategy that critically engages any construction that aims to essentialize identity or identities as "other." Such a reading strategy must begin thinking and developing alternative stances toward the biblical tradition, that is, alternative stances that aim to de-center and de-authorize the biblical tradition.

I would like to propose three such alternative stances toward the biblical tradition that emanate from the reading experience above.

Reading Strategy

The three articles we have been discussing in one way or another are engaged in a reading strategy that engages ideological criticism. They have not given up on historical criticism, as all of them (in a general way) demonstrated through their interest in the *sitz im leben* of their respective biblical tradition of study. However, they are specifically concerned with reading the texts in light of a particular community (for example, Latinos/as and Latin American women).

This type of reading strategy, I believe, needs further exploration. In other words, we need to ask how one's reading strategy of the biblical tradition, or of any tradition, for that matter, contributes to the authorization or de-authorization of that tradition. Luke Timothy Johnson correctly observes that the statement by the Pontifical Biblical Commission, "The Interpretation of the Bible in the Church," emphasizes the historical-critical approach over all other modern and postmodern approaches.[43] In so doing, I believe that the commission's statement strongly undergirds the biblical tradition by subscribing to those principles of historical criticism that support objectivity, positivism, and universality.

Mary Ann Tolbert argues that the way we read the biblical tradition, particularly along the lines of a "hermeneutics of stringing along," also contributes to how much authority is given to the biblical tradition.[44]

My point here is that one possible way to unsettle or to de-emphasize the biblical tradition is to be quite conscious of one's reading strategy and the principles and assumptions that accompany this reading strategy. These principles and assumptions must be examined closely so as not to confer more authority on the biblical tradition. Furthermore, to provide a more self-reflective analysis of one's reading strategy vis-à-vis tradition (particularly for those affiliated with a minority group) one should avoid readings that establish one's status authoritatively as an "other" (in the articles we have discussed, more so Romero than Croatto and Tamez). Instead, one should work to empower the "other" within the community (for example, more Tamez and less so Croatto) to discern how the discourse of the powerful works within the biblical tradition.[45]

Reading with Others

In the introduction to the present chapter I tried to show that social location hermeneutics has become stagnant and fixed over the years. Many of these readings focus on the identity of the reader alone and occasionally on the community being written for or about. Such a strategy also tends to place more attention on the biblical tradition in order to legitimate and authenticate the identity of the reader or the community.

I am concerned that such a strategy is now too narrow, given our globalized world. For instance, whereas Romero and Tamez were writing for their own particular, specific communities (Latinos/as, Latin American women, and women in general), Croatto's reading on the sexuality of the Divine was engaged in a larger community's struggle and experiences, namely, the community of women across the world. I believe that a "reading with others" strategy is what is needed in order to de-emphasize and unsettle the authority of the biblical tradition. In other words, in order to avoid committing hermeneutical apartheid by focusing on one community alone, and thus constructing a new "magisterium of authority" of Latinos/as, the poor, or women (to name but a few), it is important that our own histories and experiences are read along with those of *other* marginalized communities.[46]

Some of this is already occurring in the field of theological studies, and I would call for expanding such inclusion to other communities, including non-Christian communities.[47] Reading *with* others does not mean reading *for* them. I am not calling for an authoritative type of reading or for a hierarchical one; rather, I am calling for a reading that reads along with other traditions and/or texts.

Croatto's reading best exemplifies what I am proposing here. His reading with women, in my opinion, was not an attempt to privilege one group over the other. Croatto was not arguing to eradicate the masculine divine model, but rather to make space for the feminine divine model. His reading, thus, is a reading against hierarchalism. Furthermore, Croatto's reading was fully aware that the biblical tradition is an ideological, political, and theological text, and that meaning—a product between the ideological texts and readers—does change over time. Hence, his reading is also against empiricism and objectivism. This strategy, I believe, will unsettle the authority of the biblical tradition and make the biblical tradition more broadly relevant with other traditions.

Other Texts

To pay less attention to the authority of the biblical tradition, its texts need to be read along with non-canonical (Jewish or Christian) written traditions, as well as with other sacred and/or secular traditions. The three articles we have been discussing point this out somewhat, particularly Tamez's essay. Tamez, in a very brief way, began to argue for the participation of women in the *ekklesia* using a non-canonical text, *The Acts of Paul and Thecla*.

Because non-canonical texts do not paint a similar picture of the Jesus movement, but a diverse one, does not suggest that they are not worthy of critical investigation. Such belief is based on a theory of sameness rather than of difference. Non-canonical texts provide a picture of a wider spectrum of Christianity and encourage the valuing of difference (politics of identity) as well as providing an opportunity for critical analysis.

Globalization in many respects is trying to harmonize difference throughout the world. Therefore, reading different types of texts alongside the biblical tradition supports opportunities for equality and justice, both for those unrepresented in the biblical tradition and for minority groups in today's world.

The best examples of reading the biblical tradition with other texts come from postcolonial biblical scholars. Musa Dube and R. S. Sugitharajah have been reading the biblical tradition alongside the narratives of their own cultures.[48] The effect of such readings is that they weaken the potency of the authority behind the biblical tradition, thus allowing a discourse that calls for equality and justice.

Those of us working with the texts of the biblical tradition should also consider reading along the lines of intertextuality.[49] The point here is that reducing the authority of the biblical tradition will benefit minority readers who otherwise identify themselves as "other." The strategies I propose challenge this "otherness" and our own neocolonialist perspectives of ourselves as "other." Not to do so plays into the hands of those who sell our literature as "other," as we have seen done with liberation theology.[50]

It is time for under-represented readers to challenge the traditional way of understanding the authority of the biblical tradition. In other words, I am not calling for an expansion of the tradition, but rather for an overturning of the tradition by allowing a new, more inclusive line of tradition. And as we will in time find weaknesses in these new traditions, I call for others further to supplant them. Otherwise, the Bible will enslave us and not liberate us.

Notes

[1] For a discussion on tradition, see Terrence W. Tilley, *Inventing Catholic Tradition* (Maryknoll, NY: Orbis Books, 2000); John E. Thiel, *Senses of Tradition: Continuity and Development in Catholic Faith* (Oxford: Oxford Univ. Press, 2000); Sandra M. Schneiders, *The Revelatory Text: Interpreting the New Testament as Sacred Scripture* (San Francisco: HarperSanFrancisco, 1991); idem, "The Bible and Feminism: Biblical Theology," in *Freeing Theology: The Essentials of Theology in Feminist Perspective*, ed. Catherine LaCugna (San Francisco: HarperSanFrancisco, 1993); Pontifical Biblical Commission, "The Interpretation of the Bible in the Church," *Origins* 23, no. 29 (1994): 498–524; John B. Thompson, "Tradition and Self in a Mediated World," in *Detraditionalization: Critical Reflections on Authority and Identity*, ed. Paul Heelas, Scott Lash, and Paul Morris, 89–108 (Cambridge, MA: Blackwell Publishers, 1996); Orlando O. Espín, "Toward the Construction of an Intercultural Theology of Tradition," *Journal of Hispanic/Latino Theology* 9, no. 3 (2002): 22–59. For a discussion on the history of biblical interpretations, see Steven L. McKenzie and Stephen R. Haynes, eds., *To Each Its Own Meaning: An Introduction to Biblical Criticisms and Their Application*, rev. and exp. ed. (Louisville, KY: Westminster John Knox Press, 1999); R. M. Grant and David Tracy, *A Short History of the Interpretation of the Bible*, 2nd ed. (Minneapolis: Fortress

Press, 1984); Gerald O. West, "Mapping African Biblical Interpretation," in *The Bible in Africa: Transactions, Trajectories and Trends*, ed. Gerald O. West and Musa W. Dube, 29–53 (Leiden: E. J. Brill, 2000); Fernando F. Segovia, "Hispanic American Theology and the Bible: Effective Weapon and Faithful Ally," in *We Are a People: Initiatives in Hispanic American Theology*, ed. Roberto S. Goizueta, 21–50 (Minneapolis: Fortress Press, 1992); Jean-Pierre Ruiz, "Beginning to Read the Bible in Spanish: An Initial Assessment," *Journal of Hispanic/Latino Theology* 1, no. 2 (1994): 28–50.

[2] For an excellent discussion on Latin American liberation biblical hermeneutics, see Fernando F. Segovia, "Liberation Hermeneutics: Revisiting the Foundations in Latin America," in *Toward a New Heaven and a New Earth: Essays in Honor of Elisabeth Schüssler Fiorenza*, ed. Fernando F. Segovia, 106–32 (Maryknoll, NY: Orbis Books, 2003).

[3] Studies informed by social location hermeneutics since the 1980s would include, for example, *Reading from This Place: Social Location and Biblical Interpretation in the United States*, ed. Fernando F. Segovia and Mary Ann Tolbert (Minneapolis: Fortress Press, 1995), and *Reading from This Place: Social Location and Biblical Interpretation in Global Perspective*, ed. Fernando F. Segovia and Mary Ann Tolbert (Minneapolis: Fortress Press, 1995). For one of the more recent collections of essays typifying social location hermeneutics, see Elisabeth Schüssler Fiorenza, *Bread Not Stone: The Challenges of Feminist Biblical Interpretation* (Boston: Beacon Press, 1984); Itumeleng J. Mosala, *Biblical Hermeneutics and Black Theology in South Africa* (Grand Rapids, MI: Eerdmans, 1989); R. S. Sugirtharajah, *Voices from the Margin: Interpreting the Bible in the Third World* (Maryknoll, NY: Orbis Books, 1991); Cain Hope Felder, ed., *Stony the Road We Trod: African American Biblical Interpretation* (Minneapolis: Fortress Press, 1991); Leif E. Vaage, ed., *Subversive Scriptures: Revolutionary Readings of the Christian Bible in Latin America* (Valley Forge, PA: Trinity Press International, 1997); R. S. Sugirtharajah, ed., *Vernacular Hermeneutics* (Sheffield, England: Sheffield Academic Press, 1999).

[4] For an excellent discussion on the topic of representation, see Stuart Hall, ed., *Representation: Cultural Representations and Signifying Practices* (London: Sage Publications, 1997).

[5] I follow here the thesis of R. S. Sugirtharajah, presented in "The End of Biblical Studies," in Segovia, *Toward a New Heaven and New Earth*, 133–40.

[6] A number of scholars in recent years, especially Mary Ann Tolbert, have pointed to the implications of the authority of the Bible. See Mary Ann Tolbert, "A New Teaching with Authority: A Re-evaluation of the Authority of the Bible," in *Teaching the Bible: The Discourses and Politics of Biblical Pedagogy*, ed. Fernando F. Segovia and Mary Ann Tolbert, 168–89 (Maryknoll, NY: Orbis Books, 1998). For other studies that examine the question of the authority of the Bible, see, for example, James Barr, *The Scope and Authority of the Bible* (Philadelphia: Westminster Press, 1980); idem, *Holy Scripture: Canon, Authority, Criticism* (Oxford: Clarendon Press, 1983); L. William Countryman, *Biblical Authority or Biblical Tyranny? Scripture and the Christian Pilgrimage*

(Philadelphia: Fortress Press, 1981); Donald K. McKim, ed., *The Authoritative Word: Essays on the Nature of Scripture* (Grand Rapids, MI: Eerdmans, 1983); and Schneiders, *The Revelatory Text.*

[7] From the perspective of US Latinos/as, see, for example, Virgilio Elizondo, *Galilean Journey: The Mexican-American Promise* (Maryknoll, NY: Orbis Books, 1983); and David Cortés-Fuentes, "Not Like the Gentiles: The Characterization of Gentiles in the Gospel of Matthew," *Journal of Hispanic/Latino Theology* 9, no. 1 (2001): 6–26. From the perspective of Latin Americans, see Pablo Richard, *Apocalypse: A People's Commentary on the Book of Revelation* (Maryknoll, NY: Orbis Books, 1995); and J. Severino Croatto, "The Function of the Non-Fulfilled Promises: Reading the Pentateuch from the Perspective of the Latin-American Oppressed People," in *The Personal Voice in Biblical Interpretation*, ed. Ingrid Kitzberger, 38–52 (London: Routledge, 1999). And from the perspective of feminists, see Elisabeth Schüssler Fiorenza, *In Memory of Her: A Feminist Theological Reconstruction of Christian Origins* (New York: Crossroad, 1983); and Musa W. Dube, ed., *Other Ways of Reading: African Women and the Bible* (Atlanta: Society of Biblical Literature, 2001).

[8] Within my own tradition of Roman Catholic biblical scholarship, this trend to homogenize identity against the diversity within Catholicism can be found in Luke Timothy Johnson and William S. Kurz, *The Future of Catholic Biblical Scholarship: A Constructive Conversation* (Grand Rapids, MI: Eerdmans, 2002); see also Peter S. Williamson, "Catholic Principles for Interpreting Scripture," *Catholic Biblical Quarterly* 65, no. 3 (2003): 327–49.

[9] C. Gilbert Romero, "Biblical Anti-Monarchic Tradition and a U.S. Latino Theology," *Journal of Hispanic/Latino Theology* 9, no. 4 (2002): 52–69; J. Severino Croatto, "Recovering the Goddess: Reflections on God-Talk," in Segovia, *Toward a New Heaven and a New Earth*, 33–53; and Elsa Tamez, "1 Timothy: What a Problem!" in Segovia, *Toward a New Heaven and a New Earth*, 141–56.

[10] I did not want to select readings that were written by Catholics only or Protestants alone. To do so would contribute to the hermeneutical apartheid against which I am trying to argue here.

[11] The term *religiosidad popular* is not necessarily the same as "popular Catholicism." Unfortunately, Romero tends to elide the two in his article. For a clear and excellent discussion on the differences and similarities between the two terms, see Orlando O. Espín, *The Faith of the People: Theological Reflections on Popular Catholicism* (Maryknoll, NY: Orbis Books, 1997).

[12] See C. Gilbert Romero, *Hispanic Devotional Piety: Tracing Biblical Roots* (Maryknoll, NY: Orbis Books, 1991).

[13] I presume he means here Latino/a Catholics. I will keep Romero's use of "Latinos" throughout this critical review and then switch to "Latinos/as" when I am making reference to the community.

[14] Romero, "Biblical Anti-Monarchic Tradition and a U.S. Latino Theology," 53.

[15] Ibid., 64.

[16] There is no mention of Jesus in this text. Romero's theological position that the Old Testament paves the way for the New Testament is hereby revealed. Romero is not opposed to David. He is arguing that the spirit of Yahweh is opposed to the style of governance, not to David.

[17] Ibid., 60.

[18] Ibid., 63.

[19] See note 8 above.

[20] Romero, "Biblical Anti-Monarchic Tradition and a U.S. Latino Theology," 69.

[21] Croatto, "Recovering the Goddess," 39.

[22] Ibid., 40.

[23] Croatto actually argues that that these texts have nothing to do with biblical aniconism, but rather with the emphasis on excluding other Gods. It is very difficult to present rereadings of these texts because the tradition of aniconism associated with them is "too steeped in the exegetical and theological tradition to accept different readings of the texts" (ibid., 43).

[24] Ibid., 44.

[25] Ibid., 45.

[26] Ibid.

[27] Ibid.

[28] Ibid., 47.

[29] Ibid.

[30] Ibid., 48.

[31] Tamez, "1 Timothy," 142.

[32] Ibid., 141.

[33] Ibid., 142.

[34] Tamez thinks these ideas pertain to Gnosticism (ibid., 145).

[35] Ibid.

[36] Ibid.

[37] Ibid., 146.

[38] Ibid.

[39] Ibid., 149.

[40] Ibid., 152.

[41] Ibid.

[42] Ibid., 153.

[43] Luke Timothy Johnson, "What's Catholic about Catholic Biblical Scholarship? An Opening Statement," in Johnson and Kurz, *The Future of Catholic Biblical Scholarship*, 3–34. See also Pontifical Biblical Commission, "The Interpretation of the Bible in the Church."

[44] See Tolbert, "A New Teaching with Authority."

[45] For a very clear discussion on the question of power and authority vis-à-vis the church, see Chapter 2 in this volume.

[46] Sugirtharajah, "The End of Biblical Studies."

[47] See Eleazar S. Fernández and Fernando F. Segovia, eds., *A Dream Unfinished: Theological Reflections on America from the Margins* (Maryknoll, NY:

Orbis Books, 2001); and Anthony B. Pinn and Benjamín Valentín, eds., *The Ties that Bind: African American and Hispanic American/Latino/a Theology in Dialogue* (New York: Continuum, 2001).

[48] See, for example, R. S. Sugirtharajah, ed., *The Postcolonial Bible* (Sheffield, England: Sheffield Academic Press, 1998); and idem, *Asian Hermeneutics and Postcolonialism: Contesting the Interpretations* (Maryknoll, NY: Orbis Books, 1998). See also, Musa Dube, "*Batswakwa*: Which Traveller Are You (John 1:1–18)?" in West and Dube, *The Bible in Africa*, 150–62; and idem, "To Pray the Lord's Prayer in the Global Economica Era," in West and Dube, *The Bible in Africa*, 611–30.

[49] See, for example, Jean-Pierre Ruiz, "Reading across Canons: U.S. Hispanic Reflections on Globalization and the Senses of Scripture," *Journal of Hispanic/Latino Theology* 10, no. 4 (2003): 22–44; and also his essay (Chapter 4) in the present volume." See also Vítor Westhelle and Hanna Betina Götz, "In Quest of a Myth: Latin American Literature and Theology," *Journal of Hispanic/Latino Theology* 3, no. 1 (1995): 5–22; Shane Martin and Ernesto Colín, "The Novels of Graciela Limón: Narrative, Theology and the Search for Mestiza/o Identity," *Journal of Hispanic/Latino Theology* 7, no. 1 (1999): 6–26; and Elena Olazagasti-Segovia, "Judith Ortiz Cofers's *Silent Dancing*: The Self-Portrait of the Artist as a Young, Bicultural Girl," in *Hispanic/Latino Theology: Challenge and Promise*, ed. Ada M. Isasi-Díaz and Fernando F. Segovia, 45–62 (Minneapolis: Fortress Press, 1996).

[50] Marcella María Althaus-Reid, "Gustavo Gutiérrez Goes to Disneyland: Theme Park Theologies and the Diaspora of the Discourse of the Popular Theologian in Liberation Theology," in *Interpreting beyond Border*, ed. Fernando F. Segovia, 36–58 (Sheffield, England: Sheffield Academic Press, 2000).

6

Tradition as Conversation

Gary Riebe-Estrella

INTRODUCTION

Each of the essays of this volume is predicated on an understanding of tradition as first and foremost the act of handing on or of traditioning. This does not imply a denial that there is something that is handed on, some content, in what we call the tradition. However, emphasizing the "handing on" precisely discloses that the *process* of traditioning is a constitutive element of the tradition itself.

By saying that the process of traditioning is constitutive of tradition I mean that there is a mutual interaction between what is handed on and the handing on, in such a way that each influences the other. What we are dealing with in tradition is not the image of something being passed by hand from one generation to the next, wherein the *thing* remains unchanged as it passes from one set of hands to another, rather like a box being handed from a postal clerk to the person whose name appears on the address label. The handing on is not external to the content. In fact, I suggest that the very reification of tradition as consisting of some *thing* that is handed on is based on an inappropriate metaphor or at least on one that obscures the interrelationship of content and process and, therefore, of the nature of tradition itself.

In this essay I explore the use of a different metaphor for tradition, one fairly common in practical theology today, that of conversation.[1] Using principally the work of Bernard Lonergan and of James and Evelyn Whitehead, I describe the elements and interaction in the conversation and apply them to the question of tradition.

At the same time, I take a closer look at how the dynamics of this conversation might be intentionally attended to in the act of handing on the tradition, particularly in educational contexts. For, in fact, the use of the metaphor of handing on as a description of the fundamental dynamic of tradition may not only obscure how the content is changed in the very process of its being handed on. It might *also* obscure the opportunity that attention to the dynamics of the conversation presents to direct that change with intentionality. This is of particular significance in this volume in which the attempt is to speak of the tradition *latinamente*. I suggest that attention to what is Latino/a in the consideration of tradition is not determined by the concrete content of what is being handed on, for example, the practices of popular religion, but rather is made possible by the very dynamics that take place in the handing on. For example, the essay by Michelle González in this volume disputes the overemphasis on *mestizaje* that Mexican Americans bring to bear in their reflections regarding the handing on of the revelation in Jesus Christ. The Latino/a dimension of what is handed on does not come from the *what* in the revelation they are reflecting on but rather on the lived context they use within which to understand the *what*. What I hope to show in this essay is that the role of such lived context is a key part of the dynamics of the handing on.

THE NATURE
OF THE CONVERSATION

Using the term *conversation* as a way of understanding the dynamics of tradition is a metaphorical use of that word. It is true that at times the handing on of the faith is a conversation in the literal sense, an interchange between persons about their understanding of what has been revealed in Jesus Christ. Ecumenical councils are such an instance. Concrete individuals explain their understandings, debate differences, challenge what they deem to be incorrect interpretations, and come to some agreement or disagreement as to the content of the Christian revelation. Exchanges by theologians, either in writing or in live interchange, or theologians teaching their students in educational settings, are not uncommon instances of the conversation become literal. However, more often than not the handing on is not an intentional interchange between persons but rather takes the form of lived or practiced faith, as Orlando Espín so well emphasizes in his chapter in this volume—and so is a conversation in a metaphorical sense. That is, believers hand on the faith to others by practicing in their lives what they profess with their lips. It is the lived example of parents that communicates to their children the faith received from their grandparents before them.

Whether the conversation is literal or only a metaphor about passing on the faith, the image of a conversation as tradition allows us to begin to understand how it is that the very act of handing on (conversing) changes *both* what is handed on *and* those who do the handing on. That is, as each generation passes on the faith to the next, the recipients, if they accept the faith, are changed by their encounter with Christian revelation and, at the same time, if that acceptance involves the incorporation of the received faith into their lives, the content of the faith is reinterpreted by those receiving it. The content does not remain untouched by the act of transmission. In fact, the very act of handing on, because it is done by concrete people, consists of an interplay between the faith that is handed on, those who do the handing on, and those who receive what is handed on—in such a way that all three are changed in the process. Whether one takes seriously the Thomistic maxim *quidquid recipitur in modo recipientis recipitur*[2] or prefers to follow something more contemporary (such as reader-response theory or perhaps deconstructionist positions prevalent in postmodern thought), contemporary epistemological theory asserts the mutual interaction and transformation of the knower and the known in the very act of knowing.

Only if one is content to accept uncritically theories of naive realism can one so separate the components of the act of knowing into known and knower so as to assert that either one or both are unaffected in any constitutive way. As Bernard Lonergan would hold, only if one affirms what is known as *the already out there now real* can one affirm that in the act of knowing it is only the knower who is changed by conforming his or her understanding to what is *out there* while *the already out there now real* remains unchanged by the encounter with the knower.[3] Rather, Lonergan asserts that all knowing begins through the senses. However, human knowing is the process of correctly understanding those experiences in such a way that one can make a judgment on the correctness of that understanding, arriving, as Lonergan would assert, at a judgment that is virtually unconditioned.[4] One never directly accesses some *already out there now real*. The process of human knowing is actually the *construction* of meaning. What is correctly understood is *what is*.

This construction of human meaning that culminates in the making of a judgment and that, I suggest, constitutes what we mean by tradition involves at least two knowers, the one who hands on and the one who receives. In each case, according to Lonergan, the judgment made has a contextual nature. A part of that contextual nature of judgment consists in the fact that the conditions that the knowers set up for the making of the judgment are dependent on past insights and knowledge and find coherence or a lack of coherence with other present insights and knowledge.

That is, the meaning that is generated is linked inexorably to concrete past and present circumstances of the lives of the person who is handing on the tradition as well as to those of the one who is receiving it. And as is apparent, given the similarity yet uniqueness of human experience, these circumstances may have some relative similarity but are specific to the life situation of each of the knowers.[5]

Using this epistemological framework, one sees that the content of tradition is the result of the construction of the human meaning of what has been encountered in Jesus Christ and in the lives, personal and communal, of those who have self-appropriated this encounter. When that human meaning is communicated to another person through speaking, action, or the written word, its meaning is reconstituted in the knowing process of the recipient who moves from experiencing what is being communicated to correctly understanding it to reaching a virtually unconditioned judgment as to the truth of his or her understanding of what has been communicated. Obviously the recipient has been changed by coming to know something that he or she did not previously know. At the same time, however, what is known, the so-called content of tradition, is also changed by its being re-understood through the experiences and knowing process of the recipient. As such, tradition cannot be appropriately conceived of as a *thing* that is handed on in such a way that this *thing* remains unchanged. Rather the *handing on* (the knowing process) by its very nature causes what is known (the *thing*) to be reconstituted by and within the world of meaning of the recipient.[6] When the recipient hands on the tradition to another, the process of reconstitution of human meaning repeats itself. The contextual nature of the understanding of the one who is handing on the tradition is recontextualized by the recipient, given the concrete circumstances of his or her life as they have given texture to the recipient's knowing process. Thus, what is handed on is never an *already out there now* thing; rather, it is always human meaning as constructed within the specific and unique context of the human knower and his or her community.

Let us think for a moment of the concrete example of a classroom experience. The professor of theology is lecturing eloquently on the Trinity and, more specifically, on the "fatherhood" of God. Whether she attends or not to her own experiential basis for understanding what a father is, her experience of the qualities that make up fatherhood, the power relations that affect the exercise of this role in her societal framework, the psychological dynamics of her relating to her father as a daughter rather than as a son, her inability as a woman to be a biological father, these aspects of her life as they have shaped her knowing what it means to be a father have dramatically influenced what she means when she says *father*. They have provided the experiential basis from within which she has gained insight into the meaning of the word *father;* they constitute the constellation of ideas into which her insight into *father* fits or may be in an incoherent relationship; they are the material out of which the questions are formed which, when asked of her insight into fatherhood, have the breadth necessary for her to reach a virtually un-conditioned judgment as to what it means to be a father. As such, they have played a constitutive role in what she is attempting to hand on to her students about the nature of the Christian God.

This prescinds from whether or not she has paid sufficient attention in the lecture to the analogical nature of all language about God. The analogical nature of such religious language does not disembody the language from the contexts within which its meaning has been derived. Rather, in its first movement, that of affirmation, analogy relies pre-cisely on the lived experience out of which the language has been birthed as a window into the reality of the Divine. What remembering analogy does is to deny the literal equation of the human context with the divine context and then point human understanding beyond what it is able to understand conceptually.[7] However, it does not deny the contextual na-ture of all human judgments.

In fewer words, what I am suggesting is that the professor's use of the word *father* in speaking about God will inevitably bring with it the world of human meaning in which it functions for her. If she is a good peda-gogue and theologian in teaching her students about the fatherhood of God, she will articulate as clearly as possible these existential circum-stances that have shaped the construction of the meaning of fatherhood for her and for the community of which she is a member.[8] However, no matter how clearly she articulates her context, the students receiving what she is handing on are recontextualizing her message. A male stu-dent, for example, has his own experiential basis for understanding what a father is, the qualities that make up fatherhood, the power relations that affect the exercise of this role in his societal framework, the psycho-logical dynamics of his relating to his father as a son rather than as a daughter, his ability as a man to be a father; all these aspects of his life as they have shaped his knowing what it means to be a father are dramati-cally influencing what he understands when he hears *father* and, there-fore, how he understands the fatherhood of God.

The difference between the life and community contexts that have shaped the professor's understanding of fatherhood and those that have shaped the student's has become a constitutive dimension of what the student has received and, therefore, of what has been handed on, that is, the tradition. In this case it may be a more expansive understanding than that of the teacher or it may be a more restrictive one. It may be one that pays less attention to gender and more attention to qualities of care. It may be one that emphasizes authority and devalues accompaniment. Whatever the case, while still recognizing the analogical nature of that language, I suggest that what has been received is not identical with what has been given. The very process of handing on, which is really the process of human knowing and so the construction of human meaning, has affected what has been handed on. What is handed on does not exist out there somewhere, a dogmatically certain *already out there now real*. What is handed on as humanly meaningful exists in the one who gives and the one who receives, and each comprehends what is handed on differently because of the very nature of the process of human knowing.

THE PARTNERS IN THE CONVERSATION

I would like to continue my use of the word *conversation* as descriptive of what takes place in the handing on that is tradition. In light of the epistemology laid out rather simply above, what becomes apparent is that this conversation actually takes place on two levels. The more apparent one is the interaction between the one who is handing on and the one who is receiving. At another level, however, there is, in a sense, an internal conversation taking place within each of the knowers. That is, the contextual nature of human knowing as described in the above section implies that a number of dimensions of the life of the knower come into play in the knowing process. Adapting the work of James and Evelyn Whitehead, I suggest that there are three such dimensions interacting in those involved in the handing on and receiving of tradition. The interaction of these dimensions with each other is analogous to the dynamics of a conversation in which each dimension is a partner, or a voice, as it were.[9]

The first such partner in the internal conversation in the act of handing on and receiving is the content of what is being handed down. This the Whiteheads themselves term the *Christian tradition*, that is, *our* religious heritage embracing both Sacred Scripture and the long history of the Christian church with its multiple and changing interpretations of the Bible and of its own life.[10] It is interesting to note that the very content that is being handed down is identified as both changing and multiple over history. Thus, what is being passed on is, in this sense, in a constant state of flux. And, as I have argued, the flux is created precisely by the dynamics inherent in the process of handing on (the process of human knowing), which is a constitutive element of what we call tradition. That

is, each time the content is handed on it is recontextualized by the knowing process of the recipient or receiving community. While it is the same
Jesus who is passed on, that Jesus is understood anew. What has been
handed on is not contradicted, but it is conformed to be intelligible within
the context of those receiving it.

In addition, because the handing on is performed by any number of
initiators and recipients, the tradition is multiple or, as the Whiteheads
choose to call it, "pluriform." That is, the handing on is not a linear
process. Rather, multiple handings on are taking place at any given historical time. Some of those handings on are taking place among persons
within quite similar contexts, while others are happening between subjects whose lived contexts are different and perhaps different from each
other. Thus, what is sometimes mistakenly understood as a monolith,
the Tradition, is actually always composed of a number of traditions. As
we shall see, in the performance of the conversation these various
contextualized understandings shed mutual light on one another in a
way that can be mutually corrective and, at the same time, often are
interwoven to form a broader panorama, as often happens as individual
lines of thought merge in a single conversation into fuller understanding
of the theme under consideration.

The second partner in the conversation is experience. It is the experience of the individual Christian whose life is shaped by the revelation of
Jesus Christ that has been handed down to him or her. It is also the
experience of the community of faith in which what has been handed
down is reflected on and lived. These two sets of experience, that of the
individual and that of his or her community, are in constant interaction
with each other in the knowing process of receiving what is handed on.
The firsthand experience from family and school may be Julia's first
referent when her religion teacher talks about how Jesus is our friend as
he assumes our human life. However, the other third-graders in that
classroom each has his or her own personal context as well as the experiences of friendship that have occurred in the couple of years this particular class of children has been together. The task of the teacher is to
facilitate the articulation of the experiences, individual and group, that
are present in that classroom, her own and those of the children, so that
coming to know Jesus as a friend is not limited to Julia's past and present
insights into friendship but are corroborated, corrected, and expanded
by the insights that come from the context of the lives of the other students and the teacher.

In a sense, then, these two understandings of experience, individual
and communal, are actually two facets of the same reality. The very
process of handing down and of receiving presupposes the presence of at

least two individuals who, when taken together, provide the nucleus of a community. In actual fact this handing down takes place in larger group-ings of people, that is in actual communities of varying sizes. What is of particular importance here is that the experience we are speaking about is the content handed down now incorporated into the lives of those who have received it. These lives are existentially concrete. That is, they are being lived out in a given time and place with the particularities this implies. Thus, what is handed down is not only *not* changeless, but nei-ther does it have some sort of generic quality. Every time it is passed on, it is received by concrete persons whose lives are shaped by their unique circumstances. These include their socioeconomic situation, their for-mative relationships with others such as family, their educational expe-rience, the national ethos within which their consciousness of themselves has been formed, and so on. Each of these dimensions affects how the content of what is handed down is reinterpreted in its being received or known.

The third partner in the internal conversation is culture. While the definitions of culture are various, it may be viewed as *the* convictions, values and biases that form a person's social setting and therefore point to the *formative* symbols and ongoing interpretations that shape that person's world view, as well as the social roles and political structures that shape social life.[11] One of the particularities of human experience is the cultural milieu that configures it. Some might prefer to include cul-ture within the conversation partner we have named above as experi-ence, since everyone's experience is in some way *cultured*. However, cul-ture is more appropriately understood as a constellation of forces, larger than the individual or even the individual's concrete community of faith, which, through its set patterns of symbols and interpretations, exerts pressure on the way a person understands his or her experience and what has been handed down to him or her of the revelation in Jesus Christ. Thus culture is a partner with experience and the content of what is handed down in the conversation termed *the tradition*.

It would be a mistake, of course, to conceive of anyone's culture ei-ther as static or as monolithic. Cultures, by their nature, are strategies of human survival, both on the level of biology and of human meaning. As such, they are in a state of constant change as they interact with chang-ing circumstances and with other cultures. In addition, most cultures are held by groups of people large enough to allow for significant variations within a given culture. As Fred Jandt asserts, "The diversity within cul-tures probably exceeds the differences between cultures."[12] The signifi-cance here is that the world view of culture plays a role in the knowing process that reinforces the argument of the contextual nature of tradition.

As a kind of horizon of meaning, culture acts both to broaden and to limit the common-sense parameters of a person's insights and in that way both links the person profoundly with those who share this horizon of meaning and separates him or her from those whose horizon has been differently formed.[13]

A professor of ecclesiology who walks into a classroom of thirty students from eight different cultures with the intent of lecturing on the church as the body of Christ in Hans Küng's classic book *The Church* has a significant challenge with which to deal. At work in his presentation are understandings of body and bodiliness that have resulted from the personal and communal experience of Hans Küng, but which have also been shaped by his cultural world. The professor himself has his particular understandings of these same concepts, but as he has reconstituted their meaning by their being informed by his own experience and cultural horizon. He now faces thirty sets of human experience of body and eight cultural horizons that will inevitably act as filters for what those students hear of the professor's understanding of Küng's understanding of body as articulated in the letters of Paul.[14] Following the pedagogical method used in the concrete examples we have given above, the professor might rightly decide that the first part of the class needs to be employed to surface with some clarity the assumptions about and understandings of body and bodiliness that reflect the experience and culture of the text, the teacher, and the students, before he launches into an exposé of the "tradition" of the church as the body of Christ. What he attempts to hand on is itself culturally conditioned, as is his understanding of it, as is what the students will receive from his lecture.

THE STRUCTURE OF THE CONVERSATION

What I am suggesting is that each of the conversation partners sitting at the table has a distinct voice that must be listened to in the process we are calling tradition. The first step of the conversation is exploratory in nature. It demands what I might call an *unpacking* of the three dimensions that are now in conversation, that is, what is being handed down, experience, and culture. The unpacking cannot be done in the abstract, for the dimensions themselves are not abstract; rather, they flow from concrete realities.

If we were to step back into the class on ecclesiology, we might find the professor beginning with a bit of background on Hans Küng, biographical data, his cultural milieu, the major theological currents that have affected his thought, historical events in the church that have shaped

Küng's approach to ecclesiology. While the list could theoretically be endless, what the professor is looking to do is to reveal those significant elements of previous church teaching, experience, and culture that will allow the students some basic understanding of how and why Küng has developed the content of the material on body of Christ as it appears in his book. In a second move the professor brings forth those elements that he believes are significant in the way he understands and teaches Küng's theological content in this area of ecclesiology. Then he invites the thirty students into small-group discussion and asks them to focus on two basic points: (1) how they understand *body* and *bodiliness* and why (personal experience and culture); and (2) what significant experiences they have had of the church as the "body" of Christ.[15] All of this is laying the ground, getting the cards on the table. James and Evelyn Whitehead would call this first step "attending to" the voices in the conversation; that is, giving each (content, experience, and culture) a chance to speak. In my example I have built on their insight by noting that each of the three dimensions at work in the internal conversation is also at work in each of three knowers in the external conversation. So, true attending is present only when it means listening to content, experience, and culture as these are present in what is being taught, in the teacher, and in the students.

However, the conversation that is tradition is not accomplished simply by attending or listening to the voices of content, experience, and culture. Rather, these voices must be allowed to engage one another. In a way it is a move beyond the exploratory to the assertive. That is, each of the partners must be allowed to question the effect of the role of the others in the shaping of the tradition.

A fundamental assumption lies at the basis of affirming this assertive nature of the conversation of tradition. That assumption is that each of the partners in the conversation and the conversation itself are, as the Whiteheads would name it, a mixture of grace and malpractice.

As I have noted above, experience when patterned correctly leads to true knowing. However, if Lonergan's assertion that human beings are incapable of sustained development is true, then correctly understanding one's experience is not only subject to, but also is concretely affected by, defects in the knowing process. These defects, which Lonergan refers to as biases, might be the result of the unconscious repression of insights that are unwanted because of the psychological scarring that affects every human life. They may result from the pressure of one's group to favor its own well-being without adequately considering that of others. They may result from an egoism that allows preeminence to the spontaneous fears and desires that favor the self. Or they may result from the human person's penchant to take the shortsighted view of things, being satisfied with the immediate without probing the larger issues that might be at stake.[16]

Fundamentally, bias restricts the disinterested and unrestricted desire to know. As a result, what is known by persons suffering from bias is skewed by the bias itself. In the case of tradition, what is being handed down is not only reinterpreted in the process of being handed down (this is always the case), but, because of the particular bias at work in the processing of the experience of what is being handed down, the content may be re-understood in a way that causes a distortion in the new understanding of the content of what is being handed down. That is, there is a change in the understanding of what is being handed down caused not by deeper or further insight, but rather by a lack of integrity in the process of human knowing. The effect of bias is to disrupt the movement from experience to understanding either by introducing extraneous elements into the process or by keeping the subject from attending to those parts of the experience that lead to insight but which would at the same time challenge the bias.

Let us revisit for a moment the theology classroom where the professor is reflecting on the meaning of the fatherhood of God. As she reminds the students of the analogical nature of the use of the term *father* when applied to God, she pays special attention to emphasizing that the tradition holds that this term does not imply gender, that is, to call God "father" is not to assert that God is male. God can just as truthfully be referred to through female images. A rustle of tension moves among some of her male students. A couple of students raise strenuous objection to this de-gendering of God, noting that Jesus could have chosen to call God "mother" when he taught his disciples how to pray, but he did not. He stayed faithful to the heritage of the Hebrew scriptures in which God is called king, lord, judge, and father of his people. The professor gently reminds the class that God's love in those same scriptures was compared to that of a mother for her child, that the figure of God as Wisdom is effectively a feminine image of God. The students in question will have none of this feminist interpretation. Theirs is a visceral attachment to a God who is male. Their capacity to move to a new level of understanding of God is hampered, not by a lack of intellectual acuity on their part, but because the privileging of males that has been part of their experience of family and that is enshrined in the social patterns of their cultures is supported by the theological identity of God with males.[17]

No one, I dare say, would challenge the assertion that not everything in a given culture is reflective of the best of humanity. Rather, the symbol systems and world views that cultures represent are the creation of groups of individuals whose knowing process, as stated above, at times leads to genuine insight and at other times leads to blind spots. Thus, the cultural milieu that exerts its force on the knowing subject involves both truth and error.

The third conversation partner, the content being handed down (whether proposition, ritual performance, or lived practice) is itself the result of conversations held by previous generations in which the mixed nature of both experience and culture has played a significant role in shaping the content. Therefore, the content itself can never be purely graced; rather, it always bears some evidence of malpractice.

Using the metaphor of conversation for tradition, in both its internal and external modalities, allows us also to see how the assertive nature of that conversation can serve as a corrective to the malpractice. Those students whose preference for male privilege blocks their making true judgments about the place of gender in the understanding of God are invited to move beyond through the reading assignments they are given in Johnson's *She Who Is*. Their interaction in small-group work, in which the objective is to develop images of God that are liberating to diverse groups of people, pushes them to dislodge the block of privilege so that their own horizon can be enlarged for their own benefit and for that of the people they serve. Having to deal with understandings that arise out of contrary readings of the content of what is being taught, out of the experience of their female classmates, out of the presence of feminism in many areas of North American culture, stretches them and may serve as a corrective to their understanding of God, which is biased by the privileged place of males in their experience and in their cultural worlds of origin.

Those same dynamics are carried over into their course on Eucharist, as they confront the content of the tradition that asserts that only males can be ordained to the presbyterate and so preside at Eucharist. In this case, however, rather than the content attempting to push and stretch the conversation partners of experience and culture, it is these latter voices that challenge the content. As some students share the short essays they have written about women they have experienced who have been the recipients of God's compassion or the prophetic champions of God's call to liberation from poverty and racism—those students formerly so wedded to male images of God begin to question the traditional content that views only males as capable of acting in the person of Christ and, therefore, of presiding at the Eucharist.

In different words, what I am suggesting is that some voices at the table may at times try to dominate the conversation to the detriment of the contributions of the other voices. For example, past understandings of the content of what is being handed on may be so privileged as to deny legitimacy to different human experiences that, if they were allowed play in the conversation, would call for a reshaping or reinterpretation of the content. Contemporary cultural currents might enter the conversation with such force that divergent cultural perspectives already embedded in the content are displaced willy-nilly, without the constructive engagement that might allow for some mutually corrective interchange between the cultural viewpoints. It might be that the understanding of the experience to which the content is speaking has been deeply affected by individual or group bias but exerts such influence in the conversation that rather than adding insight to the content it brings distortion to bear in such a way as to disfigure the content or even to reject it. However, at the same time, the power inherent in assertive conversation can serve as a corrective to the malpractice to be found not only in the content that is being handed down, but also in the experience and the culture of the ones doing the handing on and the ones who are receiving.

My point here is really a rather simple one. The objective of the conversation that is tradition is the deepening understanding of the revelation that has taken place in Jesus Christ. That deepening is a dynamic movement and, therefore, requires a push and pull among the conversation partners. Experience and culture are each organic and developing. Therefore, one would expect that their engagement with the content being handed down would lead to new insights, confirm previous ones, and challenge current ones. The content itself is continually undergoing reshaping and reinterpretation by bringing to the conversation the strengths and weakness of its current shape and interpretation.

CONCLUSION

What has all of this to do with speaking of the tradition *latinamente?* If the reader's assumption is that what is Latino/a in the Catholic tradition are those practices, rituals, and writings that are peculiar to Latino/a communities within the church, then I suppose what I have reflected on in this essay appears to have missed the mark. However, as I mentioned at the beginning of this essay, I assert that *attention to what is Latino/a in the consideration of tradition is not determined by the concrete content of what is being handed on (for example, the practices of popular religion) but rather is made possible by the very dynamics that take place in the handing on.* I have suggested the metaphor of conversation as a way of understanding tradition because I believe that it allows us to perceive fairly clearly some of the more significant movements in the process of tradition in such a way as to open up a space for what is

Latino/a. And, I would assert that what is Latino/a in the tradition is far more ample than those specific practices, rituals, and writings found in our communities.

Analyzing the traditioning process using the metaphor of a conversation allows us to see that the experiences of Latinos/as in living out the faith in all the areas of our lives over the centuries of our peoples' existence should be a constitutive element in the handing on of the revelation of God in Jesus. Equally constitutive should be the cultural world views that mark the personalities of our peoples. Equally constitutive should be the content of that revelation that we having been handing down in our universities, in our parish halls, and in the *rinconcitos* of our homes where the *abuela* whispers to her grandchildren the prayers that have embodied her faith and that of her own *abuelita*. I have used the phrase "should be" in each of the last three sentences because I fear that Latino/a experience, cultures, and content have not been viewed in fact as part of the Catholic tradition. Rather, the reification of tradition that views it as some *thing* passed on but unaffected in the transmission process has allowed the perpetuation of the myth that the Catholic tradition is not contextual but universal.

Therefore, any contextualization of the tradition, such as a Latino/a one, is viewed as the adaptation of the universal to a particular, an application of what is truly "Catholic," a variation on a theme. Whereas, what I have been arguing in this essay is that the metaphor of conversation allows us to see that the tradition is always a particular or, better said, a set of particulars, and these particulars continually need to be placed in assertive communication with each other in order to provide correctives against bias and in order to expand the horizons of our understanding of what God has done in Jesus Christ. There is a Latino/a Catholic tradition, as there is a Euro-American one, an Indian one, and so forth. What would allow these Catholic traditions to be the catholic tradition would be to engage them intentionally in assertive conversation.

No educational example that I developed in this essay is specifically Latino/a in content. That was intentional on my part. It is simply too easy in our church, where one particular has been passed off as the universal, to reduce what is Latino/a and its role to what is content. As I have argued elsewhere, responsible theological education is best served by adequate attention to method rather than to content.[18] And that has been a second objective of this essay—not only to unpack the metaphor of tradition as conversation in order to see where what is Latino/a comes to bear, but also to give some hints on how that conversation can be conducted intentionally in educational settings.

Notes

[1] James and Evelyn Whitehead, *Method in Ministry: Theological Reflection and Christian Ministry*, rev. ed. (Kansas City: Sheed and Ward, 1995), 3–5.

[2] "Whatever is received is received according to the perspective of the one receiving." This translation is mine.

[3] Bernard J. F. Lonergan, *Insight: A Study of Human Understanding*, rev. students' ed. (New York: Philosophical Library, 1958), 424–25.

[4] Ibid., 280.

[5] Ibid., 277–78.

[6] See Chapter 7 in this volume, in which Miguel Díaz presents quite persuasively a case in which such recontextualization significantly changes the content of what is being handed on.

[7] For an understanding of analogy that recognizes the concrete specificity of the origin of language used to refer to the divine, see Elizabeth Johnson, *She Who Is: The Mystery of God in Feminist Discourse* (New York: Crossroad, 1993), 104–20.

[8] It is of critical importance in the elaboration of this epistemology to recall that the human knower is not isolated but shares in a communal life with others in the group or groups to which he or she belongs. This shared though not identical experiential basis for the construction of human meaning allows for the relative communicability of human understanding as well as for the opportunity for mutual correction in coming to judgment.

[9] One certainly could name the partners differently and expand the number depending on how one would want to nuance the dimensions being brought to bear. The point here, however, is not the partners in themselves but in how the conversation is conducted and what bearing this has on an understanding of tradition.

[10] Whitehead and Whitehead, *Methods in Ministry*, 4–5.

[11] Ibid., 5.

[12] Fred E. Jandt, *Intercultural Communication: An Introduction*, 3rd ed. (Thousand Oaks, CA: Sage Publications, 2001), 6.

[13] Lonergan himself distinguishes between common sense and culture as two quite different levels of human integration. Compare what he says about the person of common sense on page 180 of *Insight* with how he engages what he considers to be culture on page 210. However, for our purposes here his understanding of common sense is far closer to what in common parlance is called culture.

[14] The levels and sequence of reconstitution of meaning here are obviously far greater than the three mentioned, as the content has been passed down over two millennia.

[15] This second question presents the opportunity to move from exploration to engagement, because it invites students to begin to articulate the connections they have made between body/bodiliness and church.

[16] Lonergan refers to these specifically as biases: dramatic, group, individual, and general (See *Insight*, 191–226).

[17] For a particularly cogent treatment of the social function of images of God, see Johnson, *She Who Is*, 3–6.

[18] See Gary Riebe-Estralla, "The Challenge of Ministerial Formation," *Missiology: An International Review* 20, no. 2 (April 1992): 269–74; and idem, "Latinos and Theological Education," *Journal of Hispanic/Latino Theology* 4, no. 3 (1997): 5–12.

7

A Trinitarian Approach to the Community-Building Process of Tradition

Oneness as Diversity in Christian Traditioning

Miguel H. Díaz

INTRODUCTION

Within Roman Catholic circles tradition is generally conceived in relation to scripture. In turn, both tradition and scripture are conceived in light of revelation. A "two-source theory" approach to tradition and scripture was common after the Council of Trent. This approach maintained that not all revelation was contained in scripture. Rather, revelation was contained in written books and in unwritten traditions.[1] The Second Vatican Council (1962–65) moved away from this two-source theory, opting instead to conceive scripture and tradition in close relation to each other.[2] The Second Vatican Council conceived scripture and tradition as two forms of a single revelation. This single revelatory foundation was described in personal terms, namely, as God's self-revelation. Commenting on this personal approach to revelation in recent Catholic and Protestant theologies, Gerald O'Collins writes,

A squad of Catholic theologians both before and after the Second Vatican Council, not to mention many Anglican, Orthodox and Protestant theologians, moved away from a propositional view of revelation to develop the model of revelation as interpersonal encounter or—in a word—dialogue. Instead of being interpreted primarily as God revealing truths, revelation was now understood to

157

be God's self-revelation. It was expounded first and foremost as the gratuitous and saving self-disclosure of God who calls and enables us to enter by faith into a new personal relationship. Revelation is a person-to-person, subject-to-subject, I-Thou encounter. The appropriate primary question is "Who is revealed?" rather than "What is revealed?"[3]

The shift to a "who" question in matters of revelation has been central to revisioning contemporary theories of tradition. As a result of this shift, greater attentiveness has been given to the personal process of transmission. Thus, Yves Congar, in his monumental work *Tradition and Traditions: An Historical and a Theological Essay,* conceives tradition as an interpersonal process of transmission. Tradition, he argues, involves the "giving and receiving, dependence and exchange" that occurs *in community* and "brings about incorporation into a communion."[4] As *Dei Verbum* points out, as an interpersonal and community constituting process, tradition mediates, through words and deeds, God's life-giving presence (*DV*, no. 2). Together with scripture, tradition flows from "the same divine well-spring" (*DV*, no. 9) and shares with scripture one and the same mission: to communicate God's triune mystery so that human persons can come to know and "become sharers in the divine nature" (*DV*, no. 2).

According to Congar, tradition "is not primarily concerned with a particular material object, but by the act of transmission, and its content is simply *id quod traditum est, id quod traditur"* (tradition is that which is transmitted).[5] Congar's definition not only emphasizes transmission or traditioning over a static material deposit of faith (content),[6] but also invites greater attention to the question of *who* is being handed over, rather than to the question of *what* is being handed over. In turn, and perhaps as important in terms of the process of traditioning, are the following questions: Who is handing over, and to whom is the tradition being handed over?

The things handed over (the *tradita* that include words, stories, actions, doctrines, institutions, and so on) remain important human elements in the handing over of Christian faith. But the shift from a "what" question to a "who" question naturally leads to raising questions of transmission in light of personal contexts: whose words, stories, and actions are handed over, and to whom? In this sense, recent reflections that touch upon the transmission of Christian faith by Latinos/as, women, Asian Americans, and black Catholics reflect this concern.[7] In addition, this personal approach avoids the reification of tradition often encountered in the past when the focus was on the impersonal "bearers" of tradition.[8]

This essay pursues a trinitarian revisioning of tradition.[9] This approach presupposes and builds upon the personal approach to tradition just discussed. To undertake a trinitarian revisioning of tradition is to set God's self-revelation as a paradigm for a Christian understanding of community-building processes. In this sense, God's self-revelation in Christ and the Spirit can be described as a kind of handing over or traditioning of God's life. This personal handing over is a signpost for the community-building process that constitutes the very reality of God. In turn, the way that God shares and hands over God's self provides a Christian foundation for identifying authentic traditioning and community-building processes.

This essay is divided into four parts. It begins with a discussion on how the New Testament understands the notion of tradition, especially with respect to the community-building process associated with traditioning the life of God in Christ and the Spirit. This section underscores that in Christ and the Spirit, God hands over God's self to effect authentic community. Second, the essay turns to post-biblical developments in the area of trinitarian theology to explore in more detail the community-building process modeled by the triune life of God. The emergence of the doctrine of the Trinity can be read as central to understanding the kind of divine community constituted in the process of God's personal handing over of God's self.

Drawing on this trinitarian approach I then highlight how the principle of oneness in diversity is essential in this doctrine and central to understanding, appropriating, and critiquing community-building processes of Christian traditions. As a test case I briefly discuss the community-building process of traditioning the Cuban devotion to Our Lady of Charity. More specifically, following earlier arguments in this essay—which underscore the personal bearers of tradition—I focus on the identity of *los tres Juanes*. They serve as symbolic figures associated with the various communities that have traditioned this devotion. Finally, the essay concludes with some reflections that consider the contemporary relevance of embracing this trinitarian approach to tradition.

BIBLICAL REFLECTIONS: THE COMMUNITY IMPLICATIONS
OF TRADITIONING CHRIST AND THE SPIRIT

An in-depth study of the concept of tradition from a biblical perspective lies beyond the scope of this essay. As a general rule, tradition in the Bible has to do with the oral and written interpretations of faith and the community-building process of handing this faith over. In the

Old Testament this process of handing over is associated with particular persons, rituals, and key events that build community for the people of Israel. The New Testament builds upon Old Testament ideas but offers its own particular understanding of tradition, which emerges as a result of God's self-revelation in Jesus Christ and the Spirit. In New Testament writings tradition is associated with handing over the reality of Christ and the Spirit. This process of handing over God's distinct personal life effects authentic community in the divine image.

As examples of this biblical understanding of tradition the following three pericopes are highlighted here: 1 Corinthians 1:11–12, John: 14:1—17:26, and Acts 2:1–43.

1 Corinthians 1:11–12

Paul's theology, and in particular his notion of handing over what he received from the Lord (1 Cor 11:23–33), exemplifies the link between traditioning the life of God in Christ and the process of building authentic community. Paul reprimands the Corinthian community for eating the bread and drinking the cup of the Lord in an unworthy manner. For Paul, the Corinthians have failed to "discern the body" (1 Cor 11:29). Their failure to discern the body has to do with their inability to express communally Christ's reality. Underscoring the relationship between traditioning the reality of Christ and its impact on communal experiences, Jerome Murphy-O'Connor writes:

> Since the Lord's Supper involves the transformation of bread and wine into the body and blood of Christ, it would seem that for Paul the attitude of the Corinthians robbed the words of institution of validity. This is entirely congruent with the apostle's existential identification of the community of believers with Christ. In theory the community is Christ, but Paul was not concerned with this speculative aspect. His function as pastor was to ensure that the community was in fact Christ, i.e., truly animated by his life, fully penetrated by his spirit. As such the community could act with the power of Christ, and could speak with the authority of Christ. In an inauthentic community, such as that of Corinth, Christ is not present. The words of institution may be his but the voice which speaks them is not.[10]

As O'Connor suggests, for Paul traditioning Christ is above all else concerned with the communal practice of making present the reality of Christ.

Paul hints that this communal presence is realized when the members that compose the one body of Christ give and receive from one another: "For just as the body is one and has many members, and all the members of the body, though many, are one body, so it is with Christ" (1 Cor 12:12).

John 14:1—17:26

The farewell discourses and the "high priestly prayer" lend further support to the notion of tradition as a community-building process. Here, handing over is presented as a life-giving experience associated with Jesus' promises to hand himself and his truth over to his disciples in the coming of the Spirit (Jn 16:13).[11] Jesus' promise to tradition himself in the Spirit is fulfilled at the "hour" when he hands his Spirit over from the cross. In John, this hour is associated with the passion of Christ. Hence, a Spirit-centered and cross-centered experience characterizes the Johannine vision of community. Those who stand with Jesus at the cross (symbolized in John by the presence of Mary and the beloved disciple) receive the Spirit of Christ. Empowered by the Spirit, they are constituted as a community of disciples and are called to be one in service to each other (Jn 15:12–17; 19:25–30; 17:18–24). Abiding in Jesus, his disciples will be like many branches that are joined to the one fruit-bearing vine (Jn 15:1–7).

Acts 2:1–43

Beyond Paul and the Gospel of John, the Acts of the Apostles also paints a vivid picture of the community-building process that results from handing over Christ and the Spirit. In Acts, the coming of the Spirit is linked directly to what has often been described as the birth of the church. Acts suggests that the handing over of the Spirit brings about the creation of an inclusive communal body that welcomes members beyond the boundaries of the original Galilean community. The inclusive nature of this body is suggested by the list of ethnic communities that share the experience of the Spirit (Acts 2:8–9). More specifically, Peter's sermon—which affirms the outpouring of the Spirit upon "all flesh" (Acts 2:17)—evidences this inclusive vision of community. Similar to the examples drawn from Pauline and Johannine theologies, in Acts tradition can be conceived as a community-building process that results from the handing over of God's self. This handing over invites the birth of communal oneness through an experience of communal diversity.

THE DOCTRINE OF THE TRINITY AS A SIGNPOST
FOR AFFIRMING ONENESS AS DIVERSITY
IN CHRISTIAN TRADITIONING

In the years following the formation of the New Testament, Christians continued to deepen their understanding of how God's reality was handed on in the presence of Christ and the Spirit and the human and divine communal implications of this traditioning. This issue lies at the heart of the development of the doctrine of the Trinity. A historical exploration of this development lies beyond my present objective.[12] Rather, I intend to reflect upon how trinitarian theology can offer a "grammar" for understanding the relationship between traditioning and the building of authentic community.[13] This grammar will underscore the core principle without which the tradition of building authentic community "would not be recognizable."[14] In this sense these trinitarian reflections seek to describe rather than prescribe the communal reality constituted by the practice of God's self-traditioning in Christ and the Spirit.

The Christian doctrine of God emerged as a way to affirm how Christ and the Spirit "tradition" the reality of God.[15] In the East the theologians who are most credited with this development are the Cappadocian Fathers (Gregory of Nyssa, Basil, and Gregory of Nazianzus). In the West, Augustine and Thomas Aquinas receive that recognition. Much has been written regarding the similarities and differences of Greek and Latin traditioning of God's mystery. Perhaps the most controversial area lies in the theological starting points of these two traditions with respect to the life of God.

With the Cappadocians, Greek trinitarian theologies have tended to affirm the Father as the particular source for the diversity of God's life. "To exist as God is to be the Father who begets the Son and breathes forth the Spirit."[16] The Cappadocians provide important distinctions between *ousia* (roughly equivalent to what is commonly shared in God) and *hypostasis* (roughly equivalent to what is particular in God) and coin the all-important trinitarian formula *mia ousia, treis hypostaseis*. For the Cappadocians, "*ousia* expresses concrete existence. Each divine person *is* the divine *ousia*; the divine *ousia* exists hypostatically, and there is no *ousia* apart from *hypostases*."[17] Simply put, apart from the diversity of particular divine persons and their mutual communion with one another, God's oneness is inconceivable.

Augustine's trinitarian theology provides a definitive response in the West to the challenge of Arianism. Arius was a priest from Alexandria (fourth century) who embraced the subordination of the Son to the Father and, in so doing, failed to acknowledge how Jesus Christ in his own particularity "traditioned" the reality of God. By underscoring the one divine essence, equally shared by each of the divine Persons, Augustine successfully refutes subordinationism of any kind. Augustine's starting point, however, is not the biblical person of the Father but the *one* essence of God. The focus here is on "what" God is, rather than on "who" God is. The danger in this model is that the personal and communal diversity of God's life tends to be compromised at the expense of an impersonal divine unity. As Rahner notes, Augustine's theology "begins with the one God, the one divine essence as a whole, and only *afterwards* does it see God in three Persons."[18]

These Eastern and Western ways of understanding the distinct handing over of God's life carry enormous theological and practical implications. Among other things, notions of God have deeply affected anthropology, ecclesiology, and political life.[19] Their impact on Christian approaches to questions of revelation and tradition would seem undeniable. Given the emphasis that Greek theology places on the person of the Father as the source of the Godhead, this model—more than the Augustinian model in the West—is capable of engendering a more personal approach to tradition. The focus on essence in the West naturally leads to "what" questions in matters relating to revelation and tradition. Conversely, the focus on person in the Greek model immediately leads to "who" questions in these areas.

In our times Orthodox theologian John Zizioulas has retrieved the Greek trinitarian vision and written extensively on issues pertaining to human communities patterned in the image of the distinctive and personal handing over of God's life.[20] In an essay entitled "Communion and Otherness," Zizioulas reflects upon and underscores otherness as essential to the nature of divine and human personhood.[21] Zizioulas cautions that today "we feel more threatened by the presence of the other. . . . Communion with the other is not spontaneous; it is built upon fences which protect us from the dangers implicit in the other's presence." Moreover, "the fact that the fear of the other is pathologically inherent in our existence results in the fear not only of the other but of *all otherness*." Thus, "difference itself" becomes a threat and "radical otherness" an anathema. "We all," concludes Zizioulas, "want to project into the other the model of our own selves."[22]

Zizioulas's solution to this fear of the other, which he sees as leading to a lack of authentic communion and unity, reflects the Greek trinitarian notion of divine personhood. For Zizioulas, the doctrine of the Trinity evidences that "otherness is *constitutive* of unity, and not consequent upon it. God is not first one and then three, but simultaneously One and

Three."[23] Zizioulas is strongly critical of Latin traditions that have underscored oneness in the life of God at the expense of God's triune existence. For Zizioulas, diversity is essential to divine life and therefore also essential to human life. For Zizioulas, to be like God is to be catholic, that is, to exist as a community of diverse and interrelated persons. Thus, he writes,

> God's oneness or unity is not safeguarded by the unity of substance, as St. Augustine and other western theologians have argued, but by the *monarchia* of the Father. It is also expressed through the unbreakable *koinonia* (community) that exists between the three Persons, which means that otherness is not a threat to unity but the *sine qua non* of unity.[24]

Zizioulas goes on to affirm that God's oneness, which results from personal communion with others, "requires the experience of the Cross."[25] For Zizioulas, the self-emptying of God in Christ's cross is the ultimate sign of God's sacrificial movement toward, inclusion of, and communion with human persons. In a similar way our various attempts to effect unity with others cannot be realized without the "kenotic" experience of love that places us in solidarity with Jesus and the crucified of history. Ultimately, suggests Zizioulas, only a diversity that is constitutive and mindful of the cross will result in authentic oneness. This is the truth-filled meaning of authentic communal relations, for, as he affirms, "truth as communion does not lead to the dissolving of the diversity of beings into one vast ocean of being, but rather to the affirmation of otherness in and through love."[26]

These brief reflections crystalize the contribution that trinitarian theology can make to a personal approach to tradition. "Handing over" in God's image presupposes handing to and from a distinct other. This process of giving and receiving from others essentially constitutes who God is. Indeed, "oneness as diversity" *is* who God is and *is* the communal reality that results from the practice of God (the Father) handing God's self over in Christ and the Spirit. When we understand the transmission of God's life in this way, the cross becomes the supreme Christian symbol of the community-building process that emerges from the personal handing over of God. In handing God's self over to the other, including the human other, God models the process of building authentic and inclusive community. In God's life the inclusion of this other, especially the crucified and marginalized other, becomes essential to building authentic community. No human tradition that seeks to build community after the divine image can overlook this basic trinitarian principle.

A US HISPANIC TEST CASE FOR A TRINITARIAN APPROACH TO TRADITION: THE COMMUNAL SYMBOLISM OF *LOS TRES JUANES* IN THE CUBAN DEVOTION TO OUR LADY OF CHARITY

As we have argued, tradition is a community-building process. Popular traditions of faith are no exemption to this rule. The reflections of US Hispanic theologians give ample evidence for the community-birthing nature of US Hispanic popular Catholicism.[27] For Cubans and Cuban Americans the popular devotion to Our Lady of Charity serves as a locus for understanding the existential coming to be and theoretical construct of the Cuban community. As the title of a recent book on this devotion suggests, Our Lady of Charity is a symbol of what it means to be Cuban.[28]

The artistic handing-on of this popular faith in statues and holy cards commonly depicts Our Lady of Charity standing in the midst of a storm with three men rowing beneath her feet. In a similar way, through oral tradition, Cubans have heard the story of how Our Lady of Charity "saved" three salt gatherers who were about to perish in the midst of a storm. The original historical source for these representations is the finding of a statue of Mary by two Amerindian brothers and a ten-year-old African slave boy (Juan de Hoyos, Rodrigo de Hoyos, and Juan Moreno, respectively) in the early years of the seventeenth century (1612 or 1613). The events following this discovery, the evolution of this devotion, and the community of devotees that contributed to this evolution all provide insights into the community-building process of this popular tradition.

Rather than provide a detailed analysis of the process, which would require a book-length manuscript, I wish to focus briefly on the communal evolution of the identity related with those who first discovered the floating image (the Amerindian brothers and African slave boy). They are often simply and symbolically referred to as *los tres Juanes*. Properly understood, the presence of *los tres Juanes* in the devotion to Our Lady of Charity offers a sociocultural locus for understanding tradition as a community-building process. As trinitarian reflections above have shown, this process cannot authentically take place without the affirmation of oneness as diversity.

Earlier in this essay I suggested that a more personal approach to tradition should consider not only the question of who is being handed over, but also who is handing over and to whom the tradition is being handed over. These questions naturally evoke issues of authority and power, which others in this book have examined.[29] Like any other Christian tradition, the devotion to Our Lady of Charity developed as a result of a community of persons with vested interests, regardless of the ethical assessment of these interests. In light of the latter, it is interesting to consider the symbolism of *los tres Juanes*, especially highlighting how the evolution of the identity of these figures in oral, literary and iconic traditions evidences the vested interests of the various communities that have come to embrace this devotion in one way or another.

In what follows I base my arguments primarily on key literary sources that address the evolution of the symbolism of *los tres Juanes*. Similar arguments can be drawn from other sources. I want to underscore that the central theological figure in this devotion is Our Lady of Charity. Yet, I argue that, theologically speaking, it is impossible to understand her identity without understanding the symbolic representation of *los tres Juanes*. In other words, if, theologically speaking, charity or the love of God is the central theme of this devotion (represented in the symbol of Our Lady of Charity), the specific sociocultural way of understanding the traditioning of this love cannot occur apart from the community of persons that received this devotion (represented in the symbol of *los tres Juanes*).[30]

Los Tres Juanes as Symbols of Community-building Processes

A perusal of the evolution of this devotion reveals how the particular identity of the three original protagonists has changed in accordance with the various communities that have received and reshaped this tradition. Trying to make sense of the variant and oftentimes contradictory interpretations of the tradition of Our Lady of Charity, Olga Portuondo Zúñiga writes:

> It is true that . . . what could have been only one point of view became, as years went by, *the only truth*. In this sense, a legend was formed and a myth was elaborated. From the finding of the image of Our Lady of Charity until the building of her sanctuary, the story is packed with allegories and historical events, syncretic personal actions or aspirations. Up until now, the testimony of Juan Moreno in 1687 has been understood as being absolutely faithful to a past concrete reality. And yet, from this one only derives an essential truth, archetypal allusions—a useful metaphor that explains the epochal shaping of the people of Santiago del Prado. For instance, the representations of the virgin of Charity project a utopian-like ethno-cultural unity of the Cuban people when she is represented as a light *mulata*, or as many say, "a white *trigueña*."

In his introduction to his unfinished work on the *virgen* of Charity, Fernando Ortiz says that he wanted to know how she lives "in the popular soul of Cuba." *In our modest opinion, the virgin of El Cobre with her myths, legends and miracle-like experiences depends upon the very popular soul of the Cuban people* (translations of Portuondo Zúñiga are mine).[31]

Portuondo Zúñiga's qualifying remarks are significant, especially in light of the changes that take place with respect to the names and identity of the persons that symbolically represent the communal bearers of this devotion. As she suggests, the tradition of Our Lady of Charity is shaped and reshaped by specific communities of persons who relate, appropriate, and reinterpret this popular religious expression through various interests and historical circumstances. Nowhere is this more evident than in the reinterpretation of the identity of the two Amerindian brothers (Juan de Hoyos and Rodrigo de Hoyos) and the African slave boy (Juan Moreno). They have come to be known simply as the three fishermen—two *white* men and a black (adult) man, or a black, a white, and an Amerindian. Indeed, as Portuondo Zúñiga affirms, "If fervent interlocutors were asked who found the image on the waters of the Bay of Nipe almost all would assert: three fishermen, Juan, the white, Juan, the black, and Juan, the Mulato, also known as the Indian." She goes on to raise the following question: "Why has there been a change in the color and occupation of the travelers of the canoe that sailed through the waters of Nipe?"[32] José Juan Arrom begins to hint at an answer to this question when he writes:

Juan de Hoyos is reduced to Juan Hoyo without the preposition [de] and used in the singular. In this sense, "Hoyo" is on the way to being converted, as it will later become, into the adjective *criollo*: Juan Criollo. With respect to Rodrigo de Hoyos, now also known as Juan, there will be the substitution of "Hoyos" for the adjective *indio*: Juan Indio. And with respect to Juan Moreno, to avoid possible ambiguity, there is a change from *moreno* to *esclavo*: Juan Esclavo. These three *Juanes*, surnamed by gentile-like adjectives undoubtedly acquire a symbolic function: they represent the ethnic elements and the cultural values that have informed the composition of the Cuban people. The three *Juanes* thus result in a singular Juan, one Juan, one and triune: Juan the Cuban people, our indoafrohispanic people (my translation).[33]

There is no doubt that in order to understand the "handing over" of this devotion one needs to understand the community of persons that accompanies Our Lady of Charity. This is the key to understand the reasons for the change in sociocultural identity, names, occupation, and number of those that come to be portrayed at the feet of Our Lady of Charity. In turn, underlying these changes are various community interests and issues that ground creative revisions of this tradition. The catholicity of persons associated with this devotion, which influences various revisions of this tradition, can be briefly traced as follows.

Sometime in the year 1511, the Spaniard Alonso de Ojeda introduced devotion to Mary to the Amerindian natives in Cuba.[34] Anthropological and religious connections likely occurred between Atabex (supreme deity and goddess of fresh waters) and Mary (sometimes associated with the waters in Spanish devotions).[35] In 1597 Captain Francisco Sánchez de Moya was charged with overseeing the copper mines in El Cobre. Some have argued that he brought the image of La Caridad, later found in the Bay of Nipe, to El Cobre from Illescas, Spain.[36] In 1612/13 Juan Moreno, an African slave boy, and two Amerindian brothers (Juan de Hoyos and Rodrigo de Hoyos) found the floating statue of Our Lady of Charity in the Bay of Nipe in the easternmost part of Cuba. The official *Acts of 1687–1688*, recently discovered by Cuban historian Leví Marrero, confirm the Amerindian and African identities of the original protagonists of this devotion. According to the *Acts of 1687–1688*, the central protagonist is Juan Moreno, who recalls finding the statue with the two Amerindians when he was ten years old.[37]

After these originating events, subsequent communities appropriated and revisioned this tradition to mirror their own religious, sociocultural, and political interests. In 1701 Onofre de Fonseca, the first chaplain of the shrine of La Caridad, wrote a history of the appearance of the statue. This version is believed to have followed closely the *Acts of 1687–1688*. A very important historical piece is the fact that Fonseca was Jamaican. It was the Jamaicans Francisco Bejarano (vicar of the cathedral of Santiago de Cuba) and Tomás de Fonseca (diocesan vicar general and Onofre's brother) who promoted and sponsored the official *Acts of 1687–1688*.[38] To them is owed the original institutionalization and first official ecclesiastical recognition of the devotion (but not in a doctrinal sense of the term).

In 1766 an important reinterpretation of this tradition occurred, which forever marked later communal appropriations. At that time Julián Joseph Bravo offered his own version, thus originating "the myth of *los tres Juanes* when he transforms the hunter, Rodrigo de Hoyos, into Juan Diego, the Indian that carried in his *tilma* the (Mexican) *virgen* of Guadalupe. He will grant to the newly created figure of Juan Diego, the central role in the narration of finding and venerating the image of Our

Lady of Charity."[39] To Bravo is owed the "orthodox" organization of the devotion and its submission to Roman Catholic hierarchy and doctrine.[40] He seems to have had an interest in guaranteeing the orthodoxy of the devotion. Bravo also originated the myth of the violent storm, which is depicted in most iconic representations of the finding of Our Lady of Charity.[41] Ironically his version, though not historically accurate, has enjoyed the most popularity among the devotees of Our Lady of Charity.[42] Thus Portuondo Zúñiga writes:

> It is his version, not that of Onofre de Fonseca, that was imposed. An a-historical Juan Diego [a-historical with respect to this devotion] would come to be part of the three de-characterized *Juanes* that found the image of the virgin after facing a violent hurricane that almost caused their shipwreck. His voice transcended, as he would have wanted, through the dogmatic and simplistic exposition of the myth because it gained in synthesis and intensity.[43]

In spite of its widespread imposition, Bravo's version was not the last interpretative word on this tradition.[44] For instance, in 1853, following oral traditions that parallel Bravo's concerns, a new story emerged bearing the names of Juan Hoyo, Juan Indio, and Juan Esclavo. It is this version, which, as already noted above, interprets the triune identity of the protagonists of the devotion of Our Lady of Charity in light of the "indoafrohispanic" composition of the emerging Cuban nation. The communal symbol of *los tres Juanes* comes to represent the oneness in diversity of the Cuban nation. Indeed, the original identity of the figures who found the statue of Our Lady of Charity seems to recede gradually in order to yield the singular *Juan Cuba* or *Juan Pueblo*.[45]

As the above arguments demonstrate, the particular identity of *los tres Juanes* is associated with distinct communities of persons that traditioned the devotion to Our Lady of Charity. The various constructions of this identity hint at the religious, social, cultural, political, and gender interests of communities associated with traditioning the devotion. The presence of the Hoyos brothers captures the human experience of the Amerindians, which includes the particularity of their socioeconomic status as slaves, as well as their religious beliefs. Their religious particularity provides a bridge to cross over into the particularity of Christian faith. Indeed, as Arrom has observed, "it is evident that it is not Mary that 'Spanglicizes' *(españoliza)* the creed of the Indians, but rather, the Indians that indigenize the creed of Mary."[46] The relation of Caridad with Atabex (the Taíno natives' mother of the god and goddess of fresh waters) is the key to understanding Arrom's observation.

The presence of Juan Moreno and the various attempts to portray either two or all three of the *Juanes* as black raise the question of race in the catholicity of this devotion as well as the impact of religious traditions of the peoples of Africa who were enslaved and who later became associated with this devotion. As in the case of the presence of the Amerindians, the presence of various Afro-Caribbean blacks (for example, Cubans and Jamaicans) "Africanized" this devotion. In fact, if there is an invariable in the tradition, it is the presence of blacks (symbolized by Juan Moreno). The presence of Juan Moreno is a symbol of faith-traditioning processes associated with this devotion that birthed and nourished Afro-Cuban communities.[47]

The presence and inclusion of other, later *Juanes* signals a change in the sociopolitical and religious interests associated with this devotion and the identity of the Virgin. The inclusion of "white" *Juanes* signals a new way of traditioning that fosters and reflects the emergence of a new community of devotees. Indeed, the white *criollos* will increasingly embrace this devotion as a symbol of *Cubanía* (Cuban-ness) against Spanish colonial rule. After 1868, Our Lady of Charity will become known as *la Virgen Mambisa*, the nationalistic, patriotic title derived from her association with the men *(los mambises)* who fought in the Cuban wars of independence.

The changes in the identity of those associated with the finding of the statue of Our Lady of Charity undoubtedly reflect the diversity of communities that tradition this devotion. These changes suggest religious and sociopolitical elements foreign to the experience of the Amerindian and African communities originally associated with the devotion. In some cases these changes may have been brought about by communities interested in a more "orthodox" traditioning of the devotion. That may have been the reason for the substitution of and centrality given to Juan Diego in Bravo's 1766 traditioning of the narrative of Our Lady of Charity (recall earlier arguments associated with Bravo's concern to advance Catholic orthodoxy). On the other hand, it would also be reasonable to embrace these changes as evidence of ongoing intercultural and interreligious communal conversations.[48] Such polyvalent conversations result in the experience of *mestizaje/mulatez* so characteristic of communal identity in the Caribbean and MesoAmerica.

Community-Building Processes in the Image of God: A Trinitarian Critique of the Traditioning of *Los Tres Juanes*

The evolution of the identity of *los tres Juanes* in the devotion to Our Lady of Charity has been interpreted as a way to "project a utopia of ethno-cultural unity onto the Cuban people."[49] However, in what may have been a legitimate effort to include new devotees, advance their sociocultural interests, and promote unity, the particular human identities of some devotees, including the original protagonists of this devotion, have at times been forgotten and betrayed. The old truism comes to mind: to translate is to betray *(traduttore, traditore)*.[50] Seen from the trinitarian perspective that this essay embraces, betrayal suggested by the exclusion of distinct others from traditioning processes signals failed human efforts to build community in the image of God.

Because traditions build communities (authentic as well as inauthentic), the communal symbol of *los tres Juanes* serves as a crucial indicator of the kind of community envisioned in the transmission of this religious tradition. Any effort to suppress the specific sociocultural memory of the original protagonists (two Amerindians and a young African slave boy) of this devotion in oral, iconic, or written traditions seriously compromises the Christian and trinitarian significance of the devotion. Sadly, without remembering this particular humanity there is a loss of the "passional" experience that originates and ethically grounds the vision of the community-building process. As our earlier biblical and trinitarian reflections have suggested, authentic community and union with others cannot be fostered without diversity and without a kenotic experience that stems from solidarity with the cross and the crucified of history. The revelation of God in Jesus witnesses to the community-building process that constitutes the very reality of God as a kenotic process that leads to identify with (solidarity) and love of (charity) the crucified. Apart from diversity and kenosis there is no God, and no authentic community, human or divine.

The changes that take place with respect to the identity of *los tres Juanes* reflect the composition of various communities constituted by the tradition. These changes invite us to consider the inclusive nature of God's love. Since traditioning in the image of God means promoting the building of authentic community rooted in the divine practice of including others, the inclusion of other communities in this devotion could be judged to be consistent with this divine experience. But the inclusion of some cannot take place at the expense of the exclusion of others. In particular, our trinitarian reflections above have noted how the process of traditioning God's self (God's love) necessarily includes a kenotic and preferential dimension. In the devotion to Our Lady of Charity this dimension is found in the specific identity of the two Amerindians and the African slave boy who found the floating statue of Our Lady of Charity in the Bay of Nipe. As symbols of oppressed communities, their personal marginalized experiences suggest how the building of authentic community in the image of God begins with inclusion of the marginalized other.

Beyond the latter, another indication of the betrayal of tradition associated with this devotion has to do with the gender-exclusive nature of the symbol of *los tres Juanes*. While the change in the identity of these *Juanes* reflects a diversity of communities constituted by this devotion, women, who from the very beginning were the backbone of this devotion, have yet to acquire a place in the communal symbol of the devotion. In this sense, like many traditioning processes upon which communities have been built, this popular tradition clearly reflects patriarchal influences. Yet what is most perplexing is that the exclusive male transmutation of the symbol of *los tres Juanes* betrays the community of persons (women) who may have been most responsible for the survival of the devotion. Indeed, similar to other popular traditions, this tradition provides evidence that supports women as the primary yet suppressed bearers of Christian tradition. The following historical detail is worth noting:

> As a result of his [Sánchez de Moya's] good treatment, the administrator had been able to get in 1608 a legacy of 26 blacks—very few of those recently born had died. The reason for this is the fact that he maintained a midwife named Juana Ruiz, who was paid 600 *reales*, in addition to food, for her to accompany the labor of black women.[51]

How fascinating that this woman named Juana, a midwife, was charged with attending the amniotic waters and childbirth of black slave women. For among the oldest popular beliefs associated with Our Lady of Charity, still prevalent in our day, is the association of Our Lady of Charity with water and with the help of women who are in labor! It is likely that after being taken to the settlement of Barajuá, the statue of Our Lady of Charity was placed in the hospital chapel that served the needs of the copper slaves.[52] Thus one may speculate whether Juana, or other women like her, accompanied by Our Lady of Charity, helped the slave women give birth (in this hospital or in various other local homes) to the bodies of the community (Afro-Cuban) that would initially be most responsible for perpetuating the memory of this popular religious tradition. Like Juana Ruiz, there are plenty of other women (including other *Juanas*) who contributed in various sociopolitical ways to supporting the traditioning of this devotion.[53] Their identity must be remembered in any effort that seeks to address the community-building nature of this devotion and to translate symbolically such efforts into oral, iconic, or written forms of traditioning.

A trinitarian approach to the symbolic representation of *los tres Juanes*, therefore, requires a more inclusive retrieval and ongoing interpretation of particular racial, social, cultural, gender, and even generational (Juan Moreno was only ten years old when he discovered the statue) differences associated with this devotion.

The myth of sociocultural homogeneity represented in the affirmation that "the three *Juanes* thus result in a singular *Juan*, one *Juan*, one and triune: *Juan* the Cuban people, our indoafrohispanic people"[54] must be critiqued so as to recognize the distinct dangerous memories of the *Juanes* and *Juanas* that have traditioned this devotion. In doing so one can envision a future time when Cuban and Cuban American traditions that seek to symbolically represent and constitute community under the care of Our Lady of Charity will reflect more inclusively and preferentially (with respect to gender, race, and class) the image of God.

As we have argued throughout this essay, traditioning can be an authentic community-building process when the divine praxis of oneness as diversity is affirmed. But oneness, which is predicated upon diversity, requires the preferential inclusion of the marginalized others. This preferential inclusion has been suggested above by the Johannine community-building process that occurs with the outpouring of the Spirit by the crucified Christ at the foot of his cross and by the trinitarian discussion on God's kenotic movement and its symbolic representation in the cross.

In the devotion to our Lady of Charity this preferential inclusion of the other is specifically depicted by the distinct identity of the two aboriginal brothers and the African slave boy who discovered the floating image of Our Lady of Charity. The specific identity of these figures is the key that unlocks the theological significance of this devotion. While the communal evolution of the symbol into *los tres Juanes* suggests the universal traditioning of God's love, recalling the social, racial, cultural, and religious identity of those who first encountered Our Lady of Charity unveils the preferential nature that this and other forms of Christian traditioning should embrace. Indeed, this devotion, which centers upon the symbol of Our Lady of Charity, suggests that tradition ultimately has to do with handing over God's love, most preferentially to the crucified of history.

CONCLUSION: THE RELEVANCE OF A TRINITARIAN APPROACH TO TRADITION WITHIN A CULTURE OF GLOBALIZATION

In an article entitled "Toward the Construction of an Intercultural Theology of Tradition," Orlando O. Espín laments over the fact that

Catholic theologies of tradition "systematically ignore Catholic tradition as the latter is received and lived among the vast majority of Catholics, simply because they are not received and perceived as part of the First World."[55] In that article Espín seeks to underscore "the everyday faith and the faith-life of everyday Catholics" as "the ordinary means by which Catholic Tradition is interpreted and construed, Catholic identity shaped, and continuity with the past claimed." Espín underscores, however, that any Christian traditioning occurs *in* the world. He describes the world in which contemporary Christians find themselves situated in the following manner:

> Today's Christianity exists in an increasingly and irreversibly globalized world, and yet this same world seems equally and increasingly emphatic about its ethnic and cultural diversity. . . . The world in which Christianity now finds itself is increasingly "one" and increasingly "catholic" (i.e., "globalized and "diverse"). It would be a mistake to choose one facet of today's world over the other (i.e., globalization over diversity, or vice versa) as "best" category of contemporary analysis. Just as it would be a grave theoretical error to limit the interpretation and analysis of today's world to the perspectives or interests of *either* those who benefit from globalization *or* those whom globalization leaves behind.[56]

Espín is particularly interested in exploring how this worldwide experience influences theology, since no theology ever occurs in a vacuum, and more specifically Catholic theologies of tradition. Because globalization "includes forces of homogenization, of worldwide standardization at every level (cultural, social, political, economic, religious)" globalization is, in Espín's view, "inimical to true diversity and to respectful, meaningful dialogue." Given this context, Espín correctly infers the following questions: "Whose understanding and experience of Tradition is being presented as Tradition or as theology of tradition? Whose world, whose social class, whose gender, whose race, whose ethnic and cultural contexts are assumed as 'typical' of, or a 'standard' among, Catholics worldwide?"[57] In formulating these questions, Espín anticipates an answer in his intercultural approach to tradition and in his "plurichrome" and "plurivalent" understanding of "truth" in Christian traditioning.[58]

My essay proposes a trinitarian revisioning of tradition. More specifically, I have underscored the specific vision that the New Testament and later developments in trinitarian theology embrace in understanding the community-building process of traditioning God's personal life. As I have argued, God constitutes God's self by a distinct, personal, and mutual handing over. God's handing over creates the divine community, which is above all characterized by oneness as diversity. In providing a trinitarian reading of the devotion to Our Lady of Charity, I have suggested ways to appropriate properly the communal symbol of *los tres Juanes* in this popular religious tradition in accordance with this divine communal experience.

Given the fact that any tradition is always embodied and handed over by particular persons who in the process of receiving "the past in reference to a future" necessarily engage in betrayal *(traduttore, traditore)*, I find this trinitarian model for constructing theories of tradition essential and historically timely in light of the above described context of globalization. The trinitarian approach to tradition proposed in this essay resists forgetfulness, which in turn leads to betrayal and homogenization. It provides this resistance by affirming a diversity of communal experiences as essential to Christian traditioning.

In the process of acknowledging and affirming diversity, careful and preferential attention must be given to building community with marginalized others. Analogous to the role exercised by the crucified God in Jesus Christ, the marginalized are often those who have been chosen to encounter, proclaim, and anticipate the arrival of God's love (charity) among us. This is certainly the theological cornerstone of the devotion to Our Lady of Charity. While the evolution in the symbolic identity of *los tres Juanes* suggests the universality of God's love, the particularity of the original communities of persons associated with this devotion suggests the preferential nature that must be present in any authentic effort to tradition and thereby to build community according to God's image. Ultimately, the practice of traditioning *with* the other, especially the marginalized other in this increasingly diverse world, may be the surest sign that an authentic community-building process has been embraced in accordance with the triune mystery that affirms communal oneness *as* diversity.

Notes

¹ See Avery Dulles, *The Craft of Theology: From Symbol to System* (New York: Crossroad, 1996), 89.

² See Karl Rahner and Joseph Ratzinger, *Revelation and Tradition*, trans. W. J. O'Hara (New York: Herder and Herder, 1966).

³ Gerald O'Collins, *Fundamental Theology* (New York: Paulist Press, 1981), 55. See also, idem, *Retrieving Fundamental Theology: The Three Styles of Contemporary Theology* (New York: Paulist Press, 1993), 120–49.

⁴ Yves Congar, OP, *Tradition and Traditions: An Historical and a Theological Essay*, trans. Michael Naseby and Thomas Rainborough (New York: Macmillan, 1967), 241.

⁵ Ibid., 296.

⁶ Note how *Dei Verbum* abandons the use of *traditions* in the plural. As Avery Dulles argues, "Whereas Trent, interested in objective content, spoke of traditions in the plural, Vatican II, in *Dei Verbum*, speaks of tradition in the singular. Its concern is with tradition as an organ of apprehension and transmission rather than as a set of doctrines and precepts" (Dulles, *The Craft of Theology*, 94).

⁷ For instance, see M. Shawn Copeland, "Tradition and the Traditions of African American Catholicism," *Theological Studies* 61, no. 4 (2000): 632–55; Mary Catherine Hilkert, "Experience and Tradition—Can the Center Hold?" in *Freeing Theology: The Essentials of Theology in Feminist Perspective*, ed. Catherine M. LaCugna, 59–82 (New York: HarperCollins, 1993); Peter Phan, *Christianity with an Asian Face: Asian American Theology in the Making* (Maryknoll, NY: Orbis Books, 2003); and Orlando O. Espín, "Toward the Construction of an Intercultural Theology of Tradition," *Journal of Hispanic/ Latino Theology* 9, no. 3 (2002): 22–59.

⁸ This seems to me to be a basic presupposition of Orlando Espín's arguments surrounding the fundamental importance of the living witness and faith of ordinary Christian people. See Orlando Espín, "Tradition and Popular Religion: An Understanding of the Sensus Fidelium," in *The Faith of the People: Theological Reflections on Popular Catholicism* (Maryknoll, NY: Orbis Books, 1997), 63–90.

⁹ See Chapter 6 in the present volume, in which Gary Riebe-Estrella takes a different personal approach to constructing an understanding of tradition.

¹⁰ Jerome Murphy-O'Connor, "Eucharist and Community in First Corinthians," in *Living Bread, Saving Cup*, ed. R. Kevin Seasoltz (Collegeville, MN: Liturgical Press, 1982), 26–27.

¹¹ Note that elsewhere in the Gospel of John, "handing over" is presented as a death-producing experience, as is the case when Judas hands Jesus over to the guards that accompany the Pharisees (Jn 18:2).

¹² For such an exploration, see Catherine M. LaCugna, *God for Us: The Trinity and Christian Life* (San Francisco: HarperCollins, 1991); Walter Kasper, *The God of Jesus Christ* (New York: Crossroad, 1989); and Elizabeth A. Johnson, *She Who Is: The Mystery of God in Feminist Theological Discourse* (New York: Crossroad, 1992).

¹³ I use the term *grammar* in the sense that Terrence Tilley uses it to propose the principles that make up the Catholic intellectual tradition. With respect to these principles Tilley writes: "These are not principles I *want* to be the grammar of Catholic intellectual tradition. Rather, the claim made here is descriptive. These are the rules that emerge from the practices undertaken which constitute the tradition. These rules are the 'grammar' of this tradition. I do not claim that these rules are exhaustive or sufficient. Nor is their formulation

unchangeable." See Terrence Tilley, *Inventing Catholic Tradition* (Maryknoll, NY: Orbis Books, 2000), 124.

[14] Ibid.

[15] On the historical development of trinitarian theology, see William G. Rusch, *The Trinitarian Controversy: Sources of Early Christian Thought* (Philadelphia: Fortress Press, 1980).

[16] LaCugna, *God for Us*, 69.

[17] Ibid.

[18] Karl Rahner, *The Trinity* (New York: Crossroad, 1997), 17.

[19] See LaCugna, *God for Us*, 377–411. See also Justo L. González, *Mañana: Christian Theology from a Hispanic Perspective* (Nashville, TN: Abingdon Press, 1990), 101–15; Sixto García, "A Hispanic Approach to Trinitarian Theology: The Dynamics of Celebration, Reflection, and Praxis," in *We Are a People!: Initiatives in Hispanic American Theology*, ed. Roberto S. Goizueta (Minneapolis: Fortress Press, 1992); and Teresa Chávez Sauceda, "Love in the Crossroads: Stepping-Stones to a Doctrine of God in Hispanic/Latino Theology," in *Teología en Conjunto: A Collaborative Hispanic Protestant Theology*, ed. José David Rodríguez and Loida Martell-Otero, 22–31 (Louisville, KY: Westminster John Knox Press, 1997).

[20] See John Zizioulas, *Being as Communion: Studies in Personhood and Church* (New York: St. Vladimir's Press, 1985); idem, "Human Capacity and Human Incapacity: A Theological Exploration of Personhood," *Scottish Journal of Theology* 28 (1975): 401–48; idem, "On Being a Person: Towards an Ontology of Personhood," in *Persons, Divine and Human: Kings Essays in Theological Anthropology*, ed. Christoph Schwöbel and Colin Gunton, 33–46 (Edinburgh: T & T Clark, 1991); and idem, "The Doctrine of the Holy Trinity: The Significance of the Cappadocian Contribution," in *Trinitarian Theology Today: Essays on the Divine Being and Act*, ed. Christoph Schwöbel, 44–60 (Edinburgh: T & T Clark: 1995).

[21] John Zizioulas, "Communion and Otherness" (Knokke-Heist, Belgium: Apostle Andréas Press, 1994). A shortened version is available online. See also Patricia A. Fox, *God as Communion: John Zizioulas, Elizabeth Johnson, and the Retrieval of the Symbol of the Triune God* (Collegeville, MN: Liturgical Press, 2001), esp. 48–50. For a critique of Zizioulas's theological anthropology, see "Reconsidering Relational Anthropology: A Critical Assessment of John Zizioulas's Theological Anthropology," *International Journal of Systematic Theology* 5, no. 2 (2003): 168–82.

[22] Zizioulas, "Communion and Otherness."

[23] John Zizioulas, quoted in Fox, *God as Communion*, 48.

[24] Zizioulas, "Communion and Otherness." See also Zizioulas, *Being as Communion*, esp. 37–49.

[25] Zizioulas, "Communion and Otherness."

[26] Zizioulas, *Being as Communion*, 106.

[27] See Roberto S. Goizueta, *Caminemos con Jesús: Toward a Hispanic/Latino Theology of Accompaniment* (Maryknoll, NY: Orbis Books, 1995), 47–76.

[28] See Olga Portuondo Zúñiga, *La Virgen de la Caridad del Cobre: Símbolo de Cubanía* (Santiago de Cuba: Editorial Oriente, 1995).

[29] For instance, see Chapter 2 in the present volume.

[30] For a theological discussion on how Our Lady of Charity can be seen as a symbol or sacramental sign of God's love and grace, see Miguel Díaz, *On Being Human: U.S. Hispanic and Rahnerian Perspectives* (Maryknoll, NY: Orbis Books, 2001), 60–78.

[31] Portuondo Zúñiga, *La Virgen de la Caridad del Cobre*, 33.

[32] Ibid., 34.

[33] José Juan Arrom, *Certidumbre de América: Estudios de letras, folklore y cultura* (Madrid: Editorial Gredos, S.A., 1971), 210.

[34] Irene A. Wright, "Nuestra Señora de la Caridad del Cobre (Santiago de Cuba), Nuestra Señora de la Caridad de Illescas (Castilla, España)," *The American Historical Review* 5 (1922): 709–10.

[35] Arrom, *Certidumbre de América*, 192–96; Portuondo Zúñiga, *La Virgen de la Caridad del Cobre*, 58–77.

[36] Wright, "Nuestra Señora de la Caridad del Cobre," 711–13.

[37] See Mario Vizcaíno, ed., *La Virgen de la Caridad: Patrona de Cuba* (Miami: Instituto Pastoral del Sureste, 1981), 10–27.

[38] Portuondo Zúñiga, *La Virgen de la Caridad del Cobre*, 117.

[39] Ibid., 170–71. It is beyond the scope of this essay to explore further the historical connections between the devotion to Our Lady of Charity and the devotion to Our Lady of Guadalupe. The following areas of research might unveil interesting historical links between these two Latino/a devotions: (1) the pastoral concerns of the bishops of the respective dioceses at the time (of Santiago de Cuba, and of Mexico City); (2) the Franciscan and Mexican connections of the bishop who ordained El Cobre chaplain Bravo (Bishop Juan Lazo de la Vega y Cancino) and the Franciscans' pastoral activities in both Mexico and Cuba at the time; (3) the impact that the controversy surrounding the *Nican Mopohua* around 1766 may have had on Bravo's reinterpretation of the narrative of Our Lady of Charity; and (4) Bravo's personal contacts, knowledge, and pastoral interests. I am grateful to Orlando Espín for suggesting some of these initial lines of research in order to explore further what is potentially a very important intercultural connection.

[40] Ibid.

[41] Ibid.

[42] Ibid., 172.

[43] Ibid.

[44] Note the presence of other cultures (like the Chinese in Cuba in the middle of the nineteenth century), as well as other interpretations by ecclesiastical authorities (such as Bishop Morell de Santa Cruz's comments in 1756 that those who were in the boat were all black slaves, or Hippolyte Piron's comments in 1850 about the "fishermen" who found the virgin).

[45] Arrom, *Certidumbre de América*, 210–11.

[46] Ibid., 192.

[47] On the presence of Afro-Cubans, see Chapter 8 in the present volume. On the question of race, particularly in relation to class and gender oppression, see Miguel de la Torre, "Masking Hispanic Racism: A Cuban Case Study," *Journal of Hispanic/Latino Theology* 6, no. 4 (1999): 57–73. See also Thomas A. Tweed, *Our Lady of the Exile: Diasporic Religion at a Cuban Catholic Shrine in Miami* (New York: Oxford Univ. Press, 2002), 65–69. On understanding Afro-Cuban religions, see Andrés I. Pérez y Mena, "Understanding Religiosity in Cuba," *Journal of Hispanic/Latino Theology* 7, no. 3 (2000): 6–34.

[48] For an understanding of tradition that appeals to the model of conversation, see Chapter 6 in the present volume.

[49] Portuondo Zúñiga, *La Virgen de la Caridad del Cobre*, 33.

[50] See Gustavo Pérez Firmat, *Life on the Hyphen: The Cuban-American Way* (Austin: Univ. of Texas Press, 1994), 3. He writes: "'Tradition,' a term that derives from the same root as the Spanish *traer*, to bring, designates convergence and continuity, a gathering together of elements according to underlying affinities or shared concerns. By contrast, 'translation' is not a homing device but a distancing mechanism. In its topographical meaning, translation is displacement, in Spanish, *traslación*. This notion has been codified in the truism that to translate is to traduce *(traduttore, traditore)*; implicit in the concept is the suggestion that to move is to transmute, that any linguistic or cultural displacement necessarily entails some mutilation of the original. In fact, in classical rhetoric *traductio*—which is of course Spanish for translation *(traducción)*—was the term used to refer to the repetition of a word with a changed meaning. Translation/*traslación*, traduction/*traducción*—the misleading translation of these cognates is a powerful reminder of the intricacies of the concept."

[51] Portuondo Zúñiga, *La Virgen de la Caridad del Cobre*, 87–88.

[52] Ibid., 96–99.

[53] Ibid., 156.

[54] Arrom, *Certidumbre de América*, 210.

[55] Espín,"Toward the Construction of an Intercultural Theology of Tradition," 29. See also Orlando Espín, "La experiencia religiosa en el contexto de la globalización," *Journal of Hispanic/Latino Theology* 7, no. 2 (1999): 13–31; and idem, "Immigration, Territory, and Globalization: Theological Reflections," *Journal of Hispanic/Latino Theology* 7, no. 3 (2000): 46–59. For a biblical exploration of the dynamics of globalization, see Francisco Lozada, Jr., "Johannine Universalism and Particularism: Toward an Intercultural Reading of John 6," *Journal of Hispanic/Latino Theology* 10, no. 4 (2003): 5–21.

[56] Espín, "Toward the Construction of an Intercultural Theology of Tradition," 27.

[57] Ibid., 28.

[58] Ibid., 41–42.

8

What about *Mulatez?*

An Afro-Cuban Contribution

Michelle A. González

Sin el negro Cuba no sería Cuba.

—FERNANDO ORTIZ

Latino/a theologians place the contexts and cultures of Latino/a peoples at the center of their theologies—and as their starting point. Whether it is an emphasis on *lo cotidiano* (daily life), *mestizaje*, or popular religion, the particular contours of Latino/a religious expressions are the core of Latino/a theological writings. Latino/a theologians frame the prominence of their particularity in light of the contextual nature of all theological expressions. In other words, all theology is contextual, shaped by the culture and history of the theologians and the subject of their theological writings.[1] Similarly, every theological expression, whether it be written, celebrated, or performed, is organically linked to its social location.

In their retrieval of Latino/a cultures and contexts, Latino/a theologians have recovered a vital dimension of historical and contemporary Christian religious expressions. In this process Latino/a theologians have constructed a Latino/a religious identity. Whether it is Our Lady of Guadalupe, *mestizaje*, or the European conquest of the Americas, there are certain key themes that have become "canonized" in the corpus of Latino/a theology as fundamental dimensions of Latino/a religiosity and history. This has resulted in, whether intentionally or not, a traditioning

180

of Latino/a identity that foregrounds particular elements of Latino/a culture and history at the expense of, I would argue, the fullness and diversity of Latino/a peoples. Most notably, the presence of African peoples and their participation in Latino/a history and identity have been downplayed. Latino/a theologians write about Mexico, Guadalupe, *mestizaje*, and the Southwest. The Afro-Caribbean experience is strikingly insignificant within the narrative and construction of Latino/a historical identity. This has led to a depiction of Latino/a history, religious experience, and culture that privileges certain elements, erasing others in the traditioning of Latino/a identity.[2]

This essay seeks to "correct" and expand the traditioned identity of Latino/a theology by examining the Cuban face of the colonial Latin American Church. I place a strong emphasis on the African population in Cuba during the colonial era and the relationship between the colonial church in Cuba and the institution of slavery. By recovering this significant presence within the pantheon of Latino/a peoples, I hope to add another dimension to the Latino/a historical narrative. In many ways, therefore, this essay can be seen as a *ressourcement* of a particular historical moment within Latin American Church history.[3] I begin by outlining the traditioned identity of Latinos/as within Latino/a theology, emphasizing the privileging of Mexican American experience and ambiguity surrounding the term *mestizaje*. I then move to the historical Cuban context. In my concluding section I offer future directions for study in light of this Afro-Cuban retrieval.

THE TRADITIONED IDENTITY OF LATINO/A THEOLOGY

The strongest historical link that unites Latinos/as is their common Latin American heritage, including Spanish, African, and indigenous elements. As noted by church historian Justo González, "The Spanish-American Roman Catholic Church is part of the common background of all Hispanics—if not personally, than at least in our ancestry."[4] Often when Latino/a theologians trace the history of Latinos/as here in the United States, they begin with the Spanish conquest. Methodologically, as González points out, this is a sound gesture, for this shared Spanish ancestry is a strong dimension uniting contemporary Latin American and Latino/a peoples. However, too often Latino/a theologians focus on the conquest of indigenous peoples at the expense of the other dimensions of the conquest, namely, the transatlantic slave trade and the colonial era in the Americas. As a result of this, the paradigm of conquest has become normative for the history of Latino/a peoples.[5] This is not the historical case. Not all of our foremothers and forefathers were conquered; some were enslaved and brought to the Americas. In addition, a glimpse of the colonial era in the Spanish colonies reveals that the *criollo/a* population, which became the power base of independence movements from Spain, did not in fact emulate or celebrate its indigenous past, but instead affirmed a Spanish American identity that attempted to erase their racial mixture.

Since I cannot cover the breadth of these historical eras in the brief scope of this article, I would like to focus here on the normativity of the conquest as paradigmatic of Latin American history for Latino/a theologians. This, in turn, has led to the primacy of *mestizaje* within this theology. *Mestizaje* appears both as a historical category and a fundamental locus for Latino/a theology. Technically, the term refers to the biological and cultural mixture of Spanish and indigenous. However, within Latino/a theology the term has come to refer to mixture in general. My examination of *mestizaje* is twofold. First, I begin by examining its historical normativity through the historical narratives of several Latino/a theologians. I then turn to its methodological, epistemological, and hermeneutic value within Latino/a theology.

The centrality of *mestizaje* within Latino/a theology is clearly seen when one looks at the manner in which Latino/a theologians write the pre–US history of Latinos/as. Such is the case for Eduardo Fernández, in his introduction to Latino/a theology, the first book-length introductory text to this field.[6] The clash between Spanish and indigenous is the center of Fernández's account of the conquest and colonial era. The Southwest United States and the native Mexicans are the key sites and figures in his historical narrative. Turning to the late nineteenth century, Fernández broadens his narrative to include Puerto Rico in addition to the Southwest. Nonetheless, it is the Mexican American experience that remains normative in his general account of Latino/a history.

Alejandro García-Rivera's *The Community of the Beautiful: A Theological Aesthetics* offers a fundamental theology grounded in theological aesthetics informed by the ecclesial history of Latin America.[7] García-Rivera recovers the importance of symbol and Beauty as a key contribution of the Latin American Church. His account uses the image of Our Lady of Guadalupe as the centerpiece of his aesthetics; her apparition brings forth the importance of popular religion within Latin America and its underlying cosmology. "The role of the cosmic in the popular religion of the Latin American Church finds exquisite expression in Mary of Guadalupe. . . . Thus, a cosmic order and redemption intertwine in this 'form' which continues to walk with the Latin Church of the Americas in its fiery pilgrimage to the Kingdom of God."[8] In addition,

Guadalupe, through her apparition to the indigenous man Juan Diego, informs García-Rivera's notion of the "lifting of the lowly," a subversive aesthetic principle that places the suffering and marginalized at the center.

For García-Rivera, Guadalupe represents a "different Beauty," found at the intersection of the indigenous and Spanish. Her *mestiza* appearance symbolizes a "beauty of difference." Building on the difference of Guadalupe, García-Rivera recounts the history of the Latin American Church as an ecclesial tradition of difference, told through the signs and symbols of Latin American religiosity. Citing figures such as Dominican friar Antonio de Montesinos, who denounced the *encomienda* system as an unjust social structure that was little more than the enslavement of indigenous peoples, García-Rivera intertwines the theme of justice within his narrative. Franciscan Bernardino de Sahagún is also featured prominently for his ethnography of the Nahuatl world view. Sahagún's twelve-volume study of the symbols and culture of the Nahuatl people is a priceless resource for scholars today and is, for García Rivera, a "semiotics of culture."[9] García-Rivera then turns to the contemporary Latin American Church through the documents of Medellín and the writings of Latino/a theologians to emphasize further the intersection of Beauty and Justice in the Latin American ecclesial tradition. Centering in particular on Virgilio Elizondo's work on Our Lady of Guadalupe, the aesthetic and the call for justice remain intertwined as a key contribution of the Spanish Americas. Like Fernández, we once again find a "Mexicanized" account of Latin American history.

While the history of Africans and their role in Latino/a identity is often downplayed, it is not entirely absent from the narratives of Latino/a theologians. In his overview of the ecclesial history of the Americas, Justo González aptly mentions not only Spanish attitudes toward the indigenous, but also toward the slave population. Nonetheless, his history remains centered around the indigenous, the church in the Southwest, and Our Lady of Guadalupe.[10] In a similar vein, Miguel A. De La Torre and Edwin David Aponte's more recent introduction to Latino/a theology incorporates African traditional religions as one of the three major sources to Latino/a religiosity, the other two being Spanish and indigenous elements.[11] Nonetheless, their historical narrative remains focused on the conquest, the *encomienda* system, and the indigenous.

The root of the primacy of *mestizaje* within Latino/a historical narratives can be traced to the writings one of the founders of Latino/a theology, Virgilio Elizondo. Born in his doctoral dissertation, this theme is one of the central theological loci within Latino/a theology.[12] For Elizondo, *mestizaje* is representative of the border reality that characterizes the

Latino/a experience of being people "in between." Even in his early writings, while remaining grounded in the Mexican American reality, Elizondo described *mestizaje* in terms of general mixture: "*Mestizaje* is simply the mixture of human groups of different makeup. . . . *Mestizos* are born out of two histories and in them begins a new history."[13] *Mestizos/as* must not see their racial and cultural mixing as a source for feelings of inadequacy. Instead, Elizondo argues in his Christology, *mestizaje* becomes a privileged site of God's self-disclosure. Therefore, the *mestizo/a* has an honored role in salvation history.

The major themes in Elizondo's Christology are outlined in his text *Galilean Journey: The Mexican-American Promise*.[14] Here Elizondo grounds his christological reflection on Jesus' Galilean identity, giving Jesus' social, cultural, and political particularity theological value. For Elizondo, Jesus' identity as a Galilean is not accidental; it is revelatory of his life and ministry: "Like every other man and woman, he was culturally situated and conditioned by the time and space in which he lived. . . . Jesus was not simply a Jew, he was a Galilean Jew, throughout his life he and his disciples were identified as Galileans."[15] Born in Galilee, Jesus was not born at the center of Jewish life and society—namely Jerusalem—but on the border. Elizondo connects this marginal border reality to the contemporary context of Latinos/as, more specifically Mexican Americans. As a *mestizo* figure, Elizondo contends, Jesus reveals the border as the site of God's revelation: "The *mestizo* culture of the borderland is the privileged locus of God's self-revelation."[16] Christ's incarnation as a man within a marginal region reveals the theological significance of that context. In Elizondo's Christology the ambiguity and pluralism that characterize *mestizaje* become key dimensions of God's revelation. The hybridity of Galilee calls us to a new understanding of community and consequently of church.[17]

The category of *mestizaje* has come to saturate Latino/a theology. Anthropologically, *mestizaje* functions to name the ambiguity and in-betweenness of Latino/a identity. Contesting a monolithic understanding of Latinos/as as a single race, De La Torre and Aponte note, "Hispanics are a *mestizaje* (racial mixture or combination of ethnicities), a *mestizaje* of races, a *mestizaje* of cultures, a *mestizaje* of kitchens, a dense stew of distinct flavors."[18] In the concluding section of their text, Aponte and De La Torre describe the diversity of the current Latino/a community as an "evolving *mestizaje*." The category, for them, no longer represents the mixture of indigenous and Spanish—it now refers to cultural mixture in any sense of the word, as long as it applies to Latino/a communities.

The 1995 anthology of Latino/a theology *Mestizo Christianity* cemented the primacy of this category for Latino/a theologians.[19] As Arturo

Bañuelas states in the opening paragraph of his introduction:

> In this theology, *mestizaje*, the mixture of human groups, is a core
> paradigm because Latino history begins in the early sixteenth cen-
> tury with the Spanish conquest and the religious and cultural
> confluence of the Spaniards, Amerindians, and Africans in the
> Americas. This paradigm of the mixing of bloods and cultures also
> marks the birth of *mestizo* Christianity, the experience of God from
> within *mestizaje* reality. *Mestizo* Christianity is the Latino's heri-
> tage. Presently, Latino theology is attempting to elaborate the link
> between *mestizaje* and God's design for humanity.[20]

Like Aponte and De La Torre, Bañuelas sees *mestizaje* as encompass-
ing mixture in general, not merely Spanish and Amerindian. However,
there remains a strong ambiguity within Latino/a theology on the use of
this term. In the more recent *From the Heart of Our People: Latino/a
Explorations in Catholic Systematic Theology*, the editors note this ambiguity in their glossary.[21] *Mestizaje* is defined as the cultural and racial
mixing of Spanish and indigenous. However, they note that "the term is
often used, in Latino/a theology, to refer to a much broader and deeper
mixing of cultures, religious traditions, and so on." The following entry,
mulataje, refers to the cultural and racial mixing of African and Spanish.
"Although occasionally used in Latino/a theology, the terms *mulataje*
and *mulato/a* are often and inaccurately subsumed into the categories of
mestizaje and *mestizo/a*."[22]

Even when it is not explicitly named as *mestizaje*, the paradigm of
indigenous-Spanish mixture remains a normative category for Latino/a
experience. This is seen, for example, in Justo González's notion of the
"non-innocent history" of Latino/a peoples. "We always knew that our
ancestors were not guiltless. Our Spanish ancestors took the lands of
our Indian ancestors. . . . Some of our Spanish forefathers raped our
Indian foremothers. Some of our Indian foremothers betrayed their people
in favor of the invaders. It is not a pretty story."[23] Gonzalez's contribution remains extremely vital for Latino/a peoples, yet we must not erase
the experiences of African slaves and their place in our "non-innocent
history."

Not all Latino/a theologians collapse *mulatez* into *mestizaje*. For
mujerista theologian Ada María Isasi-Díaz, these terms remain distinct.
Highlighting the mixture of African cultures and races within the Spanish-speaking Americas, the use of *mulatez* accounts for this history. Isasi-
Díaz sees "*mestizaje* as a hermeneutical tool and paradigm," which contributes to an understanding and representation of who Hispanics are.[24]

Mestizaje and *mulatez* are the theological locus of *mujerista* theology. They contribute to a new understanding of plurality, diversity, and difference. In a more recent work Isasi-Díaz transforms the nature of both terms:

> The importance of difference for Latinas and Latinos is made obvious by the insistence in Hispanic/Latino theology, including *mujerista* theology, on recognizing the importance of *mestizaje/ mulatez*, a concept which originally referred to the mingling of Amerindian and African blood with European blood, but which now also includes the present-day mixtures of people from Latin America and the Caribbean both among ourselves and with people of other ethnic/racial and cultural backgrounds here in the United States.[25]

This new conceptualization of *mestizaje/mulatez*, Isasi-Díaz argues, opens avenues for discussions with other marginalized groups and grounds an understanding of difference that is not exclusive or oppositional. Her sentiments are echoed in the writings of Roberto S. Goizueta, who sees the coming together of Latin America and the United States as a second *mestizaje* and the convergence of Latino/a cultures in the United States as a third *mestizaje*.[26]

This racial and cultural mixture, the sense of people living between two worlds, reflects the context from which Hispanic theology emerges. "Because we choose *mestizaje* and *mulatez* as our theological locus, we are saying that this is the structure in which we operate, from which we reach out to explain who we are and to contribute to how theology and religion are understood in this society in which we live."[27] *Mestizaje/ mulatez* not only portrays the Latino/a context, but these terms also reflect the epistemological standpoint from which Latinos/as exist in the world, their way of being. This mixture and ambiguity becomes the hermeneutical lens through which Latinos/as see the world.

Perhaps no other Latino/a theologian has attempted explicitly to maintain the categories of *mestizaje* and *mulataje* more than biblical scholar Fernando F. Segovia. Segovia describes Latinos/as a "hybrid people," both *mestizo* and *mulato*. "On the one hand, we are children of Spain and thus of Europe, Mediterranean and Catholic Europe. . . . On the other hand, we are also the children of pre-Columbian America and Africa—deeply rooted as well in other ancient cultures, histories, and languages."[28] Segovia continues by noting that *mestizaje* and *mulatez* permeate all aspects of Latino/a culture and identity, including religion, art, and epistemology. In his own work he resists the trend within

Latino/a theology to collapse *mulatez* into *mestizaje*. Noting that *mestizaje* is often used to speak metaphorically of all mixture, he says, "I prefer, however, to use the two terms to point to the different fusions of 'races' that have taken place in the whole of Latin America."[29]

The hermeneutic and methodological implications of *mestizaje* for Latino/a theology are highlighted in María Pilar Aquino's excellent essay on Latino/a theological method in *From the Heart of Our People*. In this essay Aquino lists three fundamental hermeneutic-epistemological principles and three sources and loci that she understands as framing the methodological coherence of US Latino/a theology.[30] The three principles must be understood jointly. "Together, these principles govern faith's *epistemic locus* by granting theology its methodological coherence; because they are rooted in the *sociocultural locus* of Latino/a communities, these principles also determine the selection and interpretation of theological contents."[31] The first principle is a focus on the faith of the people, primarily through the study of popular Catholicism. Second, Aquino highlights an option for the poor and oppressed. An emphasis on liberating praxis is the third principle. The three sources and loci Aquino lists are seen as the privileged contexts of Latino/a theological knowledge. They are Latino/a popular Catholicism, the reality of *mestizaje*, and *lo cotidiano*. Aquino speaks of an intellectual and theological *mestizaje* as a way of addressing the interculturality of the Latino/a people.

The normativity of *mestizaje* is also seen in the primacy given to Our Lady of Guadalupe and Elizondo's Galilean *mestizo* Jesus. One only has to look at the Cuban theologians who have written about Guadalupe to support this claim. They include Alejandro García-Rivera, Orlando O. Espín, and Roberto S. Goizueta. The normativity of Guadalupe is also seen in Arturo Bañuelas's claim that "even Cuban-American theologians, for whom Our Lady of Charity and not Guadalupe is the central marian symbol, now accept Guadalupe as somehow normative for U.S. Hispanic Theology."[32] Roberto S. Goizueta's *Caminemos con Jesús* centers on the predominantly Mexican American community of San Fernando Cathedral in San Antonio Texas, emphasizing *mestizaje* and Guadalupe. In Gloria Inés Loya's *mestiza* feminist theology, she argues for Guadalupe and Malinalli/Malintzin as central figures for all Latinas: "I am aware that as a Mexican-American, the presence of Guadalupe and of Malintzin are interpretive keys for a Latina-Hispanic-*mestiza* theology. Having presented much of this information to other Latina-Hispanas, I have consistently found support in that Malintzin and Guadalupe are core figures for all *mestizas*, not only for those of us of a Mexican-American or Chicana heritage."[33]

Whether it is in the symbols recovered by Latino/a theology as normative for Latino/a religiosity, or the history constructed by Latino/a theologians, or the categories used to describe Latino/a identity, hermeneutics, and epistemology, there is a clear normativity given to Mexican and Mexican American experience. Latino/a theologians of all backgrounds, not just Mexican Americans, perpetuate this normativity. In many ways this is understandable, given that Mexican Americans constitute the majority of Latino/a peoples. However, as "minority" peoples in the United States, Latinos/as have constantly struggled to have their voices and stories heard within the dominant discourse. Therefore, within our own theologies, we must not allow the majority to rule, erasing the complexity of Latino/a identity. As the authors of this volume contend, tradition, whether it is of identity or religiosity, is a process that creates identity.

In the following more historical section, I retrieve another dimension of Latino/a ecclesial history, namely, Cuba. I begin by examining Afro-Cuban culture and the manner in which it contributed to the preservation of African religiosity.[34] I then move to the Catholic church in Cuba and its relationship to the slave population. While I cannot cover the entirety of Cuban ecclesial history, I hope this snapshot into Cuban Catholicism is an invitation both for further study in this area and an initial step in addressing the constructed, traditioned identity of Latino/a theology.

AFRO-CUBA

Sociologist Fernando Ortiz, in numerous studies, discovered the African contribution to Cuban culture in the island's art, religion, and language and "in the tone of the collective emotionality." Writer and folklorist Lydia Cabrera would later ask not waiting for an answer, "What piece of our soil is not saturated with secret African influence?" Fidel Castro would more recently declare, "We are Latinoafroamericans!" In the structures of perception and discourse, in the everyday language of thought and feeling, Africanity runs through and colors everything that can be called uniquely Cuban.[35]

The history of slavery in Cuba must be contextualized in light of the indigenous population and its extermination in the early years of the conquest. There were approximately 112,000 indigenous people in Cuba in 1492. By 1510, half of this population was gone, forcing the Spanish to hunt and capture indigenous people in what is today known as the Bahamas. By 1555 the indigenous population was down to 5,000.[36] When the natives became too few and far between, the Spanish turned to African slaves as a source of labor on the island. Historian Arthur F. Corwin notes that one of the earliest references to African slavery in the Antilles was by King Fernando in 1511; he allowed fifty black slaves to work in Santo Domingo. African slaves were seen as stronger and better workers than the natives.[37] By 1534 there were 1,000 African slaves in Hispaniola. In 1531 the Crown outlawed indigenous slavery, thus creating the need for more African slaves.[38] Between 1512 and 1761, 60,000 slaves were imported to Cuba from West Africa; 400,000 were imported between 1762 and 1838. According to the 1841 census the entire population of Cuba comprised 418,291 whites, 152,838 freed blacks, and 436,495 slaves.[39] For a period of time, then, the black population outnumbered the white population of Cuba. Even though Spain abolished slave trafficking in 1835, an estimated 190,000–240,000 slaves were illegally brought to Cuba between 1840 and 1867.[40] Slaves from more than twenty different African nations were brought to Cuba, but four African regions were significantly represented.[41] In 1880 the law abolishing slavery in Cuba was passed, although the total abolition of slavery did not occur until 1886.

Afro-Cuban historians and ethnographers Jorge and Isabel Castellanos divide slavery into two eras in Cuba: the first period, pre-plantation, was during the sixteenth, seventeenth, and the first half of the eighteenth centuries; the plantation era was from the latter half of the eighteenth century until the abolition of slavery in 1886.[42] However, between 1846 and 1862 the white population in Cuba increased dramatically. The 1846 census shows that whites still remained the minority of the island, but by 1862 they are the majority.

The dramatic increase in the Cuban slave trade during the plantation era is due to the sugar revolution of the latter eighteenth to early nineteenth centuries. As noted by historian Franklin W. Knight, "Over the years from 1763–1838, Cuba changed from an underpopulated, underdeveloped settlement of small towns, cattle ranches, and tobacco farms to a community of large sugar and coffee plantations."[43] Cuba had become the world's leading producer of sugar. This led, in turn to an economy entirely dependent on slave labor. "In no other Spanish colony was the local economy so totally dependent on slavery; in no other Spanish colony did African slaves constitute so large a part of the population; in no other Spanish colony did the total population of color constitute a majority."[44] One can thus directly trace the overall increase in Cuba's population to the plantation system.

The white population in Cuba was divided into two groups: criollos/ as and *peninsulares*. *Criollos/as* were of Spanish descent but born in the Americas. The *peninsulares* were born in Spain. *Peninsulares* dominated the colonial bureaucracy and commerce. *Criollos/as* were the landholders and planters.[45] In the sixteenth and seventeenth centuries there were very few white women in Cuba. Relationships between African women and white men led to a *mulato* population that later constituted a significant portion of free people of color.[46] In contrast to other areas of the Spanish empire, such as Mexico, in the early half of the colonial era these two groups of whites coexisted in relative harmony. However, with the growing wealth of the island in the nineteenth century and a growing *criollo/a* nationalism, tension began to rise as each group sought to defend its own political and economic interests. *Criollos/as* sought to rid themselves of Spanish rule. However, they were in agreement on the issue of slavery and opposed any attempt to abolish it.

Colonial slave society in Cuba had its own particular flavor, with spaces for African slaves to maintain their cultural and religious heritages; various aspects of Spanish colonial society allowed African identity to survive. The urban population of slaves, some of which were able to buy their freedom, was able to gather in *cabildos*. These brotherhoods of Africans date to as early as 1598 (for example, Nuestra Señora de los Remedios, in Havana). Their predecessors are the Andulasian brotherhoods known as *cofradías*. Cuban ethnographer Fernando Ortiz traces the formation of *cabildos* of Africans to the fourteenth century in Seville, long before the conquest of the Americas. It is this structure that the Spanish brought to the Americas. In Andalusía the term *cabildo* often referred to a religious brotherhood, throughout the rest of Spain it referred to a city council.[47] *Cabildos* were associations of Africans (men and women) from the same tribe living in a city, a representative body of a particular nation. They were social societies and were very active on religious feast days.[48] In Havana they were also known as *reinados*, for during festivals one woman was made queen of the *cabildo*. The elder of the community was known as the king of the *cabildo*.

Philip A. Howard highlights the role of the *cabildo* within the Afro-Cuban community:

> After arriving in Cuba, Africans, particularly those in the principal cities and towns of the island, established mutual aid societies known as *cabildos de naciones de afrocubanos*. As early as the middle of the sixteenth century, these voluntary associations were created in order to mitigate the psychological and cultural shock of transplantation from the familiar context of traditional African societies to

the uncertainties of life in the Americas as slave laborers. In the countryside, plantation owners with government approval, even permitted their slaves to gather on days of rest or holidays to allay their sense of alienation. These reunions were spontaneous affairs without structure, however, and consisted only of recreational activities. But in the towns and cities of the island, individuals who spoke the same or related languages—such as Yoruba, Mandinga, Arará, and Carabalí—came to form and employ their mutual aid societies to promote the maintenance of African languages, customs, and heritage. The associations also provided assistance to sick members and assured them a decent funeral and burial when they died. Thus, these language- and group-based associations not only provided a sense of community to members and cushioned them from the blow of cultural dislocation, but they also provided a forum for the transmission of African cultures in Cuba.[49]

Cabildos were not directly linked to the Catholic church and were headquartered in members' households. This distance from the institutional church allowed members to enjoy more freedom, including using the *cabildo* as a site for political resistance. While women did not have leadership roles in *cabildos,* they did participate in their activities (including ceremonial roles). *Cabildos* thus played a central role in the preservation of African culture, religion, and identity.

In addition to *cabildos,* Afro-Cuban religion maintained Africans' identity and was also a site of resistance. Eugenio Matibag's work examines the manner in which Afro-Cuban religious traditions shaped modern Cuban identity, especially in the early half of the twentieth century. Building on the work of scholars Jorge and Isabel Castellanos, Matibag identifies seven features of Afro-Cuban religion: the combination of monotheism and polytheism; a belief in divine supernatural power that can manifest itself in objects; ritual as the mediation between humans and the gods; divination; magic; the importance of music and dance in liturgy; and a sense of belonging to a religion, though not necessarily to a church.[50] As noted by the Castellanos, "One of the most important contributions of African culture to Cuban culture is the gift of popular religion."[51] For Latino/a theologians, any study of Latino/a popular religion that failed to include the African dimension of these religious practices would be remiss.[52]

Although the African population in Cuba originally enjoyed relative freedom, with its continuing growth the colonial government tried to increase its control over them. In 1785 the Código Negro Carolino was passed, limiting African rituals, celebrations, and gatherings. This

coincided with the increase in the slave trade to Cuba and Cuba's growing prominence within the Spanish empire. Historian Philip A. Howard
cites the 1792 Bando de buen gobierno y policía as one of many efforts
to regulate the activities of *cabildos*. "The central point conveyed by
the 1792 proclamation is that the Spanish authorities, although granting the *cabildos* the right to exercise some of their traditional religious
activities, would not tolerate any amalgamation of African and Christian customs and beliefs."[53] This was one way to exert Spanish dominance in the face of the sheer number of Africans on the island. By the
late nineteenth century the colonial government was "cracking down,"
attempting to impose its control over the *cabildos*. The Cuban war of
independence, beginning in 1895, marked the demise of the *cabildo* system.

The history of the Catholic church in Cuba is ambiguous, tainted by
an institutional church that remained tied to the Spanish crown and to
plantation owners. Yet the church also voiced its prophetic tradition by
denouncing the exploitation of Africans and the indigenous. From the
beginning of the conquest ecclesial leaders in Cuba denounced violence
toward the indigenous. One of the great liberators of the indigenous,
Bartolomé de Las Casas, was converted to his cause by the River Arimao
in Cuba. Cuban church historian Manuel Maza Miquel states that the
year 1680 is pivotal in the ecclesial history of Cuba. In that year the
Capuchin friars Francisco José de Jaca and Epifanio de Moirans preached
against the possession of slaves and against slavery as an institution.[54]
Jaca refuted the notion that Africans are born to serve and that there is
some sort of philosophical or theological justification of slavery. For
Jaca, the institution had to end in its entirety. The two Capuchins were
suspended from all priestly functions in December 1681.They had not
only condemned slavery, but they refused to give absolution to those
who did not liberate and give retribution to their slaves. They were returned to Spain and imprisoned. In time they were absolved, but they
were prohibited from ever returning to the Americas.

However, Maza Miquel depicts the history of the church in Cuba as
mostly saturated by the power interests of the Spanish crown until 1899.[55]
This was so much the case that the church, with few exceptions, consistently opposed independence from Spain. The church in Cuba was marked
by the system of royal patronage. For Maza Miquel, one cannot understand the colonial church without understanding this system.

Beginning with the 1508 papal bull *Universalis ecclesiae*, the crown
controlled ecclesial leadership, including the presentation of candidates.
Bishops did not communicate directly with the Holy See, except by way
of Spain's royal government. The life of the early Cuban church was

rigidly monitored by the Spanish crown, including clergy expeditions to the Americas, the activities of congregations and religious orders, and the internal governance of dioceses. The crown controlled ecclesiastical budgets and made or approved all personnel appointments.

One has to contextualize the sixteenth-century church in the Americas in light of the Christian *Reconquista* of Iberian territories from the Muslims. "It is an over-simplification to identify the *Reconquista* directly with the general model of the crusade, but there was in it the same interplay of worldly enterprise and religious purpose. There was also the idea that the faith could and should be propagated by military means."[56] Maza Miquel dates the first era of the Catholic church in Cuba as beginning with Diego Velázquez's first expedition (1511–15) through the first diocesan synod of 1680. He suggests that this synod was a first step in pastoral institutionalization. The 1680 date also coincides with the first denunciation of slavery by the Capuchins Jaca and Moirans.

For Maza Miquel the period from 1685 to 1832 can be understood as the Golden Age of the Cuban church, for it was under the leadership of visionaries. This is also the era that gives birth to native clergy in Cuba.[57]

The Cuban clergy members were very lax and superficial in their evangelization of slaves. However, along with the "boom" in the slave trade in the late 1700s came a surge in the financial situation of the Cuban church—financial gains based on slavery. Plantations went so far as to build private chapels, where clergy acted and were paid much like employees rather than evangelizers. During the nineteenth century the areas with the greatest slave populations had the fewest priests. Matanzas, for example, in 1846 had one priest for every 2,707 slaves. Clergy neglected the rural slaves, for parishes catered to the white urban population. "In 1860, of the 779 clergymen ministering to a population of 1,396,530 (a ration of 1:2,000) more than 50 percent (401) lived in Havana."[58] Clergy preferred to live in urban settings, while the slave population was located primarily on sugar plantations.[59]

Plantation owners eventually began to feel that any sort of religious worship (including the Catholic Mass) was a disruption of the workday.[60] With the sugar boom the influence of the Catholic church as a voice of dissent on slavery faded into the background. Due to a shortage of clergy, much of the church's influence deteriorated in the nineteenth century. This affected the entire Cuban population, though the evangelization of slaves was especially neglected. "The Church fought and lost the struggle for orthodoxy in the countryside at the turn of the century when the crown agreed with the planters' demand to liberate the plantation from religious burdens such as meatless Fridays, work-free Sundays and holidays, and the all-important tithe."[61]

Within two hundred years of the beginning of the conquest, the church began to feel threatened by the presence of Africans on the island. The 1680 diocesan synod explicitly sought to regulate the cultural and religious influences of Africans on the church, controlling, for example, certain African rituals and practices. "The Church was a part of the system of slavery. It supported, reinforced, and reflected the status quo."[62] Historian Johannes Meier highlights that the church did not question slavery: "In fact, the church benefited from slavery. The slaves were employed as domestics in the residences of clergy, they worked in the construction of cathedrals and convents and cultivated the land of the property of the convents."[63]

This neglect for African evangelization is in sharp contrast to the church's efforts to convert the indigenous. The church's complicity with slavery was not passive, for the church itself owned slaves. As noted by Armando Lampe:

> In the French and Spanish colonies, the slaves were incorporated into the Catholic Church through baptism and the other sacraments, and efforts were made to keep them to some degree in touch with the parishes. But the Church had no real interest in evangelizing the blacks, mainly because it was too deeply involved in the slave system. There is a long list of bishops and priests who owned sugar mills and large numbers of slaves in the French and Spanish Caribbean. . . . The seminary in Havana, for example, still drew its revenue from the sugar industry in the nineteenth century.[64]

Researching in papal documents dated between the fifteenth and nineteenth centuries, Gutiérrez Azopardo notes that it was not until Pius VII's 1814 letter to the king of France that the enslavement of Africans was condemned (but, in this document, only partially and with conditions). While earlier documents condemned the slavery of the indigenous, Africans were not mentioned.[65] What is also particularly shocking is the manner in which slavery has been written out of the history of the colonial church. Many twentieth-century monographs do not even mention it.[66] Traditioning, as Miguel H. Díaz and Gary Macy emphasize in this volume, includes forgetfulness and suppression. Too often the connection between slavery and the church has been forgotten in ecclesial histories.

This brief overview of Afro-Cuban religious culture in colonial Cuba and the church's relationship to slavery provides a snapshot of this historical era. Plantation culture in Cuba, unregulated by ecclesial authorities, became a space for Afro-Cubans to preserve their religious and cultural identities.[67] The absence of clergy on plantations, where the majority of slaves resided, contributed to the formation of Afro-Cuban popular religious practices, many of which continue to influence Cuban Catholicism today. *Cabildos* provided an institutionalized space for the preservation of African identity. The church, while offering a prophetic voice in the early years of colonialism, was virtually silenced through its complicity in the slave trade. While as an institution it attempted to regulate and control the mixture of African and Spanish religious world views, due to neglect and the sheer number of Africans on the islands the church failed in this endeavor.

CONCLUSION

As the contributors to this volume frequently emphasize, tradition is understood as a process, a dynamic active practice that perhaps is best understood as traditioning. When communities tradition their identity, beliefs, and practices, they engage in a process in which the present draws from the past in the shaping of its current and future reality. Within this practice, power, as in every human endeavor, is at play, and certain voices are privileged over others.

This chapter attempted to "correct" the traditioning of Latino/a identity within Latino/a theology by broadening our understanding of Latino/a culture and history, specifically in light of its heavy Mexican American influence. The Cuban reality, one that differs sharply from the Mexican, challenges the normativity given to Mexican American experience. For Cubans and Cuban Americans, it is not the *mestizaje* of Spanish and indigenous that shape our identity, but African and Spanish *mulataje*.

As noted by Jorge and Isabel Castellanos, one can only define and understand Cuban culture if one considers the interrelationship of two poles: *eurocubano* and *afrocubano*. With origins in European and African cultures respectively, these two poles exist on a continuum. Cuban culture, they argue, is indistinguishable from Afro-Cuban culture.[68] This in turn, influences the very nature of *all* Cuban religiosity. "If you ask a Cuban (here or there [on the island]) what his or her religion is, the majority will respond Catholicism. But if one examines in detail the theological content of their beliefs and ritual practices, one will immediately see that in many cases they are distant from orthodox Catholicism."[69] While the Castellanos perhaps draw too sharp a line between orthodox Catholicism and Cuban religiosity, the impulse underlying their point is sound. African culture and religiosity have left an indelible mark on Cuban religiosity as a whole.[70] This has often led to a false description of

Cuban Catholicism as syncretic. Cuban Catholicism is no more syncretic than Catholicism as a whole, which throughout its history has become incarnate in the cultures in which it lives and breathes. This particularity often is most clearly seen in popular religious practices. Latino/a theologians, therefore, with their heavy emphasis on popular religion, are remiss in their scholarship if they do not incorporate the vital African dimension of Latino/a religiosity.

By way of conclusion I offer three implications of this essay that point to further directions for study. First, Latino/a theologians must become more nuanced in their elaboration of Latino/a identity. We cannot afford to erase and marginalize portions of our own population in favor of a more generalized description of our shared identity. To do so is to do violence to those communities that we ignore and forget. It is to deny the dangerous memories within our traditions. This emphasis on particularity within community is both theological and ethical. As seen in Díaz's contribution to the present volume (Chapter 7), catholicity implies diversity. Díaz offers a trinitarian model for respecting the particularity and catholicity of communities, with an emphasis on God as one and diverse. Thus, to emphasize particularity within one's tradition is to be catholic in the truest sense of the word. Roman Catholic theology, therefore, must embrace this principle of unity amid diversity as a central feature of the catholic nature of theology.

There are also ethical dimensions to traditioning that must be raised. As theologians standing in the heritage of Latin American liberation theology, the ethical dimensions of the theological task are not new to Latino/a theologians. As Gary Macy highlights in his contribution to this volume (Chapter 3), writing history is a moral (as well as political, social, and economic) act that must be placed in an ethical framework. The ethics of Latino/a traditioning must be at the forefront of our theologies. While it is important to maintain the coalitions that exist between and among different Latino/a groups, it is equally important not to subsume certain sectors of our population at the expense of others.

Second, an examination of the African elements of Latino/a culture, it is to be hoped, will open a pathway of dialogue and collaboration between African American and Latino/a theologians. Within black theology the Afro-Latin is glaringly absent.[71] Future collaborations are vital if one is to further research on this topic. However, such collaborations would force an entire transformation of the understandings of black and Latino/a identities functioning within these theologies. As this essay has emphasized, there are certain key themes that have become "canonized" in the corpus of Latino/a theology as fundamental dimensions of Latino/a religiosity and history. In a similar vein, black liberation theology has strongly emphasized race as a central analytic lens through which to interpret the experience of African Americans in the United States. While recent scholarship has sought to nuance this depiction of African American identity, race remains a central marker of the African American experience. Afro-Latin religiosity and culture forces black and Latino/a theologies to recast their construction of identity within their respective communities.

Third, through my highlighting the traditioned identity within this particular context, I hope that theological scholars will further address the question of how we construct identity within theology, often at the expense of excluding certain groups and privileging others. Returning to the morality of traditioning, the way we construct identity is not ethically neutral. Too often, minority groups within Catholicism are seen as unorthodox, as if their particularity somehow detracts from the Catholic nature of their religiosity. Dominant Catholicism, which is just as "particular," is accepted uncritically as the norm by which other forms of Catholicism are judged. Theologians need to be aware of the power dynamics of traditioning in all contexts and cultures throughout the history of Catholicism.

Traditioning identity is a vital aspect of what we do, for it builds identity, community, and a sense of historical context. The construction of identity, whether cultural, racial, or ecclesial, is an exclusionary process; one group's identity is set apart from others. We must be mindful, however, of the manner in which power functions in the construction of identity. The identity that is traditioned is too often the identity constructed by the elite. Whether it is ecclesial leaders or academic theologians, the official, traditioned narrative of a people is often in the hands of a few. This is also the narrative often accessed by "outsider" groups.

As theologians informed by a preferential option for the marginalized and the contextual nature of all theology, Latino/a theologians must be vigilant of the identity we tradition and how we risk denying the identity and humanity of some of our fellow Latino/a brothers and sisters.

Notes

[1] The prominence of culture in Orlando O. Espín's essay, Chapter 1 in this volume, resonates with this emphasis on the contextual nature of all theology.

[2] As noted by Gary Macy in Chapter 3 of this volume, history involves choosing and taking active control of self-identity.

[3] The *ressourcement* movement in twentieth-century Roman Catholic theology was an appeal for theologians to return to historical sources to inform contemporary understandings. But *ressourcement* does not represent a return

to historical sources applied uncritically to the present. Instead, it entails a revival of historical sources. *Ressourcement* engages an innovative reading of the Christian sources in light of the questions of the contemporary era. Some of its most notable proponents were Yves Congar, Karl Rahner, and Hans Urs von Balthasar. Though not named *ressourcement*, the same spirit of historical retrieval is a key methodological gesture of various liberation theologians in their attempt to write theology from the underside of history.

⁴ Justo L. González, *Mañana: Christian Theology from a Hispanic Perspective* (Nashville, TN: Abingdon Press, 1990), 55.

⁵ Refuting an objective understanding of history, Gary Macy argues that ultimately history is whatever historians decide to write about. This constructive dimension of history informs my critique of the historical narrative of Latino/a theology.

⁶ Eduardo Fernández, *La Cosecha: Harvesting Contemporary United States Hispanic Theology (1972–1998)* (Collegeville, MN: Liturgical Press, 2000).

⁷ Alejandro García-Rivera, *The Community of the Beautiful: A Theological Aesthetics* (Collegeville, MN: Liturgical Press, 1999).

⁸ Ibid., 192.

⁹ Ibid., 48. See Bernardino de Sahagún, *Historia general de las cosas de la Nueva España*, ed. Angel Maria Girabay K. (1956; repr. Mexico City: Editorial Porrúa, 1981).

¹⁰ See González, *Mañana*, chap. 3.

¹¹ Miguel A. De La Torre and Edwin David Aponte, *Introducing Latino/a Theologies* (Maryknoll, NY: Orbis Books, 2001).

¹² The scope of the contribution of *mestizaje* is perhaps best described by the incredulity with which Elizondo's dissertation director, Jacques Audinet, responded to the former's request to write on the topic. "First of all, *mestizaje* is not a traditional theological theme. As far as I knew at the time, there was not one reference, one book, not even a theological passage written on the subject. In theology, as in other disciplines, *mestizaje* was at best a marginal topic, if not nonexistent. It had nothing to do with the grandiose deployment of God's design from creation to parousia which is usually considered the domain of theology." Jacques Audinet, "A *Mestizo* Theology," in *Beyond Borders: Writings of Virgilio Elizondo and Friends*, ed. Timothy Matovina (Maryknoll, NY: Orbis Books, 2000), 143.

¹³ Virgilio Elizondo, "*Mestizaje* as a Locus of Theological Reflection," in Matovina, *Beyond Borders*, 160–62.

¹⁴ Virgilio Elizondo, *Galilean Journey: The Mexican-American Promise* (Maryknoll, NY: Orbis Books, 1994).

¹⁵ Elizondo, *Galilean Journey*, 49. In his 2003 Catholic Theology Society of America presentation "Good Fences and Good Neighbors? Biblical Scholars and Theologians," New Testament scholar Jean-Pierre Ruiz explores the influence of Elizondo's *Galilean Journey* on Latino/a systematic theology. Ruiz critiques Elizondo's construction of Galilee, and Latino/a systematic theology's uncritical acceptance of it, for drawing broad generalizations that are at times

embellished. Ruiz also highlights that due to Elizondo's uncritical use of West-ern European biblical scholarship, sections of *Galilean Journey* border on anti-Judaism. While not discarding Elizondo's *mestizo* Jesus, Ruiz does call for a closer examination of the biblical notions underlying this Christology and for more explicit collaboration between theologians and biblical scholars. See Jean-Pierre Ruiz, "Good Fences and Good Neighbors? Biblical Scholars and Theolo-gians," paper presented at the 2003 Annual Convention of the Catholic Theo-logical Society of America. Unpublished paper cited with the permission of the author.

[16] Roberto S. Goizueta, "A Christology for a Global Church," in Matovina, *Beyond Borders*, 155. In his later work, most notably his book on Our Lady of Guadalupe, Elizondo offers a more synthetic notion of *mestizaje*. See Virgil Elizondo, *Guadalupe: Mother of the New Creation* (Maryknoll, NY: Orbis Books, 1997).

[17] Goizueta sees Elizondo's Christology as representative of a global Chris-tianity that is no longer centered in Europe. At the heart of this Christianity is the *mestizo* Christ, and consequently, the *mestizo* church. "Beyond the Christ of kings and princes, beyond the Christ of the theologians and philosophers, beyond the Christ of the clerics and bishops, is the Christ of Juan Diego. This Christ is not found primarily in Jerusalem but in Galilee." In an increasingly globalized world the church must turn to the borders, not to the centers of power, in an effort to discover the true church (Goizueta, "A Christology for a Global Church," 150).

[18] De La Torre and Aponte, *Introducing Latino/a Theologies*, 13.

[19] Arturo Bañuelas, ed., *Mestizo Christianity: Theology from the Latino Per-spective* (Maryknoll, NY: Orbis Books, 1995).

[20] Arturo Bañuelas, "Introduction," in Bañuelas, *Mestizo Christianity*, 1. María Pilar Aquino defines Latino/a identity as *mestizo/a*, a combination of indig-enous, African, and European (María Pilar Aquino, "Directions and Founda-tions of Hispanic/Latino Theology: Toward a Mestiza Theology of Liberation," in Bañuelas, *Mestizo Christianity*, 192–208).

[21] Orlando O. Espín and Miguel H. Díaz, eds., *From the Heart of Our People: Latino/a Explorations in Catholic Systematic Theology* (Maryknoll, NY: Orbis Books, 1999).

[22] Orlando O. Espín and Miguel H. Díaz, "Glossary," in Espín and Díaz, *From the Heart of Our People*, 262. This position is a development of Espín's thought, for in earlier writings he uses the category of *mestizaje* to designate *mulato/a* realities. "Hispanic communities with their roots in the northeast, Florida or the Spanish-speaking Caribbean tend to be the result of *mestizaje* between Span-iards and Africans. Those communities with roots in the West and Southwest or in Mexico and central America tend to be the outcome of *mestizaje* between Spaniards and Native Amerindian populations (Orlando O. Espín, "Tradition and Popular Religion: An Understanding of the *Sensus Fidelium*," in Bañuelas, *Mestizo Christianity*, 151).

[23] González, *Mañana*, 40.

[24] Ada María Isasi-Díaz, *En La Lucha/In the Struggle: Elaborating a Mujerista Theology* (Minneapolis: Fortress Press, 1993), 186.

[25] Ada María Isasi-Díaz, "A New *Mestizaje/Mulatez*: Reconceptualizing Difference," in *A Dream Unfinished: Theological Reflections on America from the Margins*, ed. Eleazer S. Fernández and Fernando F. Segovia (Maryknoll, NY: Orbis Books, 2001), 203.

[26] Roberto S. Goizueta, *Caminemos con Jesús: Toward a Hispanic/Latino Theology of Accompaniment* (Maryknoll, NY: Orbis Books, 1995), 8.

[27] Ada María Isasi-Díaz, "*Mujerista* Theology: A Challenge to Traditional Theology," in *Mujerista Theology: A Theology for the Twenty-First Century* (Maryknoll, NY: Orbis Books, 1996), 66.

[28] Fernando F. Segovia, "Two Places and No Place on Which to Stand: Mixture and Otherness in Hispanic American Theology," in Bañuelas, *Mestizo Christianity*, 32.

[29] Fernando F. Segovia, "In the World But Not of It: Exile as Locus for a Theology of the Diaspora," in *Hispanic/Latino Theology: Challenge and Promise*, ed. Ada María Isasi-Díaz and Fernando F. Segovia (Minneapolis: Fortress Press, 1996), 196n6.

[30] María Pilar Aquino, "Theological Method in U.S. Latino/a Theology," in Espín and Díaz, *From the Heart of Our People*, 28–39.

[31] Ibid., 29.

[32] Arturo Bañuelas, "U.S. Hispanic Theology: An Initial Assessment," in Bañuelas, *Mestizo Christianity*, 59.

[33] Gloria Inés Loya, "Pathways to a *Mestiza* Feminist Theology," in *Religion and Justice: A Reader in Latina Feminist Theology*, ed. María Pilar Aquino, Daisy L. Machado, and Jeanette Rodríguez (Austin: Univ. of Texas Press, 2002), 219. Malinalli/Malintzin is also known as La Malinche. She was Hernán Cortéz's interpreter and translator.

[34] Due to the limited space of this essay, I will not be covering here the Lukumí religion, popularly known as Santería. Nor will I be addressing the other Afro-Cubans religions that thrived, and continue to do so, in Cuba and its diaspora. For some overviews of Afro-Cuban religion, see George Brandon, *Santería from Africa to the New World: The Dead Sell Memories* (Bloomington: Indiana Univ. Press, 1993); Joseph Murphy, *Santería: African Spirits in America* (Boston: Beacon Press, 1993); and Eugenio Matibag, *Afro-Cuban Religious Experience: Cultural Reflections in Narrative* (Gainesville: Univ. Presses of Florida, 1996).

[35] Matibag, *Afro-Cuban Religious Experience*, xii.

[36] See Louis A. Pérez, *Cuba: Between Reform and Revolution* (New York: Oxford Univ. Press, 1988).

[37] Arthur F. Corwin, *Spain and the Abolition of Slavery in Cuba, 1817–1886* (Austin: Univ. of Texas Press, 1967), 4.

[38] Matibag, *Afro-Cuban Religious Experience*, 20.

[39] Manuel P. Maza Miquel, "Clero católico y esclavitud en Cuba: Siglos XVI al XIX. Ensayo de síntesis," in *Esclavos, patriotas y poetas a la sombra de la*

Cruz: Cinco ensayos sobre catolicismo e historia cubana (Santo Domingo: Centro de Estudios Sociales Padre Juan Montalvo, 1999), 90, citing Kenneth F. Kiple, *Blacks in Colonial Cuba, 1774–1899* (Gainesville: Univ. Presses of Florida, 1976), 88. Kiple's text offers a wealth of resources on the demography of Cuba between 1777 and 1899.

[40] David R. Murray, *Odious Commerce: Britain, Spain, and the Abolition of the Cuban Slave Trade* (London: Cambridge Univ. Press, 1980), 244.

[41] For a detailed study of the different African nations brought to Cuba, see Franklin W. Knight, *Slave Society in Cuba during the Nineteenth Century* (Madison: Univ. of Wisconsin Press, 1970).

[42] Jorge Castellanos and Isabel Castellanos, *Cultura Afrocubana*, vol. 1, *El negro en Cuba, 1492–1844* (Miami: Ediciones Universal, 1988), 61.

[43] Knight, *Slave Society in Cuba during the Nineteenth Century*, 3.

[44] Pérez, *Cuba*, 101.

[45] "But they were not only the cattle raisers and planters of tobacco, sugar, and cotton. They spanned a very wide range from highly professional people such as lawyers, journalists, and educators in Havana to simple, solitary workers wringing a difficult living from a small mountainous plot in the eastern provinces" (Knight, *Slave Society in Cuba during the Nineteenth Century*, 89).

[46] Pérez, *Cuba*, 47.

[47] Fernando Ortiz, *Los cabildos y la fiesta afrocubanos del Dia de los Reyes* (1921; repr. Havana: Editorial de Ciencias Sociales, 1992), 4.

[48] The January 6 festival of Epiphany, *El Día de Reyes*, was perhaps the most significant feast day for Afro-Cubans. As described by renowned ethnographer Fernando Ortiz, "That day black Africa, its people, its costumes, its music, its tongues, its song and dance, its ceremonies, its religion and political institutions, were brought across the Atlantic to Cuba, especially Havana"(Ortiz, *Los cabildos y la fiesta afrocubanos del Dia de los Reyes*, 1).

[49] Philip A. Howard, *Changing History: Afro-Cuban Cabildos and Societies of Color in the Nineteenth Century* (Baton Rouge: Louisiana State Univ. Press, 1998), xii–xiv.

[50] Matibag, *Afro-Cuban Religious Experience,* 10–16, citing Jorge Castellanos and Isabel Castellanos, *Cultura Afrocubana*, vol. 3, *Las religiones y las lenguas* (Miami: Ediciones Universal, 1992).

[51] Castellanos and Castellanos, *Cultura Afrocubana*, 3:11.

[52] Many Roman Catholic scholars have held the distinction between popular religion and popular Catholicism in their writings. While there are certainly differences between non-Catholic popular religious practices and popular Catholicism in Latino/a communities, there is also a gray area where elements of indigenous and African religiosity enter into Spanish Catholic practices. For further reading on this distinction, see Orlando O. Espín, "Popular Catholicism among Latinos," in *Hispanic Catholic Culture in the U.S.: Issues and Concerns,* ed. Jay P. Dolan and Allan Figueroa Deck (Notre Dame, IN: Univ. of Notre Dame Press, 1994), 308–59. Also, as Espín notes in Chapter 1 of the present volume, popular religion is one of the key bearers of cultural identity.

[53] Howard, *Changing History*, 54.

[54] Manuel Maza Miquel, "Iglesia cubana: Cinco siglos de desafíos y respuestas," in Maza Miquel, *Esclavos, patriotas y poetas a la sombre de la Cruz*, 26.

[55] Manuel Maza Miquel, "Iglesia cubana," 10.

[56] Josep M. Barnadas, "The Catholic Church in Colonial Spanish America," in *The Cambridge History of Latin America*, vol. 1, *Colonial Latin America*, ed. Leslie Bethell (Cambridge: Cambridge Univ. Press, 1984), 511.

[57] Manuel Maza Miquel, *Iglesia cubana: Cinco siglos de desafíos y respuestas* (Santo Domingo: Editorial Amigo del Hogar, 1995).

[58] Knight, *Slave Society in Cuba during the Nineteenth Century*, 107.

[59] Maza Miquel, "Clero católico y esclavitud en Cuba," 97.

[60] "Even in Cuba, with its strong clerical traditions, the church's influence was nullified by the advent of the slave plantation system in the nineteenth century. What appears to emerge from these data is that the religious education of slaves in prosperous sugar colonies was viewed as an alarming intrusion into the affairs of the estates, inconsistent with maintaining social order and stability. The isolation of the plantation slave and his lack of contact with authority other than the master or the overseer was an elementary condition for maintaining the system. The advantages which religious conversion of the slaves offered in promoting stability were offset by this higher consideration essential to the maintenance of the slave system once the society became prosperous and the slaves in rural areas began to substantially outnumber whites." See Gwendolyn Midlo Hall, *Social Control in Slave Plantation Societies: A Comparison of St. Domingue and Cuba* (Baltimore: The Johns Hopkins Press, 1971), 51.

[61] Robert L. Paquette, *Sugar Is Made with Blood: The Conspiracy of Escalera and the Conflict between Empires over Slavery in Cuba* (Middleton, CT: Wesleyan Univ. Press, 1988), 62.

[62] Knight, *Slave Society in Cuba during the Nineteenth Century*, 106.

[63] Johannes Meier, "The Beginnings of the Catholic Church in the Caribbean," in *Christianity in the Caribbean: Essays on Church History*, ed. Armando Lampe (Barbados: Univ. of the West Indies Press, 2001), 42.

[64] Armando Lampe, "Christianity in the Caribbean," in *The Church in Latin America 1492–1992*, ed. Enrique Dussel (Maryknoll, NY: Orbis Books, 1992), 204.

[65] Ildefonso Gutiérrez Azopardo, "La Iglesia y los negros," in *Historia de la Iglesia en Hispanoamérica y Filipinas (Siglos XV-XIX)*, vol. 1, *Aspectos generales*, ed. Pedro Borges (Madrid: Biblioteca de Autores Cristianos, 1992), 322–23.

[66] Not one of the following books deals with the question of slavery and the Roman Catholic Church in colonial Latin America: Richard E. Greenleaf, ed., *The Roman Catholic Church in Colonial Latin America* (Tempe, AZ: Center for Latin American Studies, 1977); Enrique D. Dussel, *Desintegracion de la cristianidad colonial y liberación* (Salamanca: Ediciones Sígueme, 1978); Consejo Episcopal Latinoamericano, *La evangelizacion fundante en America Latina* (Bogotá: CELAM, 1990); Alberto de la Hera, *Iglesia y corona en la América*

española (Bilbao: Editorial MAPFRE, 1992); and Elisa Luque Alcaide and Josep-Ignasi Saranyana, *La Iglesia Católica y América* (Bilbao: Editorial MAPFRE, 1992).

[67] "Indeed, as developments in religious forms have perhaps most clearly demonstrated, the amalgamation, synthesis, symbiosis, or crossing of diverse West African and Hispanic cultural elements in the American setting produced a new religious culture. In Cuba as elsewhere in the Antilles, the 'peculiar institution' of slavery made possible the birth of this distinctly Afro-Caribbean culture" (Matibag, *Afro-Cuban Religious Experience*, xii).

[68] Castellanos and Castellanos, *Cultura Afrocubana*, 1:13.

[69] Ibid., 1:178–79.

[70] A study is urgently needed on the influence of African religiosity within the Cuban exile and Cuban American communities, and on the manner in which Cubans in the United States have or have not become more doctrinalized.

[71] Black theology has overwhelmingly remained wedded to the United States, and, within the United States, to non-Spanish-speaking peoples. The Afro-Latin is nonexistent within the writings of black theologians.

9

Traditioning

The Formation of Community, the Transmission of Faith

Nancy Pineda-Madrid

Accounts of the history of the Catholic faith reveal an evolving under-standing of the idea of tradition, particularly in terms of the intrinsic relation of process and content. Semantically, this is the distinction be-tween *traditio* and *traditum*. *Traditio* refers to the process of transmis-sion, the process by which tradition remains dynamic. *Traditum*, on the other hand, concerns that which are handed on, all that encompasses the true life of the church. Obviously, *traditum* includes the teachings of the church, but it likewise includes the church's life of worship and all that is the church, which extends to attitudes, practices, virtues, and so forth.

Even though the *traditio-traditum* intrinsic relation has been long rec-ognized, the study of tradition has been generally limited to patristic writings, the work of theologians, conciliar documents, and writings of the magisterium, in other words, a crucial but nonetheless limited slice of *traditum*. In the twentieth century both Yves Congar, OP, in his semi-nal work on tradition and the Second Vatican Council's constitution *Dei Verbum* (1965) put forward an understanding of tradition that empha-sized the act of transmission and critiqued the idea of tradition as equated only with content.[1] More recently, Orlando Espín has argued that "the living witness and faith of the Christian people"[2] are just as important to the study of tradition as are the written texts of tradition. Today, more than ever, we need to continue to examine the ways in which popular religious practices may break open our understanding of tradition. This chapter represents a modest attempt to consider anew how the tradition is claimed and passed on, in a word, traditioning. I examine traditioning as it is exemplified in the popular religious practice of the Latino/a devotion to Guadalupe. For as Terrence Tilley posits, "Traditions are not reified 'things' that can be known apart from practice, any more than languages are 'things' that can be known apart from linguistic performance and competence."[3] A tradition is only a tradition to the extent that it has been received and internalized through some practice.

This chapter examines the dynamic of traditioning in a popular religious practice using the methodological approach of United States North American pragmatist Josiah Royce (1855–1916).[4] Royce offers an atypical but useful way to think about traditioning. He has developed a philosophical systematic approach in which he assumes that all experience is not only essentially individual but also essentially social. Because experience is viewed as social, then traditioning, an inherently social idea, entails processes of interpretation that necessarily and invariably create community. Community comes into being and renews itself only through ongoing processes of interpretation, which concurrently facilitate traditioning. These processes take place ad infinitum. Using the approach he outlines, we can gain a deeper understanding of how popular religious practice furthers traditioning. Such an approach resonates strongly with the claims made by US Latino/a theologians regarding the communal character of the Latino/a culture.[5]

This essay argues that we can extend our understanding of traditioning, the process by which tradition is claimed and passed on, through an examination of ritual practices by means of a Roycean approach. More specifically, I intend to make clear that when participants engage in popular religious practices, they (1) interpret their life history toward a hope-filled future in the context of their present; (2) claim a shared event of faith, in this case Guadalupe, as part of their own lives in such a way that their lives take on a larger meaning and significance; and (3) recognize Guadalupe as an expression of Christian faith in that she deepens their insights into the Christian mystery of Jesus' life, death, and resurrection.

This essay comprises four sections. In the first section I share stories from two different periods in my life in which I participated in a practice that celebrated Guadalupe, and in the last section I offer an account of how these specific ritual practices serve as living examples of traditioning the Catholic faith. The second section lays the conceptual groundwork for my use of a Roycean approach to traditioning. In this section I rely particularly on Catherine Bell to clarify what it means to identify the

Guadalupan devotions as ritual practices. I then review Royce's conception of interpretation and argue that ritual practices can be understood legitimately as an interpretation of sign. The third section, which is the pivotal section of this essay, delineates Royce's theory of interpretation and its implications for traditioning. In short, ritual practices, understood as sign interpretation, create and sustain community in such a way as to facilitate the transmission of faith.

TRADITIONING GUADALUPE

I grew up on the US-Mexico border in El Paso, Texas, the daughter of parents who maintained not only a devout Catholic home replete with images of Guadalupe and Jesus on the cross but also an active schedule of church commitments at our local parish, St. Matthew's. In short, I lived in a world saturated with US Mexican American Catholicism of the borderlands variety. I cannot recall a time in my life when Guadalupe was not part of my religious imagination. The following examples of Guadalupan practices, one private and the other public, reveal the transmission of tradition in quite different settings. Together they break open some of the depth of traditioning.

While attending high school at Loretto Academy, I would take a twenty-five minute bus ride to and from school each day. On the first day back after the Christmas break of my freshman year, I jumped on board looking forward to my daily morning visit with my good friend Cecilia. Perhaps her most striking feature was her beautiful, perfectly straight, dark hair, which stretched down the length of her body almost to the back of her knees. She and her family had gone to Mexico City during the Christmas holidays, and I wanted to hear all about her trip. But when she boarded the bus I hardly recognized her. "Cecilia, what happened to your hair?" "I know. I miss it. But, my mom and I had to cut it off because of a *promesa* my mom made to *la Virgen* when I six years old. I guess I never told you. When I was six I got very sick, and the doctors thought that I was going to die. My mom promised Guadalupe that if I lived she would not cut my hair until I was fourteen. Then, when I turned fourteen, we would cut off my hair and take it to *la Virgen* in thanksgiving for allowing me to live. That is why we were in Mexico City."

In my early twenties I had been living in the small dusty Mexican border town of Palomas, Chihuahua, Mexico, for just under a year. It was the night of December 11, close to midnight. Along with almost everyone who lived in town, I braved the dry, cold, desert night air and huddled with the rest to take part in a ritual that had taken place ever since there was a Palomas, namely, the annual offering of *flor y canto (flower and song) to Nuestra Señora de Guadalupe*. Along with the other choir members in the balcony, I had been singing my lungs out. We had a bird's eye view of the whole event. After much song; many flowers, mostly plastic; and a sporadic dose of poetry, the energy in the too-small church subtly shifted. A group of mariachis was offering its musical rendition of "Mi Virgen Ranchera."[6]

In the middle of this song the large crowd began to part down the middle, making way for a group of women whose arms were overloaded with dozens and dozens of red roses. As they made their way toward the front of the church, a delicate, velvety scent spread throughout. Looking around, I knew that this was not the first Guadalupe celebration in which these women had come bearing their gift of roses. With nods and sympathetic glances, several of the community members acknowledged the presence of these women. However, the body language of others made it clear that some devotees present wanted nothing to do with these women. I knew virtually everyone in town, but I did not recognize these women. I was puzzled. Who were they? Where did they get such richly fragrant roses in the middle of this desolate and sun-scorched Chihuahua desert? And most important, why had they chosen to honor Guadalupe with the rest of us? "*Las cantineras* [barmaids],"[7] whispered my companion Socorro. Throughout the year these women remained unseen, indoors, waiting for their mostly US male clients in one of the bedrooms attached to the local bars. They faced a number of challenges in order to offer Guadalupe their gift. They negotiated with the local police, getting them to turn a blind eye so that they could leave the cantina and present their offering in the church. In addition, they ordered fresh roses from out of town and made arrangements for their delivery to Palomas.

Shortly after the Guadalupe celebration I talked to some of the townspeople. I learned that almost all of the women were from desperately poor families, many from small ranchos. They became *cantineras* because someone in the family needed money for surgery or because there was no other way to feed and clothe their extended family. What an outrage, some townspeople remarked, that these women had no choice but to make a living as *cantineras*. Their presence on the feast of Guadalupe served as an annual reminder of the egregious injustices wreaked upon poor people, especially upon poor women. Moreover, some noted, with their presence in church the *cantineras* publicly professed their own human dignity, a dignity they could affirm through Guadalupe.

RITUAL PRACTICES UNDERSTOOD AS INTERPRETATIONS

These Guadalupan devotions are examples of Latino/a popular Catholicism in the form of ritual practices. They have much to teach about how partakers struggle with their Catholic faith, come to terms with it, and in the process make it their own. What does it mean to identify these devotions as expressions of popular Catholicism and, more particularly, as ritual practices? Indeed, why is it not only legitimate but also valuable to view these ritual practices as interpretations? This question, of course, presumes an understanding of interpretation. So, what is the nature of interpretation? For if ritual practices are in fact interpretations, then their central role in traditioning can be made clear. Thus, identifying them as interpretations has wide-ranging and significant implications. In this section I address these questions and concerns.

As expressions of popular Catholicism, these Guadalupan devotions represent a path that runs parallel to official, institutionally sanctioned beliefs and liturgical practices. This parallel path grows out of a need to frame Catholicism so that it responds in a personal way to the people's sorrows and joys. It is likewise a group's response to the experience of being treated as subordinate.[8] As Espín explains, "Latino/a popular Catholicism is . . . the religion of those treated as subaltern by both society and Church in the United States. . . . Popular religion is *founded on the claim that the divine (identified by the people as the Christian divine) has been and is encountered by them in and through the symbols (ritual, ethical, and doctrinal) of popular Catholicism.*"[9] Moreover, it is through popular Catholic practices that most US Latinos/as become Catholic and sustain their Catholicism. When in the midst of life's struggles, Latino/a Catholics will turn to popular religious practices and in the process negotiate their Catholic identity and lay claim to it anew. "Partakers of popular religion may be seen as putting their faith 'on the line.' Disease, family unrest, or even social conflict may be typical motivation for popular religious practice, but they also happen to be challenges to faith, a struggle where faith is at stake. The result of that struggle is a reinterpretation or reevaluation of that faith, . . .which is then willingly, consciously, made one's own."[10] The women at the center of the Guadalupan devotions exemplify attempts to negotiate faith in the face of extreme hardship.

We can further distinguish these Guadalupan devotions as ritual practices. As ritual practices they manifest a particular set of characteristics and a given dynamic process. These characteristics form the basis for my claim that ritual practices are interpretations. In order to clarify the nature of a ritual practice I turn to the work of Catherine Bell. (I use the phrase "ritual practice" to designate ritual understood as practice.)

In her classic text *Ritual Theory, Ritual Practice* Bell offers a list of characteristics that apply to ritual practices. The following three characteristics are among those Bell identifies. First, practice can be described as situational; namely, what is crucial to a practice can only be understood from within the context out of which it arises. In other words, a given practice is historically situated. "When abstracted from its immediate context, an activity is not quite the same activity."[11] For example, in the case of Cecilia, the *promesa*, the healing, and the pilgrimage take on meaning in context of a Mexican American Catholic family and society with a multi-generational devotion to Guadalupe, as well as other key historical factors. Outside of this social location, the ritual practice would be understood differently and perhaps even appear incongruent.

Second, practice is "inherently strategic, manipulative, and expedient."[12] Practice manifests a logic that is practical and instrumental and yet one that eludes the grasp of those employing only analytical tools. In the second example of Guadalupan devotion, the community gathered and the *cantineras* both seek an experience of the sacred and of affirmation through their participation in the ritual. This public celebration of Guadalupe offered partakers the possibility of a transformed experience of self and of community.

Finally, practice reveals "the will to act"; namely, partakers engage in practice as a means of restoring what they understand to be righteous authority. Practice reveals an orientation embedded in the doing of action. Inherent in practice are "unexpressed assumptions that constitute the actor's strategic understanding of the place, purpose, and trajectory of the act."[13] In both examples of Guadalupan devotion the various partakers seek to create and participate in a world that reflects their own vision of divine justice.

Moreover, ritual practices involve producing ritual acts, in a word, *ritualization*. Ritualization is "a strategic reproduction of the past in such a way as to maximize its domination of the present,"[14] whether by designated authorities who take on the mantle of protecting the integrity of the past, or by the people who desire to make the tradition their own, to enable it to respond to their circumstances. While ritual practices are not the only way that tradition is passed on, they "*can* be a strategic way to 'traditionalize,' that is, to construct a type of tradition but in doing so [ritual practices] can also challenge and renegotiate the very basis of tradition"[15] to the point of radically questioning what before had been deemed foundational and permanent.

Indeed, the dynamic process of ritualization concerns the ordering of power. Ritualization brings to the fore questions of boundaries and authority. Who creates the "strategic reproduction of the past"? And whose interest does this reproduction serve? Whose experience counts? Theologians, like Rosemary Radford Ruether, have rightly called our attention to the silencing effects of the patriarchal culture that so marks the Christian tradition and, most assuredly, its ritual practices. "Throughout patriarchal culture there reverberates the constant demand the women keep silent. Women should not speak, certainly in the company of men, but also not too much to each other. The repression of women, not only into marginality, but into silence; the deprivation of speech, of the capacity to articulate their own experience and communicate it; this is essential to the definition of women as objects rather than as subjects."[16] As expressions of the Christian tradition (albeit "subaltern" expressions) do these Guadalupan ritual practices promote the full humanity of women, or do they once again suppress women's voices, rendering women objects of the Christian tradition's patriarchal hegemony? No pat answers exist. Interpretation, to which I will turn next, provides the means to engage this question deeply and repeatedly.

In short, ritual practices reflect the historical context out of which they emerge; they attempt to convince partakers of a particular way of viewing the world; they reflect a purpose inherent in the world view they embody; and finally, they may generate in partakers a mixed reaction. They demand of their partakers an evaluation or a judgment, one that is unique to each person and consists of a combination of both consent and resistance. All of these features of ritual practices are consonant with the understanding of interpretation I will delineate next. I adopt a Roycean conception of interpretation because it affords a cogent understanding of traditioning.

The dominant perspective on the idea of interpretation has been shaped primarily by the European Continental hermeneutic tradition, and often more specifically by Hans-Georg Gadamer, its most influential thinker.[17] However, the pragmatic tradition of interpretation,[18] in which Royce stands, begins with a significantly different set of assumptions.[19] According to Royce, above all else interpretation concerns the human drive to be in communion with others and to be self-possessed. Royce's conception of interpretation has its roots in his fascination with the Civil War, the assassination of Abraham Lincoln, and most significantly, his research on the social networks that developed among the "Spanish, Anglo-Americans, Indians and Chinese peoples"[20] in California from 1846 to 1856.[21] In an insightful article Kenneth Stikkers identifies some of the differences between these two views of interpretation. Briefly,

Royce calls into question at least three central features of Gadamer's hermeneutics: (1) the givenness of "tradition," and with it "community," (2) the givenness of "self," and (3) the primacy of texts taken broadly as any object of interpretation. That is, first, while Gadamer assumes the givenness of tradition and community within the fore-structure of understanding, such are highly problematic for Royce and, instead, are seen as *continuously constituted and renewed* [emphasis added] through the processes of interpretation. Second, and similarly, Gadamer assumes the givenness of "self," while for Royce "self," too, is highly problematic. Third, while for Gadamer the central task of hermeneutics remains getting at the meaning of texts, the disclosure of Being in and through texts, interpretation for Royce is first and foremost the artistic constitution of community, and always, simultaneously, the constitution of selves.[22]

In short, a Gadamerian approach to interpretation entails getting at the meaning of texts, while a Roycean approach to interpretation concerns how humans express their drive to be in communion with others and how the self is formed.

If we think about interpretation as the way in which community is formed and sustained, this approach will afford us greater clarity about the intrinsic process-content relation that I am calling traditioning. So, what is the task of interpretation understood as such? As human beings we are inherently social creatures and thus given to being in relation with one another. Yet, we find ourselves frustrated by the estrangement that marks the difference between our ideas and purposes and those of others. We likewise see a similar frustration in others. Essentially, interpretation seeks to create a vision that enables us to bridge our experience of estrangement. Processes of interpretation allow distinct selves to enter into a communion with one another. These processes inevitably and necessarily endeavor to forge "communities of interpretation." This process involves three selves each central to interpretation. "The interpreter, the mind to which he addresses his interpretation, the mind which he undertakes to interpret—all these appear, in our explicitly human and social world, as three distinct selves."[23] The members of the emergent community of interpretation, the interpreter and the other selves as well, together seek out a vision of unity, their goal. This goal may be thought of as a common ideal future event. In the second example of Guadalupan devotion, some among the community gathered and among the *cantineras* viewed their ritual practice as their declaration of hope for a future in which the dignity of all, the least as well as the greatest, is

fully affirmed. To state the obvious, this would certainly not be the interpretation of everyone or even most of those present. And even for those
who espoused such an interpretation, each would understand it distinctly.

Because interpretation always involves three terms, it is a triadic relation and thus, necessarily, a social process and a historical process:

> You cannot express any complete process of interpreting by merely
> naming two terms,—persons, or other objects,—and by then tell-
> ing what dyadic relation exists between one of these two and the
> other. . . . An interpretation is a relation which not only involves
> three terms, but brings them into a determinate order. One of the
> three terms is the interpreter; a second term is the object—the per-
> son or the meaning or the text—which is interpreted; the third is
> the person to whom the interpretation is addressed.[24]

If we think of interpretation in strictly dyadic terms—that is, as an interpreter who seeks the meaning of a text or of an object—then we tend to
presume that interpretation can take place in the abstract. In other words,
a dyadic approach creates the illusion of the possibility of an ahistorical,
acontextual interpretation. But interpretations invariably reflect some
purpose, some intent on the part of the interpreter. Thus, interpretations
are always historically situated and therefore properly understood as a
triadic relation. Moreover, the process of interpretation produces a new
interpretation or a new sign, creating the need for future interpretations.
Consequently, someone interprets this new sign to another self, which in
turn leads to the need for further interpretations ad infinitum. Any inter-
ruption to the process would be arbitrary. Interpretation generates rich
discoveries and varied possibilities that are "constantly renewed by the
inexhaustible resources of our social relations."[25] It is the social nature
of interpretation that makes traditioning possible.

Significantly, since an interpretation necessarily incorporates some
purpose or aim, then, of its essence, every interpretation is a moral act.
It is a moral act, according to Royce, in that gaining insight into another
requires transcending my ego, and, second, it involves seeking out a third
idea that mediates between the two. While, ideally, this third reflects a
wider horizon, this third, nonetheless, invariably reflects some idea and
purpose of the interpreter. Accordingly, every interpretation both bears
some measure of adequacy in relation to the good and is conditioned
by some historical reality.[26] Yet, I would argue, it is a moral act in
another sense as well. Because interpretations reflect a purpose, that of
the interpreter, we must ask whose experience counts? Whose experience is privileged, and whose is overlooked? While Royce's conception

of interpretation takes us a long way, it needs to be developed much further so as to take into account the questions of power raised by contemporary feminist (and other liberationist) theologies. While this critique must be made, addressing it is well beyond the bounds of this chapter.

Interpretation begins with comparison. After observing likenesses and differences one realizes that a comparison is needed and that the presenting problem is one of mediating difference. Difference may be attributed to conflict, to distinct ideas, to experiences of alienation, and so forth. The difference means that without an explicit mediation, estrangement would simply continue indefinitely. A new idea or new act or new sign thus becomes desirable.[27] "This new act consists in the invention or discovery of some third idea, distinct from both the ideas which are to be compared. This third idea, when once found, interprets one of the ideas which are the objects of the comparison, and interprets it to the other, or in the light of the other."[28] This third idea mediates between the two former ideas. And if this third idea genuinely mediates between the two former ideas, then a community of interpretation is forged.[29]

The new act or idea functions as a mediating third and makes a more substantive contribution than any that could result from a simple comparison. This new third idea enables us to develop a vision of greater expanse and enables the forging of community. We come to know idea "A" in light of "B," and in the process "A" takes on new meaning. For example, both Guadalupan devotions begin with an experience of suffering (a life-threatening illness; a pattern of abuse and objectification of women). These experiences of suffering run counter to what the women in each instance deeply want. They want healing, dignity, and self-respect. The ritual practices serve as a mediating third for the partakers who perceive these practices to be creating a deeper understanding of a history of suffering in light of a hope for a transformed future. This implies neither that these partakers in the ritual practices agree with regard to the efficaciousness of the rituals practices, nor that these partakers interpret their experience identically. Even so, a fragile vision of unity can emerge that did not exist before.

As we have seen, the desire for a mediating third idea occurs on the social level, but it occurs on a personal level as well. For example, a person experiencing some inner struggle, through interpretation as the fruit of authentic comparison, can strive after and attain a greater truth about himself or herself. As Royce explains, "We are wider than any of our ideas, and can win a vision which shall look down upon our own inner warfare, and upon our own former self-estrangements, as well as upon our own inner contrasts of exact definition."[30] We can come to terms with ourselves because we see ourselves as we are, and as a result, our capacity for self-consciousness expands and deepens. In other words, through the interpretive process an altered "self" also emerges.

Given the foregoing conception of interpretation, on what basis can I claim that ritual practices are interpretations? Fundamentally, ritual practice and interpretation can be distinguished by essentially identical characteristics. While ritual practices reflect both the situational context from which they emerge and an expedient yet symbolic logic, interpretations necessarily reveal their historical location. And because interpretations invariably address someone, they incorporate some aim. Furthermore, ritual practices also attempt to convince partakers of a particular way of viewing the world, just as processes of interpretation strive to create a vision of unity. This renders both always morally telling. Finally, ritual practices generate in their partakers mixed reactions of consent and resistance whereas processes of interpretation yield new interpretations that create the need for further interpretations ad infinitum. In short, given the Roycean conception of interpretation I have adopted, ritual practices are examples of interpretations. Therefore, as interpretations, ritual practices create communities and selves in such a way as to make traditioning possible.

INTERPRETATION, COMMUNITY, TRADITIONING

In the process of interpreting Guadalupe these ritual practices concurrently forge community and produce tradition. But, how is tradition produced? What is the dynamic of interpretation that forges a traditioning community?

Only a *community* of human beings produces a tradition. Through the act of interpreting—that is, through the efforts of a community of human beings that functions in an organized fashion—"products" like tradition, language, custom, and culture are created, modified, and shared. Interpretation, conceived socially as Royce has argued, thus allows us to assert that a community possesses a "mind" and that this mind changes and reinvents itself time and again.[31] Similarly, a community possesses a "will." A community makes its mind and will known as it expresses itself in an ongoing fashion through processes of interpretation.

Interpretation, then, serves as the foundation and sustenance for traditioning communities. Three central conditions of traditioning communities illustrate the principal role of interpretation.[32] First, a community comes into being through a time process whereby it bears a consciousness of its past, present, and future. It interprets its past toward the future in the present. Second, a community comes into being when individual members extend their lives in time well into the past and the future so that all the individuals claim events as their own which exist beyond the span of their lifetimes. These ideally extended selves are not simply a collection of past and future events or experience but an interpretation of those events and experiences. Finally, a community exists when its members claim at least some identical events as significant for them. Even though all members agree that particular events are central, each member will interpret the meaning of the events differently. These three conditions make traditioning possible. As we will see in the concluding section, the Guadalupan ritual practices embody each of these conditions.

Time Process

Through a complex and lengthy social process a community develops some consciousness of its past, whether real or ideal, and has hopes and intentions for the future. Consciousness of a time process allows a community to come into existence and to sustain itself. Obviously, memory plays an important role. Moreover, a community also distinguishes itself not only by its history but also by its hopes and intentions for the future.[33]

Therefore, community is *not* a "compounding of consciousness." If it were, it would become synonymous with a crowd, amorphous and lacking stability. To equate a community with a crowd would imply that the individual consciousness of each participant is absorbed, even if only temporarily. A crowd is *not* a community because even though a crowd has a mind, it has "no institutions, no organization, no coherent unity, no history, no traditions."[34]

While a community must possess a consciousness of both its history and its hope for the future, this is insufficient. A community is formed and sustained when each member interprets the community's past and present experience in a more or less coherent fashion toward some ideal future the members envision.

The Ideal Extension of the Self

In the life of such a community, individuals not only cooperate with one another, but they ideally extend their own lives such that the work they do together, along with its past, present, and future, represents for each participating member his or her life writ large. Each individual, therefore, sees his or her particular life as extended to include events that existed beyond the limits of his or her conscious memory, and beyond his or her lifetime. This extension in time has no clear limit. Each individual's work in community then serves as a manifestation of his or her particular destiny, significance and legacy.[35]

This ideal extension of the self necessitates an interpretation. One must develop some sort of reason, which can be drawn from any of several realms of human experience, for taking on or resisting past glories and future promises. Thus, one must make a judgment concerning the extent to which the ideal past and future enter into one's life and enhance it. Physical things, such as the image of Guadalupe in our case, become a part of this ideal extension of the self.[36]

This formation of the individual human self requires a time process. At any one moment in time the self is conscious to only a fragment of the self. For the self is "by its very essence, a being with a past" and with "a pursuit of its own chosen good." Thus I can recognize myself as a historical continuity, as made up of the goals that I sought out yesterday and still seek today. Over time I continue to pursue an idea of myself. "In brief, my idea of myself is an interpretation of my past—linked also with an interpretation of my hopes and intentions as to my future."[37] The ideally extended self is one whose destiny and significance looms larger than what may be contained in the brief time of earthly existence.

A group of human beings working together in an organized fashion do not in and of themselves constitute a community, even when their cooperative activities tend to be complex in nature. A community comes into existence *only* through the emergence of a tradition, which necessitates a long period of time, and *only* when participants are conscious of their collective life as a community. Such is the case when cooperating members remark, "This activity which we perform together, this work of ours, its past, its future, its sequence, its order, its sense—all these enter into my life and are the life of my own self writ large."[38] And, such is the case when cooperating members desire that their collective activity as a community continue. Accordingly, each member will look back into the past and rejoice in his or her forbearers and heroes on whose shoulders the current community stands, and each member will look forward with hopeful anticipation.[39]

Shared Events

In addition, community depends upon the existence of some event (or events) of the past or future that ideally extended selves hold as identical. On the occasions that a community commemorates this event of its common past or its hoped for future, it sustains and invigorates its united life. The event must be recognized not only as central in the life of the community but also central to the life of each individual community member.[40] Community depends for its very existence upon its members believing that specific events, which occurred long before and will occur long after their lifetimes, bear meaning in their lives now. Individual members must interpret these common events as somehow belonging to their lives now, and as they interpret these events they constitute a community. Shared events play a central role in creating "communities of memory and hope." Royce writes:

> When many contemporary and distinct individual selves so interpret, each his own personal life, that each says of an individual past or of a determinate future event or deed: "That belongs to my life;" "That occurred, or will occur, to me," then these many selves may be defined as hereby constituting, in a perfectly definite and objective, but also in a highly significant, sense, a community. They may be said to constitute a community *with reference* to that particular past or future event, or group of events, which each of them accepts or interprets as belonging to his own personal past or to his own individual future. A community constituted by the fact that each of its members accepts as part of his own individual life and self the same *past* events that each of his fellow-members accepts, may be called a <u>community of memory</u> . . . [and] a *community of expectation*, or . . . a *community of hope.*[41]

In short, the interpretation of specific events enables the coherency of a community.

However, while each member recognizes the identical shared event as significant, each member, nonetheless, interprets and understands the event differently. Differences of interpretation do not necessarily undermine or threaten the cohesiveness or stability of the community. Just because all members hold the same event as significant does not mean that all need to understand it to mean the same thing. Agreement is not required, but some mutual understanding of the differences in interpretation is valuable. Such understanding allows members to work together toward the same end but for diverse reasons. Kathryn Tanner offers the following perspective.

> Christians may . . . come together over the form of things if not their substance. They may agree, for example, that Jesus saves or that ritual meals should be eaten in church, even if they do not agree about what those statements or those gestures mean. . . . They feel solidarity with one another in that each person knows that

every other person will gladly affirm, for example, *that* Jesus saves.
Such solidarity is achieved despite the fact that no two of them
would develop the sense of such a statement in exactly the same
way. . . . Far from threatening the stability of a Christian way of
life, the fact that Christians do not agree in their interpretation of
matters of common concern is the very thing that enables social
solidarity among them. . . . Just to the extent that [symbolic forms
and acts] remain ambiguous, amendable to a variety of interpretations, are they able to unify a diverse membership, to coordinate
their activities together in the relatively nonconflictual way necessary for a viable way of life.[42]

Interpretation does *not* seek a synthesis. Differences are not erased
but take on new meaning. Interpretation seeks out the meaning of one
distinct idea in light of the other so as to invent a "realm of conscious
unity which constitutes the very essence of the life of reason."[43] A new
consciousness results, which can only come about through a genuine
understanding of the motivation, value, and contribution of each distinct idea. The integrity of the formerly estranged ideas is not compromised in the attainment of a higher unity of consciousness; the integrity
of each takes on new meaning.

We may agree that through ongoing processes of interpretation the
differences among distinct interpretations can take on new meaning, can
be productive of an expanded consciousness, and can preserve the integrity of each distinct interpretation. Yet, this claim does not resolve the
challenge presented by differences in power. Obviously, some interpretations both command hegemony and lend legitimacy to relationships of
subordination. Oppression ensues. For example, within the Catholic tradition, even though women as well as men are understood as created in
the image of God, there still persist tenacious "misogynist traditions in
which women are considered less than fully human, less than fully re-
deemed, [and] symbolic traditions in which women are 'glorified' as more
than human but still denied full Christian personhood."[44] Such oppressive interpretations must be critiqued and dismantled, but this cannot be
adequately undertaken without recognition of the power interests that
influence every process of interpretation. Thus, our understanding of
traditioning must take power interests into account. However, in this
brief chapter I can do no more than acknowledge the imperative to address this challenge.

These three conditions, all crucial to the creation of community, make
clear that a tradition is claimed when the traditioning community consciously interprets its history and future, and when its members interpret

their lives such that they lay claim to events that fall outside the temporal limits of their earthly existence.

Moreover, traditioning communities, like all genuine communities, draw members through the possibilities they hold open. All communities, by virtue of being both "an object of interpretation and a life interpreting itself,"[45] provide some measure of coherence and meaning that an individual alone cannot access. Because such communities allow individuals to escape the limitations that result from the "natural narrowness of our span of consciousness,"[46] they are the means by which the notions of meaning, significance, and value become relevant. Consequently, over time members typically develop a love of community.

Yet, the human drive to be in relation with one another, sometimes experienced as the desire to be in a type of mystical union with other selves, cannot be reduced simply to an emotion. Love of community consists in an interpretation that expresses itself actively through *deeds* in the world. The ideal extension of the self takes on full meaning only when expressed through deeds. "Unless each man knows how distinct he is from the whole community and from every member of it, he cannot render to the community what love demands,—namely, the devoted work."[47]

While ultimately traditioning communities seek final truth, this, of course, remains beyond reach in this life. We do not reach this goal in any one moment during our earthly lives. Nevertheless, continuously prompted by our desire for spiritual unity we do interpret the goal of final truth. If we presuppose, as does Royce, "a certain unity in the meaning and coherence of experience taken as a whole—a unity which can never at any one moment be tested by any human being,"[48] we can claim the existence of a sort of truth of which we cannot give an adequate account. Even our most adequate interpretations of final truth, while not wholly false, are always insufficient.

For the Christian traditioning community, final truth concerns the meaning and significance of the mystery of Jesus' life, death, and resurrection.[49] Therefore, in addition to considering the three aforementioned conditions of a traditioning community, which admittedly apply to a wide variety of communities, we must ask if the aforementioned Guadalupan ritual practices provide insight into the Christian mystery of Jesus' life, death, and resurrection? And if so, how?

TRADITIONING GUADALUPE, AN ACCOUNT OF OUR HOPE

In this final section, I return to the two Guadalupan ritual practices noting how they reveal the three conditions of a traditioning community (e.g. time process, ideal extension of the self, and shared events) and suggesting some of the ways in which these ritual practices break open the Christian mystery.[50]

Cecilia and *La Promesa*

When Cecilia's mom made a promise to *la Virgen* in hope of her daughter's healing, she situated herself and her daughter among a longstanding historical community of pilgrims who have offered promises and experienced healing. Like Cecilia and her family, many who have been healed have journeyed to Mexico City to express their gratitude through prayer and homage. Indeed, several huge picture frames with velveteen canvases have been hung within the Mexico City basilica honoring Guadalupe. Each canvas displays a decorative pattern created by hundreds of small metal figures in the shape of hearts, heads, arms, legs, eyes, torsos, hands and feet. Each of these metal figures signifies a promise and a healing. Some are recent; others are quite old. All publicly witness to the long history of petitions and corresponding healings. They serve not only as a public account of the community's history of healings but also as a beacon of hope that future petitions will likewise be answered. Moreover, there is also a tradition of offering a sacrifice as an expression of gratitude. Cecilia cut off her long, beautiful hair, leaving it behind, and her family made the journey at some sacrifice to themselves.

As a young sickly girl, Cecilia's life, through the efforts of her mother, became extended to include Guadalupe and the promises of healing. Guadalupe first made a promise to Juan Diego that his uncle Juan Bernardino would be restored to health and would live. She also told Juan Diego that she wanted to remain with the people, responding to their needs.[51] This promise, Cecilia's family prayed, would somehow include Cecilia as well. Through this ritual practice and the efforts of her family, Cecilia imagined a life for herself marked by health and longevity. As Cecilia matured, the event of Guadalupe entered even more deeply into her life and consciousness when she cut off her hair and offered it. In fact, she may even to this day interpret Guadalupe as the active presence of the Spirit of God in the struggle for life, her own and others.

The "Guadalupe vision," writes Virgilio Elizondo, "is not something totally new [but] the ideal of the kingdom of God as lived and proclaimed by Jesus."[52] More specifically, the effect and message of Guadalupe closely parallels that of Jesus as recorded in the gospels. So, we may inquire, in what ways does Cecilia's story call attention to the gospel message? How does her experience of suffering, of a desire for healing, of God's gratuitous love, help us to understand the Christian faith more fully? As we pursue these questions we may discover how Cecilia's experience of healing takes on greater meaning and coherence not only in light of Guadalupe but also in light of the Christian mystery of Jesus' life, death, and resurrection.

The *Cantineras'* Offer of Roses

The community gathered and the *cantineras* in their gift of roses participated, as devotees have for hundreds of years, in honoring Guadalupe on her feast day with *flor y canto*. And, similar to generations of devotees that preceded them, many of those gathered recognized that beauty has the capacity to transform a hardened heart, to slow us down, and to enable us to see the world differently. Like modern-day Juan Diegos, the *cantineras* went through a great deal of trouble (and personal sacrifice) in order to be able to present roses in honor of *la Virgen*, dozens and dozens of roses of exceptional beauty and exquisite fragrance. When the *cantineras* processed in with their offering many of us present were taken aback, perhaps a bit like the bishop and those with him when Juan Diego offered roses and Guadalupe's image as a sign. Yet, also like those present at the first offering of *flor y canto*,[53] many of us found ourselves transfixed and transformed by the beauty of the roses and the image. While not all present described it this way, some did. Admittedly, though, many in Palomas were not able to get beyond their anxious, uneasy reaction to the presence of the *cantineras*, and consequently they could not receive the gift of beauty being offered. When some present saw the *cantineras*, they quickly and narrowly equated these women with one of the town's most serious manifestations of sin. Yet, the procession of these women into the church with armsful of long-stemmed red roses gave a number of us pause. The experience challenged us to extend our hearts a bit beyond our comfort level to imagine a future more hopeful than our present, a future in which the dignity of all is revered.

When they took the initiative to present roses to Guadalupe, the *cantineras* laid claim to Guadalupe as somehow part of their extended lives. In honoring Guadalupe they recognized that she first claimed them. Like Juan Diego, the world looks upon the *cantineras* as nobodies.[54] Even though Guadalupe could choose anyone, she chose Juan Diego, and in some sense she and the *cantineras* chose one another. Through their gift of roses the *cantineras* claimed and affirmed their own God-given human dignity. They publicly acknowledged that they are far more than instruments for someone else's pleasure. Like all humans they too long for genuine relationships marked by interpersonal intimacy and relationality. In Guadalupe they found this longing affirmed. Consequently,

Guadalupe extends to the *cantineras* a reason to honor her. Why else would they go to the trouble?

Traditioning only occurs through a process of interpreting our past toward a hope-filled future in the context of our present, and through our willingness to risk believing that our life has some higher purpose, some wider significance. As such, it concerns an account of our hope. Hope is the existential orientation of our whole self toward the future. It is our will to live, to believe that life is worth living even in the face of evidence to the contrary. Guadalupan ritual practices, when considered in light of the Christian mystery, encourage Christian believers to hope, to see in the human lives that God restores now, evidence that God's reign is at hand.

Notes

[1] Yves Congar OP, *Tradition and Traditions: An Historical and a Theological Essay*, trans. Michael Naseby and Thomas Rainborough (New York: Macmillan, 1967); *Vatican Council II: The Conciliar and Post Conciliar Documents*, Austin Flannery, OP, ed., New Revised Study Edition 1992 (New York: Costello Publishing Co., 1992), *Dei Verbum* 750–65. For a discussion of the idea of *traditio* as it relates to the origins of popular Catholicism among Latinos/as, see Orlando O. Espín, *The Faith of the People: Theological Reflections on Popular Catholicism* (Maryknoll, NY: Orbis Books, 1997), 111–55.

[2] Espín, *The Faith of the People*, 65.

[3] Terrence W. Tilley, *Inventing Catholic Tradition* (Maryknoll, NY: Orbis Books, 2000), 45.

[4] For a general introduction to Royce and his thought, see John Clendenning, *The Life and Thought of Josiah Royce*, rev. ed. (Nashville, TN: Vanderbilt Univ. Press, 1999). For the uninitiated reader interested in reading Royce, see Josiah Royce, *The Philosophy of Loyalty*, ed. John J. McDermott (1908; Nashville, TN: Vanderbilt Univ. Press, 1995). For major works by Royce, see *The Religious Aspect of Philosophy: A Critique of the Bases of Conduct and of Faith* (Boston, MA: Houghton, Mifflin, and Company, 1885); *The Feud of Oakfield Creek: A Novel of California Life* (1887; New York: Johnson, 1970); *The World and the Individual, First Series* (1899; New York: Dover Publications, 1959); *The Sources of Religious Insight* (1912; Washington, DC: Catholic Univ. of America Press, 2001); *The Principles of Logic* (1913; New York: Philosophical Library, 1961); *The Problem of Christianity* (1913; Washington, DC: Catholic Univ. of America Press, 2001); *Metaphysics (Royce's Philosophy 9 Course of 1915–1916)*, ed. William Ernest Hocking, Richard Hocking, and Frank Oppenheim (Albany: State Univ. of New York Press, 1998); *The Basic Writings of Josiah Royce*, ed. John J. McDermott, 2 vols. (Chicago: Univ. of Chicago Press, 1969). For a scholarly overview of Royce's contributions see Frank M.

Oppenheim, SJ, *Royce's Mature Ethics* (Notre Dame, IN: Univ. of Notre Dame Press, 1993); idem, *Royce's Mature Philosophy of Religion* (Notre Dame, IN: Univ. of Notre Dame Press, 1987).

[5] Some may find my use of Josiah Royce anomalous. Throughout the spectrum of US Latino/a theological writings, relationality or community consistently appear as fundamental to a Latino/a understanding of reality. And, while US Latino/a theologians define and describe relationality differently from one another, it nonetheless holds a place of prominence in this body of work. The following are but a few examples: Alejandro García-Rivera, *The Community of the Beautiful: A Theological Aesthetics* (Collegeville, MN: Liturgical Press, 1999); Roberto S. Goizueta, *Caminemos Con Jesus: Toward a Hispanic/Latino Theology of Accompaniment* (Maryknoll, NY: Orbis Books, 1995), esp. chaps. 3, 6 and 7; Ada María Isasi-Díaz, *Mujerista Theology: A Theology for the Twenty-First Century* (Maryknoll, NY: Orbis Books, 1996), 128–47; Anita De Luna, MCDP, *Faith Formation and Popular Religion: Lessons from the Tejano Experience* (Lanham, MD: Rowman and Littlefield, 2002), 47, 52, 56, 166; Miguel H. Díaz, *On Being Human: U.S. Hispanic and Rahnerian Perspectives* (Maryknoll, NY: Orbis Books, 2001), esp. chap. 2; Ismael García, "Hispanic Experience and the Protestant Ethic," in *Protestantes/Protestants: Hispanic Christianity Within Mainline Traditions*, ed. David Maldonado, Jr., (Nashville, TN: Abingdon Press, 1999), 148–53. Moreover, recently an affinity has begun to emerge between the US American pragmatist intellectual tradition, on the one hand, and the interests and concerns of US Latino/a theology, on the other. See, for example, Alejandro García-Rivera, *A Wounded Innocence: Sketches for a Theology of Art* (Collegeville, MN: Liturgical Press, 2003); Nancy Pineda-Madrid, "In Search of a Theology of Suffering, *Latinamente*," in *The Ties That Bind: African-American and Hispanic-American/Latino Theology in the United States*, ed. Anthony B. Pinn and Benjamin Valentin, 187–99 (New York: Continuum, 2001); and Robert Lassalle-Klein, "The Potential Contribution of C. S. Peirce to Interpretation Theory in US Hispanic/Latino and Other Contextualized Theologies," *Journal of Hispanic/ Latino Theology* 6, no. 3 (1999): 5–34.

[6] A popular song sung in honor of Guadalupe.

[7] This term is often used as a euphemism for prostitutes.

[8] Espín, *The Faith of the People*, 113–15; and Alejandro García-Rivera, *St. Martin de Porres: The "Little Stories" and the Semiotics of Culture* (Maryknoll, NY: Orbis Books, 1995), 20–21.

[9] Espín, *The Faith of the People*, 92.

[10] García-Rivera, *St. Martin de Porres*, 20–21.

[11] Catherine M. Bell, *Ritual Theory, Ritual Practice* (New York: Oxford Univ. Press, 1992), 81.

[12] Ibid., 82.

[13] Ibid., 85; see also Catherine Bell, *Ritual: Perspectives and Dimensions* (New York: Oxford Univ. Press, 1997), 80–83.

[14] Bell, *Ritual Theory, Ritual Practice*, 123, 140.

[15] Ibid., 124. As an example of a radical questioning process, Bell cites the Reformation's "challenge to papal authority by recreation of the free outpouring of the spirit to the early church."

[16] Rosemary Radford Ruether, *Women-Church: Theology and Practice of Feminist Liturgical Communities* (San Francisco: Harper and Row, 1986), 58–59.

[17] See especially his seminal work, Hans-Georg Gadamer, *Truth and Method*, trans. Joel Weinsheimer and Donald G. Marshall, 2nd rev. ed. (New York: Continuum, 1997). Note also the work of Jürgen Habermas, one of Gadamer's most influential critics: Jürgen Habermas, *Knowledge and Human Interest*, trans. Jeremy J. Shapiro (Boston: Beacon Press, 1971). For a historical survey of many of the most influential thinkers of the European Continental hermeneutic tradition, see Kurt Mueller-Vollmer, ed., *The Hermeneutics Reader* (New York: Continuum, 1988).

[18] For a discussion of the pragmatic tradition of interpretation, see Robert S. Corrington, *The Community of Interpreters: On the Hermeneutics of Nature and the Bible in the American Philosophical Tradition*, 2nd ed. (Macon, GA: Mercer Univ. Press, 1995). See also, Donald L. Gelpi, *Varieties of Transcendental Experience: A Study in Constructive Post-Modernism* (Collegeville, MN: Liturgical Press, 2000); Cornel West, *The American Evasion of Philosophy: A Geneology of Pragmatism* (Madison: Univ. of Wisconsin Press, 1989); Bruce Kuklick, *The Rise of American Philosophy: Cambridge Massachusetts, 1860–1930* (New Haven, CT: Yale Univ. Press, 1977); John J. Stuhr, *Genealogical Pragmatism: Philosophy, Experience, and Community* (Albany: State Univ. of New York Press, 1997); Donald Francis Boehn, "Interpretation and Community: Josiah Royce and the Reconstructive Tradition in American Philosophy" (Ph.D. diss., Vanderbilt University, 1988), 49.

[19] For an extended discussion of the distinctions between the European Continental hermeneutic tradition and the Pragmatic tradition, see Wayne Proudfoot, *Religious Experience* (Berkeley and Los Angeles: Univ. of California Press, 1985), 41–74; and Robert S. Corrington, "A Comparison of Royce's Key Notion of the Community of Interpretation with the Hermeneutics of Gadamer and Heidegger," *Transactions of the Charles S. Peirce Society* 20 (1984), 279–302.

[20] Oppenheim, *Royce's Mature Ethics*, 27.

[21] A few of Royce's early publications examine these concerns. See, for example, Josiah Royce, *California from the Conquest in 1846 to the Second Vigilance Committee in San Francisco [1856]: A Study of American Character* (1886; New York: Knopf, 1948); Royce, *The Feud of Oakfield Creek;* and idem, *Race Questions, Provincialism, and Other American Problems* (New York: Macmillan Company, 1908). For an overview of Royce's personal moral development and the development of his ethics, see Oppenheim, *Royce's Mature Ethics*.

[22] Kenneth W. Stikkers, "Royce and Gadamer on Interpretation as the Constitution of Community," *The Journal of Speculative Philosophy* 15, no. 1 (2001): 14.

[23] Royce, *The Problem of Christianity*, 314.

[24] Ibid., 286–87.

[25] Ibid., 290. See also Oppenheim, *Royce's Mature Ethics*, 94.

[26] Royce based his ethics on a metaphysics of logic or in his own term of art, the "logic of relations." He developed his notion of the logic of relations using the concept of negation, and through this notion he was able to distinguish good and evil. See Josiah Royce, "Negation," in Oppenheim, *Josiah Royce's Late Writings: A Collection of Unpublished and Scattered Works*, ed. Frank Oppenheim SJ, vol. 1 (Bristol, England: Thommes Press, 2001), 92–108 (originally published in 1917); Josiah Royce, "Order," in Oppenheim, *Josiah Royce's Late Writings*, 1:109–28 (also originally published in 1917); Royce, *The Principles of Logic*; Royce, *Metaphysics*. See my discussion of the metaphysical basis of Royce's ethics in Nancy Pineda-Madrid, "The Problem of Evil: Considering a Roycean Approach," in *The Hope for the Great Community: The Possible Contribution of the Philosophy of Josiah Royce to Catholic Theology*, ed. Alejandro García-Rivera and John Markey, OP (Washington, DC: Catholic Univ. of America Press, forthcoming).

[27] According to Royce, we live in a vast sign system that is our world. We constantly send signs, receive signs, interpret signs, and are interpreted through signs. Royce holds that the objects of interpretation are signs, which certainly include texts, but indicate a field of concern much more extensive than texts. Signs are expressions of the meaning of some mind. It is well beyond the bounds of this brief essay to explain Royce's semiotic world view. See Royce, *The Problem of Christianity*, 321–62; idem, "Mind," in Oppenheim, *Josiah Royce's Late Writings*, 1:56–78 (originally published in 1916). For his semiotic world view, Royce adopts and develops the semeiotic system of Charles S. Peirce. For a comprehensive overview of Peirce's contribution, see James Jakob Liszka, *A General Introduction to the Semeiotic of Charles Sanders Peirce* (Bloomington: Indiana Univ. Press, 1996); and Gelpi, *Varieties of Transcendental Experience*, 227–87.

[28] Royce, *The Problem of Christianity*, 304.

[29] An important nuance is that a Roycean conception of interpretation does not yield a synthesis of the two formerly estranged ideas. Following the work of Charles S. Peirce (the progenitor of the Pragmatist tradition) Royce carefully distinguishes his more general process of interpretation from Hegel's specialized dialectical method of thesis, antithesis, and higher synthesis. For Royce's discussion of this potential misunderstanding of his work, see Royce, *The Problem of Christianity*, 304–35; see also Oppenheim, *Royce's Mature Philosophy of Religion*, 43–53, 247.

[30] Royce, *The Problem of Christianity*, 312, 305.

[31] Ibid., 80–83; see also Royce, "Mind," 76.

[32] In addition to the three conditions that I examine, Royce identifies three more: (1) communities must be capable of real communication, (2) communities need the voluntary cooperation of their members, and (3) communities must be loved first by their members. Royce terms this genuine love of community "loyalty to loyalty." For Royce's more comprehensive overview of his theory of community, see Royce, *The Problem of Christianity*, 75–98, 229–72. Because community is the cornerstone for all of his work, Royce explained some dimension of his theory of community in virtually every text he wrote. See, for example,

Royce, *The Sources of Religious Insight*, 37–75, 166–210, 257–97; Royce, *Metaphysics*, 24–32; Royce, "Mind." For a straightforward, succinct summary of Royce's theory of community, see John J. Markey OP, *Creating Communion: The Theology of the Constitutions of the Church* (New York: New City Press, 2003), 127–40.

[33] Royce, *The Problem of Christianity*, 243–45.

[34] Ibid., 243, 242–45.

[35] Ibid., 253.

[36] Ibid., 253–54.

[37] Ibid., 245.

[38] Ibid., 263.

[39] Ibid., 263–65.

[40] Ibid., 256–58.

[41] Ibid., 248.

[42] Kathryn Tanner, *Theories of Culture: A New Agenda for Theology* (Minneapolis: Fortress Press, 1997), 121–22.

[43] Royce, *The Problem of Christianity*, 306.

[44] Anne E. Carr, *Transforming Grace: Christian Tradition and Women's Experience* (San Francisco: HarperCollins, 1988), 38.

[45] Royce, *The Problem of Christianity*, xviii.

[46] Royce, *The Sources of Religious Insight*, 259–62.

[47] Royce, *The Problem of Christianity*, 268.

[48] Josiah Royce, "Error and Truth," in Oppenheim, *Josiah Royce's Late Writings*, 1:371 (originally published in 1912). See also Royce, *The Problem of Christianity*, 332.

[49] For an examination of the nature of truth in light of Hispanic popular Catholicism, see Goizueta, *Caminemos Con Jesus*, 132–72.

[50] For a translation of the *Nican Mopohua*, the written account of the Guadalupe story, see Lisa Sousa, Stafford Poole, and James Lockhart, eds. and trans., *The Story of Guadalupe: Luis Laso de la Vega's "Huei Tlamahuiçoltica" of 1649*, Nahuatl Studies Series 5 (Stanford, CA: Stanford Univ. Press, 1998). Generally speaking, scholars today recognize Laso de la Vega as the author of the *Nican Mopohua*. However, the origins of the narrative account have been disputed, with at least three versions each attributed to different authors, namely, Laso de la Vega, Miguel Sánchez, and Antonio Valeriano. For a discussion of the different versions and the political interests that each furthered, see D. A. Brading, *Mexican Phoenix: Our Lady of Guadalupe: Image and Tradition across Five Centuries* (Cambridge, UK: Cambridge Univ. Press, 2001).

[51] Sousa, Poole, and Lockhart, *The Story of Guadalupe*, 77–79, 87–89; see also Virgilio Elizondo, *Guadalupe: Mother of the New Creation* (Maryknoll, NY: Orbis Books, 1997), 60–78.

[52] Elizondo, *Guadalupe*, 115.

[53] Sousa, Poole, and Lockhart, *The Story of Guadalupe*, 79–85; see also Elizondo, *Guadalupe*, 34–38, 75–77.

[54] See Elizondo, *Guadalupe*, 48–53.

10

The Politics of Tradition
in the Protestant Educational Endeavor
for Colonial Puerto Rico

José R. Irizarry

INTRODUCTION

Michael de Certeau's *L'ecriture de l'histoire* opens to an allegorical etching by Jan van der Straet depicting the encounter between the Italian voyager Amerigo Vespucci and a native woman in the land to be named Latin America.[1] The scene is familiar in the iconography of conquest. A heavily dressed conqueror carries in his hands the symbols of the European tradition.[2] Whether a cruciform standard, a scientific instrument, a machine, or a weapon, these symbols represent the cultural products of the European mind, and they are displayed before the curious gaze of the naked conquered as a reminder of difference, superiority, and power. There is no indication in such representations that the conqueror desires to offer those symbols to the conquered and make her a participant of the historical tradition they represent. On the contrary, the hands of the conqueror hold tight and close to his body those symbols that grant him a sense of identity, ownership, and power before the overwhelming and enigmatic presence of bare *alterity*.

Since the concept of *traditum* connotes the act of "handing down," it naturally infers an activity whereas those who hold tradition in their hands, due to power or ascription, retain the authority to decide the what, how, and when of that transference[3] of tradition. The conqueror assumes the power to choose what part of tradition, if any, will be shared, and to what degree the conquered will participate in the conqueror's cultural and religious legacy, and therefore, the conqueror's identity, as

227

well as their rightful place in the continuity of history. Tradition, from the point of view of the European subject depicted in the imagery of conquest, serves as a tool of seduction, where those with power and self-ascribed authority display the desirability of their cultural possessions in order to exercise control over the body (model behavior through discipline) of the conquered and to regulate access to knowledge. In short, the conqueror and the conquered delimit the boundaries of their respective identities as they engage the *politics* of tradition.

In order to interpret tradition as *politics,* that is, as a process by which social relations are regulated and organized rather than as historical content, attention should be given to the method of shaping and communicating traditions.[4] My contribution to this communal reflection, as a practical theologian, moves beyond the contours of tradition as what Edward Shils calls "the transmitted thing,"[5] to address tradition as a socioreligious praxis. This essay attempts an exploration of the politics of religious traditioning by studying the process by which tradition is "handed on," *social communication*, through one of the primary forms used by the church to model and achieve the communication of tradition, *education*. I will situate this discussion in the Puerto Rican context and will address the missionary enterprise of North American Protestant churches at the turn of the twentieth century as they responded to the colonization of the Caribbean island after the conclusion of the Spanish Cuban American war.

Moreover, by looking at Protestant missionary education, this article furthers the hypothesis that, absorbed into a socially progressive *Zeitgeist* that supported the new imperialist politics of North American overseas expansionism, the Protestant churches obscured the distinctiveness of the historical reformed traditions and paid little attention to delivering the Protestant dogmatic and religious tradition (theology, rituals, symbols, history) to the Puerto Rican population they attempted to evangelize. While constantly pointing to the "inadequacy" and "poverty" of Puerto Rican "Catholic" religiosity, the missionary rarely rendered a Protestant "tradition" as a substitute. While missionary politics were accompanied by a deliberate effort to "de-tradition" native religious culture, as the article by Machado in this volume suggests (see Chapter 11), there was a lack of systematic agency in religious "re-traditioning." We have to be extremely cautious not to suggest naively that lack of exposure to Protestant tradition was a positive element of the missionary enterprise, amounting to a "good will" expression that allowed Puerto Ricans to construct their own Protestant identity. While a lack of exposure to "classic" Protestant tradition undoubtedly allowed for creative reformulations of doctrine and for the contextualization of theology and religious practices, we should consider what was intended by the retention of knowledge and authority by those who adhered to a tradition.[6] In the case of Protestant education in Puerto Rico, one motive for suspending the communication of tradition was to expose Puerto Ricans to their apparent "nakedness" (void of positive traditions) and to keep it bared of any tradition, so that blank colonial bodies *(corpora rasa)* could be established in order to be inscribed with the colonizers' history, seduced by their progress, and disciplined by their political institutions.

It can be argued that, to some extent, the Protestant church defined itself since its inception *vis-à-vis* the ecclesial tradition of the Roman Catholic magisterium, and that the doctrine of *sola scriptura* was a counterbalance to the heavy emphasis on tradition that came to characterize Tridentine thought.[7] However, with the exception of some movements of radical reformation, an incisive rupture with tradition was not supported by "mainstream" Protestant reformers.[8] Not only did reformers sustain the continuity of their doctrinal stances with some elements of ecclesial tradition, but the Reformation, as a religious movement, early on achieved a high degree of *canonization* and systematization of its own particular tradition.

Since the European and North American Protestant churches were deliberately *traditioned* into the canons of Reformed thought and of the historical narratives of Protestant denominationalism, the question of why the Puerto Rican *evangélico/a* was not immersed in a similar process of *traditioning* raises the issue of politics. I contend that the amalgamation of Americanizing and Christianizing ideologies superseded the doctrinal formulations of Protestant faith in the missionaries' minds.[9]

We can but speculate what may have resulted of a missionary education that focused on the communication of Reformed thought and Protestant identity. On one side, knowing the religious tradition of the missionary could disclose the internal rationale and religious beliefs generating colonial politics and therefore bring into awareness a significant source of colonial legitimization, opening a space on the Puerto Rican consciousness for re-politicization. Or perhaps the potentially subversive elements of that tradition, if owned, interpreted, and carried out into social implications by Puerto Rican subjects, would be counterproductive to the Americanizing and colonizing efforts. In any case, to accomplish the goals of colonial politics, the colonizing nation needed an institutional matrix experienced in the technologies of *traditioning* in order to engage the process of shaping a new political identity in the colonized. The Protestant educational project established by missionaries and carried out through public education and Sunday Schools stepped forward to serve that role.

EDUCATION AND THE RECASTING
OF PROTESTANT TRADITION
IN LIGHT OF MISSIONARY IDEOLOGY

June 1898. A month before the American invasion terminated the hegemony of Spain over the island of Puerto Rico, the Presbyterian Board of Foreign Missions invited other Protestant missionary bodies to convene a meeting in order to design a strategy for evangelizing the soon-to-be American territories. The American Baptists, Episcopalians, Methodists, and Congregationalists responded to the invitation.[10] The fact that this strategic planning started before the actual military campaign on the island demonstrates that Protestant churches were intentionally collaborating in shaping the politics of American expansionism and that, to some extent, they shared the national ethos of cultural imperialism.[11]

In order to participate in the new colonizing process, the Protestant churches had to reassess their doctrinal traditions and their ecclesial traditions—because the missionary context became a point of discontinuity with the past, a virgin laboratory of progress, the pristine sign of the American *novus ordo*. While recasting their historic *doctrinal* traditions, Protestant churches retained one of the most *practical* traditions of the church of the Reformation: the utilization of educational institutions to establish a relationship between the community of the baptized and the political community. It is in the educational efforts of the Protestant missions that we can clearly see the obliteration of the Reformed doctrinal tradition and the substitution of ideological principles that support the colonial enterprise. These ideological principles were paradoxically legitimized with modernist theological language, on the one hand, and strict evangelical values, on the other. Three foundational ideologies seem to be pervasive in the Protestant educational model for the new colonial territory: centralization, democratization, and Americanization. The fact that such principles emerged from a liberal interpretation of faith and religion, and not from historic Reformed principles, accounts for the critique that neo-orthodoxy came to pose for these political tendencies in the midst of the twentieth century.

A pivotal idea promoted by the educational discourse of American imperialism, adopted by the Protestant missionary church, was the idea of educational centralization. Centralization was the means by which the United States federal government maintained control over crucial directions and policy-making processes in the educational system of the nation.[12] With the United States expanding its territory and seeking unification after the Civil War, not only on the mainland but also across the sea, the oversight of state and local education became more complex.

As early as 1870 a bill was introduced into the US House of Representatives pressing for federal participation in the establishment of a national system of education.[13] However, as Robert Church argues, centralization was not fully achieved due to the strong district school organization that solidified throughout the whole century. Church states that "tentative moves toward more centralization still left the power over educational decisions dispersed through the districts."[14] This means that the United States government was dealing with the complex issue of centralization and the rational coherence of its principles on the mainland when the idea of a centralized school system for Puerto Rico was promoted.

The idea of public schooling in Puerto Rico became a colonial experiment in centralization in a newly occupied territory. The colonial situation was an adequate context for such experimentation for various reasons. First, Puerto Rico's small territorial extension made possible the oversight of schools and school governmental organisms. Second, the tradition of liberal and conservative educational reformers and theorists, which made the centralization of mainland American education difficult due to differing political views, was nonexistent in Puerto Rico. And third, the political and social instability of the colonial territory made its institutions more manageable and susceptible to control. Since the common school system aimed toward social control through governmental centralization of education, it served as a primary tool of colonization. In this respect, Robert Church argues,

> the essence of the common school movement was its rhetorical commitment to the deliberate use of education as a tool for social manipulation and social progress. Educational control had to be centralized and educators trained to adhere to a single professional standard in order to accomplish the manipulation of society. This emphasis on schooling for social manipulation explains the most distinctive element in the common school movement's rhetoric—the imperative to get all children, and especially urban children, into school.[15]

In Puerto Rico the proposal for a centralized system of education functioned as a colonial initiative to achieve social control. This was accompanied by other governmental measures of administrative centralization. Church historian Daniel Rodríguez Díaz suggests that in Puerto Rico "the politics of administrative centralization has the double purpose of guaranteeing the ideological homogenization of the whole system and of separating the landowner class from the municipal control of education."[16]

Whereas centralization operated as a structural strategy for colonial control, there were also ideological strategies impelling centralizing measures. Moving the policy-making forces toward centralization was the influence of *patriotic sentiment* in education. In order to secure public approval for American imperialist politics, confidence in the purposes of the nation and patriotic pride had to be fostered.[17] The old colonial emphasis on religious orthodoxy, with its clear connections to historic Protestant tradition and its diverse theological perspectives, was progressively replaced by a shared discourse on citizenship and loyalty to the American nation. Not only was religious orthodoxy, in its support of distinctive dogmatic traditions, detrimental to national unification, but it also remained nonoperative in the scheme of the emerging ideology of progressivism. Progressivism, the idea that promotes public interest in social amelioration, served as the foundational construct of an education entrusted with the task of improving the quality of American life.[18]

The discourse on education that combined principles of centralization, loyalist citizenry through Americanization efforts, and lay democracy was adopted by almost every US social institution—including the Protestant church. Protestant theologians constructed their religious discourse on the basis of these foundational principles of educational thought. The movement toward centralization was seen as a democratic process intended to solve the social flaws of aristocratic and monarchic systems that were assumed to be the byproducts of the Catholic tradition in European countries. Defending centralization, religious thinker Josiah Strong wrote that "so general a tendency toward the centralization of population, political power, of capital, and of production, manifested in ways so various, can indicate nothing less than a great movement toward a closer organization of society, a new development of civilization."[19]

Beyond achieving social organization and governmental control, centralization would provide the centrifugal force that would attract divergent interest sectors to the ideal of nationhood. Protestant theologians gave an ethical basis to nationhood by stressing the ideas of Christian fraternity and of the moral relations that hold the Christian society together. It was the Christian ideal of "brotherhood" that, according to influential American preacher Henry Ward Beecher, would form "habits of common thought, common purposes, and common government."[20] It is clear, then, that a missionary enterprise based on the ethics of brotherhood would need to ameliorate the doctrinal and ecclesial distinctiveness of the diverse Protestant traditions.

Undertaking the idea of divine sanction for national politics, many theologians and clergy contended that the democratic state was the paradigm of the *civitas Dei*. This theological correlation induced some Christian theologians to make bold statements about the democratic society. On a particular occasion, a respectable professor of systematic theology at Yale declared, in clear Deweyan fashion: "A pure social democracy is the political fulfillment of Christianity; the political organization of Christ's law of love; the order through which faith in the right manifests itself in the freedom of man. The old Hebrew idea of God dwelling in the midst of the people constituted in a free common-wealth expresses the fact and method of democracy."[21]

Since in this line of theological reflection "the democratic state is on its ethical side identical with the ideal of the kingdom of God,"[22] the United States would embody this ideal by compelling the "people to work out a new peculiar destiny" as Americans; therefore every citizen or inhabitant of the democratic state needed to be "Americanized."[23] The invitation to follow this historical course for the United States, and for the sake of the world, came out of pulpits and theological texts. The "white man's burden" was the sacrificial expression of the religious vocation of a democratic society. It was also the legitimating force of imperialism, as demonstrated by the words of theologian and religious educator Horace Bushnell:

> Thank God we have a country, and that country has the chance of a future! Ours be it henceforth to cherish that country, and assert that future; also, to invigorate both by our own civilization, adorn them by our literature, consolidate them in our religion. Ours be it also, in God's own time, to champion, by land and sea, the right of this whole continent to be an American world, and to have its own American laws, and liberties and institutions.[24]

PROTESTANT EDUCATION AND THE DISPLACEMENT
OF TRADITIONS IN PUERTO RICO

The Protestant missionaries who arrived in Puerto Rico as a result of the North American occupation were informed, and to a great extent influenced, by the functionalist notion of society fostered by American liberal theology and by an educational system that sustained and promoted the aforementioned American foundational principles of education. Trust in the educational system, its values, and its grounding principles is represented in the emphasis that missionaries gave to schooling, public communication, and publishing.

As in many other countries where American missionaries settled, the establishment of parish schools and Sunday Schools preceded the establishment of worship houses; throughout the initial decades of missionary work the number of attendees to Sunday Schools surpassed the number of church members.[25] The missionary educational philosophy followed a catechetical model in which instruction in faith rubrics (primarily biblical) preceded full participation in the new Protestant communities. In fact, it was through education that the need for Protestant congregations was fostered. Reading the religious context of Puerto Rico, Joseph B. Clark perceived that "the people are practically without churches and must be made ready by education to feel their need and their blessing."[26]

Another sign of confidence in the American educational system, and a clear example of the surrendering of Protestant religious traditions to the missionary ideology, was the rapid transference of parish schools into the hands of the government to be used as centers of public education. This was the case with Congregationalist Sunday Schools in the central towns of Puerto Rico—which predate by years the establishment of the first public schools in their surrounding rural areas.[27] The Methodist Mission documented its commitment to lend its resources to the public schools in order to provide primary education to children.[28] The Disciples of Christ made a decision to turn over church educational facilities, in which the Latin *quadrivium* was taught along with the Bible, to the public school system.[29] The Presbyterians, followed by the United Brethren Church, decided to cease most of their educational work once the public educational system was in place within their missionary fields.[30] Only in the second half of the twentieth century did Protestant churches again start to establish parochial schools with purposes distinct from those of the public school.

Although the transference of religious educational institutions to the colonial administration reflects Protestant church support for the ideals of common public schooling, above the teaching of their respective theological traditions, the churches also reflected some of the foundational principles of American education in various areas of their own ministerial practice. One of the first demonstrations of institutional centralization was the unification efforts of various Protestant denominations to present a common ideal of Christian social demeanor on the island. Initial interdenominational cooperation developed soon into structural organization. As another indication of the surrendering of distinctive Protestant traditions (denominational identities), the Protestant churches moved immediately toward ecumenical cooperation in the missionary field, even when the ecumenical movement was not yet mature on the mainland and would gain its momentum only by the end of World War II.[31] The Federation of Evangelical Churches of Puerto Rico, the first ecumenical body in Puerto Rican history, and, for that matter, the first Latin American council of churches, was created a few years later in order to foster a common Protestant culture within a fragmented Catholic country.[32] This form of centralization, achieved through ecumenical relations, pretended to regulate missionary objectives as well as to formulate religious-political strategies for the missionary field.

While retaining their own administrative autonomy, Protestant denominations became more influential in the public sphere when they spoke through representative organizations. Those organizations included, besides the diverse interdenominational organizations, the most widely known Protestant newspaper on the island, *El Puerto Rico Evangélico*, as well as shared boards of evangelism and education. Interdenominational cooperation in education systematized the methods and content of Protestant religious education. It also centralized into a single public voice the opinions of congregations and clergy regarding education. When church opinions regarding education were published in the Puerto Rican secular press, they were prefaced with such phrases as "the evangelical church thinks."

Sunday Schools cooperated in the process of Protestant centralization by teaching Bible content which de-emphasized doctrinal and theological differences among the traditional historical churches.[33] Denominationalism was not known by the average Puerto Rican, who perceived at that time, and to some extent still does today, all Protestant churches as evangelical; the average Puerto Rican lacked the knowledge of theological distinctions and particularities within Protestant traditions. The educational policies of the various Protestant denominations, as Samuel Silva Gotay says, showed little variation, if any at all, while uniform lesson series were readily accepted as curricular resources.[34] Missionary educational efforts were centralized within an ecumenical organization and also determined within the respective missionary boards in the United States that controlled the production and distribution of Protestant literature on the island. That educational material was developed and written by US educators and then translated for Puerto Rican consumption.[35]

With the establishment of Sunday Schools, the missionaries also advanced the educational centralization pursued by the colonial administration. In the early years of its formation, the Puerto Rican Department

of Education saw as one of its major challenges the dispersion and inac-
cessibility of the island's population. The isolation of great parts of the
population from the centers of governmental control was responsible, in
part, for the failure of the Spanish colonial administration to provide
adequate education and for the Catholic churches to attend to the spiritual and instructional needs of the population.[36] As Josiah Strong suggested, within expansionist politics any form of political or social centralization necessitates the centralization of the population.[37] Missionaries
started to solve this problem by establishing small congregations in those
unreachable rural areas under the leadership of a Puerto Rican, and by
erecting Sunday Schools to serve their most immediate educational needs.

The Sunday School was able to reach the dispersed areas of the population because, as an institution, it was more "portable" than the public
school which depended on buildings and educational materials. Sunday
Schools brought people together in a way that few other institutions
could manage during that period. This was due to various elements: (1)
the eagerness of Puerto Ricans to know the Bible, and the need for spiritual direction among a population that was relatively abandoned by the
institutional church; (2) the provision of a means of social encounter
when there was a lack of public spaces in rural areas; (3) the teaching of
a new religious subject matter besides the distribution of clothes and
food, and hygiene instruction in a society characterized by disease and
high infant mortality due to malnourishment and poor hygiene; and (4)
the incorporation of innovative educational approaches, such as the inclusion of music, which has been always appreciated by the Puerto Rican
population.[38]

The missionary educational effort supported the idea of Americanization by fostering loyalty to the United States and a religious zeal for
American patriotism. Again, the Protestant churches were more apt to
advance this Americanizing process with their theological emphasis on
evangelical obedience and inclusion. Sunday Schools were the guardians
of public morals by teaching obedience to authority (re-implanting a
new version of the Catholic tradition of moral teaching the Puerto Ricans
had already experienced vis-à-vis the Reformed principle of freedom of
conscience). In addition, by offering a social space where every person
belonged, regardless of race or social status, they immersed the Puerto
Rican in the democratic experience.

The president of the Sunday School Committee of the Presbyterian
Church, the Rev. J. L. Santiago Cabrera, reflected the strong influence of
Americanization thought in religious education. In a letter to the Rev.
Harold Robinson, secretary of the Presbyterian Board of Publication
and Sabbath School Work, Santiago Cabrera asks for assistance because

if "the United States wants to make good and loyal citizens of the United States out of Porto [sic] Ricans, we have to pay attention to the formation of their moral character."[39]

Missionary boards entrusted religion teachers with the responsibility of developing the moral character necessary to make Puerto Ricans apt participants in a new public life defined by US values and ideals. In this way Protestant missionaries worked in the shaping of a new *paideia*, in which literacy formation was solely a means to a political end: the character formation of the soon-to-be citizens of the United States.[40] As Stella Wyatt Brummitt pointed out in her history of the Woman's Home Missionary Society of the Methodist Episcopal Church, the task of education is defined by teaching habits of mental and physical conduct. She then discloses the purpose of this training: "To see these bright-eyed children stand to pledge allegiance to our flag, gives one courage and hope for the Porto [sic] Rican American citizen of tomorrow."[41]

Regardless of its own distinctiveness as an educational project, the US educational endeavor reflected the same mode of political control and colonial intervention that characterized the Spanish colonial administration. Historians and sociologists may immediately connect such politics to the theological perspectives of both Catholic and Protestant traditions, which respectively supported the Spanish and the US colonial administrations on the island. Certainly, the obvious theological and dogmatic differences between Catholic and Protestant traditions conveyed the idea that some elements of these traditions were re-created through socially motivated hermeneutics, or "re-traditioned," as Dale T. Irvin would say,[42] in order to create what seems to have been a similar political project of imperialist expansionism. The variant that particularized the US colonial administration's educational policies was the establishment of a public school system that was centralized, Americanized, and democratized.

Nevertheless, the way the US educational project in Puerto Rico could validate its own uniqueness and value was to contrast the potential progress brought by the new system to the stagnant social conditions found under Spanish rule. The different social experience produced by distinct approaches to education would be necessarily attributed to the mutually opposed Protestant-Catholic traditional orientations toward reality. In other words, to communicate the positive value of the American way of life, the Protestant establishment needed to stress, in its educational model, the inadequate values of the Catholic tradition that fostered the apparently precarious way of life experienced under Spanish rule. We should not be surprised, then, to discover that Protestant missionaries expounded *more* of the classic Catholic tradition in their teaching (explaining to Puerto Rican *evangélicos/as* what the Catholic church believed in terms of dogma and doctrine) *than* the Reformed tradition (already replaced by political ideologies and rote biblical teaching). For this reason a brief comparison of the Protestant educational approach and the Catholic one yields the distinctive uses of tradition to further politics in a colonial context.

THE CATHOLIC TRADITION
AND THE POLITICS OF THE "OTHER"

The *content* of Spanish colonial education, modeled by the Catholic church, was based on a clear exposure to its religious tradition, understood as both dogma and moral/liturgical practices, with a particular emphasis on doctrinal teaching. The new Protestant establishment declared that the context of its education was equally religious, but that it was now defined by the liberal discourse that expounded democratic ideals as a new secular religion. The *form* of Spanish colonial education was understood as authoritarian, placing the teacher at the center of pedagogical decisions. In contrast, US colonial education was seen as technical, placing method and measured management at the center of pedagogical decisions. Educational practice during the years of Spanish rule served the colonizing purpose of forming the intellectual and moral leadership of the incipient colony, with a clear emphasis on higher education, while the US educational practice served the imperialist needs of shaping new loyal citizens by forging the consciences of children through an overt process of Americanization. There is no doubt that the educational ecology shifted with the change of colonial administrations—from the dispersed parish schools and the institutions of learning for the elite to a mass-oriented and centralized school system.

Before the creation of a public school system modeled on US schooling, and even before the first missionary attempts to engage Puerto Ricans in educational projects, educational efforts within Puerto Rican society were already in place. The education envisioned by these efforts was inherently religious. Religious education during the period of Spanish colonial rule responded to the interests both of the Spanish regime and of its ally, the Catholic church. Even at moments when more liberal proposals of educational policy were impelled by constitutional measures, the subject matter of religious tradition remained at the core of the learning corpus. This remained the case even when the institutional church started to break its relationship with the colonial state, at the end of the nineteenth century, due to issues of financing and of state appropriation of church properties.[43] At the time that the Protestant establishment initiated its educational project on the island, based on the principle of church-state separation, although practically manifesting the tight connection between the interests of the state and the ministry of the church, Protestants encountered a Catholic church that, in principle, promoted relations between church and state—but a Catholic church that was suffering from the fragmentation of those relations.

The fact that religious education, as a referent, disappeared from the historical narrative of Puerto Rican educational history is explicated by the unfitness of the religious educational practice, as previously described, within the discursive framework of education as defined by US expansionist and imperialist practices. This discourse—defined by the separation of religious subject matter from secular education, control of educational institutions by the state, citizenry formation, and democratic ideals—was unknown to the Spanish colonizer. The educational practice engaged in by the Spanish regime in Puerto Rico during four centuries of colonial control was antithetical to this discourse. The Spanish educational practice was characterized by the dogmatic principle of church and state integration, de-centralizing control over schooling matters, and clear distinctions among social classes.

The educational project of the US administration and the efforts of Protestant missionaries would be presented as one of the many social innovations that would bring "civilization." It is important to emphasize this, because in the process of defining its own educational policy, the US colonial administration felt the need to construct Puerto Rican "otherness." The Puerto Rican subject was defined by the new colonizer within a shorthand understanding of Catholicism in order to objectify Puerto Rican identity and, consequently, to gain better control over it; in other words, using Paulo Freire's illustrative phrase, in order to discover it outside themselves.[44] The US establishment constructed, by propaganda, literature, and public oratory, an idea of Puerto Rican Catholic society—an idea that was not yet articulated by the island's populace. In fact, Puerto Rican Catholicism was more fragmented and diversified on the island than the discursive representation provided by US leaders and missionaries.

According to the American representation of Puerto Rican Catholic society, it was this society's "Romanist" posture that limited the social, moral, and economic progress of the island.[45] The first pedagogical objective of the missionaries was to substitute the "Romanist" culture found in Puerto Rico with an "Americanist" one. Little consideration was given to the fact that the influence of "Romanism," as defined by the head of the Roman Catholic Church, was irrelevant at that time within Puerto

Rican society. First, the Catholic church in Puerto Rico was under the jurisdiction of the Spanish Crown through the *patronato regio,* and the Roman See had little interest in matters regarding the island. Second, even if there were any indirect influence of "Romanism" on the Puerto Rican Catholic church, this influence did not impinge upon the majority of the population, which was isolated from the ministerial work of the parishes.[46]

The accusations that the missionaries directed against "superstitious and backward" Catholicism were misplaced, for it was popular religion and not the Catholic church that represented the religious experience of the majority of Puerto Ricans. However, antagonism with the institutional Catholic church was expected in the American colonial project, for this institution was the most visible because it was strongly allied with the Spanish regime. Besides, the United States lacked a discourse or even a practice that could confront the Puerto Ricans on the basis of their popular religion.[47] This may account for the fact that even when the Protestant establishment was accepted, its Americanizing project was never fully achieved.

Another problem with the US educational discourse was that it obviated the fact that, apart from the Catholic Spanish establishment, there was a colonized subject defining his or her own cultural identity as Puerto Rican. As US educational ideals were introduced on the island, emerging ideas of Puerto Rican education, separated from the Spanish colonial practice and the conservative stance of institutional Catholicism, already existed. The Puerto Rican society in formation already practiced many of the educational ideas that were introduced by the American administration as "civilizing" innovations. Concepts of liberalism, national unification, citizenry, and democracy were part of the language that the Puerto Ricans were constructing during the nineteenth century.[48] Since that was the case, there was nothing inherently Protestant in such ideals and, therefore, the contribution of the Reformed tradition to the implementation of those ideals was obscured. Notions of liberal education, introduced by the American discourse as innovations of common school practice, were already part of the Puerto Rican intellectual tradition, as demonstrated by the works of Eugenio María de Hostos, José Julián Acosta, and Salvador Brau.[49] A variety of critical pedagogical treatises were written by the black Puerto Rican Celedonio Delgado, who reflected a neo-Darwinian inclination in his emphasis on biological determination, environmental adaptation, and heritage.[50]

The development of a "counter-colonial" discourse was not only the domain of the educated Puerto Rican classes but also of Puerto Rican religious movements represented by all classes and faith traditions, as demonstrated by the creolized Kardecian Spiritists, the pre-missionary Protestant movement of Los Bíblicos, and the Catholic popular movement of Los Hermanos Cheos. Religious instruction seemed to be a practice that initiated Puerto Ricans into the development of a local religious tradition. It also assisted the social classes represented in these religious movements to achieve their social and political projects.

The most critical change effected by the discourse of American education was the implementation of a pedagogy that attempted to tamper with the conscience of Puerto Rican children, substituting new American cultural values for the cultural values with which they were socialized. Americanization was pursued not only as a process of axiological and ideological subversion, but also as a process of appropriation of the children's consciousness by naming for them, and on their behalf, their own thoughts and sentiments about the new cultural configuration. Not only in educational literature but also in religious literature written by missionaries, ideas on how children "felt" under the new social and cultural arrangements were a recurrent theme. From the description of children pointing "triumphantly" to a map to identify their new motherland, singing the American national anthem "heartily and enthusiastically," and being "anxious" to learn the English language, documentation presents us with an undeniable picture of this imposition on and appropriation of consciousness.[51] With this pedagogy American teachers inscribed their own patriotic sentiments in the consciousness of Puerto Rican children as a projection of the imperialist pride that accompanied the new colonial enterprise. It is clear, then, that emphasis was placed on the education of children, since in light of new theories of child-centered education and experimental psychology in the United States, the child's consciousness-in-formation was the potential developer of a new concept of progressive culture.[52] Spaniards, interested more in cultural stability and solidification, directed their educational efforts to the training and instruction of adults.

This observation on the educational effects of US pedagogy on the children's conscience calls us to reevaluate the taken-for-granted thesis among many historians and sociologists that the Americanization process in Puerto Rico produced a crisis of consciousness contrasting the Catholic tradition to the Protestant one.[53] To suggest that such a crisis existed is to suggest that the effects of Americanization were felt explicitly by Puerto Ricans who had a psychological and emotional system in place to resist the Americanizing imposition at a conscious level. Furthermore, these historians and sociologists need to imply that such a psychological and emotional system was provided by the Catholic colonial establishment.

So far, historians and sociologists who continue to sustain the thesis of a "crisis of consciousness" have been unable to provide enough evidence to demonstrate formative processes that transferred Catholic tradition or at what levels this tradition embedded itself in the collective consciousness of Puerto Ricans. The history of education problematizes this issue, since it recognizes the lack of Catholic formative institutions and the alienation of those few Catholic institutions—which supposedly forged that consciousness—from the majority of the Puerto Rican populace. What some of these historians and sociologists seem to overlook is that the "crisis" hypothesis supports the colonialist discourse of elites that needed to create, for political reasons, the illusion of antagonism between two historical traditions. The Spanish colonial regime supported the idea of a Catholic tradition to attract the Puerto Rican population to its political interests on the basis of "cultural" loyalty. The American colonial regime also sustained the idea of a Puerto Rican Catholic tradition in order to contrast it with its own national conscience and as proof of its "cultural" superiority. At the center of the discursive tension between a Catholic tradition and a Protestant tradition, the Puerto Rican child was educated within a pedagogical practice that implicitly and subtly was forming, in practice and apart from the child's agency, the real conscience of the quintessential colonized subject.[54]

CONCLUSION

While from the perspective of some classic schools of systematic theology tradition is primarily conceived as a received datum (whereas its source is historical or transcendent), from the point of view of this practical theologian, tradition is presently constituted and uses elements of the past in the process of selecting, interpreting, and creating a *usable* tradition. Because of the intentionality engaged in this process of forging a tradition, whose primary function is, according to Madan Sarup, "to defend identity against the threat of heterogeneity, discontinuity and contradiction . . . to bind and necessarily, therefore, to exclude,"[55] we can assert that it involves and carries *politics* with it.

The context of colonial relations between a hegemonic culture and a "dependent" culture puts in place a complex political organization that legitimizes the unequal power balance of this arrangement. Such political organization necessitates a "tradition" that can generate the controlling social metaphors of authority and truth that need to be accepted as "given." In the politics of traditioning the dominant tradition feeds its authority with claims of permanence and immutability. When such a tradition overtakes the imagination of both the colonizer and the colonized, other traditions that genuinely forge their respective cultural and religious identities are obscured and even transformed in the process.

In this essay I have proposed that the political organization of the colonial relation between Puerto Rico and the United States, after the Spanish Cuban American War, established an educational system in order to hand down the tradition of the new Manifest Destiny ideology and, in doing so, not only transformed the Catholic tradition(s) of the Puerto Rican subject but also the Protestant traditions brought by the missionaries who collaborated in the colonizing process. As a result, the newly baptized Puerto Rican *evangélicos/as* received a socially morphed Protestant tradition from which the foundational documents, histories, and doctrines of the rich Reformed traditions were absent. The *evangélicos/as* struggled to build an identity, bared of any *substantial* tradition, out of elements of the Puerto Rican popular culture and theological trends adopted by their sponsoring denominations in the United States.

It is accurate to say that the Protestant churches in Puerto Rico, as well as Protestant Hispanic churches in the US mainland, continue to search for a Protestant identity rooted in a sense of continuity with the Reformed traditions. Another look at the educational programs and educational resources created by American denominations to be consumed and implemented by Puerto Rican and US mainland Hispanic churches betrays an equal absence of the theme of tradition. In fact, for many of us engaged in the pastoral practices of Hispanic Protestant congregations and attentive to denominational support for these faith communities, it is obvious that these have been excluded from the overall project of theological traditioning, understood as the deliberate process of sharing a common historical religious identity. Far from being an unfortunate oversight, this exclusion obeys an implicit and rarely articulated fear of seeing the "other" as part of ourselves, as well as the equalizing claims of that new relation.

Equality would have blurred the line between the missionary and the missioned, the colonizer and the colonized. In this sense, keeping control over tradition allows the church to play a vital part in the current structures of neocolonial politics. Therefore, learning from our past, the question remains pertinent: What are the politics behind the absence of a tradition in the traditioning process? Or, framed within the question of colonial relations, we may ask, What does the dominant church gain from the nakedness and absence of tradition in that "other" church that is its subject?

Notes

[1] Michel de Certeau, *L'ecriture de l'histoire* (Paris: Gallimard, 1975).

[2] Similar illustrations abound in nineteenth-century historical material. See examples in Peter Wood, *Diversity: The Invention of a Concept* (San Francisco: Encounter Books, 2003), book cover and 51.

[3] Aware of the surplus of meaning for terms frequently used in cultural theory after the "linguistic turn," I want to limit the use of the term *transference* to the activity of passing on. By doing this I separate the term from its strictly psycho-analytic usage (Freudian), although Lacan's claim that transference necessitates a "subject presumed to know" may support my argument that there is a position of power and authority (knowledge stakeholder) in the transference of tradition.

[4] In his Aquinas Lectures, Jorge J. E. Gracia surfaces the three analytical domains to be explored when discussing any form of tradition: group identity, knowledge, and communication. The process of communication is framed as the primary problem to be solved in discussing tradition, since it is on the basis of the rules and expectations of linguistic and behavioral exchanges that identities are negotiated and knowledge is shared. See Jorge J. E. Gracia, *Old Wine in New Skins* (Milwaukee: Marquette Univ. Press, 2003).

[5] Edward Shils, *Tradition* (Chicago: Univ. of Chicago Press, 1981), 12–15.

[6] For a more comprehensive description of the effect of authority and knowledge production in the development of a tradition, see John E. Thiel, *Senses of Tradition* (Oxford: Oxford Univ. Press, 2000).

[7] The Council of Trent demanded assent to and veneration of the received traditions (written and unwritten) under the claim that those traditions were preserved in unbroken succession by the Roman Catholic Church, the depository of truths that were passed "per manus traditae." See H. J. Schroeder, *The Canons and Decrees of the Council of Trent* (Rockford, IL: Tan Books and Publishers, 1978).

[8] Of common knowledge among scholars of Luther's and Calvin's work is the great debt of these reformers to medieval and renaissance ecclesial thought. Patristic tradition is often quoted as a respectful source of doctrine and faith by both reformers. A comprehensive discussion of such influences is found in Robert J. Bast and Andrew C. Gow, eds., *Continuity and Change: The Harvest of Late Medieval and Reformation History* (Leiden: Brill, 2000).

[9] I am borrowing the term *amalgamation,* in relation to tradition, from Edward Shils, who states that "amalgamations occur by renunciation and modification of elements hitherto regarded as integral to one of the traditions and by replacements of those elements by corresponding elements" (Shils, *Tradition,* 276).

[10] *Christian Work in Latin America* (New York: Christian Missionary Education Movement, 1917).

[11] This author recognizes the historical distinctions associated with both movements: expansionism and imperialism. Some authors circumscribe their

expansionist language to the events regarding the acquisition of territories within the American mainland. Such authors see imperialism as an advanced stage in which extraterritorial dominion is sought in order to establish international hegemony in the areas of culture, economy and defense. I assume in this essay that both movements are contingent and that they take root in a shared ideological framework that holds the United States as the bearer of a historical vocation—"civilizing" and bringing progress to the world.

[12] Lawrence A. Cremin, *The Transformation of the School: Progressivism in American Education 1876–1957* (New York: Vintage Books, 1964), 274–76.

[13] R. Freeman Butts and Lawrence Cremin, *A History of Education in American Culture* (New York: Holt, Rinehart, and Winston, 1953), 370–79.

[14] Robert Church, in ibid.

[15] Ibid., 58–59. Historians argue about the source of the centralizing concern. Church says that the root of the problem (the need for centralization) is the diversification of urban America. According to many other educational historians, like Freeman Butts and Lawrence Cremin, especially those interested in the social phenomenon of immigration, the root of the problem was urbanism and the impossibility of controlling the increasingly diverse value system created by the racial diversity of the big cities. A variety of historical documents support this argument, especially Jane Addams's articles on the education of the immigrant child and Elwood P. Cubberly's pro-Americanist historical interpretations. Although recognizing it as an urban problem, other historians, like David B. Tyack, state that it was equally a rural problem because local management of schools could not advance the educational system that was disintegrating along with other aspects of rural social life as progress became measured by technical and industrial skills. See David B. Tyack, *The Best One System: A History of American Urban Education* (Cambridge, MA: Harvard Univ. Press, 1974), 21–27.

[16] Daniel Rodríguez Díaz, *La primera evangelización norteamericana en Puerto Rico, 1898–1930* (Mexico City: Ediciones Boriquén, 1986), 158.

[17] See the still pertinent work by Arthur Schlesinger, *Political and Social Growth of the United States, 1852–1933* (New York: Macmillan, 1935), 274–91.

[18] The intellectual work on progressivism in education was advanced by Francis W. Parker in *Talks on Teaching* (New York: Kellogg's Teachers Library, 1883) and in *Talks on Pedagogics* (New York: E. L. Kellogg, 1894). Its major exponent was American philosopher John Dewey in his extensive work on education. See particularly, John Dewey, *The School and Society* (Chicago: Univ. of Chicago Press, 1899); and idem, *Democracy and Education* (New York: Macmillan Company, 1916).

[19] Josiah Strong, *The New Era* (New York: Baker and Taylor, 1893), 8.

[20] Henry Ward Beecher, *The Original Plymouth Pulpit* (Boston: Pilgrim Press, 1871), 5:203–19. Reprinted in Conrad Cherry, ed., *God's New Israel: Religious Interpretations of American Destiny* (Englewood Cliffs, NJ: Prentice-Hall, 1971), 233.

[21] Samuel Harris, *The Kingdom of Christ on Earth* (Andover, MA: W. F. Draper, 1874), 76.

[22] Laurence H. Schwab, *The Kingdom of God* (New York: Dutton Press, 1897), 260.

[23] Isaac Wise, "From a Lecture Delivered before the Theological and Religious Library Association in Cincinnati," January 7, 1869. Printed in Cherry, *God's New Israel*, 227.

[24] Horace Bushnell, *An Oration in Honor of a Civil War Soldier on Building Eras in Religion* (New York: Charles Scribners Sons, 1881).

[25] J. Merle Davis, *The Church in Puerto Rico's Dilemma* (New York: Department of Social and Economic Research and Counsel/International Missionary Council, 1942).

[26] Joseph B. Clark, *Leavening the Nation* (New York: The Baker and Taylor Co., 1903), 259.

[27] See H. P. Douglass, *Congregational Missionary Work in Puerto Rico* (New York: American Missionary Association, n.d.).

[28] B. S. Haywood, "Informe Anual del Superintendente," *El Defensor Cristiano* 128 (May 1, 1909), 15–16.

[29] In the *Puerto Rico Evangélico*, August 10, 1913, 2:16, the author of an article entitled "Un campo de Cristo" mentions that a school that was established by the Disciples of Christ in the Dajaos sector of the city of Bayamón, at the town's request, became a public school under the control of the American administration.

[30] For an analysis of the Presbyterian Missionary work on the island, see Edward A. Odell, *It Came to Pass* (New York: Board of National Missions, Presbyterian Church U.S.A., 1952). For the description of the educational ministry of the United Brethren, see Philo W. Drury, "Annual Report of the Mission of the United Brethren Church in Porto [*sic*] Rico for the Year 1910–1911."

[31] The beginnings of the ecumenical movement among the Protestant churches can be dated to the World Missionary Conference in Edinburgh in 1910. The Amsterdam Conference in 1948 gave the major institutional shape to the movement with the establishment of the World Council of Churches.

[32] Regarding this organization, see Donald T. Moore, *Puerto Rico para Cristo* (Mexico City: Centro Intercultural de Investigación, 1969).

[33] The statement that the missionaries in Puerto Rico were not interested in denominationalism was clearly presented by the concluding report of the 1916 Latin American missionary congress in Panama. See specifically the report presented by the Rev. Philo Drury, *Regional Conferences in Latin America: The Report of a Series of Seven Conferences following the Panama Congress in 1916* (New York: The Missionary Educational Movement and the Committee of Cooperation in Latin America, 1917).

[34] Samuel Silva Gotay, *Protestantismo y política en Puerto Rico, 1898–1930* (Río Piedras: Editorial de la Universidad de Puerto Rico, 1997), 197. Silva Gotay establishes that "all denominations define their mission in analogous form," and then proceeds to discuss the issue of education as a singular, shared manifestation of the Protestant project in Puerto Rico.

[35] Rodríguez Díaz, *La primera evangelización norteamericana en Puerto Rico, 1898–1930*, 218–20.

[36] Nélida Agosto Cintrón, *Religión y cambio social en Puerto Rico* (Río Piedras: Ediciones Huracán, 1996), 22–31.

[37] Strong, *The New Era*.

[38] Regarding the use of music for gathering Puerto Rican peasants, a peculiar description was given by C. Manly Morton: "During the early days, the missionaries had an old fashioned gramaphone and a few records with which they called people together. Many a person who came to listen to the little talking-machine remained to accept the message of salvation. The missionaries also had a little folding organ which was a great mystery to the people. On one occasion, a woman who had been intently watching Miss Siler play nudged her neighbor excitedly and said, 'See, she makes music with her feet, too!'" C. Manly Morton, *Kingdom Building in Puerto Rico* (Indianapolis: The United Christian Missionary Society, 1949), 44.

[39] Letter by the Rev. MacRobinson, dated June 1, 1920. Cited in Rodríguez Díaz, *La primera evangelización norteamericana en Puerto Rico, 1898–1930*, 221.

[40] I use the word *paideia* in relation to religious education in the sense used by Jack L. Seymour, Robert T. Gorman, and Charles Foster when they refer to the "substance and character of a culture" that becomes the essential form and content of education. The church participates in this *paideia* by being a public agent of character formation within the culture. See Jack L. Seymour et al., *The Church in the Education of the Public* (Nashville, TN: Abington Press, 1984).

[41] Stella Wyatt Brummitt, *Looking Backward—Thinking Forward* (Cincinnati: The Woman's Home Missionary Society, 1930), 213.

[42] Dale T. Irvin, *Christian Histories, Christian Traditioning: Rendering Accounts* (Maryknoll, NY: Orbis Books, 1998).

[43] See Elisa Julián de Nieves, *The Catholic Church in Colonial Puerto Rico* (Río Piedras: Editorial Edil, 1982).

[44] Paulo Freire, *Pedagogy of the Oppressed* (New York: Continuum, 1990), 31. It goes without saying that the same dialectics Freire applies to the oppressor-oppressed relation are operative in colonial relations.

[45] The Protestant newspaper *El Puerto Rico Evangélico* editorialized the anti-Romanist sentiment of the missionaries during the first three decades of the American occupation of Puerto Rico.

[46] Cintrón, *Religión y cambio social en Puerto Rico*, 22–31.

[47] The acknowledgment and study of popular religion as a social phenomenon within the American context are modern expressions of an intellectual interest in the sociology of knowledge. This scholarly tradition can be traced back to the work of Max Weber and is represented more recently in the work of Robert Redfield and Robert Bellah. See Peter W. Williams, *Popular Religion in America: Symbolic Change and the Modernization Process in Historical Perspective* (Urbana: Univ. of Illinois Press, 1989).

[48] For a description of the evolution of liberal ideals and the emergence of a "new thought" in Puerto Rican culture, see Edward J. Berbusse, *The United States in Puerto Rico, 1898–1900* (Chapel Hill, NC: Univ. of North Carolina Press, 1966).

[49] Ibid., 21–26.

[50] See Celedonio Delgado, *Apuntes sobre el problema educacional puertorriqueño* (Ponce: Tipografía El Día, 1918).

[51] Although the selected examples can be found in Joseph Seabury's works, they seem to be common in a long series of documents that includes reports of missionary societies and the religious press. The Protestant newspaper *El Puerto Rico Evangélico* reproduced some of these examples in its first few issues.

[52] See Parker, *Talks in Pedagogics.*

[53] This position is derived from an anthropological theory of cultural confrontation. It is also congenial with Hegelian dialectics presenting reality as a confrontation of forces. This theory, which relies heavily on psychological notions of cultural identity and on national and religious consciousness, has been the assumed position of authors like Samuel Silva Gotay and Luis Torres Oliver. The case of Puerto Rico defies such theory, and some Puerto Rican scholars, like Gervasio L. García and José Luis González, have called for a reevaluation of this "crisis" theory, especially when there is lack of evidence of that crisis in historical events. See Gervasio L. García, *Historia crítica, historia sin coartadas* (Río Piedras: Ediciones Huracán, 1989), 122–23; and José Luis González, *El país de cuatro pisos* (Río Piedras: Ediciones Huracán, 1989).

[54] The "crisis of consciousness" theory raises an educational problem—that of prescription. By "prescription" Paulo Freire means the assimilation of the consciousness of the oppressor by the oppressed, denying the possibility of conscious subjectivity and agency by the oppressed (*conscientização*). The "crisis" theory overlooks that the two consciousnesses in contestation are shaped by the world views and values of the colonizer and not necessarily by the subjective experience of consciousness formation of the colonized people (see Paulo Freire, *Pedagogy of the Oppressed*).

[55] Madan Sarup, *Identity, Culture and the Postmodern World* (Athens, GA: Univ. of Georgia Press, 1996), 182.

11

El gran avivamiento del '33

The Protestant Missionary Enterprise, Revival, Identity, and Tradition

Daisy L. Machado

INTRODUCTION

In the last few weeks of 1932 and throughout 1933 there erupted a period of revivalism in Puerto Rico in the Protestant denominational body known as the Christian Church (Disciples of Christ). Today this revival is called *el avivamiento del '33*. The Reverend Joaquín Vargas, who was present when the revival began in the city of Bayamón, described this unique event as "the cornerstone of the history of the Christian Church (Disciples) in Puerto Rico."[1]

Yet if one were to compare it to the earlier revivals that had taken place in the United States in the nineteenth century, *el avivamiento del '33* was not a large revival. It did not encompass a large geographical area or a large number of people and churches. The Puerto Rican Disciples churches in 1932 numbered only thirty-one, with fourteen ministers to serve 1,780 members.[2] Its impact, however, should not be underestimated, because it motivated the development of indigenous lay and ministerial leadership, helped to create a new sense of Christian identity, brought about a new understanding of Christian stewardship, and increased numerical church growth.[3] A growth that began in 1933 and continues to this day is evidenced in the more than ninety congregations with over twenty thousand members who today make up the Disciples in Puerto Rico. In addition, the denomination also has an Instituto Bíblico for the training of lay leaders, nine church-owned elementary schools, two high schools, a camp and conference center, a radio program heard throughout the island, as well as missionary projects in Haiti, the Dominican Republic, and Venezuela.[4] Surely the seed of renewal and growth planted in 1933 has given much fruit. But even more important than subsequent growth, what transpired in Iglesia Calle Comerío in 1933 and spread to other congregations forever changed the Puerto Rican Disciples' understanding of church and of their place in that church. With this understanding there also emerged a new identity and a strong conviction that the time had come for the end of United States missionary control over the Puerto Rican Disciples.

In an attempt to understand the factors that led to this period of revivalism and to the many changes it produced, the first statement that must be made is that this revival was a complex event possessing its own distinctive characteristics. However, before any interpretations are made, I want to say that the revival of 1933 was foremost a very deeply spiritual event. Those involved in the revival believed and stated that "God wanted to bless the church."[5] As the noted scholar on revivalism William McLoughlin argues, "In all awakenings the concept of divine immanence as opposed to divine transcendence becomes a central issue."[6] What this means is that revivalism stresses the immanence or presence of the deity. For those who were present in Iglesia Calle Comerío in 1933, it was the real presence of the Holy Spirit that fueled revival. In other words, God *was* present with those women and men who met and prayed in the small church building.

Revivals can also be understood as events that go beyond the religious experience by incorporating the daily life reality of the people who experience it. Understood in this way the 1933 revival in Puerto Rico was a shared activity that "held the promise of guidance in a socially disordered world."[7] Not only were the Puerto Rican Disciples facing economic hardships and natural disasters, but they were also dealing with a missionary leadership that did not always understand the people to whom it ministered. That is why one also finds in this revival event an "inner directedness" that had nothing to do with the missionaries themselves. R. C. Gordon-McCutchan, scholar on revivalism, says that the inner directedness of a revival event is guided by what he calls an "inner gyroscope (i.e., biblically guided conscience)."[8] This inner directedness or gyroscope was a combination of the tradition or teaching brought to them by the missionaries *and* the interpretation of that tradition based on the real-life experience of the Puerto Rican Disciples. That is why revivals can also be described as being "rooted in the past and in existing church institutions and tradition."[9] What this tells us is that the inner directedness of the 1933 revival made it an event that, while profoundly relevant to the Puerto Rican churches, was ultimately not understood by the US missionaries because it did not reflect their experience. As a result, the missionaries saw the revival as a "domestic broil in the house of faith"[10] that caused a great divide between the indigenous Puerto Rican Disciples and the missionaries who had evangelized them. However, despite US missionary opposition or criticism, what must be understood is that the revival had such significance for the Puerto Rican Disciples that it moved beyond the control of the North American missionaries. Therefore, in summary, we can say that the revival of 1933 can be understood as a spiritual event led by the Holy Spirit that ultimately produced some very concrete human results.

Indeed, it can be said that revivalism gives people the courage needed to take bold steps that "break the crust of custom" and adapt a culture to changing social conditions.[11] The most significant results of the 1933 revival in Puerto Rico were independence from US missionary control and the creation of a new Protestant identity expressed in a new liturgy and especially in a new hymnody. This newly forged identity is very significant because it not only led to the rejection of the Protestant identity created by the North American missionaries but also led to the creation of a *Puerto Rican* Protestant identity now reflected in a more endemic style of worship expressed in an autochtonous hymnody. It is important to recognize that this hymnody gave voice to the new theological understandings about the Puerto Rican faith community's relationship with God, as well as its perception of God's presence with and among that community. One of the most important and long-lasting results of the 1933 revival was that a new Puerto Rican Protestant tradition came into being.

INTERPRETING REVIVALS: A BRIEF HISTORICAL OVERVIEW

In the 1980s arguments and counter-arguments about the nature of religious revivals interested historians and sociologists of religion. In these debates some even insisted that the "Awakening construct," which holds that revivalism in the United States passed through periods of stagnation and renewal, was no longer valid. Yet William McLoughlin held that the Awakening construct possesses interpretive value because it helps church historians and others to understand the various shifts that have taken place in North American Protestantism. Nevertheless, the debate continued. Are revivals to be understood as cyclical or linear movements of socio-historical change? Are they to be interpreted as microcosmic or macrocosmic views of history and society? Should one argue, as did church historian Timothy Smith, that revivals should be understood as having an energy and life of their own, which is rooted in the existing religious traditions and institutions themselves and not in the disorder of the secular world? Or should one argue, as did Gordon-McCutchan, that revivals are cyclical phenomenon that are directly related to social conditions that are seen as threatening or disruptive, and that revivals "are useful to those in an anomic social condition"?[12]

I return to these now historical arguments about how to interpret revivals because I think that the revival that took place in Puerto Rico in 1933 combines the arguments put forth by both Smith and McLoughlin. The revival was not only rooted in the theological foundations laid by the US missionaries and gained its energy from that very tradition and theology, but it was also a lived (real) event that took place in a very specific historical time and space; as such it was also a cultural event. This means that when we examine the revival of 1933, we must see it as taking place on two levels. On one level it was a real-life event that was experienced and interpreted by a number of people, specifically the Puerto Rican Disciples and missionaries. Joaquín Vargas, who was in attendance in the church in Puerto Rico in 1933, believed the revival event was a miraculous outpouring of God's Spirit. To the missionaries it was an activity that they had never encountered before, did not fully understand, could not control, and it produced the many changes in the church that led to their eventual displacement as leaders. Yet on another level the revival of 1933 happened in a particular setting—Puerto Rico in the early 1930s, a time period shaped by the political, economic, and social realities that had preceded this decade. Understood this way the revival was also a response to the changes caused by the many factors in Puerto Rican society that produced stress, instability, and dissatisfaction. The revival also had repercussions on the religious culture being created by the US missionary enterprise in Puerto Rico. The revival served as the pivotal event in which the religious culture of the colonizing US Protestant missionary enterprise collided with an emerging Puerto Rican Protestant culture.

What were some of the conflicts and stresses faced by the Puerto Rican society during this time period? The first stress factor that can be identified within Puerto Rican society was the 1898 Spanish American War. The war served as a signal to the Roman Catholic hierarchy that its survival depended on renewal. The loyalty of many Spanish priests to Spain throughout the 1800s as Latin America and the Latin Caribbean struggled for independence created a great amount of suspicion of the Roman Catholic Church. This was true not only in Puerto Rico but also in all of Latin America. So with the end of Spanish rule after the war in

1898, the number of priests began declining, as many returned to Spain. In 1930, when the Roman Catholic Church was at its lowest level, there were only forty-five diocesan priests in Puerto Rico.[13] The Roman Catholic Church in Puerto Rico also faced a second stress: the immediate intervention of the Protestant missionary enterprise led by US mainline denominations at the close of the war. Undoubtedly the Protestant missionary enterprise led to renewal and change. And change was to be a continual part of Puerto Rico's history during the first decades of the 1900s, when under the rule of the United States, Puerto Rico was evolving, changing, being reshaped. Not only were the culture, language, and government of the United States being introduced to the island, but so was its religion. The shifts taking place were linguistic, cultural, and religious: to the English language, to a North American world view, and to Protestantism. These forced changes represented for Puerto Ricans a *conquista* that instead of being European was North American, and instead of being Roman Catholic was Protestant. And it is precisely in the midst of these political, economic, and social shifts that the *avivamiento del '33* takes place.

Life in Puerto Rico prior to 1933 was one of upheaval, change, and conquest that certainly touched the lives of every one of those that began meeting at noon for prayer during the last weeks of December 1932 and into 1933. Therefore, it is not surprising that this revival was understood by those present as a divine response to the pains and struggles of Puerto Rican Disciples. Yet for the missionaries what proved to be an unexpected byproduct of this revival was the fact that the revival became a powerful means for self-identity, for self-definition, for autonomy, and for the affirmation of hope for a community that was "experiencing bitterness and suffering."[14] What took the missionaries by surprise was that the revival gave the Puerto Rican Disciples new theological insights, which in turn legitimated their "engaging in behavior made necessary by new social conditions but uncountenanced by the directives of tradition."[15] The Puerto Rican Disciples were in a very real sense re-traditioning themselves.

This becomes especially important for a country that had moved from Spanish to United States domination despite its own struggles for independence. It is also important to point out that this difficult political reality was also being reenacted in the Puerto Rican Protestant churches themselves. All Protestant churches on the island were under the leadership of foreign missionaries. These missionaries had an advantage in that they could always appeal to their missionary boards for economic support as needed or simply choose to leave if life in Puerto Rico became economically unfeasible. This is not to say that the missionaries frequently

abandoned their work or that they did not share some of the hardships of
the Puerto Rican Disciples to whom they ministered. However, the fact
remains that the presence of North American missionaries was representative of the loss of autonomy and self-determination that Puerto Rico as
a nation experienced politically following the Spanish American War.

Therefore, if we place the revival of 1933 within the context of the
many political and historical changes and stresses Puerto Ricans had
been experiencing since 1895, when they began their push for independence from Spain, we can see that the revival did not simply occur all at
once. The revival was yet another expression of change, a response to
the instability and stresses (anomie) the members of the Disciples congregations were living. Therefore, many saw the revival of 1933 in the
Disciples churches as an outward burst of emotion and spirituality that
was in reality both gradual and continuous. On a deeper level the revival
was about change. It was about a change that had been shaped by the
forces, secular and religious, that made up the Puerto Rican reality of the
early twentieth century. In addition, this revival also had an energy of its
own, an inner directedness, as I previously stated, that allowed it to spread
from congregation to congregation, becoming a force of its own and hold-
ing great significance for the community. Because internally the revival
was also an amalgam of the tradition and theology laid down by the missionaries that was now being reinterpreted through the lens of experience,
it also became a product and expression of Puerto Rican Protestantism
that could not be contained or stopped by the missionaries. As a result,
the revival became the key experience that shaped and defined the Puerto
Rican Disciples church in 1933 as authentically Puerto Rican.

In order to better understand the model I have presented of the revival of 1933 as being both a movement that responded to social instability and stress yet also possessed an internal energy of its own, I would
like to examine some of the history of Puerto Rico. This will help the
reader to better understand the stresses or the forces that were present
before the revival and that contributed to it. This general history then
needs to be paralleled to the history of the Protestant missionary effort
in Puerto Rico in order to see how church and state were in service to
one another and how both helped create the forces that led to the period
of revivalism within the Disciples church.

EL CONQUISTADOR Y CRISTO: PART I

Columbus set foot on Borínquen[16] November 14, 1493, as he traveled to Fort Natividad in Hispaniola. The island was given the European

Christian name of San Juan Bautista de Puerto Rico. As Spain thrust its might upon the New World, the interests of the state moved hand in hand with those of the church and "missions were often used as a means to extend Spanish culture and power. . . . For their Catholic Majesties and their subjects, European culture—and especially Spanish culture— was synonymous with the Christian faith. Therefore the Hispanization and the Christianization of the American Indians were for them one and the same thing."[17] Puerto Rico quickly acquired the reputation of being both the cockpit and the shield of the Caribbean and the Greater and Lesser Antilles.[18] In 1582 a military garrison was established at El Morro, thus converting Puerto Rico into a military base.[19]

Through its years under Spanish rule Puerto Rico was attacked by British, French, and Dutch navies, making it clear that Spain was not the only country aware of the island's strategic importance. Some of these attacks were successful and brought new elements to the island. For example, the first Protestant services to be held in Puerto Rico took place in 1598, when the British took San Juan and held it for five months.[20] This, however, was a very brief and rare incident in an otherwise long history of Spanish Roman Catholic domination. Always vigilant, Spain continued to keep Puerto Rico from having any direct contact with Protestantism: "Thus, when in 1846 the Board of Commerce and Development requested from Spain that non-Catholic foreigners be allowed to settle in Puerto Rico, the government agencies in Madrid, following the recommendations of the bishop of San Juan, refused to grant the authorization requested."[21]

Despite its stronghold on the Caribbean, the nineteenth century was to see Spain's power in the Western hemisphere come to an end. The Spanish empire finally came apart in 1898, and the history of Puerto Rico would thereby be altered forever. As Spain lost her strengths, a new power, the United States, was on the rise in the Western hemisphere. By the mid-nineteenth century the United States began to flex its diplomatic muscles and to pursue a very active role in the politics of Latin America and the Latin Caribbean. For example,

> Simón Bolívar, the liberator of a continent, intended to free Puerto Rico and Cuba from the Spanish yoke. He demonstrated this intention at the Congress of Panama (1826), and on January 25, 1827, he resolved to send an expedition to Puerto Rico and Cuba. . . . But the United States declared its determined opposition to any alteration of the status quo in Puerto Rico and Cuba, a position she would maintain throughout the nineteenth century.[22]

As Spain lost its power in the Latin Caribbean the United States government saw some new and desired opportunities in the making:

> Throughout the nineteenth century U.S. interest in having Cuba and Puerto Rico fall within direct influence of the North American empire—whether by purchase or by conquest—manifests itself. . . . In 1867 Blaine . . . said: "I believe that there are three non-continental places of enough value to be taken by the United States. One is Hawaii; the others are Cuba and Puerto Rico."[23]

So despite Puerto Rico's Grito de Lares[24] on September 23, 1868, in which it declared itself a nation free from Spanish rule, and despite the many years of diplomatic negotiations with Spain to obtain its freedom from foreign domination, the United States had its own agenda.

> Luis Muñoz Rivera (1859–1916), after ten years of effort, obtained from Spain the Sagasta Pact of 1897 or "Charter of Autonomy." Much is made of this grant because on paper it was rather broad, giving Puerto Rico dominion status and theoretically the right and power to bring about effective change. But it never had a chance to prove itself. One-year later [North] American troops landed near Ponce on the southwestern coast and were warmly welcomed by the people who did not realize that a new brand of colonialism was in the offing.[25]

This new colonialism was not all that different from the old one. Despite the obvious differences of language and religion, both powers were intent on keeping Puerto Rico a colony and both used the church as an important tool in their process of colonization. The Treaty of Paris signed in 1898 gave Puerto Rico to the United States despite the initial hesitation by the Spaniards to include Puerto Rico as part of a peace treaty.

This new "people of Puerto Rico" were given United States citizenship as a result of the Jones Act, passed on March 2, 1917, "although it was opposed in Puerto Rico by the majority Unionist Party, because it was felt to be inconsistent with a demand for independence."[26] Puerto Ricans still held out for independence. They still envisioned a future as a republic of free citizens, but this was not to be. Not only had they lost their struggle for independence from Spain, but by 1930 there was a new firmly rooted flag over the capitol building in San Juan, and it was not Puerto Rico's.

An already bad situation worsened when another destructive hurricane, San Felipe, hit the island in 1928. Storming across the island, it dealt the coffee industry a deathblow. . . . As a result of [North] American colonialism coupled with natural disasters Puerto Rico by 1930 was on the edge of socioeconomic disaster. . . . Possibly some 35,000 on the island suffered from tuberculosis, some 200,000 from malaria.[27]

History had indeed repeated itself. The miserable conditions existing before 1898 under Spanish domination had not improved by 1930 under United States domination.

EL NUEVO CONQUISTADOR Y CRISTO: PART II

On October 18, 1898, two days after the Spanish government withdrew, the US military government took control of the island and, two months later, after signing the Treaty of Paris, guaranteed complete freedom of worship.[28] By 1900 the Foraker Act had not only established a civilian government under US control, but "that same year President McKinley clearly averred that the occupied island would enjoy complete separation between church and state."[29] This not only abruptly disestablished the Roman Catholic Church but also opened Puerto Rico to a new type of enterprise, the Protestant missionary enterprise.

On June 10, 1898, the Board of Foreign Missions of the Presbyterian Church in the U.S.A. took the initial step toward the formation of a comity agreement. The Presbyterians met with four other mission boards and sat down to review and establish "a frank and mutual understanding as to the responsibilities of the American Christians to the people of Cuba, Puerto Rico, and the Philippine islands, and an agreement as to the most effective distribution of the work among the several boards."[30] The denominations involved in that initial phase were the Presbyterians, American Baptists, Congregationalists, and Methodist Episcopalians. At a second meeting, in 1899, "they knelt around the map . . . upon the table and prayed that God might help us to enter Puerto Rico in such a way that there might never be any missionary hostility of any kind in that island."[31] The denominations then proceeded to divide the island into four sections, thereby hoping to eliminate any sense of competition or friction. By 1900, however, a "readjustment of the original agreement took place on the field and on the mainland to permit territorial assignments for the Disciples of Christ, the Christian and Missionary Alliance, the United Brethren in Christ, The Christian Church of the United States, and the Evangelical Lutheran Church."[32] Puerto Rico was then divided into nine sections of missionary work of which the Disciples received the north central section of the island, with Lutherans to the east, Christian and Missionary Alliance to the west, and Presbyterians to the south.

Disciples work began when at "the forty-ninth convention of the American Missionary Society . . . in October 1898, it was announced that the society was sending Rev. J. A. Erwin to Puerto Rico for exploratory work."[33] Following the convention Rev. Erwin left for Puerto Rico and upon his return filed a report that urged that missionaries be immediately sent to this new mission field. At a special meeting held on January 6, 1899, by the board of managers of the society, Mr. and Mrs. Erwin were appointed the first missionaries of the Disciples of Christ to Puerto Rico.[34] They landed in Ponce, on the southwestern end of the island, and made their way to San Juan. By December 1899 the authorities of Bayamón, a suburb of San Juan, "tendered the use of the municipal building on the condition the [missionary] society would establish and maintain an orphanage for girls in it."[35] The Erwins sent the offer to the society's office in the United States. It was accepted, and the Disciples invested eight hundred dollars for the repair of the buildings and grounds. In August 1900 the Disciples became the first Protestant denomination to run an orphanage on the island; it was under the direction of Mrs. A. M. Fullen. This orphanage became an especially useful community service especially after Puerto Rico was devastated by hurricane San Ciriaco on August 8, 1899. Over twenty-five hundred people were killed, and thousands were left homeless as a result of this natural disaster.[36] The orphanage opened with twenty-eight girls in residence.

In regard to the work of evangelizing, due to the many United States soldiers in Puerto Rico in the years immediately following the war, "Mr. Erwin conducted regular English services for them, and Mrs. Erwin opened a day-school for the children of the community."[37] These first missionaries did not speak Spanish and because of this concentrated their initial efforts on the English-speaking people, but by June 1900 they baptized their first Puerto Rican converts. The first church was organized in 1901 and met in rented quarters until 1908, when a building was erected with part of the centennial offering of the Kentucky Christian Woman's Board of Missions.[38]

During this first decade of Disciples work there were two major setbacks: "that there were not more workers and funds . . . and the frequent changes in the missionary personnel."[39] This was certainly the case from 1899 to 1906, when there were four changes in missionary personnel. Yet what the missionaries perceived as a tragedy the Puerto

Rican Disciples perceived as an opportunity. The frequent changes created the need for developing Puerto Rican leadership so that there would be continuity to the work begun by the missionaries. By 1907 the newly forming congregations provided men like Manuel Torres, the first convert to Protestantism in the town of Dajaos, and others, who, though lacking formal education, provided leadership to these new churches.

The arrival in 1906 of Vere C. Carpenter and his wife marked a change in Disciples work. Carpenter, who came from Kentucky, felt most at home in the country, and it was in rural evangelizing that he worked most arduously to expand the Disciples missions. By 1922 the Disciples had three missionary couples working all along the northeastern coast of the island, and there were 847 members, in mostly rural areas.[40] In that same year a decision was made by the missionaries, in agreement with the missionary board in the United States, to permit the two ordained Puerto Rican ministers to attend their missions meetings. They were to represent their Puerto Rican colleagues at these monthly meetings and were given voice but not vote. Correspondence from several meetings held in 1922 give evidence that, despite the missionaries' awareness of the need for a national voice in decisions about Disciples work, "secret meetings were held to discuss matters behind the Puerto Rican pastors' backs."[41] The establishment in 1919 of the Seminario Evangélico de Puerto Rico helped to create a larger and educated pool of Puerto Rican Disciples ministers, so that by the 1920s there were seven Puerto Rican Disciples seminary graduates. These new pastors began to assume leadership roles within their congregations and became spokesmen for their churches. As they increased their participation, they "made the missionary presence all the more dispensable."[42] By 1930 there were eighteen Puerto Rican pastors attending thirty-one congregations, rural and urban. The Disciples church in Puerto Rico was undergoing important changes in spite of the missionary stronghold yet change was to come sooner than many had anticipated.

The year 1932 was to be difficult yet decisive for the Puerto Rican Disciples. Hurricane San Felipe had hit the island in September 1928 and had destroyed sixteen church buildings. Some were repaired and others abandoned. Between 1929 and 1930 five new buildings were erected, paid for with a generous fifty-two thousand dollar gift from congregations in the United States.[43] But 1932 was to change everything. Responding to a global economic crisis, church giving plummeted and the $12,500 contributed annually to Puerto Rico for ministerial support was cut to $4,400 used to pay eighteen pastors a monthly income of $20.37.[44] Four pastors chose to leave their positions in the church because of the economic crisis, but the other fourteen stood firm. Rev.

Ortiz, pastor of Iglesia Calle Comerío, who had the most numerous family, was only able to provide one meal a day; at the other meals the family gathered around the table of empty dishes and prayed.[45] Morale was low, and both pastors and congregations experienced great economic hardships and hunger. In the midst of these very difficult times in the early hours of September 26, 1932, the island was hit by yet another hurricane, San Cipriano, "filling to the brim the bitter cup of suffering of laity, pastors and all the Puerto Rican community."[46] The hurricane left in its wake an outbreak of tuberculosis and malaria that affected almost every home on the island.[47]

In the midst of all this suffering at the end of December 1932 Leonardo (Lolo) Castro, a Disciples lay leader from Iglesia Calle Comerío in Bayamón, began to meet at noon for prayer in the church building. At first only two other people joined him, but as the weeks passed the numbers grew and by 1933 the group filled the church. The mood, one of confession of sin and reconciliation with God, soon spread to the other churches.[48] The revival was described as an "explosion . . . an operation of the Holy Spirit, a marvelous thing. There was great clamor, much crying, speaking in tongues and manifestations previously unknown to all who were present."[49] In a Sunday evening worship service, much to the preacher's surprise, as he called for the final prayer, the entire congregation fell to its knees and people began to pray aloud.

In February 1933 the 25th Convention of the Christian Church (Disciples of Christ) in Puerto Rico was celebrated in the town of Ciales. There the fervor and rare enthusiasm of the delegates from Iglesia Calle Comerío affected many of the other delegates, and soon this same fervor was reflected in all the events of the program of that assembly.[50] Rev. Vargas remembers:

> In that Convention there was lit the flame that would remain lit throughout the rest of that memorable year and the years to come. There was not however, speaking in tongues, or clapping, or hysterical expressions. Yes there was much joy and a contagious as well as overflowing enthusiasm. There was much singing there was also much praying.[51]

The missionaries, however, were not happy. Rev. Carpenter saw this as a total departure from Disciples tradition and immediately wrote to Dr. Morton, a Disciples professor at the Evangelical Seminary who was on sabbatical in the United States. When Morton returned to Puerto Rico in 1934 he found a totally new and invigorated Puerto Rican Disciples church. Everything had changed, especially the music and worship services. A new revival hymnody had developed, written mostly by musicians who had been infected by tuberculosis after the hurricane of 1932. These new hymns not only had a different melody and rhythm, but their message was one of hope and victory as seen from the inside of suffering. There was also a new wave of evangelistic outreach by the local churches, which now depended on local leadership.

The missionary reaction to the changes taking place was totally negative, and a letter was written, dated October 12, 1934, to the executive secretary of the Department of Overseas Ministries, Lela Taylor. Dr. Morton made the following recommendation to Taylor:

> I would suggest that you write a letter to the Puerto Rico Mission stating that because of departure from the traditional and scriptural position which Disciples have always occupied that the present mission will have to subject itself again to a superintendent of the mission . . . and that the final word with reference to doctrine and church polity will be with the superintendent. . . . I also recommend that you name Mr. Carpenter as superintendent of the mission.[52]

It is not at all surprising that the missionaries reacted adversely to the revival in Puerto Rico and particularly to public expressions of religious fervor and emotion. After all, the Christian Church (Disciples of Christ) was a denomination that had its beginnings in the westward frontier of the mid-nineteenth century United States (1832). Because its founders were European Protestants, foundational to Disciples theology were the threads of Lockean philosophy and Enlightenment concepts, especially the importance of rational thought as basic to the religious experience. Biblical interpretation was also not understood to be literal. Therefore, the missionaries were not open to the claim that there had been actual manifestations of "speaking in tongues" (glossalia) in the revival.

And so it was that Taylor's letter to the Puerto Rican pastors, dated October 29, 1934, stated exactly what Dr. Morton had recommended. By December 1934 a document was drawn up that stated the purpose, practices, and beliefs of the Disciples as they were to be practiced in the Puerto Rican churches. Pastors were asked to sign an agreement to keep with the established guidelines or to leave the Disciples church. On December 28, 1934, the local pastors met to discuss the document, and three said they would sign. In the first week of January 1935 Morton and Carpenter went to Iglesia Calle Comerío during a worship service to inform the congregation that Rev. Vicente Ortiz, who was home with pneumonia, was being relieved of his pastoral duties and that the congregation was being assigned a new pastor. The congregation was told to stop the worship service, and the missionaries proceeded to put a padlock on the church doors. Some members of the congregation immediately went to get a municipal judge, who was a member of a Baptist congregation, to try to stop the action of the missionaries. At the same time the missionaries themselves returned with police agents to enforce the vacating of the temple. As judge and missionaries faced one another, the judge used his jurisdiction, ordering that none of the Disciples churches in his municipality of Bayamón be interrupted in its worship.[53] The judge then met with all the Disciples ministers and recommended that they register church buildings and parsonages with the state to impede outside control of those properties.

Needless to say, relations between the missionaries and the pastors were unfavorably affected by this encounter. Taylor made a special trip to Puerto Rico that same year, and she brought with her Dr. Samuel Guy Inman to act as intermediary. Taylor and her department judged Dr. Inman to be "someone who understood the Hispanic temperament and who was also an effective diplomat."[54] This was probably due to the fact that Dr. Inman had been involved with Disciples missions in Texas and then in Mexico since the early 1900s. However, no immediate solution was obtained, even though both Puerto Ricans and missionaries attempted to move toward common ground. As tempers cooled and the situation was reevaluated the following steps were mutually agreed upon: the written document that the Puerto Rican pastors saw as a "straitjacket" to their ministry was to be discarded; no pastors were to be removed from the congregations they were serving; the position of superintendent of missions was to be eliminated; and a board of eleven (four missionaries, six local pastors, one local layperson) was to oversee the administrative work of the churches.[55]

There was, however, no acknowledgment by the missionaries or by the Department of Overseas Ministries of the revival itself or of what the local pastors and their churches considered to be the positive effects that the revival had had on the Disciples churches. This meeting preceded a period of "peaceful coexistence between 1935 and 1941 in which missionaries used greater diplomacy and local leaders were just as gracious without giving up their right to an indigenous Disciples church."[56] As proof of how far the Puerto Rican Disciples had moved toward self-determination, in 1941 Mae Yoho Ward was named to fill the vacant position of executive secretary to Latin America, and under her leadership came changes in the missionary personnel in Puerto Rico. Rev. Carpenter was to retire in 1944 after thirty-eight years of service, and Dr. Morton was to take a seven-month leave. Ward consulted the pastors in

Puerto Rico in April 1943 about replacing both men. In that consultation Rev. Marcelino Pollock stood up and said, "If you are sending to Puerto Rico missionaries who will act as overseers of the Puerto Rican pastors, then you need send no one. If, however, the new missionaries come as our colleagues and equals, send us as many as you would like."[57]

This very short statement is evidence of how much had changed on two important issues. One was the dynamics and relations of power between the missionaries and the Puerto Ricans. The other was how Puerto Ricans now understood the dynamics of leadership within the Disciples churches. The understanding of missions and missionaries had also undergone transformation. The indigenous leaders now claimed their right to be treated as colleagues and as equals in the missionary enterprise. In the revival of 1933 the forces of colonialism, economic upheaval, natural disaster, and higher education came together to change the Puerto Rican Disciples church as a whole. It was a religious phenomenon understood as divine intervention sent by God to pronounce renewal for a people whose hope was ebbing away as they encountered a difficult social, economic, and political reality. The revival of 1933 also had an inner force of its own, an inner directedness, that gave the revival relevance to the community despite its rejection by the North American missionaries. This internal cohesion and energy made the revival of 1933 a historical event that not only outlived the decade, but is also remembered today as "the year when the disciples in Puerto Rico began to grow up."[58]

THEOLOGICAL IMPLICATIONS: TRADITION AND IDENTITY

To revisit *el avivamiento del '33* is much more than an intellectual exercise that seeks to examine the phenomenon of revivals within a Latino context. It is really about trying to understand and to explain the genesis of a Latino Protestant tradition that came into being and stood in defiance of the missionary legacy. The product or result of the revival of 1933 went above and beyond what the mainline Protestant missionaries gave to their Puerto Rican converts. This is especially important because the revival not only gave Puerto Rican Disciples a new Protestant evangelical[59] identity but also a new tradition. What I am saying is that the new Protestant evangelical tradition born from the revival experience provided the Puerto Ricans with a new understanding of what is normative (guidelines of behavior) as well as a new interpretation of the authority of that tradition. This, of course, represented two important shifts. One was a theological shift as the Puerto Ricans began to express a new worship style shaped by new theological insights. The second was a shift in the relations of power between the missionaries and the Puerto Rican Christians. For scholars of revivals, the changes that took place in the theology of the community as well as in their relations with the missionaries was to be expected. As McLoughlin has argued, "Awakenings begin in periods of cultural distortion and grave personal stress, when we lose faith in the legitimacy of our norms, and the viability or our institutions, and the authority of our leaders in church and state."[60] The social conditions that McLoughlin identifies are not difficult to find in the Puerto Rico of 1933, as I have already shown. For example, there was the political crisis over Puerto Rico's future as a colony. This uncertainty and dissatisfaction came from the reality that the US military force in 1898 had effectively wiped out any autonomy that Puerto Rico had achieved. Proof of this loss is found in the fact that it would not be until 1946 that Puerto Ricans would see one of their own named as governor, and not until November 2, 1948, that Puerto Ricans would elect their first governor. Added to this was also the realities of poverty and hunger. "Up to 1898 the economy of the island was dependent on decentralized agriculture. With the transfer of possession from Spain to the United States, Puerto Rico became economically dependent on its new colonizer."[61] Surely the devastation left by the hurricanes of 1928 and 1932 could only have exacerbated the reality of despair and unrest expressed by Rev. Joaquín Vargas when I interviewed him.

But I want to add another level to this analysis and examine the relationship between the North American Disciples missionaries and the Puerto Rican converts. What were some of the issues in these relations that were also causing stresses and dissatisfaction? I have already mentioned that the missionaries had been reluctant to accept the Puerto Rican pastors as equal partners in the church work being done. This, of course, was a point of contention between the groups, but we cannot fully address this issue without examining how the missionaries saw the Puerto Ricans and how they dealt with the preexisting religious identity of the Puerto Ricans. What I call the *missionary imaginary* must be carefully examined, because in it we will find that the missionaries were using definitions of "other" to create their relations of power. For Disciples missionaries in Puerto Rico this same imaginary greatly influenced how the missionaries related to the indigenous population and the kind of leadership model they developed.

In 1949 C. Manly Morton, who served as a Disciples missionary in Puerto Rico for twenty-five years (1923–49), wrote *Kingdom Building in Puerto Rico*, in which he told of Disciples work on the island. Morton admits that the Disciples missionary enterprise to Puerto Rico was launched without a clear understanding of the many realities of the task ahead, including an understanding of who were the people and what was expected of the missionary. However, despite this lack a missionary agenda was set. Morton writes:

> Few had any understanding of the significance of what their country was doing, or of the magnitude of the task. To most people it was a simple matter to be accomplished within a few decades: the elimination of Spanish and the establishment of English as the language of the people; the reorganization of the social and political life; the transferring of loyalties from Spain, oppressor, to the United States, savior and benevolent uncle. Reports emanating from occupation authorities and from visitors emphasized the backwardness of the people of the island, the hunger and filth and disease. . . . Confronted by this confusion, the first missionaries began their work.[62]

Notice how the social/political agenda for Puerto Rico—to Americanize it, to change the language spoken by the people, to bring Puerto Rico into the orbit of US influence and control—was also described as part of the missionary agenda. Also notice the identity given to the United States as "savior and benevolent uncle." What is significant here is that the missionary imaginary was not only used to define the "other" of the mission field, but was also used to define the missionary and the work he or she was doing. When examining this missionary imaginary I agree with Native American scholar George Tinker, who says that to chastise the missionaries for their response to the people of color they evangelized serves little purpose. I also agree when he argues that the "missionaries were people of their own times and especially of their own cultural heritage."[63] Nevertheless, it is precisely because the missionaries were directly shaped and influenced by their time and culture that one must be critical of the agendas they incorporated into the missionary enterprise.

> If we concede good intentions to the missionaries in general, we also must be careful to recognize them as people of their own times. . . . That they confused their spiritual proclamation of the gospel of Jesus Christ with the imposition of new and strange cultural models for daily life is today inexcusable. But a century and more ago, the distinction between gospel and Euroamerican culture was far less clear.[64]

In this process of making the Puerto Ricans into Protestants one finds evident an anti–Roman Catholic bias that was transmitted to the new converts (which, of course, does not imply that the Roman Catholic Church was also not anti-Protestant). The missionary imaginary placed the two groups, Roman Catholics and Protestants, in an oppositional relationship. The contrasts or dichotomies being formulated were democracy versus authoritarianism, progress versus backwardness, neglect versus pastoral care, morality versus immorality. Morton writes:

> Spanish control meant Roman Catholic control, and both meant spiritual and material exploitation. Since the priests received their living directly from the government, it mattered little to them whether anyone came to mass. Although 82 per cent of the population was rural, the priests built no rural churches, nor did any of them relocate in remote communities. The people of the mountains received little or no religious instruction or inspiration. . . . The dead were buried without a religious service, and couples mated without the sanction of church or state. Witchcraft prevailed. . . . There can be no doubt as to the importance of the moral and spiritual emancipation which the Protestant church has brought Puerto Rico since the change in sovereignty. Protestantism has built churches, distributed Bibles, published literature, fostered education. It has brought to the Puerto Ricans a personal, approachable God, through communion with whom the most humble individual can receive inspiration and strength and a realization of his own divinity. Protestantism, with its deep interest in the individual, has championed the rights of the weak against the strong, has insisted upon a vital connection between moral living and spiritual growth, has endeavored to show that democracy is possible in all walks of life by practicing it in the church.[65]

In the missionary imaginary Protestantism would also give the Puerto Ricans a new model for behavior. The missionaries were very conscious of how Puerto Ricans responded to life on a daily basis. For example, when describing a death that occurred in the Disciples orphanage in the city of Bayamón, Morton shares this report from the orphanage's superintendent, Mrs. A. M. Fullen:

> Rosario Sorrel, a four-year-old child in our orphanage, died the twenty-third of August [1900]. . . . I went to San Juan to get lumber for a coffin. No coffins are kept in stock here. Almost all of the poor are buried without them. . . . It is the custom here for the

people to scream and cry when the angel of death has laid his hands on any loved ones, but I had talked to the girls as best I could and had taught them why they should not do this.[66]

Observations are even made about the Puerto Rican diet. Morton's wife, who was a nurse and dietician, was assigned the task of creating a "healthy, balanced diet" for the seminary students. Morton observed: "As a general rule the Puerto Rican does not eat green vegetables. To him such foods as lettuce and carrots are *yerba* (grass), and unfit for human beings. He much prefers rice and beans and bread and coffee."[67] While this may seem a trite observation, what is really at play here is the missionary imaginary judging a culture and its people. The conclusion reached is that the Puerto Rican population being imagined (interpreted) is "less than." Therefore, the missionary imaginary assumed the responsibility for creating a new identity, a new culture for the convert, as well as a new religious tradition. The irony is that this new religious culture never totally accepted the Puerto Rican convert, and as a result the tradition given to the new convert never really became meaningful and satisfying. Both the Protestant culture of the missionary and the Protestant tradition given by the missionary remain foreign to the Puerto Rican convert, and an inequity between the missionary and the convert is created. In addition, because the Puerto Rican is never really accepted as equal, the Protestant missionary enterprise ultimately converted the people into a religious system that was foreign to them and continued to view them as inferior, uncivilized, in need of not only spiritual redemption but also of cultural redemption.

Missiologist Carlos Cardoza-Orlandi has identified five implications of the relationship between "mission and civilization." Of these five I think that three implications can be applied to the missionary enterprise in Puerto Rico:

1. *The demand upon new converts to exhibit discontinuity with their culture.* It is expected that new converts, upon accepting the Christian faith, will break with lifestyles, cultural and religious practices, and standards of conduct of the society in which they live.

2. *The new "Protestant" culture replaces the culture of the converts.* Through a process of "civilization," the missionaries teach new converts the standards of conduct of the new Christian faith.

3. *The new "Protestant" culture is the culture of Western Christendom.* It was very common for the missionaries who trained the new converts to assume that Protestant culture is that which emerges from

the Bible. However, today we know that the "Protestant" culture we have learned corresponds with the values of Western Christendom.[68]

I believe that what Cardoza-Orlandi is describing is the process of "de-traditioning," which takes place when the convert moves into Protestantism. The Puerto Rican Disciples adopted the liturgy of the missionary; sang hymns written by Europeans or Euro-Americans that had been translated into Spanish; began receiving biblical instruction that responded to the values of Western Christendom held by the missionaries; began to work in church structures imported by the missionaries; and Puerto Rican seminary students even were introduced to a new diet, considered healthier than what was customarily eaten. The question now is, how successful were the missionaries?

I have already mentioned the tension between the Puerto Rican pastors and the missionaries as experienced and described by Rev. Joaquín Vargas. Morton admits that "there was a tendency for the missionaries to feel sometimes that the nationals were not altogether frank with them, and for the nationals to feel that the missionaries thought themselves superior."[69] Things were not going as smoothly as anticipated and the missionaries were becoming aware of the tensions and dissatisfaction that were building. It would seem that internally, that is within the denomination itself, the stage was being set for the revival the Puerto Rican Protestant church needed. As scholars of revivals will argue, "Social turmoil turned the [Puerto Rican Disciples] from trust in external authority to an evangelical pietism centered on instantaneous rebirth and inner guidance by the Holy Spirit."[70] What this means is that the revival experience was totally theirs; foreigners did not give it to them. It did not happen in a language that was not theirs, using symbols or rituals they did not create or understand. The revival made it possible for Puerto Rican Disciples to become the subjects of their own religious rebirth. The Puerto Rican Disciples were now the creators of their own religious tradition and would now determine how that tradition would be expressed.

As I have already said, missionary records shed little light on what the missionaries personally thought about the revival. What we have is the official denominational response, which was negative but remained understated. Morton, who was in Puerto Rico during this period of revival, makes only very brief and veiled comments in his book. For example, he writes, "Before anyone realized what was happening, the difficulties ceased to be entirely physical and became emotional."[71] We can infer from his previous paragraphs that he is talking about the devastating effects of the worldwide depression on Puerto Rico and the Puerto Rican Disciples churches. He is describing great hardships and poverty among the congregations and their pastors. Since the depression took place in 1932, we can only guess what "physical difficulties" Morton is alluding to in his book—hunger, disease, malnourishment. However, what is significant for Morton is that these had now become "emotional." It is not hard to imagine that the Disciples missionaries from North America, who came with a Eurocentric world view, a denominational tradition of rational thought, and a strong focus on education would interpret the revival as "emotional" and interpret these "emotions" in a negative light. However, for scholars of revival movements, the fact that the external hardships would lead to an internalized emotional response is to be expected. "This is the irony of evangelical history: 'Charismatic religious forms emerging to meet psychological needs born of social dislocation have become, in a few short steps, themselves agencies for vastly accelerating the pace of social change.'"[72]

The revival of 1933 accelerated the changes that were beginning to take place in the Disciples missionary enterprise, including the emancipation of the Puerto Rican Disciples leadership from missionary control. What were some of the results of the revival for the Puerto Rican Protestant church? I think that among the most significant results of the revival were the changes in the theology, liturgy, and hymnody of the Puerto Rican Protestant church. But before I examine these I want to look briefly at the gender issue, because I think that a broader impact of the revival had to do with the participation of Puerto Rican women in ministry. While church historians and sociologists have mostly ignored this area, there is some evidence that the role of women was empowered by the revival experience. The most prominent woman to emerge from the revival was Leoncia Rosado Rousseau (1911–), who today is affectionately known as Mama Leo, a respected Pentecostal preacher in the northeastern United States. The Rev. Rosado came to New York City in 1935 with her husband-pastor, and together they founded the Concilio de Iglesias Cristianas de Damasco (Council of Damascus Christian Churches). After her husband was drafted in World War II, the church called on her to be its minister, making her perhaps the first Latina Pentecostal pastor in New York City.[73] To her credit Rosado not only broke out of her prescribed cultural role as a woman and Latina, which is quite remarkable given the fact she began her ministry in the 1940s, but she did the same as a pastor. Unlike other ministers of her time, Mama Leo aimed her ministry at Puerto Rican youth who were gang members and/ or drug addicts. What is significant about the Rosados' ministry is that she was able to combine the charismatic theological discourse about the Holy Spirit with a commitment to social justice.

There is still much investigation and analysis to be done in the area of revivalism and gender empowerment within the Latina/o context; however, the power of the experience of the immanence of the Divine during a revival cannot be discounted. Mama Leo's strong conviction that God had called her and that she had experienced a *personal* manifestation of the Holy Spirit, which she experienced for the first time during the revival of 1933, empowered and emboldened her to begin an evangelistic ministry of preaching and even to leave Puerto Rico for New York City. I believe that this same conviction, the revival experience of the immanence of the Divine, also made it possible for the Puerto Rican men to stand up to the missionaries. While for the men this experience was about how to claim power from the missionaries, for women like Mama Leo it was about claiming worth as a woman who was called by God despite the objections or disbelief of the men in her community, whether in Puerto Rican or New York City. I also think that this new theological understanding about the presence of the Divine and how the Christian experiences that presence became important components of the new theological production that resulted from the revival. God was no longer manifested through the experience of the missionary church. The revival allowed for a direct, personal, and immediate manifestation of God's presence that did not require mediation. The Puerto Rican Protestants were now involved in a powerful and deeply personal experience of and with God that freed them to move ahead on their own. The experience of the divine presence created a sense of renewal or rebirth, the coming of something new.

This new theological insight was expressed in the creation of a new worship style for the Puerto Rican Protestant church. This worship style, incorporating indigenous instruments and a new hymnody, remains one of the long-lasting results of the revival. In many ways it can be said that the hymnody is the voice of the revival. The hymns written by Puerto Rican Protestants are not only about praise or an exaltation of God and the Holy Spirit, but many of the hymns that come from the revival event are about suffering and about pain as experienced by Christ, who is now identified with the community in a very personal way. Given the many stresses and hardships the Puerto Rican community was living with and also given the fact that many of the composers had survived tuberculosis or malaria, it is to be expected that they wrote about what they knew best. For example, Ramón (Moncho) Díaz, whose lungs were destroyed by tuberculosis, "always carried in his pockets paper, ink bottles and a pen, archaic even in those days, in case any inspiration got to him."[74]

The hymns reflected the suffering they had endured and survived. In a very concrete way their hymns are perfect examples of contextual theology. What images or symbols appear in the hymns? One of the most prominent is the cross with the suffering Christ. Puerto Rican composers translated the meaning of the cross so that Christ not only suffered for them in the act of redemption, but Christ also shares in their human sufferings. This type of imagery is found in one of the better-known hymns of the revival, written by Ramón (Moncho) Díaz, who is known to have written at least six hymns. The hymn is titled "Hizo blanco la cruel amargura" (he made as his target cruel suffering):

Hizo blanco la cruel amargura en la carne del buen Salvador oportó humillación y tortura, vil agravios, tristeza y dolor. Cruenta lanza hiere su costado, sed intense le obliga a expirar, al sepulcro después fue llevado para luego El resucitar.

He made as his target cruel suffering in the flesh of the Good Savior who withstood humiliation and torture, vile sufferings, sadness, and pain. The cruel sword wounds his side, intense thirst forces him to die, to the tomb he was then taken so later he could rise.

Coro:
¡Alabanzas, gloria a Dios!
Por los siglos demos Gloria
Al Señor que conquistó la más gloriosa Victoria.[75]

Chorus:
Praises to God!
Through the centuries let us say glory
To the Lord who conquered the greatest victory.

In his analysis of the hymns of the revival, missiologist Cardoza-Orlandi[76] argues that the Roman Catholic roots of the composers is made evident when one begins to see how the hymns replace the Roman Catholic crucifix so that Christ is ritualized in a new way. The importance of the crucifix is highlighted in the hymns, but it is now also connected to the eschatological hopes of the Protestant Puerto Rican community. So, while there is an acknowledgment of human suffering, symbolized by the cross, once that suffering is connected to the resurrection the hope of the community is made clear: Christ's Second Coming will end all suffering, all pain, all despair. Even though the converts have left Roman Catholicism to embrace Protestantism, their new religious location does not mean a total discontinuity from their Roman Catholic roots. However, because they were no longer concerned about the reaction of the missionaries, the composers were free to speak with their own theological voice, a voice that had in some ways been shaped by Roman Catholicism.

The hymn "A la final trompeta" (at the final trumpet), whose author is unknown, tells about the moment of eschatological encounter:

A la final trompeta todo el pueblo de Dios se llenará de gozo cuando venga el Señor. Con vestiduras blancas estaremos allá allí no habrá más lágrimas, allí no habrá dolor.	At the final trumpet all the people of God will be filled with joy when the Lord comes. Dressed in white we will all be there. There will be no more tears. There will be no pain.
Coro:	*Chrous:*
¡Gloria sea al Señor que aparece en las nubes en las nubes viene con poder, su corona ya brilla en el alba y los ángeles vienen con El![77]	Glory be to God who appears in the clouds In the clouds he will come with power, his crown shines in the dawn And the angels will come with him.

Another important element in the hymnody of the revival is that this very Protestant experience created a space that was not otherwise available for the creation of indigenous religious music. The writing of these hymns could not have happened in the Roman Catholic Church of Puerto Rico in the 1930s. It is also important to note that there were at least two women who contributed to the production of this native hymnody. Ramona Alamo is credited with six hymns, her best-known titled "A empezar de Nuevo" (to begin anew). María Luisa Rivera wrote the hymn "El poder de Dios levantó" (the power of God lifted up). The Protestant revival experience provided an outlet for these local musicians, and the music poured forth, going beyond the Disciples congregations to influence the other Protestant denominations on the island. As a result, one can accurately say that this new hymnody belonged to all the Protestant Puerto Ricans. At the same time, we must also acknowledge that as these hymns spread into other Protestant denominations and then into Latin America, they served to reinforce the tradition created in the revival. This means that the theological content produced by the revival event, now the new Protestant tradition, was moving across oceans and borders. This was certainly the case with the hymns written by Rafael Cuna, who was born in 1907 in Corozal, Puerto Rico. He became a Protestant around the time of hurricane San Felipe in 1928 and was baptized by a Disciples missionary, Mr. Granger, in 1929. He wrote a series of hymns that crossed all denominational lines and were sung throughout Latin

America. One of his more popular and widely known hymns is "El que habita al abrigo de Dios," which is based on the words of Psalm 91 ("He who dwells in the shelter of the Most High"). In 1942 Cuna compiled all his compositions in the hymnal *Cuna de Flores*.

The eschatological hope expressed in the hymns of the revival was also expressed in a call to renewal, rebirth, and conversion. And this call was not just to the Protestant community but to the entire nation. The shift to a national call to conversion represents another of the elements produced in the revival—evangelistic zeal. It was no longer the missionaries who were called to evangelize and preach. The transfer of authority in the church in Puerto Rico from the missionaries to the local leaders meant that it was now up to them to continue the evangelistic mission. And the Puerto Rican pastors and lay leaders assumed their evangelistic responsibility with joy and with new music to give them hope, to remind them of the task ahead, and to fill their hearts with enthusiasm. After all, had not God's Spirit been poured upon them in the miraculous revival of 1933?

Ha llegado a la Isla del Cordero	There has come to Island of the Lamb
Un momento de grande confusión,	A moment of great confusion,
Cumplimiento de muchas profecías,	The completion of many prophecies,
De profetas que el Señor iluminó.	From the prophets that the Lord illuminated.
Y tenemos que estar bien preparados;	And we have to be well prepared;
No durmamos y velemos con valor,	Let us not sleep, let us bravely watch,
Que el Señor no tarda su promesa;	Because the Lord does not delay his promise;
Lo veremos con su Gloria y gran Poder.	We will see him in his glory and power.
Coro:	*Chorus:*
Puerto Rico, nuestra patria redimida	Puerto Rico, our redeemed nation
Es el lema de toda alma fiel.	Is the motto of all faithful souls
Levantemos de Cristo la bandera,	Let us raise Christ's flag,
Y Borínquen transformada ha de ser.[78]	And Borínquen will be transformed.

Notes

[1] Joaquín Vargas, *Los Discípulos de Cristo en Puerto Rico—1899–1987* (San José: Depto. Ecuménico de Investigaciones, 1988), 73. All translations are my own.

[2] Ibid., 70.

[3] Phone interview with Joaquín Vargas, Puerto Nuevo, Puerto Rico, March 1, 1991.

[4] Vargas, *Los Discípulos de Cristo en Puerto Rico—1899–1987,* 19.

[5] Ibid., 73.

[6] William McLoughlin, quoted in R. C. Gordon-McCutchan, "Great Awakenings?" *Sociological Analysis* 44 (1983): 90.

[7] Ibid., 92.

[8] Ibid., 90.

[9] Ibid., 85.

[10] William G. McLoughlin, Jr., *Modern Revivalism* (New York: The Ronald Press Co., 1959), 5.

[11] Gordon-McCutchan, "Great Awakening," 92.

[12] Ibid., 90.

[13] Justo González, *The Development of Christianity in the Latin Caribbean* (Grand Rapids, MI: Eerdmans, 1969), 100.

[14] Vargas, *Los Discípulos de Cristo en Puerto Rico—1899–1987,* 71.

[15] Gordon-McCutchan, "Great Awakenings?" 92.

[16] Original Taíno Indian name for what is today known as Puerto Rico.

[17] González, *The Development of Christianity in the Latin Caribbean,* 17, 18.

[18] Clifford A. Hauberg, *Puerto Rico and the Puerto Ricans* (New York: Hippocrene Books, 1974), 15.

[19] Manuel Maldonado-Denis, *Puerto Rico: A Socio-Historic Interpretation* (New York: Vintage Books, 1972), 18.

[20] González, *The Development of Christianity in the Latin Caribbean,* 101.

[21] Ibid., 101.

[22] Maldonado-Denis, *Puerto Rico,* 37–38.

[23] Ibid., 55.

[24] "The Cry of Lares," known as the cry for independence and the declaration of the Republic of Puerto Rico.

[25] Hauberg, *Puerto Rico and the Puerto Ricans,* 25.

[26] Ibid., 42.

[27] Ibid., 48.

[28] Donald T. Moore, *Puerto Rico para Cristo: A History of the Progress of the Evangelical Missions on the Island of Puerto Rico,* Sondeos 43 (Cuernavaca: Centro Intercultural de Docomentación, 1969), section 15.

[29] Ibid.

[30] Ibid., p. 2, section 1.

[31] Ibid., section 3.

[32] Ibid., section 3.4.

[33] C. Manly Morton, *Kingdom Building in Puerto Rico* (Indianapolis: The United Christian Missionary Society, 1949), 13.

[34] Ibid., 14.

[35] *Survey of Service,* International Convention of Disciples of Christ (St. Louis: Christian Board of Publication, 1928), 471.

[36] Vargas, *Los Discípulos de Cristo en Puerto Rico—1899–1987*, 32.

[37] Morton, *Kingdom Building in Puerto Rico*, 14.

[38] *Survey of Service*, 472.

[39] Morton, *Kingdom Building in Puerto Rico*, 15.

[40] Vargas, *Los Discípulos de Cristo en Puerto Rico—1899–1987*, 61.

[41] Ibid., 65 n 27.

[42] Ibid., 67.

[43] Ibid., 70.

[44] Ibid.

[45] Vargas, interview.

[46] Vargas, *Los Discípulos de Cristo en Puerto Rico—1899–1987*, 71.

[47] Vargas, interview.

[48] Ibid.

[49] Vargas, *Los Discípulos de Cristo en Puerto Rico—1899–1987*, 75.

[50] Vargas, interview.

[51] Ibid.

[52] Vargas, *Los Discípulos de Cristo en Puerto Rico—1899–1987*, 194.

[53] Vargas, interview.

[54] Ibid.

[55] Vargas, *Los Discípulos de Cristo en Puerto Rico—1899–1987*, 96, 97.

[56] Ibid., 97.

[57] Ibid., 98.

[58] Vargas, interview.

[59] It is very important to clarify that the term *evangelical* is used here as it is used and interpreted in the Latino community, *evangélico*. This changes the definition of the term from how it is commonly used and defined in the United States by Euro-American scholars and church leaders. An *evangélico* in the Latino experience is a person who is Protestant and who recognizes the charisma of the Holy Spirit as central to the Christian experience. It is not about fundamentalism or a literal reading of the Bible, and it is not necessarily related to more conservative political views. It is a tradition of Latino Protestantism that may be mainline, whether Disciples, American Baptist, Presbyterian, or Methodist, yet expresses itself in a charismatic style of worship and the open acknowledgment of the immanence of God (through the Holy Spirit) in the life of the individual Christian and of the church community.

[60] William McLoughlin, as quoted in Gordon-McCutchan, "Great Awakenings?" 89.

[61] Domingo Zapata, "The Puerto Rican Experience in the United States: A Pastoral Perspective," *Dialogue Rejoined: Theology and Ministry in the United States Hispanic Reality*, ed. Ana María Pineda and Robert Schreiter (Collegeville, MN: Liturgical Press, 1995), 47.

[62] Morton, *Kingdom Building in Puerto Rico*, 41, 42.

[63] George E. Tinker, *Missionary Conquest: The Gospel and Native American Cultural Genocide* (Minneapolis: Fortress Press, 1993), 8.

[64] Ibid., 9.

[65] Morton, *Kingdom Building in Puerto Rico*, 10, 11, 108.

[66] Ibid., 22, 23.

[67] Ibid., 91.

[68] Carlos E. Cardoza-Orlandi, *Mission, An Essential Guide* (Nashville, TN: Abingdon Press, 2002), 39.

[69] Morton, *Kingdom Building in Puerto Rico*, 57.

[70] Gordon-McCutchan, "Great Awakenings?" 91.

[71] Morton, *Kingdom Building in Puerto Rico*, 66.

[72] Gordon-McCutchan, "Great Awakenings?" 92.

[73] María E. González y Pérez, "Latinas in the Barrio," *New York Glory: Religions in the City*, ed. Tony Carnes and Anna Karpathakis (New York: New York Univ. Press, 2001), 291.

[74] Julio Vargas-Vidal, "Puerto Rico's Native Hymnody," published online. My thanks to Julito, who has so graciously shared his writings on the *avivamiento*.

[75] "Hymn #7," in *Himnos del Avivamiento,* ed. Luis Del Pilar, which was presented at the fiftieth-anniversary celebration of the 1933 *avivamiento*, Christian Church (Disciples of Christ), Puerto Rico, July 1983. I am grateful to Rev. Del Pilar for his willingness to make this hymnal available to me. The translation of the hymn is mine.

[76] I thank Carlos Cardoza-Orlandi for sharing with me the research he has done on the Puerto Rican revival hymns. Our conversations have been very rich.

[77] "Hymn #18," in Del Pilar, *Himnos del Avivamiento*. The translation of the hymn is mine.

[78] Lucas Torres, "El Avivamiento: Toma de conciencia en cuanto a nuestra identidad puertorriqueña expresada en la adoración y música," presentation at 100th Assembly, Christian Church (Disciples of Christ) in Puerto Rico, February 15, 1999. The translation of the hymn is mine. Note that "Isla del Cordero (island of the lamb) refers to Puerto Rico, which was named by Spain San Juan Bautista de Puerto Rico. Because the island bears the name of John the Baptist, it has a lamb on its seal.

12

La Quinceañera

Traditioning and the Social Construction of the Mexican American Female

Theresa L. Torres, OSB

High heels and lipstick. A beautiful ball gown. The dreamy rhythm of a waltz. A bejeweled crown sparkles in the spotlight as a proud father whirls his fifteen-year-old daughter out of childhood and into adolescence. Her family and friends applaud; her mother dabs a handkerchief to her eye. Life that night is a fairy tale, with ladies and chamberlains in attendance. She is a real-life princess—*la quinceañera*.[1]

The *Quinceañera* is a common practice for many Mexican and Mexican American families and is often compared to a debutante ball. The celebration, however, is more than a "coming out to society" practice because it includes a religious ceremony and is one example of an activity in which Mexican Americans maintain their cultural identity. Ordinarily, the celebration takes place during a Eucharist and is followed by a fiesta that includes a reception and dance.

While *Quinceañera* is popular among Mexicans and Mexican Americans, it is also celebrated in various Latin American countries: Brazil, Cuba, the Dominican Republic, El Salvador, Guatemala, Peru, and Puerto Rico, to name a few. In the United States the celebration is quickly becoming a part of Latino/a popular culture and is targeted by United States retail business, which is evident in the more than 100,000 *Quinceañera* websites that appear on the Internet.[2] Although some of the websites are educational, religious, or personal examples of a particular

277

young woman's celebration, the majority are part of the business of marketing religious items, clothing, how-to books, fiesta products, receptions, and even cruises.[3] A recent development in the evolution of this celebration is the observance of the *Quinceañera* within various Christian churches, Baptists, Lutherans, and Anglicans, among others, which is an example of Latino/a religious and popular culture influencing denominational religious practices.[4]

This chapter is one example of Latino/a traditioning, the *Quinceañera*.[5] The celebration of the *Quinceañera*, which comes from popular Catholicism and popular culture, is a clear example of the fluid, evolving, and ambiguous nature of the traditioning process. The *Quinceañera*, while it is placed in a familial and communal context, is about the expression of religious and cultural meanings and the fostering of individual and gender identity for the young woman. As an example of popular Catholicism, the *Quinceañera* is one of the sources of Latino/a theology and is also part of young adolescent Latino/a experience. The ongoing evolution of the religious celebration of the *Quinceañera*, while promoted by "official and/or religious professionals" along certain lines, remains ambiguous. Each celebration has its own interpreters. The many levels of meaning present are defined by the participants and their expression and celebration of the event. Each of the participants has a particular role and is important to the overall determination of the meanings expressed and claimed.

I see myself as both an insider and an outsider to understanding the experience of the *Quinceañera*. Because I did not grow up in a Mexican American community, I did not attend a *Quinceañera* until the 1990s, when I was working in a metropolitan Roman Catholic parish in Kansas City, Missouri. As a Mexican American and because of my work in the parish, I had an insider position. But I was considered an outsider to the community because I was not originally from Kansas City and because I was an "official" member of the parish staff.

During the four years that I was a pastoral associate, I prepared the young women, their families, and their friends for the celebration of the *Quinceañera*. While I did not officially preside at the ceremony, because most of them were in the context of the Eucharist, I did help the families plan the liturgy and assisted the priest during the service. I also assisted the young women and the participants through a formal or informal religious education on the celebration and practiced with them before the service.

I did not believe that it was my role to interpret the meaning of the celebration, nor did I try to determine what the "essential elements" of the celebration were. I believe it is important for the families and participants to assist as much as possible in the preparation of the celebration and to be the ones to determine the meaning and elements of the popular religious celebration.[6] Most of the families had clear ideas about the essential elements of the *Quinceañera* service, namely, the content of traditioning, and why they wanted the celebration.

Many of the young women expressed their reasons for wanting to celebrate the event: to meet family expectations, particularly those of their grandparents and parents; and to receive support from family and friends who wanted to participate in the fiesta and to participate in the religious nature of the service. They were less clear about the religious meaning of the event, so we would take time to reflect and to prepare for the ceremony through a retreat, meetings, and participation in our religious education/youth ministry program at the parish. As the young woman and her friends became more comfortable with the process, they began to share their expectations and hopes for the *Quinceañera*.

This chapter is divided into several sections. The first section is an analysis of what is known regarding the origins of the *Quinceañera*. The second section is an analysis of the religious, gender, communal, and cultural meanings present in the religious texts of the ritual of the *Quinceañera*. The third section is an analysis of the popular cultural expressions that are part of the fiesta and fostering of gender and individual identity. The final section is a discussion of the possible innovations in the ongoing process of traditioning the *Quinceañera*.

LOCATING "HISTORY" WITHIN A POPULAR TRADITION

The search for the origins of the *Quinceañera* is an elusive quest. While numerous claims are made about the origins of the ritual, these explanations are rooted in oral history, which makes it difficult to locate the bases of their claims. In 1980, as an attempt to respond to the pastoral need for a ritual formula and to answer questions on the history of the ritual, the Mexican American Cultural Center produced one of the first books on the topic in the United States. In *Religious Celebration for the Quinceañera*, Sr. Angela Erevia gives these explanations of possible origins of the celebration:

The custom probably dates back to a custom of the Mayas and the Toltecas. It was considered that the *muchacho* [young man] was not a person until he reached the age of 15. . . . Now, he legally belonged to the community. The young lady was also presented to the community because she was looked upon as a vital force of the tribe. Because of her power of motherhood, she gave warriors to the community. For the young lady, the ceremony included the commitment and responsibility she had to the community. The community in turn accepted her as a committed and responsible member.[7]

This custom dates back to the Jewish custom of presenting the young lady in the temple. The ceremony symbolizes the responsibility of the young lady at this time of her life to the human group of which she is a member. The way this custom is popularly understood today is the presentation of the young lady to society. In order to bring out the religious and spiritual dimensions, Catholics celebrate this custom with special emphasis on the awareness and sensitivity of the young lady in dealing with the values, concerns, and challenges of the Christian community.[8]

While she notes indigenous Mayan and Toltec origins and connections with the Jewish custom of presentation in the Temple, Erevia does not give much detail about Mayan and Toltec religious practices or explain why she finds this ritual consistent with the Jewish custom of presentation at the Temple. While Erevia does not offer supporting evidence, she implies that this history is well known among those who are familiar with this cultural expression. Liturgical scholar Raúl Gómez's articulation of the historical roots includes most of Erevia's suggested origins. He, however, links these indigenous origins to Spanish rituals. He argues that a variety of groups may have contributed to the *Quinceañera* because "its contemporary expression is like Hispanics: a *mestizaje*, a blend of European, African, and American blood, language, and culture."[9] Gomez's arguments are plausible, but he has not located direct connections to support his reading of this history.

In one of the first formalized *Quinceañera* religious education books, *My 15th Birthday: Teaching Material for Quinceañera Formation*, the following description of the history and development of the celebration illustrates the difficulties of defining and tracing a historical explanation:

Its origin can be traced back to the indigenous traditions of Mexico that revolved around the dedication of young people to their gods. The actual celebration now, however, evolved from the colonial era, especially from the last part of the 19th century, when the customs of European society were prominent. . . . Daily life focused on the emulation of a European atmosphere. One example of this was the formal introduction of young women into society, while the painful reality of social inequality was ignored. . . . The current celebration of the Quinceañera is a far removed replica of the cotillion dances of the Viennese courts, where young ladies were introduced into society as they symbolically danced their first waltz in public.

Fr. Raúl Mora, Ph.D., a historian from the Jesuit University of Guadalajara, recounts how the lower classes of Mexico were silent onlookers at their landlord's Quinceañera celebrations, admiring the splendor only from afar. Eventually, some landlords began allowing their workers to have their photograph taken once in their lifetime. For most workers, the chosen occasion was their daughter's fifteenth birthday. . . . However, it was not until the post-revolutionary period in Mexico and the Batista era in Cuba (1940–1950), that the celebration became a social event among the middle and lower classes. The presentation of a young lady during the Quinceañera was transformed and democratized from what was previously a strictly "high society affair" into an opportunity for affirmation or recognition among the extended family and surrounding community. In post-modern Mexico (1970–2000), the upper class stopped celebrating the Quinceañera, whereupon the middle and lower classes adopted the custom with fervor.[10]

This is among the most descriptive and plausible explanations of the origins and historical developments of this tradition, and yet, except for the reference to the Jesuit University historian in Mexico, it gives little supporting evidence.

Chicana studies scholar Norma E. Cantú gives a cogent explanation of the development of the *Quinceañera* and the reasons for differing opinions regarding its historical foundations. She believes that the celebration has evolved from European influences in Mexico, the Spanish court dances, and native Mexican initiation rites, which later spread to the southwestern United States, probably over the last century.[11] Cantú notes that the *Quinceañera* is a unique celebration that probably did not originate in Spain, because historically there is no known ritual celebration like it that includes both the religious and initiation rituals in a single celebration. She argues that the names of the elements of the rite have a definite European, if not French, influence. "Words taken from royalty or at least the practices of the nobility, like *paje, damas, chambelán,* and elaborate choreographed dance that resembles a seventeenth century court dance, appear to be remnants of earlier celebrations."[12] These terms, she believes, may be part of French support of previous Spanish cultural influences on the local populations.

Cantú's study of the *Quinceañera* is part of her own experience as a young woman growing up in Laredo, Texas. Through her family stories, church records, and newspaper articles, Cantú can date the tradition's existence for several generations to the 1920s. In her research on indigenous initiation ceremonies, she has not located a coming-of-age ritual that includes the specific elements of the *Quinceañera* as practiced in Laredo. The celebrations may have similarities with indigenous or Spanish court celebrations, but no direct connection can be made. She argues that the reason the *Quinceañera* continues to be important to Mexican Americans "is that [it serves] a particular function in the community on an individual and communal level, while other folk religious cultural practices that have ceased to have a viable function, such as the wearing of saints' habits, have all but disappeared from the community."[13]

Relating to her ethnographic research of Mexican and Mexican American women in Chicago, Chicana scholar Karen Mary Davalos argues that the significance of the *Quinceañera* is not dependent on our knowing the origins of the celebration but on the meaning of the event. Her ethnographic interviews with participants in the celebrations show that the importance of the fiesta is found in their interpretation of the event, its actual celebration, and the innovations that are expressed in each ritual and celebration.[14] Davalos concludes that the women do not believe that an understanding of the origins or an "officially correct interpretation" of the meaning of the *Quinceañera* is important.

Even if it were possible for scholars to locate the exact meaning of the ceremony as it was first celebrated, the new meanings and evolving dynamics of popular religions are part of the nature of the celebration. The historical or official traditional meanings are not of greatest import. The most important thing is the significance of the celebration in the lives of the young women, their families, and their friends. The apparently contradictory oral history of the *Quinceañera* is not a problem to those who participate in the celebration. Hence, as with most interpretations of oral history, the *Quinceañera* is a developing notion that is determined by those who are the purveyors of the traditioning process.

INTERPRETING THE RELIGIOUS TEXTS AND CONTEXTS OF THE RITUAL OF THE *QUINCEAÑERA*

In the following section I analyze the religious, cultural, communal, and gender dimensions of the *Quinceañera* religious service. The religious ritual of the *Quinceañera* text by Erevia includes the Mass service with suggested prayers for the *Quinceañera*.[15] While the actual celebration of the ritual may have numerous additions, as determined by local custom and the participants, who may bring new innovations to the celebration, Erevia's text is among the most commonly used and allows for variations.[16]

I do not intend to put an emphasis on an official text; my goal is to show the multivocal dimensions of the celebration even within a study of what is generally used as a text for the religious ceremony. While the focus of this section is on two prayers, these texts must be seen within a ritual that is part of the larger event of the *Quinceañera*. This discussion will not be limited only to the texts but will take into account various actions of the ritual and the role of the participants.

In the first part of her book Erevia explains the meaning of the *Quinceañera*: "To bring out the religious and spiritual dimensions, Catholics celebrate this custom with special emphasis on the awareness and sensitivity of the young lady in dealing with the values, concerns, and challenges of the Christian community."[17] The *Quinceañera's* central purpose is to celebrate the young woman's growth and development within the Christian community through the presentation and dedication of her faith as a young adult.

During my time working at the Latino/a parish in Kansas City, most families requested that the celebration of the Eucharist be part of the *Quinceañera* service.[18] The service begins with a procession of the court of honor, which may consist of fifteen couples, the *damas* (young women) and the *chambelanes* (young men), followed by *la quinceañera* with her escort (a *chambelán* or her father) and the priest. After their entrance procession, the priest begins the service with a welcome and a special prayer in honor of the celebration. Specific prayers for the ritual of the *Quinceañera* follow the homily. The priest reads the first text, inviting the young woman to renew her baptismal promises:

> *(Name),* when you were an infant, your parents and godparents brought you to the waters of baptism to be initiated into the new life of our Savior, Jesus Christ. At that moment they made a profession of faith for you and in your name, in the same faith which now brings you to this altar. Therefore the Catholic Church now asks you to renew and affirm this same commitment of faith of your own free will and conviction.[19]

The priest invokes the symbols of water and new life while calling to mind the original promise to Christ that the young woman's parents and godparents made for her at the time of her baptism. These Christian symbols are tied to the symbols of the *Quinceañera* initiation ritual as a way to support the young woman's commitment and responsibility to her Christian faith as she grows into young adulthood.[20] The symbols of the ritual include the gifts that will be given to her following her prayer of dedication. These gifts symbolize the passing from childhood to her new status as a young Christian woman. The religious gifts that are given to her during the religious service may include a religious medal (usually of Mary, often of Our Lady of Guadalupe), a rosary, and a bible and/or missal. Other gifts are sometimes blessed: a doll, a crown, high heels, a pillow, roses. The gifts, if not carried in the entrance procession, are brought forward at the time of the blessing, which follows the prayer of dedication. After the young woman affirms her baptismal promises, she proclaims the second text, titled "A Prayer of Dedication of the Girl."[21] "The Prayer of Dedication" reveals the religious meaning of the *Quinceañera:*

> I offer you, O Lord, my youth. Guide my steps, my actions, my thoughts. Grant me the grace to understand your new commandment to love one another, and may your grace not be wasted in me. I ask you this through Jesus Christ, your Son, our Savior and Redeemer.
>
> Oh, Mary, my Mother, present my offering and my life to the Lord; be my model of a valiant woman, my strength and my guide. You have the power to change hearts; take my heart then and make me a worthy daughter of yours. Amen.[22]

Of interest is the equal manner in which this prayer addresses the Lord and Mary. The two images, Lord and Mary, are comparable in their abilities, except that the Lord is given the additional roles of giver of grace, savior, and redeemer. This image of Mary is multivocal because Mary is a mother and has the qualities as a model, force of strength, and guide. This comparison highlights the ambiguity within Mary's liminal status because she appears to have divine qualities and yet is not Lord or Savior.

The purpose of the ritual is to effect the meaning of the text, which is evident as the young woman is called to give testimony to her beliefs. She responds affirmatively, proclaiming her baptismal promises as a Christian. Following this testimony she declares her commitment to her future role as an adult Christian woman within her Latino/a family and community. Her public proclamation of the prayer of dedication is the testimony of her beliefs and the acceptance of her role. Before the *Quinceañera* the young woman has received preparation from her family, friends, and church leaders in support of her honest choice to proclaim her commitments in the ceremony. Whether this proclamation is a source of peace or tension depends on the young woman and her own level of acceptance or rejection of the purpose of the religious ceremony.

The complexity of these texts is revealed when one looks at the public nature of the prayers. The prayers address several levels. First, they address God; second, and in several sections, they address Mary; third, they address the young woman; and fourth, they address the community that is assembled. Likewise, each level corresponds to specific roles a person or group plays in the ceremony. God is called upon to effect the petitions within the prayers. The role of Mary, as noted previously, is ambiguous, because Mary appears to have divine qualities, while not a deity; she is a role model and given special powers of intercession.

The role of the young woman and her status within the ceremony are complex because she is in a liminal state.[23] As neither child nor adult, she has an undetermined place in the community. The celebration of her coming-of-age is, in fact, part of the community's support of her personhood. In a surface reading of the ritual the young woman's role forces her into a submissive stance whereby she is to accept her role as a future mother and the traditional role as helper, guide, and possessor of the qualities ascribed to Mary. Like Mary, the young woman is to accept her responsibilities as a mother and her place in her community and Christian faith. While on one level this stance could be seen as merely passive, it could also be a stabilizing role because her place within society is secure. From this complementary understanding of the nature of women, the *Quinceañera* reinforces the gender role of women in society as helpmates, wives, and mothers.[24]

While some feminists might declare the *Quinceañera* inherently patriarchal, and therefore devoid of value for young women, others, myself included, might use a hermeneutics of reconstitution to note ways to develop the liberating aspects of the ceremony.[25] The *Quinceañera* has moments that allow the young woman to claim her voice. Within the ritual, she has the opportunity to use her voice, if she is allowed sufficient time, preparation, and agency. Her understanding of the meaning of the event is significant, and she needs to speak out of her true voice and not out of a role prescribed for her. The relationships with her family, friends, religious leaders, and the Latino/a community are pivotal in helping her develop this voice. The fiesta has moments when the young woman is affirmed by family and friends through the reception of gifts that support her as she moves into another chapter of her life. The support that she receives both at the religious service and at the fiesta creates a platform for her to liberate herself from false images and insecurities, a place where she can develop her own image of self that has agency, self-confidence, and inner strength.

In a literary analysis of the verbs used throughout the texts of the ritual service for this celebration, one sees that all of the verbs used in relation to the young woman are receiving verbs. Alternatively, the verbs used for the priest's role are active. Similarly, the role of the priest needs to be evaluated so that he can be a true representative of the community as well as one who supports, rather than gives, the young woman her agency. If the *Quinceañera* is to be an opportunity to develop agency and voice, the aspects of the ritual that promote silence and subservience need to be redefined and reconstituted.

The priest is a major figure within the ceremony, and yet his presence appears contrary to the emerging womanhood of the young girl. The central figure of the ritual is a man, the priest, who bestows his blessing on the young woman in order for her to be accepted into her new position within society and places her under the protection of—and subordination to—men.[26]

The priest represents both the sacred realm and public nature of the assembly; the latter is also present in the community that is gathered to witness and participate in the celebration of the religious service and fiesta. The priest's role may be ambiguous, depending on his support or lack of interest in the event. The priest can be a discordant presence if he subverts the importance of the *Quinceañera*. Likewise, while the role of the priest is central, if he is not an active participant in the community—except for his role as the official religious leader of the ceremony—then there is a contradictory nature to his presence as a representative of the community.

When the priest does not represent the intent of the community, then the family and friends of the young woman may try to play a stronger leadership role within the ceremony or within the preparation of the *Quinceañera*. These additional roles are a means of agency for the community and are attempts to strengthen the lines of force within the ritual and the impact of the event on the young woman.

Besides the two main participants, the priest and the young woman, several other voices are present within the ceremony itself. The service usually has a congregation of family and friends whose presence is a way of honoring and supporting the young woman. This presence, however, can either support or subvert the ritual's effects.[27] Neither the family nor the community is merely a passive receiver of the testimony of the young woman in the ritual. Their presence is a supportive presence for the young woman as she enters the next stage of her life.[28] During the

Mass the young woman is given gifts by her *padrinos* (her sponsors, who are generally older members of her family and friends and close friends of her parents) that symbolize her growth, commitments as a young Christian Mexican American, and her responsibilities as she develops the next stage of her life.[29] Similarly, the young couples, who are the attendants in her court of honor, display their public support of her by their participation in the celebration.

This analysis of the celebration reveals the delineation of the role for the young woman as noted within the religious service. The development of the ritual and the interpretation of the meanings can be viewed from various perspectives that can effectively change the direction of the ritual. While the meaning of the celebration may be the construction of *la quinceañera* as subservient and submissive to the men in her life, the direction of the ritual does not necessarily have to be developed or interpreted in this manner. The obvious ambiguities and sources of tension are part of the liminal quality of the celebration and can be moments for instruction, change, and transformation.

In reconstructing the *Quinceañera* as a means of agency for the young woman, careful analysis needs to be done in order to address the exact nature of the ambiguities present in the prayers and the ritual itself, such as, what images of young women is this ritual promoting? One needs a view of the young woman as a strong Mexican American person who is capable of being a force of agency for herself and others.

The *Quinceañera* is an example of popular Catholicism, and while it is not an official sacrament, its sacramental nature is one way Latinos/as express their view of life, or, as Espín calls it, their "epistemology of life."[30] Latino/a theologians focus on these popular religious expressions because they are one way that Latinos/as find the incarnation, the Divine in *lo cotidiano* (daily life). Hence, all of life is capable of revealing the sacramentality that is the communication of the divine principle underlying creation.

This view of life does not separate the corporeal, the human, from the divine. The false attitudes in Christianity, the Jansenist approach, are inherently rejected in this sacramental world view and in popular religions.[31] The celebration of life in the *Quinceañera* is about a young woman's body. She has reached the age of fecundity, she has begun menstruation, and her family and community acknowledge and rejoice in her potentiality and new state of being. This rejoicing in her fecundity also creates a certain tension/ambiguity within religious traditions, particularly among some members of religious authority, because although bodies are good, bodies are also dangerous, which is part of the carryover from a Jansenist perspective within the church.[32]

The sacramental nature of this celebration of *Quinceañera* is an ambiguous reality because it has the character of revealing the infinite within the finite.[33] The both/and character of the celebration of a young woman's coming of age is shown by the transcendent nature of the universal as expressed in a particular experience. The transcendent sacramental nature of God-with-us is found in the moment of celebration of a young woman's life, and yet the sacramental nature is also opaque in the particular experience of a finite present moment.[34] This sacramental celebration of life and community points to the revelatory character of the larger community of faith and the saving nature of God's actions as they are made present in person, family, and community. Thus, the *Quinceañera* is revelatory because it points to the saving presence of God in creation, particularly in the person of the young woman and her family's and her community's support for her.

As previously noted, the figure of Mary is ambiguous. Within the texts Mary is a role model, but her exact role is unclear unless one accepts the view of women as only helpmates, guides, and mothers. As Latinas and other feminist theologians are looking at the image of Mary, we need to incorporate their new interpretations of the image of Mary, which go beyond the image of passive receiver and include the images of Mary as a woman of strength and courage. These new images need to be incorporated within evolving popular religious expressions, liturgies, and especially within homilies.

THE *QUINCEAÑERA* AND THE IMPORTANCE OF CULTURAL MEANING AND IDENTITY FOR MEXICAN AMERICANS

One reason that families and young Mexican Americans participate in *Quinceañeras* is to promote the young person's cultural identity. This celebration plays a role in the adolescent's larger search for identity within US society, which is often at dissonance with Mexican and Mexican American culture. Mexican American youth live within the dynamics of social, cultural, and economic factors that interact within a larger dominant culture in the United States. While these youth cannot be characterized as a single monolithic group, they can be described by the life situations that illustrate their perspectives and affect the choices they make, as well as the struggles that many of them face to advance in educational and economic status.[35] While some Mexican American youth may strongly identify with the Mexican culture, others may chose not to identify themselves as Mexican or Mexican American, and an additional number may choose to combine their identities as Mexicans and Americans to create their own unique youth subculture that is separate from both dominant culture and family identity.[36] A *Quinceañera* can be one way for families and youth to develop a sense of ethnic identity in the midst of hegemonic discourse that pushes them away from their Mexican and Mexican American identity.[37]

The continuing interest in *Quinceañera* celebrations and the ongoing development of the tradition surrounding this popular religious and cultural event are examples of the persistence and strength of cultural identity. Based on her research Davalos concludes that these rituals are ways for families and youth to find their own cultural identity.[38] Cantú stresses the importance of this life cycle ritual within border communities in Texas and Mexico. She argues that for borderland communities the *Quinceañera* serves a different function than for immigrants living elsewhere in the United States. The *Quinceañera*, while it is part of the affirmation of culture, is part of the ongoing popular traditions that have existed since before 1848, when the Southwest became part of the United States.[39]

Cantú describes the various elements of the *Quinceañera* and focuses on the relationships and networks that are part of the *compadrazgo* system.[40] This system of family and friend relationships refers to a communitarian system whereby these relationships sustained the village during economic times. Continuing this system of support in a contemporary setting is part of Mexican American culture and fostering of community.

From my experience of working with Euro-American priests and pastoral agents, one of the problems they have with the celebrations is that the fiestas are "too wild" or distort what they feel is the religious meaning of the *Quinceañera*. Part of the difficulty, I believe, is that they lack understanding of the multivalent character of the *Quinceañera* and the sacramental nature of the fiesta with its moments of religious expression and fun. The fiesta is a liminal time, a transforming time and place, or, as Roberto Goizueta calls it, "life in the subjunctive."[41] The mentality of fiesta came out of a medieval culture and developed around the liturgical season of Lent, when fast and simple living are interspersed with moments of fiesta (the celebration of feast days of saints).[42] The season of Lent concludes with Holy Week events (the Triduum) and the high feast of Easter. The feast days were times of breaking the fast with celebrations of much food and drink. This allowed everyone, not merely the wealthy or royalty, to have times of work and of play. Yet to sacralize times of play seems very difficult in a society that is utilitarian in nature or that looks for the ultimate party or escape. The fiesta is truly a time of "play and work."[43]

Goizueta articulates the features of fiesta that are helpful for under-standing *la fiesta Quinceañera*:

(1) an expression of *communitas*; (2) human action "in the sub-junctive mood"; (3) the confluence of play and work; and, there-fore; (4) a form of liturgical action. . . . As an act of reception and response for the gift of life, the fiesta—whether expressly civil or religious—is a fundamentally religious act.[44]

The Mexican culture incorporated this idea of times of feast and fam-ine, and it is evident in the celebration of the rites of initiation: baptism, first communion, *Quinceañera*, weddings, and so on. The ritual of fam-ine and feast is still evident within the popular expression of the celebra-tion; *la quinceañera* enters a period of preparation before the event, similar to a fast time. This may be a time when she goes for a retreat or is taught by her elders regarding the meanings of the rituals in which she will participate, as well as practice of the various rituals, whether those in the church or part of the dance. The dance includes a formal waltz, for which all of the couples—*damas, chambelanes*, and *la quinceañera*—practice for hours to have the correct choreography for the event.

Difficulties with the fiesta still exist, and I do not wish to romanticize the fiestas that are overt expressions of excess and consumerism. Latino/a popular culture has its moments both of resistance and of acceptance of hegemonic materialism. I have attended *Quinceañeras* that have turned into angry fights among youths that ruined *la quinceañera's* reception. From my experience, I believe that one part of this disparity of speech and action is a distortion that comes out of a fractured community in need of more than a fiesta to heal the wounds of youth growing up amid poverty and discrimination. Although I note these contradictory aspects, the *Quinceañera* celebration has the potential to offer moments for heal-ing, building community support systems, and empowering relationships within religious communities and across cultures and genders.

Davalos describes the contradictory character of the celebration as part of the experience of Mexicanas living in the United States. They move, she says,

between their Mexico and their United States, between patriarchy and equality in order to make sense of their lives. It is a territory that permits two or more cultures, multiple meanings, and compli-cated constructions of a Mexicana. It is a site of negotiation where people and cultural practices are not coherent, whole, or distinct. The discourse and practice of the *quinceañera* encourage us to examine the paradoxical and ambiguous nature of "tradition." The discourse and practice suggest that what we intend as "cultural" is fluid, slippery, contradictory, spontaneous, and chaotic.[45]

Davalos is describing what is essentially the "messy nature" of sacramentality, popular religion/*Quinceañera*, which is expressed in the embodiment of *lo cotidiano*, the lived reality of a people. *La quinceañera* experiences this reality with her very being and the dialectic of "almost but not yet." Some young women seek to engage in adult rituals as soon as possible through drinking, sexual experimentation, having children, or living independent of their families. The sacramental character of the celebration is one way to ritualize the importance of "life in the subjunctive" that allows for and does not move to completion of tensions/ambiguity. This fiesta is about sacramental nature of life and can mean that the young woman is given support, through family and friends, to live with the inner questions of her own journey, through this state of liminality.

CONCLUSION

The *Quinceañera* is an important example of traditioning *latinamente*. In their study of the *Quinceañera*, Davalos and Cantú recognize that the meaning and lived expressions of these celebrations are not dependent on the historical origins or on the "officially correct" celebration of the *Quinceañera*, even if such origins were located and exact following of "official rules and rubrics" of any liturgical celebration were possible. What is at stake are the new meaning systems that each participant and generation adds to the evolving nature of the celebration as determined by their own needs and cultural demands. Rituals have their own nature and meaning apart from any particular rite book or official text. Popular Catholicism adds its own flavor to the rituals because by their very nature they are more flexible and adaptable; few of the rituals are official, and few of them have texts that are published and promoted for uniform celebration. While the *Quinceañera* is one example of the development of a formalizing/institutionalization of a popular Catholic ritual, there is still much debate and evolution found concerning various levels of participation in the celebration, whether among the families, young women and friends, official religious leaders, parishes, and/or dioceses' rules regarding the celebration.

The evolving nature of the *Quinceañera* is a challenge to anyone who wishes clarity regarding the official or original meaning of the celebration.

Perhaps the questions asked about this tradition reveal more about the character of the individual than what is involved in the actual celebration. While some religious leaders and ritual texts promote the subservience of the young woman as part of the purpose, symbolism, and direction of the ritual, others—myself included—argue that the *Quinceañera* can allow an opportunity for those who love the young woman to affirm her and to allow a place for her to exercise her developing voice. This event is a way of reinforcing young women's self-concept and development. The process can be a source of hope and is life-giving because a young woman is empowered to use her agency, and in so doing, she becomes a role model for other young women. This action can also be a stance of resistance against the oppressive forces that seek to silence her and others like her. As a ritual, the *Quinceañera* is about effecting the very meaning of the event so that amid all of the ambiguities, the presence of God is truly liberating, and thus effects the agency and voice of the young woman.

In preparing and leading *Quinceañera* services, I always felt ambivalent toward the event, but at the time I was not clear about my difficulties with the entire process. I now believe that the liturgical rites and the preparation process for the celebration need to be refocused on the liberating and hopeful dimensions of the *Quinceañera*. This traditioning process needs to include a different understanding of the role of women, one that includes agency and voice, which could be inserted into the preparation and the ritual itself. Essentially, I am calling for continued discussion of the *Quinceañera,* taking into account the lines of force and the religious, gender, and cultural implications. While I originally wanted a rewriting of the ritual, I now argue that we need to create various rituals that allow for the developing expression of roles of women and men and allow for the celebration of culture, youth, and the human body, as well as religious faith—essentially the honoring of popular religious sacramentality, rather than a concretizing of the ritual into a sterile notion of Mexican American young women or men.

Notes

[1] Michele Salcedo, *Quinceañera! The Essential Guide to Planning the Perfect Sweet Fifteen Celebration* (New York: Henry Holt and Company, 1997), xi. The term *quinceañera* is used to describe both the young woman who is celebrating her fifteenth birthday and the celebration itself. For clarity, I use the term *la quinceañera* to refer to the young woman and *Quinceañera* to refer to the fiesta.

[2] While I did not review all the websites, I did cover over ten thousand websites. The overwhelming majority are commercial.

³ For examples of the types of commercial websites, enter "quinceanera" in any search engine.

⁴ See various websites. See also Tomas Chavez, "Quinceañera: A Liturgy in the Reformed Tradition," *Austin Seminary Bulletin* 98 (1983): 40–47.

⁵ A focus of this book is to express various ways to understand the process of tradition, which is the means of passing on meaning from one generation to another. The term *traditioning,* refers to the dynamic processes that occur within time, place, and culture in which people fashion their memories and interpret their past experiences while expressing their interpreted meaning systems in the present as they look forward to the future. Because of the contextual nature of the human condition, traditioning can never be described as universal or uniform, because it is a part of the developing and ongoing nature of meaning systems and memories of a people's faith. See Orlando O. Espín's explanation of tradition in Chapter 1 in this volume; and idem, "Mexican Religious Practices, Popular Catholicism, and the Development of Doctrine," in *Horizons of the Sacred*, ed. Timothy Matovina and Gary Riebe-Estrella, SVD (Ithaca, NY: Cornell Univ. Press, 2002), 142.

⁶ Unlike the preparation of other liturgical services, such as baptisms, first communions, weddings, and funerals, where the essential aspects of the rituals/liturgies are more formally determined by the Roman Catholic Church, the preparation for the *Quinceañera* liturgy is more open to alternative ways of celebrating by the inclusion of various rituals into the service.

⁷ Angela Erevia, *Religious Celebration for the Quinceañera* (San Antonio: Mexican American Cultural Center, 1980), 3.

⁸ Ibid.

⁹ Raúl Gómez, "Celebrating the Quinceañera as a Symbol of Faith and Culture," in *Misa, Mesa y Musa: Liturgy in the U.S. Hispanic Church*, ed. Kenneth G. Davis, OFMConv. (Schiller Park, IL: World Library Publications), 108.

¹⁰ *Mis 15 Años/My 15ᵗʰ Birthday: Teaching Material for Quinceañera Formation* (Boston: Pauline Books and Media, 2002), 16.

¹¹ Norma E. Cantú, "*La Quinceañera:* Towards an Ethnographic Analysis of a Life Cycle Ritual," *Southern Folklore* 56, no. 1 (1999): 74–75.

¹² Ibid., 75.

¹³ Ibid., 76–77.

¹⁴ Karen Mary Davalos, "*La Quinceañera*: Making Gender and Ethnic Identities," in *Velvet Barrios: Popular Culture and Chicana/o Sexualities*, ed. Alicia Gaspar de Alba (New York: Palgrave Macmillian, 2003), 149–50.

¹⁵ The *Quinceañera* rite is a popular religious tradition and as such has been orally passed down through generations, but it has never been designated as an official rite within the Roman Catholic liturgy. Erevia's book is perhaps the most widely known written text of the ritual in the United States (see Erevia, *Religious Celebration for the Quinceañera*, 15–50). In 1998 a more standardized formula was developed by the Mexican American Culture Center and has been endorsed by the US Bishops' Committee on the Liturgy (*Quinceañera: Celebration of Life—Guidebook for the Presider of the Religious Rite* [San Antonio: Mexican American Cultural Center, 1999]).

[16] As the evolution of the ritual of the *Quinceañera* develops, some of the leaders in Latino/a Catholicism and liturgists have produced other formal books.

[17] Erevia, *Religious Celebration for the Quinceañera*, 3.

[18] The religious celebration of the *Quinceañera* does not have to be within a Mass. It can be part of a prayer service, communion service, or blessing in the home. See the options noted in *Quinceañera: Celebration of Life—Guidebook for the Presider of the Religious Rite*, 29–60.

[19] Ibid., 17.

[20] Another reason for the evolution of the *Quinceañera* within Hispanic Catholicism is its similarity to confirmation, which addresses the need for a young-adult faith commitment. In Latin America confirmation is received either at the time of baptism or at the time of first communion; therefore, the *Quinceañera* meets the need for a young-adult faith commitment. In the United States most dioceses confirm youth during their adolescent years, so confirmation fulfills this need.

[21] Erevia, *Religious Celebration for the Quinceañera*, 19.

[22] Ibid., 19.

[23] The liminal state is the experience of being in transition, which anthropologist Victor Turner calls the "betwixt and between." One example of this ambiguous period is puberty, the period between childhood and adulthood. This period is also a time in some cultures when the neophyte would go through a ritual before being accepted as an adult. The *Quinceañera* is a ritual expression of that transition from the ambiguous liminal state between childhood to adulthood. See Victor W. Turner, "Liminality and Communitas," in *Readings in Ritual Studies*, ed. Ronald L. Grimes (Upper Saddle River, NJ: Prentice-Hall, 1996), 512–13.

[24] John Paul II has promoted the image of complementary of women and men. See John Paul II, *On the Dignity and Vocation of Women (Mulieris Dignitatem)*, *Origins* 18, no. 17 (October 1988): 261–83.

[25] Elisabeth Schüssler Fiorenza, *In Memory of Her: A Feminist Theological Reconstruction of Christian Origins* (New York: Crossroad, 1984), 68–92.

[26] I am not advocating this perspective of women's place within society. I am noting the outlook that some leaders and women take regarding the meaning of the *Quinceañera*.

[27] An example of subversion would be their emphasizing certain aspects of the *Quinceañera* but not focusing on the religious texts and the underlying significance of the texts and ritual. Instead, the family and community could focus on the clothes, reception, and dance while hurriedly rushing through the religious ceremony without preparation on the religious nature and meaning of the ritual. Or, the family might focus on the religious meaning and not prepare the young woman as a young adult who is going into society to meet the expectations of her peers and community.

[28] Not all *Quinceañeras* are large lavish events. If the *Quinceañera* were limited to a very small group of only nuclear family members, it would not erase the public nature of the event. The presence of the priest, who is a leader/

representative of the larger community, and the location of the church as a public space are two ways to bring forth communal dimensions of celebration even without the young woman's extended family and friends.

[29] *Padrinos* and *madrinas* are part of the larger *compadrazgo* system. See George M. Foster, "*Cofradía* and *Compadrazgo* in Spain and Spanish America," *Southwestern Journal of Anthropology* 9, no. 1 (1953): 1–28.

[30] Orlando Espín, *The Faith of the People: Theological Reflections on Popular Catholicism* (Maryknoll, NY: Orbis Books, 1997), 156–69.

[31] For a brief explanation of the Jansenist movement within the Roman Catholic Church, see Konrad Hecker, "Jansenism," in *Encyclopedia of Theology: The Concise Sacramentum Mundi,* ed. Karl Rahner, 727–30 (New York: Seabury Press, 1975).

[32] Susan A. Ross, *Extravagant Affections: A Feminist Sacramental Theology* (New York: Continuum, 2001), 34–42.

[33] Roberto Goizueta, *Caminemos Con Jesús: Toward a Hispanic/Latino Theology of Accompaniment* (Maryknoll, NY: Orbis Books, 1995), 49–50.

[34] Ross, *Extravagant Affections,* 37–42.

[35] Roberto Ramirez, author of *The Hispanic Population in the United States, March 1999,* Current Population Reports, U.S. Census Bureau, Washington, DC (Spanish version), notes the diversity of the Latino/a population, "In many respects, people with origins in Cuba, Mexico, Puerto Rico, Central America and South America, as well as other Hispanic countries, had wide variations in their social and economic characteristics, from educational attainment and marriage, to employment and income" (quoted in Roberto Ramirez, *Census Bureau Updates Profile of Nation's Latino Groups, March 8, 2000,* press release, US Census Bureau Report, Washington, DC).

[36] George P. Knight et al., "Family Socialization and Mexican American Identity and Behavior," in *Ethnic Identity: Formation and Transmission among Hispanics and Other Minorities,* ed. Martha E. Bernal and George P. Knight, 105–6 (Albany: State Univ. of New York Press, 1993). Five aspects of ethnic identity are given: First, ethnic self-identity is a person's membership within a particular ethnic group. Ethnic identity refers to a person's knowledge, understanding, values, and feelings toward one's particular ethnic group in relation to the individual. Second, ethnic constancy is the awareness that a person's ethnic identity is unchanging over time, place, and setting. Third, ethnic role behaviors are those behaviors that exhibit ethnic values, styles, customs, tradition, and language. Fourth, ethnic knowledge is the knowledge regarding role behaviors and traits, values, styles, customs, traditions, and language that are part of one's ethnic group. Fifth, ethnic preferences and feelings pertain to the feelings about members of one's ethnic group and preference regarding ethnic members, behaviors, values, traditions, and languages. Ethnic identity is a complex issue. No single theory can account for its continuation and the continuation of ethnic communities. A number of theorists refer to the isolation of the ethnic group, which serves to preserve and defend against loss of identity, while others point to threats—perceived and real—that exist against the group, which serve to

preserve the boundaries and reinforce the group identity. While no single theory can thoroughly describe the complexities of ethnicity, a number of Chicano/a scholars address the context of Mexican Americans identity. See Norma Alarcón, "Theoretical Subjects of This Bridge Called My Back and Anglo-American Feminism," in *Making Face, Making Soul: Haciendo Caras*, ed. Gloria Anzaldúa, 356–69 (San Francisco: Aunt Lute Books, 1990); Gloria Anzaldúa, *Borderlands: La Frontera*, 2nd ed. (San Francisco: Aunt Lute Books, 1999); Irene I. Blea, *La Chicana and the Intersection of Race, Class and Gender* (New York: Praeger, 1992); Adela De la Torre and Beatríz M. Pesquera, eds., *Building with Our Hands: New Directions in Chicana Studies* (Berkeley and Los Angeles: Univ. of California Press, 1993); Olivia Espín, "Cultural and Historical Influences on Sexuality in Hispanic/Latin Women: Implications for Psychotherapy," in *Race, Class, and Gender*, 2nd ed., ed. Patricia Hill Collins, 423–38 (Washington, DC: Wadsworth Publishing Co., 1995); Mario T. García, *Mexican Americans Leadership, Ideology, and Identity, 1930–1960* (New Haven, CT: Yale Univ. Press, 1989); Roberto Goizueta, "*Nosotros*: Toward a U.S. Hispanic Anthropology," *Listening: Journal of Religion and Culture* 27 (1992): 55–69; Louise Año Nuevo Kerr, "Mexican Chicago: Chicano Assimilation Aborted, 1939–1954," in *Ethnic Chicago*, 3rd rev. and enl. ed., ed. Melvin G. Holli and Peter d'A. Jones, 269–98 (Grand Rapids, MI: Eerdmans, 1984); Edward Murguía, *Assimilation, Colonialism and the Mexican American People* (Austin: Center for Mexican American Studies, Univ. of Texas at Austin, 1975; repr. Lanham, MD: Univ. Press of America, 1989); George J. Sánchez, *Becoming Mexican American: Ethnicity, Cultural and Identity in Chicano Los Angeles, 1900–1945* (New York: Oxford Univ. Press, 1993); Anthony M. Stevens-Arroyo and Gilbert R. Cadena, eds., *Old Mask, New Faces: Religion and Latino Identities* (New York: Bildner Center for Western Hemisphere Studies, 1995); José Vasconcelos, *The Cosmic Race: A Bilingual Edition* trans. Didier T. Jaén (Los Angeles: Centro de Publicaciones, California State Univ., 1979; Baltimore, MD: The Johns Hopkins Univ. Press, 1997); and Mary C. Waters, *Ethnic Options: Choosing Identities in America* (Berkeley and Los Angeles: Univ. of California Press, 1999).

[37] Mexican American culture develops across successive generations and cannot be called a linear assimilation, as ethnic identity is often described by scholars of immigrant Europeans. Mexican American culture involves some aspects of both Mexican and U.S. cultures and is its own unique culture. While Mexican Americans born in the United States do acculturate, they often retain many of their ethnic traits. Gradual acculturation occurs from the first generation through successive generations, but this does not mean that acculturation into American society is a linear process over time and generations. Researchers Susan E. Keefe and Amado M. Padilla studied three cities in California—Santa Barbara, Oxnard, and Santa Paula—as representative of cities and smaller agricultural towns in California. All three of the communities have a broad Mexican American population. They interviewed over six hundred individuals in thirty- to forty-minute interviews. They completed further in-depth research on a smaller number of respondents. Fourth-generation respondents retained some

ethnic cultural patterns and in some cases strengthened their cultural ties. Family ties appeared to strengthen over generations, which was particularly evident for those with greater income. Even those respondents who focused on their American identity continued to show pride and affiliation with the Mexican culture. Those who did not identify with the Mexican culture still participated in cultural activities and social gatherings with mainly Mexican Americans. The most acculturated of the respondents, those who have the greatest social interaction outside of their ethnic group, continued the maintenance of their ethnic identity. Also, because of the need to live between two cultures, there is "situational ethnicity," whereby the individuals self-identify and participate within their culture according to time, group, and place. Susan E. Keefe and Amado M. Padilla, *Chicano Ethnicity* (Albuquerque: Univ. Press, 1987), 190, 195.

[38] Davalos, *"La Quinceañera,"* 153–58.

[39] Cantú, *"La Quinceañera,"* 76.

[40] Ibid., 78. See also Norma E. Cantú, "Chicana Life Cycle Rituals," in *Chicana Tradition: Continuity and Change*, ed. Norma E. Cantú and Olga Nájera-Ramírez, 15–34 (Chicago: Univ. of Illinois Press, 2002).

[41] Roberto S. Goizueta, "Fiesta: Life in the Subjunctive," in *From the Heart of Our People: Latino/a Explorations in Catholic Systematic Theology*, ed. Orlando O. Espín and Miguel H. Díaz (Maryknoll, NY: Orbis Books, 1999), 84.

[42] See William A. Christian, Jr., *Apparitions in Late Medieval and Renaissance Spain* (Princeton: Princeton Univ. Press, 1981), 12–16.

[43] Goizueta, "Fiesta," 94.

[44] Ibid., 91.

[45] Davalos, *"La Quinceañera,"* 158. Davalos uses the term *Mexicana* because her interviewees used it to describe themselves (159 n 1). Davalos refers to Anzaldúa's description of their contradictory experience between two nations (Gloria Anzaldúa, *Borderlands/La Frontera* [San Francisco: Aunt Lute Books, 1987], vii).

Index

Abner of Burgos, 63
abuela, 28–29, 31, 154
Acosta, José de, 73, 99, 240
Acts 2:1–43, 161
Acts of 1687–1688, 168
Acts of Paul and Thecla, The, 133, 135
afrocubano, 195–96
Albo, Joseph, 63
Alegre, Francisco Javier, 76
Alfonso X, king of Castile and Léon, 64
Alfred of Sareshel, 64
Americanization, 241, 265; education and, 232, 236, 238; foundational ideologies, 230
American Missionary Society, 258
Andreu, Antoni, 66
Anna in the Tropics (Cruz), 83–87, 89, 104, 105 n3, 105 n4
anticlericalism, 90
Anzaldúa, Gloria, 103
Aponte, Edwin D., 183, 184
Apringius of Beja, 60
Arianism, 162–63
Arnald of Vilanova, 66
Arrillaga, Basilio, 78
Arrom, José Juan, 167–68, 169
Asbaje y Ramona, Juana de. *See* Juana Inés de la Cruz
Asherah, 124
Atabex, 168–69
Augustine, Saint, 162–63
authority: abuses of, 37–38; church structures, 36–37; ritual, 30–32; scriptural, 25–26; social location, 34–36; texts, 26–30

Averroes. *See* Ibn Roshd, Abul Wabid Mohammed ibn Ahmad ben Mohammed Hafid
Avicebron (Avicebrol). *See* Ibn Gabirol, Solomen
"Awakening construct," 250–51
Azriel of Gerona, 62
Aztec traditions, 99–102

Bacalzo, Dan and Anna, 84
Balbuena, Bernardo de, 74
Bando de buen gobierno y policía, 192
Báñez, Domingo, 70
Bañuelas, Arturo, 184–85
bar Hyya of Barcelona, Abraham, 62
Beecher, Henry Ward, 232–33
Bejarano, Francisco, 168
Bell, Catherine, 205–6; *Ritual Theory, Ritual Practice*, 209
ben Abraham Hayyun, Joseph, 63
Benavides, Alonzo, 74
ben Barzilai of Barcelona, Judah, 62
Benedict XIII, 66–67
ben Isaac Ha-Levi, Zerahiah, 62
ben Judah, Isaac, 62
ben Meshullam, Samuel, 62
ben Samuel Abulafia, Abraham, 63
ben Sem Tov of León, Moses, 63
ben Sheshet, Jacob, 62
ben Solomon d'Escola, Moses, 62
Bertano, Piero, 94
Bévenot, Maurice, 91
bibles, 40 n14, 95; *Biblia de Alba*, 95; *Biblia del Oso*, 95; *Complutensian Polyglot Bible*, 95; King James Version, 93; Vulgate, 94–96, 110 n52

"Biblical Anti-Monarchic Tradition and a U.S. Latino Theology" (Romero), 116–22

biblical tradition: feminism and, 122–27; identity construction and, 115; kyriarchy and, 123, 125, 127; Latino/a, 40 n14; monarchism and, 116–22; other texts and, 135–36; patriarchy and, 123, 125, 127, 128–29

bisexuality of the Divine, 126–27

Blancarte, Roberto, 59; *Historia de la Iglesia Católica en México*, 59

Bolívar, Simón, 255

Bonuccio, Agostino, 92

Boone, Elizabeth Hill, 98–99

Borges, 58

Brau, Salvador, 240

Braulio, Bishop of Zaragoza, 61

Bravo, Julián Joseph, 168–69

Browne, Walden, 98

Brummitt, Stella Wyatt, 237

Bushnell, Horace, 233

cabildos, 190–92, 195

Caminemos con Jesús (Goizueta), 187

Campo Lacasa, Cristina, 59; *Historia de la Iglesia en Puerto Rico*, 59

Cano, Melchor, 69

Cantú, Norma E., 281–82, 289

Capetillo, Luisa, 88, 105

Cappadocian Fathers, 162

Cardoza-Orlandi, Carlos, 267–68, 271

Caridad, La, 168–69

Carpenter, Vere C., 259, 260–62

Castellanos, Jorge and Isabel, 189, 195–96

Castro, Alfonso de, 93–94

Catholicism, popular, 6–11, 165, 187, 201 n52, 278; *Quinceañera* and, 287, 293 n15, 294 n20; *religiosidad popular* and, 138 n11, 201 n52; ritual practices and, 208–14; women and, 20 n13. *See also* Roman Catholic Church

Cavanaugh, Darien, 87

centralization, educational, 230–33, 245 n15

Cernadas, Remigio, 78

Certau, Michael de, 227; *L'ecriture de l'histoire*, 227

Charity, Our Lady of, 165–73, 175, 178 n39

Charter of Autonomy. *See* Sagasta Pact

Christ, Jesus, 160–61; Goizueta and, 159–64; human suffering and, 271; *mestizaje* and, 142; redemptive work of, 129; revelation and, 147–53, 159; traditioning of, 159–64

Christian Church (Disciples of Christ), 249; 25th convention (1933), 260; North American, 264; in Puerto Rico, 249–54, 259–72. *See also* missionaries

Christianity: core messages, 1–3, 10–14, 19; devotional and ritual practices and, 6–7; evangelical, 19 n12; Iberian, 90–91; as lifestyle, 10–11; necessary memories, 1–3, 10–14, 19; in New Spain, 97–102; popular, 6–11; reception of doctrines, 21 n24; reform movements, 11–14, 21 n23; social hegemony and, 8. *See also* Catholicism

Church, Robert, 231

Church, The (Küng), 149–50

church structures, authority of, 33–34

Cisneros, Francisco Ximénez de, 67, 95, 96

Código Negro Carolino, 191–92

colonization, tradition and, 97–102

Coloquios y doctrina cristiana (Sahagún), 100, 103

"Communion and Otherness" (Zizioulas), 163–64

Community of the Beautiful (García), 182–83

Congar, Yves, 158; *Tradition and Traditions*, 158

Constitution on the Sacred Liturgy (Sacrosanctum concilium), 32
conversation dimensions, unpacking of, 149–53
Corwin, Arthur F., 189
cotidiano, lo, 85, 291; Latino/a theology and, 180–88; popular Christianity and, 7–8, 19 n11; traditioning and, 5, 10–11, 12, 15; women and, 18 n8
Council of Trent. *See* Trent, Council of
Crescas, Hasdai, of Barcelona, 63
criollo/a population, 167, 182, 190
"crisis of consciousness," 241–42, 248 n54
Croatto, J. Severino, 122; "Recovering the Goddess," 122–27
Cruz, Juan de la, 49
Cruz, Nilo, 90; *Anna in the Tropics*, 83–87, 89, 104
Cuba, 50–52, 85, 165–67, 173; Africanity and, 188; Afro-Cuban religion, 191; Catholic Church in, 192–95; *criollos/as* and peninsulares, 190; indigenous population, 188–89; slavery, 189–90
Cuban Americans, 88–90, 165–67
cultures, 18 n4, 155 n13; confrontation of, 248 n53; Latino/a, romanticization of, 18 n6. *See also under* tradition; *under* traditioning
Cuna, Rafael, 272–73; "El que habita al abrigo de Dios," 273
curanderos/as, 36

daily life. *See cotidiano, lo*
Davalos, Karen Mary, 282, 289, 290–91
Davidic tradition, 117–19
Decree concerning the Canonical Scriptures. See Dei Verbum
Decree on the Acceptance of the Holy Scriptures and the Apostolic Traditions, 91–92

Dei Verbum, 39 n11, 92–93, 120, 158, 176 n6, 204
De La Torre, Miguel, 183, 184
Delgado, Celedonio, 240
democracy, Christianity and, 233
denominational identity, 1–3, 11–13, 15–16, 17 n2, 19 n12, 50–51
Día de Reyes, El, 201 n48
Díaz, Ramón (Moncho), 271
Disciples, Puerto Rican, 259–60; hardships and, 259–60; hymnody, 271–73; indigenous music and, 272–73; missionaries and, 260–63; role of women, 269–70; worship styles, 270–71
DMA, 58
Doctor Dulcifluus. *See* Andreu, Antoni
Doctor Eximius et Pius. *See* Suárez, Francisco
Doctor Fundantissimus. *See* Andreu, Antoni
Dogmatic Constitution on Divine Revelation. See Dei Verbum

educational centralization, 230–33, 245 n15
education in Puerto Rico, Spanish *versus* US, 227–48
EEC, 58
Eimeric, Nicolás, 66
Eiximenis, Francesc, 66
EJ, 58
Elizondo, Virgilio, 183–84; *Galilean Journey*, 184, 187
"El que habita al abrigo de Dios" (Cuna), 273
Enlightenment, the, 80 n4
Erevia, Angela, 279; *Religious Celebration for the Quinceañera*, 279–80, 282
Erwin, J. A., 258
Espada y Landa, Juan José Díaz de, 77
Espín, Orlando O., 23, 28, 48, 97, 187, 204; "Toward the Construction of

an Intercultural Theology of Tradition," 173–74
Espinoza, Isidro Félix de, 75
established structures, authority of, 36–37
Eucharist, women and, 152
Eugenius, Bishop of Toledo, 61
eurocubano, 195–96
Eutropius, Bishop of Valencia, 60
Eutropius the Presbyter, 60
evangelical versus *evangélico*, 275 n59
expansionism versus imperialism, 244 n11
experience, knowing and, 40 n14, 143–44, 147–48, 150

Federation of Evangelical Churches of Puerto Rico, 235
Ferrar of Catalonia, 65
Ferrer, Vincent, 66
Florencia, Francisco de, 75
Fonesca, Onofre de, 168, 169
Fonseca, Tomás de, 168
Foraker Act, 257
Freire, Paulo, 239
From the Heart of Our People (Espín and Díaz), 26, 30, 185
Fronteras, 58
Fructuosus, Bishop of Braga, 61
Fullen, A. M., 258, 266–67
functionalism, 233–34

Gadamer, Hans-Georg, 210–15
Galilean Journey (Elizondo), 184
Gandhi, Leela, 102–3
Gante, Pedro de, 98
García, Bartolomé, 76
García, Gregorio, 98; *Orígen de los indios del Nuevo Mundo*, 98
García-Diego y Moreno, Francisco, 78
García-Rivera, Alejandro, 187; *Community of the Beautiful*, 182–83
Garibay Kintana (Quintana), Angel María, 79–80

Gerald of Cremona, 64
globalization, 23–24, 37, 115, 174–75
God: analogical language and, 145; fatherhood, 145–46, 151; gender, 122; life of, 162–64
Goddess, 124–25
Goizueta, Roberto, 30, 186, 199 n17, 289; *Caminemos con Jesús*, 187
González, Justo, 25–26, 181–88
Gordon-McCutchan, R. C., 250, 252
Grafton, Anthony, 97
Gramática de la lengua castellana (Nebrija), 96
Gregory, Bishop of Elvira, 49, 59
Grito de Lares, 256
Guadalupe, Our Lady of, 182–83, 187, 205; traditioning of, 206–7
Gundisalvo, Domingo, Archdeacon of Cuéllar, 64
Gutiérrez y Gutiérrez, Alonso. *See* Vera Cruz, Alonso de la
Guzmán, Luis de, 95

Ha-Levi, Solomon, 63
Ha-Levi of Toledo, Judah, 63
Hechavarría y Peñalver, Manuel, 77
hegemonic groups, traditioning and, 16
Herman the German, 64–65
hermeneutics, 188, 237, 285; Gadamer and, 210–11; social location and, 113–36
Hewitt, Nancy A., 87–88
Hidalgo y Costilla, Miguel, 76–77
Hispanic theologians, sources, 58–59
Historia de la Iglesia Católica en México (Blancarte), 59
Historia de la Iglesia en Puerto Rico (Campo Lacasa), 59
Historia de la teología española (Melquíades Andrés), 59
history, study of, 45–46, 198 n5; lack of innocence and, 44–48; social location and, 35–36

Holy Spirit, 21; *gran avivamiento del '33, el,* and, 250–52, 260, 268, 273; reading strategies and, 120; tradition and, 159–64
Hosius of Córdoba, 59
Hostos, Eugenio María de, 240
Howard, Philip A., 190–91
Hydatius. *See* Idatius, Bishop of Chaves

Ibn Daud, Abraham. *See* John of Spain
Ibn Daud of Toledo, Abraham, 62
Ibn Gabirol, Solomen, 62
Ibn Roshd, Abul Wabid Mohammed ibn Ahmad ben Mohammed Hafid, 62
Idatius, Bishop of Chaves, 60
incarnation, theology and, 57, 184, 287
institutional structures, authority of, 36–37
interculturality, theology and, 55–56
interpretation, tradition of, 210–15
Isabella, Queen, 95–96
Isasi-Díaz, Ada María, 185–86
Isidore, Bishop of Seville, 49, 61

Jaca, Francisco José de, 192–93
Jandt, Fred, 148–49
Jansenism, 287
John, Abbot of Biclaro and Bishop of Gerona, 61
John 14:1–17:26, 161
John of Avila, 69
John of Spain, 64
John of the Cross, 70–71
John XXI, 65
Jones Act, 256
Josiah, 124–25
Juana Inés de la Cruz, 75
Juanes, los tres, 165–66; community-building and, 166–71; race and, 170; women and, 172
Julian, Bishop of Toledo, 61

Justinian, Bishop of Valencia, 60
Justus of Urgel, 60
Juvencus, 59

Kabbalist School of Gerona: Azriel of Gerona, 62; ben Isaac, Solomon, 62; ben Isaac Ha-Levi, Zerahiah, 62; ben Judah, Isaac, 62; ben Meshullam, Samuel, 62; ben Sheshet, Jacob, 62; ben Solomon d'Escola, Moses, 62
Kingdom Building in Puerto Rico (Morton), 264–65
Knight, Franklin W., 189
knowing and meaning, 143–44; communal life and, 155
Küng, Hans, 149; *The Church,* 149–50
kyriarchy, 125–27

Laínez, Diego, 69
Las Casas, Bartolemé de, 95
Las Casas, Bartolomé de, 71–72
Latino/a cultural identity: *abuela* and, 28–29, 31; romanticizing of, 18 n6; traditioning and, 153–54, 278; women and, 278–79, 285–88, 292
Latino/a theology, 43–44; Africans and, 181–88; *cotidiano, lo,* and, 180; heritage streams of, 52–57; intercarnation and, 57; sin and, 57; social justice and, 56
Leander, Bishop of Seville, 61
learning, bias and, 151
L'ecriture de l'histoire (Certau), 227
lectors and *oidores,* relationships between, 83, 87–88
León, Luis, 70
Leo X, 95
Licinianus of Cartagena, 60
Lonergan, Bernard, 141, 143
López de Haro, Damián, 74
Lorenzana, Francisco Antonio de, 75–76
Lorki, Joshua, 63

Loya, Gloria Inés, 187
Loyola, Ignatius, 67–68
Lull, Ramón, 49, 65
Luna, Pedro de. *See* Benedict XIII
Luther, Martin, 50, 91, 93, 109 n33,
    244 n8

machismo, 82 n24
Maimonides, Moses, 62–63
Maldonaldo, Juan, 70
Mallá, Felip de, 67
Mama Leo. *See* Rosada Rousseau,
    Leoncia
Manifest Destiny, 243
Marcos of Toledo, 64
Marrero, Leví, 168
Martí, Ramón, 65
Martin, Bishop of Braga and Abbot of
    Dumium, 60
Martín of Córdoba, 67
Martini, Raymond. *See* Martí, Ramón
Mary of Nazareth, 125
Masona, Bishop of Mérida, 61
Materialis, 58
Maza Miquel, Manuel, 58
McLoughlin, William, 250, 251, 264
Medina, Bartolomé de, 70
Meier, Johannes, 194
Melquíades Andrés, 59; *Historia de la
    teologia española*, 59
Mendieta, Gerónimo de, 73, 98
Mesnier, Desiderio, 79
mestizaje, 141, 198 n12; definitions of,
    182, 184–85; historical normativity
    of, 182–88; Jesus Christ and, 142;
    Latino/a theology and, 184–88;
    mulataje and, 185–88
Mexican American cultural identity,
    277, 295 n36, 296 n37
Mexico, 50, 51–52
Michael the Scot, 64
Mignolo, Walter D., 100–101
missionaries: education and, 238–48;
    European, 97–105; North Ameri-
can, 229–30, 233–38, 251, 254,
    263
missionary imaginary, Puerto Rico,
    264–68
Moirans, Epifanio de, 192–93
Molina, Luis de, 70
Montesinos, Antonio de, 71, 183
Mora, Raúl, 281
Morton, C. Manly, 260–61, 262, 268–
    69; *Kingdom Building in Puerto
    Rico*, 264–65
Mota y Escobar, Alonso de la, 73–74
Motolinía (Toribio de Benavente), 99–
    100
mulataje, 185–88, 195. *See also
    mestizaje*
Muñoz Rivera, Luis, 255
Murphy-O'Connor, Jerome, 160–61
Murray, 58
music, 247 n38

Nacchianti, Giacomo, 92
Navarra, Francisco de, 92
NCE2, 58
Nebrija, Elio Antonio de, 67, 98;
    Gramática castellana, 95–96;
    *Gra–mática de la lengua caste-
    llana*, 96
New Testament, tradition and, 92,
    159–60, 159–61; doctrine of Trin-
    ity and, 159–60, 174
nouvelle theologie, 33

O'Collins, Gerald, 157–58
ODCC, 58
Ojeda, Alonso de, 168
Oliver, Bernard, 66
Orígen de los indios del Nuevo Mundo
    (García), 98
Orosius, Paul, 60
Ortiz, Fernando, 167, 187
Ortiz, Vicente, 259–60, 261–62
Osius of Córdoba. *See* Hosius of
    Córdoba

otherness, 114–16, 122, 123
ousia and *hypostasis*, 162

Pacheco, Pedro, 93–94
Pacianus, Bishop of Barcelona, 60
Palau, Francisco, 76
Palomo, 84–86
Pané, Ramón, 71
Pareja, Francisco, 74
patriarchy, 82 n24, 122, 125–26, 130–31
Patristic period, 27
Paul, Saint, 160–61
Paul the Christian, 66
Peter of Alcántara, 68–69
Peter of Spain. *See* John XXI
Peter of Spain, the Elder, 65
Peter of Spain, the Younger, 66
Philip II, King, 98
Pilar Aquino, María, 187
plantation system, 189, 193, 202 n60
Plato of Tivoli, 64
"poder de Dios levantó, El" (Luisa Rivera), 272
Polcari, 59
popular religion, 6–8, 19–20, 138n11, 142, 247 n47; Catholicism and, 201 n52; Latino/a theologians and, 180–82, 196; Puerto Ricans and, 240; *Quinceañera* and, 291. *See also* Christianity; *under* Catholicism, popular
Portuondo Zúñiga, Olga, 166–67, 169
Potamius of Lisbon, 60
Presbyterian Board of Foreign Missions, 230
Priscillian, Bishop of Avila, 60
Protestant tradition, 37; Americanization and, 236; "de-traditioning" and, 268; education and, 233–48; *gran avivamiento del '33, el*, and, 263; missionary ideology and, 228–33
Prudentius, 60

Prudentius of Galindo, 63
Puerto Rican Americans, 88–90
Puerto Rico, 50–53; church membership, 249–50; conflicts and stresses, 252–53; education in, 227–48; Latino Protestant tradition, 263; lectors, 88; living conditions, 257, 259–60; missionaries, 257–68; Protestantism, 255, 257–58; revival impacts, 249–50, 269–71; revival origins, 250–54; Roman Catholic Church, 252–53, 255, 257, 266; Spain and, 50, 254–57; United States and, 256–63. *See also* Americanization; missionaries, North American
Puerto Rico Evangélico, El , 235
Pym, Anthony, 96

Quiroga, Vasco de, 72–73

race, theological differences and, 196–97, 203 n71
Rahner, Karl, 163
Raíces, 59
Raymond, Archbishop of Toledo, 63
Raymond of Peñafort, 65
reading strategies, 133–35; Rule of St. Benedict and, 108 n29
Rebolo, Pedro Juliano. *See* John XXI
reception of doctrines, 16, 21 n24
reform movements, 11–14; Reformed churches, 50–51, 82 n17; Reformed tradition, 82 n17
Reina, Casiodoro de, 95
religiosidad popular, 116–17, 120–22, 138 n11
Religious Celebration for the Quinceañera (Erevia), 279–80, 282
ressourcement movement, 197 n1
re-traditioning, 237
revelation, 4–5, 9–10, 91–92, 120, 157; handing on, 142–43, 159; Jesus Christ and, 147–48, 153–54;

tradition and, 95, 104; tradition-bearing texts and, 25; Vatican II and, 39 n11, 157

Ríos, Juan Julian, 83–87, 89–90, 104

ritual, 6–9, 30–33, 41 n27, 194–95; Our Lady of Guadalupe and, 205–14, 219–22; Protestantism and, 41 n32; *Quinceañera* and, 291–92

ritualization, 209–10

Rivera, María Luisa, 272; "El poder de Dios levantó", 272

Robert of Chester, Archdeacon of Pamplona, 64

Rodríguez Díaz, Daniel, 231–32

Roman Catholic Church: in Cuba, 192–95; intellectual tradition, 176 n13; popular, 6–11; in Puerto Rico, 266; slavery and, 192–95; women and, 210. *See also* Catholicism, popular

Romero, C. Gilbert, 116; "Biblical Anti-Monarchic Tradition and a U.S. Latino Theology," 116–22

Rosada Rousseau, Leoncia (Mama Leo), 269–70

Royce, Josiah, 205, 210–17, 219, 225 n26, 225 n27, 225 n29, 225 n32

Rubio, William, 66

Rudolf of Bruges, 64

Ruiz, Jean-Pierre, 26

Ruíz y Flores, Leopoldo, 79

Sacrosanctum concilium, 32

Sagasta Pact, 256

Sahagún, Bernardino de, 72, 183; *Coloquios y doctrina cristiana*, 100, 103

Sánchez, Tomás, 71

Sánchez de Moya, Francisco, 168

Santa Fe, Gerónimo de. *See* Lorki, Joshua

Santa María, Pablo de. *See* Ha-Levi, Solomon

Santiago Cabrera, J. L., 236–37

Saranyana, 59

Schottroff, Luise, 26

Segovia, Fenando F., 186–87

Seminario Evangélico de Puerto Rico, 259

sensus fidelium, 8, 9, 24–25

Servetus, Miguel, 69

Severus, Bishop of Málaga, 60

Severus, Bishop of Minorca, 60

Sibiuda, Ramón de, 67

sin, 4; incarnational theology and, 57; Latino/a theology and, 57; priests and, 29; traditioning and, 4–6, 9

Sinaitic tradition, 117–19

slavery, 181–82, 185; in Cuba, 189–90; plantation system and, 202 n60; Roman Catholic Church and, 192–95

Smith, Timothy, 252

Smith, Wilfred Cantwell, 103–4

social justice, theology and, 56

social location, 34–36; hermeneutics, 113–36

sola scriptura, 91–94, 104, 229

Soto, Domingo de, 68

Stagaman, David, 24

Strong, Josiah, 232

Suárez, Francisco, 71

Sugirtharajah, R. S., 103

Sunday School Committee of the Presbyterian Church, 236

Sunday Schools, 229, 234–36

tabaquerías, 84–85, 88, 90, 104

Taio, Bishop of Zaragoza, 61

Tamez, Elsa, 135; "1 Timothy," 128–33

Taylor, Lela, 261–62

Tenochtitlán, 98

Teresa of Avila, 49, 69–70

texts, 25–26, 40 n14, 97–105, 128, 133–36, 204, 212–14; colonialism and, 102–3; feminism and, 40 n16; secular, 22–29

textuality and orality, 85, 109 n41
Theatermania, 84
theologians, 48–53; annotated list of, 57–80; Latin American, 130–31
theological differences, 43–44; Afro-Latin identity and, 196–97, 203 n71; context and, 5–14; historical research and, 197 n3–98; ideological hegemony and, 16–17; interculturality and, 56, 235; life of God and, 162–64; traditional *versus* Latino/a, 43–44, 180–81, 184–88. *See also* Catholicism, popular; *cotidiano, lo*
Thiel, John, 91
Thirty-Nine Articles, 50
Thomas Aquinas, Saint, 143, 162
Tilley, Terrence, 24, 205
Tinker, George, 265
Tolbert, Mary Ann, 133–34
Toledo School of Translators, 63–64
Torres, Manuel, 259
"Toward the Construction of an Intercultural Theology of Tradition" (Espín), 173–74
tradition, 2–3, 81 n5, 93; analytical domains of, 244 n4; authority and, 23–24; biblical, 113–15; classical theology and, 242; colonization and, 97–102; communication and, 81 n7; Council of Trent and, 91–97; cultural hegemony and, 242–43; definitions of, 38 n1, 179 n50; historical research and, 39 n10; meaning and value of, 85–86; normativity and, 23; reform of, 81 n6; scriptural, 83–105, 93, 113–15, 159–61; streams of, 53–56; theologies of, 17 n2; traditioning and, 15–16, 100, 204
traditioning, 2–3, 142–46, 292, 293 n5; community-building and, 160–61, 205, 215–19; content and, 146–47, 204–5; *cotidiano, lo*, 5–6; culture and, 3–5, 148–49, 151–52;

dimensions of, 146–49; doctrinal differences and, 16; doctrinal error and, 7–8; experience and, 143–44, 147–48; grace and malpractice and, 150–53; hegemonic groups and, 16; historical research and, 29–30; identity, 197; Jesus Christ, 159–64; Latino/a elements and, 153–54; partners in, 146–49; as politics, 228; popular Christianity and, 6–11; process, 141, 195, 204–5; *Quinceañera* and, 291; religious texts and, 25–29; ritual and, 30–33; role of ministers in, 13–14; secular texts and, 27–29; sin and, 5–6; structure of, 149–53; tradition and, 15–16, 100, 204
Treaty of Paris, 257
Trent, Council of, 21, 50, 91–95, 103–4, 157, 176 n6, 244 n7

United Brethren Church, 234, 258
Universalis ecclesiae, 192–93

Valadés, Diego, 73
Valdés, Juan de, 68
Vallerius of Bierzo, 61
Valverde y Telles, Emeterio, 58, 79
Varela, Félix, 77–78
Vargas, Joaquín, 249, 252, 260, 264
Vatican Council II, 32–33, 41 n27; revelation and, 157
Vázquez, Gabriel, 71
Vázquez de Arce, Martín, 74
Velásquez Hernández, Pedro, 80
Vera Cruz, Alonso de la, 73
Vieira, Antonio, 75
Vilanova, 59
Virgen Mambisa, la. *See* Charity, Our Lady of
Vitoria, Francisco de, 68
Vives, Juan Luis, 68

Ward, Mae Yoho, 262–63

Whitehead, James and Evelyn, 141, 146, 150

women: *cotidiano, lo,* and, 18 n8; Eucharist and, 152; popular Catholicism and, 20 n13, 37; Puerta Rican, in ministry, 269–70; *Quinceañera* and, 283–85, 287–88, 292, 294 n26; scripture and, 131. *See also abuela*

Yermo y Parrés, José María de, 78–79

Zizioulas, John, 163–64; "Communion and Otherness," 163–64

Zumárraga, Juan de, 72